"Apostolicity is associated with th[illegible] has been distorted by faulty interp[illegible] ving the binary definition—cultivation of the faith, communication of the faith—for most of the past two millennia the priority has been firmly placed on cultivation, making communication subsidiary. This has had profoundly negative consequences for both church and mission. In this pioneering study Dr. John Flett shows with multiple examples—historical, theological and cultural—how pervasive and influential this traditional view has been. Today's pluriform and polycentric global Christianity will continue to move with a limp so long as a true apostolicity is not appropriated. This work boldly and constructively points the way forward."

Wilbert R. Shenk, senior professor of mission history and contemporary culture, Fuller Graduate School of Intercultural Studies

"This is a highly original work in the theology of Christian mission, which deserves the serious attention of missiologists, theologians and New Testament scholars. Flett has issued a weighty challenge to all attempts—from whatever ecclesiastical stable—to ground the apostolic being of the church in ecclesiological form or some static essence. The church is apostolic only to the extent that its testimony to Jesus Christ is severally received and embodied by diverse peoples and cultures. The diversity of world Christianity today is thus not a problem for the apostolicity of the church, but rather integral to its very being as the body of Christ, the one sent into the world to redeem it."

Brian Stanley, professor of world Christianity, University of Edinburgh

"Following John Flett's incisive critique of the missio Dei paradigm in *The Witness of God*, *Apostolicity*—a further interrogation of post-war ecumenical theology—does not disappoint. In this challenging book Flett tackles the theological significance of the diversity recognized in the study of world Christianity. This leads him to question an ecumenical understanding of apostolicity as based on historical origins and the continuity of church cultures. He does so on the grounds that it leads merely to church replication and not mission, which, following Christ in the Spirit, is anything but smooth and predictable. The book encourages serious engagement at the interface of church history, mission realities and Christian doctrine."

Kirsteen Kim, professor of theology and world Christianity, Leeds Trinity University, editor of *Mission Studies*

"The missiological movement in the nineteenth century was a powerful force in the creation of the ecumenical movement in the twentieth. Today, it would seem that missiological theology gives promise of reorienting an ecumenical movement that is threatening to retreat into a form of splendid isolation, making itself unwittingly supportive of the attitudes of colonization that missiologists (through a lengthy period of self-criticism) have largely left behind them. At the heart of this book lies a searing indictment of those 'communion ecclesiologies' that, through their identification of the being of the church with practices internal to them, foster an understanding of mission in terms of the cultivation of precisely those practices in other contexts, without regard for the fact that the church itself is being treated in the process as a culture whose task then becomes the subsumption of other cultures into itself. This is a book that is bound to make some folks angry. Hopefully, it will awaken many others to the need for more culturally sensitive accounts of Christian mission."

Bruce L. McCormack, Princeton Theological Seminary

"The nature of apostolicity has been a vexing question in ecumenical discourse with significant consequences for our understanding of the church and its unity. In this volume John Flett challenges many of the common assumptions of this conversation in order to construct a more fully Christological notion of apostolicity that resists colonizing conceptions of mission and embraces the diversity and plurality of Christian witness in the world without sacrificing the unity of the church. This is a significant contribution to ecumenical and missiological literature that is sure to provoke much conversation."

John R. Franke, theologian in residence, Second Presbyterian Church, Indianapolis

"In many respects, this work by John Flett is an outstanding contribution to international ecumenism and to the discussion on current issues in mission theology. The topic of apostolicity touches on the question of continuity, and it also touches on the question of crossing boundaries in the service of mission. As Swedish bishop and mission studies scholar Bengt Sundkler was wont to say, 'Transplantation means mutation.' John Flett outlines the different positions of various denominational traditions (Protestant, Roman Catholic, Orthodox, etc.) and he relates perspectives from the southern hemisphere to those from the northern hemisphere. In so doing, the book builds bridges and contributes toward mutual understanding. Flett's approach is as integrative as it is innovative and will certainly stimulate the ongoing discussion. This is a remarkable effort that deserves the highest praise."

Henning Wrogemann, Protestant University Wuppertal/Bethel, author of *Intercultural Theology*

APOSTOLICITY

The Ecumenical Question in
World Christian Perspective

JOHN G. FLETT

IVP Academic
An imprint of InterVarsity Press
Downers Grove, Illinois

InterVarsity Press
P.O. Box 1400, Downers Grove, IL 60515-1426
ivpress.com
email@ivpress.com

InterVarsity Press® is the book-publishing division of InterVarsity Christian Fellowship/USA®, a movement of students and faculty active on campus at hundreds of universities, colleges and schools of nursing in the United States of America, and a member movement of the International Fellowship of Evangelical Students. For information about local and regional activities, visit intervarsity.org.

Scripture quotations, unless otherwise noted, are from the New Revised Standard Version of the Bible, copyright 1989 by the Division of Christian Education of the National Council of the Churches of Christ in the USA. Used by permission. All rights reserved.

Cover design: David Fassett
Interior design: Beth McGill
Images: Markwippach by Lyonel Feininger (American, 1871–1956)

ISBN 978-0-8308-5095-2 (print)
ISBN 978-0-8308-9973-9 (digital)

Printed in the United States of America ∞

Library of Congress Cataloging-in-Publication Data

Names: Flett, John G., 1972- author.
Title: Apostolicity : the ecumenical question in world Christian perspective / John G. Flett.
Description: Downers Grove, IL : InterVarsity Press, 2016. | Includes bibliographical references and index.
Identifiers: LCCN 2016007932 (print) | LCCN 2016008842 (ebook) | ISBN 9780830850952 (pbk. : alk. paper) | ISBN 9780830899739 (eBook)
Subjects: LCSH: Church--Apostolicity.
Classification: LCC BV601.2 .F59 2016 (print) | LCC BV601.2 (ebook) | DDC 262/.72--dc23
LC record available at http://lccn.loc.gov/2016007932

P   23   22   21   20   19   18   17   16   15   14   13   12   11   10   9   8   7   6   5   4   3   2   1

Y   36   35   34   33   32   31   30   29   28   27   26   25   24   23   22   21   20   19   18   17   16

For Darrell L. Guder

A better friend and colleague a person could not want.

Contents

Acknowledgments

This text is an edited version of my Habilitationsschrift undertaken at the Kirchliche Hochschule Wuppertal/Bethel. Working in a second culture and second language is only possible with the grace, generosity and encouragement of others. In this respect, I am very much indebted to the whole of the Kirchliche Hochschule community, faculty, staff and student body. This is a wonderful place, my adopted home. I can only encourage readers of this text to spend a season there. I am proud to have been a recipient of the Karl Immer Stipendium; my work would not have been possible without this. Special thanks is due to Prof. Dr. Alexander Ernst, who went out of his way to make my family welcome, along with the library staff, and especially Katrin Grosskurth, who secured for me an endless procession of books and articles. I am also thankful to my fellow "Assies" and Tijmen Aukes for his help with translating Dutch-language materials. The external readers of my Habilitationsschrift, Prof. Dr. Daniel Cyranka and Prof. Bruce McCormack, both expended a good deal of constructive energy in working through the text, and for this I am grateful.

My most profound thanks, however, is reserved for Prof. Dr. Henning Wrogemann and his family. I have benefited not only from his scholarship but also from his friendship. It would be difficult to overstress his importance for my own academic and personal development.

Though my work took place within the Kirchliche Hochschule Wuppertal/Bethel, my debt of gratitude stretches beyond its borders. It was my privilege to spend some small time with the Evangelische Kirche im Rheinland, in Elberfeld-Nord, and under the supervision of Dr. Hermann-Peter Eberlein. This was a great moment of learning for me. Preaching and conducting the liturgy in a second language I found a challenging exercise, and I am honored to have been a small part of this community and grateful for the patience. I benefited from contact with the Vereinte Evangelische Mission and, through both this institution and the Institut für Interkulturelle Theologie und Inter-religiöse Studien, remain indebted for the connections with the Université Libre des Pays des Grands Lacs, Goma, DRC. My thanks extends to both Dr. Clifford Anderson, director of Scholarly Communications at the Jean and Alexander Heard Library, Vanderbilt University, and to Kenneth Henke, ar-chivist at Princeton Theological Seminary, for helping me secure some rare ecumenical documentation. Prof. Dr. Dr. Günter Thomas, Dr. Robert Brandau, Prof. Christophe Chalamet, Prof. Dr. Marco Hofheinz and Dr. Gudrun Löwner all contributed to the progression of the work. In terms of critical reading, Dr. John Hitchen and Dr. Sarah Wilson read through the whole work and mea-sured its readability. Prof. Darrell Guder, as ever, assisted with the clarity of the German translation. Stone Hill Church of Princeton offered financial support at a time when it was much needed, as did Eric and Annemiek Meinsma. As to my new friends and colleagues at Pilgrim Theological College, a warmer welcome could not have been given. For the space to finish the manuscript, and the fresh eyes of Dr. Sean Winter and Dr. Geoff Thompson, I am also here indebted. As for David Congdon at IVP Academic: simply fantastic, an engaged editor with an eye for detail and supreme patience. I could not have asked for more.

Finally, to Priscilla, Trinity and Mila, you carried a load that was not yours to bear. I can only acknowledge the debt, for it is not redeemable.

Abbreviations

BEM	*Baptism, Eucharist and Ministry* (1982)
CD	Karl Barth, *Church Dogmatics*
CTCV	*The Church: Towards a Common Vision* (2013)
CWME	Commission on World Mission and Evangelism
GAIII	*The Gift of Authority: Authority in the Church III* (1998)
IMC	International Missionary Council
KD	Karl Barth, *Die kirchliche Dogmatik*
Louvain	Catholicity and Apostolicity (1971)
Niagara	The Niagara Report: Report of the Anglican-Lutheran Consultation on the Episcope (1987)
MSC	The Missionary Structure of the Congregation (1961–1968)
NMC	*The Nature and Mission of the Church* (2005)
Porvoo	The Porvoo Common Statement (1992)
RM	*Redemptoris Missio* (1990)
STI	Robert W. Jenson, *Systematic Theology I: The Triune God*
STII	Robert W. Jenson, *Systematic Theology II: The Works of God*
TEV	*A Treasure in Earthen Vessels* (1998)
WCC	World Council of Churches

1

· ·

The Problem of Apostolicity

The community of faith witnesses to its foundation by caring for its institu-
tions. This witness is its mission. So the church fulfils its mission by caring
for the institutions in which Christian certainty and freedom can grow.

EILERT HERMS[1]

It is a cultural imposition on peoples of other cultural matrix
to have to embrace these Eurocentric modes of being
church to the detriment of their cultural heritage.

TERESA OKURE[2]

1.1 THE PRIMACY OF CULTIVATION IN RELATION TO COMMUNICATION

The following is a meditation on the critical import of world Christianity for
fundamental theology. It considers the pluriformity of the world Christian
communion, its evident richness of theologies and structures, to be of material theological significance. Such significance will be tested in relation to
apostolicity. The choice is deliberate. Apostolicity sets the parameters of
Christian identity, underlying what it means to be catholic. It constitutes an

---

[1]Eilert Herms, "Unity, Witness, Mission: A Hypothetical Statement on Each of the Terms in the
Title and Some Remarks on Further Possible Developments in the Meissen Process," in *Einheit
bezeugen: Zehn Jahre nach der Meissener Erklärung: Beiträge zu den theologischen Konferenzen von
Springe und Cheltenham zwischen der EKD und der Kirche von England*, ed. Ingolf Dalferth and
Paul Oppenheim (Frankfurt am Main: Verlag Otto Lembeck, 2003), 478.
[2]Teresa Okure, "The Church in the World: A Dialogue on Ecclesiology," in *Theology and Conversation: Towards a Relational Theology*, ed. Jacques Haers and P. De Mey (Leuven: Peeters, 2003), 425.

evaluative measure, composed of interpretive means and structural limits, by which a particular communion is received as a member of Christ's body. Apostolicity, defined as faithfulness to origins expressed in the continuity of mission, often prioritizes historical continuity and its associated institutional means. Precise limits are consequently applied to the cross-cultural engagement and appropriation of the gospel. However celebrated the diversity of Christian expression may be, when presented as a question of apostolicity, a received orthodoxy prevails, one which makes claims on, but remains uninformed by, the developments of world Christianity.

While the aspects of "continuity" and "being sent" both belong to apostolicity, a controlling opposition directs formal treatments of the concept. This results from the "tendency," identified by Rowan Williams, "to think of 'mission' and 'spirituality' as pointing in different directions—the communicating of the faith and the cultivation of the faith."[3] Much more than a simple tendency, this reflects an ordering whereby apostolicity is identified first with the cultivation of the faith and so in relation to historical continuity, stability, order and office. Cultivation, in other words, is the governing factor beside which all others are asymmetrically ordered. Its priority shapes the nature and purpose of structures and the ends to which the sacraments and the accompanying interpretive measures, such as order and liturgy, are directed. It conditions theological formulations of the church's "visibility," the nature of its historical continuity and the relationship of the local to the universal. It promotes a precise definition of witness, one contingent on growth in the faith and the practices deemed essential to such.

The primacy given to cultivation in the definition of apostolicity both directs and establishes a range of controls over the second direction: the communication of the faith. Communication, especially with the flexibility of form the occasion of cross-cultural translation demands, assumes a secondary and derivative position. As not itself the primary form of Christian witness, mission becomes an "external" act, one detached from the practices associated with formation in the faith. Such mission often enters treatments of apostolicity through a concern for "limits." The general necessity of mission might be granted, but when considered in relation to unity, to

---

[3]Rowan Williams, "Doing the Works of God," in *A Ray of Darkness: Sermons and Reflections* (Cambridge, MA: Cowley, 1995), 221.

historical continuity or to the processes variously termed "inculturation" or "contextualization," it is evaluated against its potential negative effect over the cultivation of, and maturity in, the faith.[4] Mission, by this binary, is not only properly distinguished from Christian spirituality—it is to be approached with an enduring theological caution.

Dominant ecumenical definitions of apostolicity, Protestant and Catholic alike, exploit this ordering of cultivation over communication. The immediate focus of the ecumenical discussion has shifted from the contentious issue of episcopal order to the nature of the Christian community and its mission. Apostolicity is first defined by naming the range of practices and institutions that belong to the "apostolic tradition" before identifying their significance with their "permanence" and service to "Christ's mission."[5] Apostolicity becomes the expression, the gestalt, of the whole life of the church and the essence of its mission. To cite the Faith and Order study *Episkopé and Episcopacy and the Quest for Visible Unity*, "within the total life of the church, the gifts of apostolic continuity form parts of a single system of identity, a single system of communication."[6] As this "total life," apostolicity encompasses the complex of interpretive measures accompanying these practices and institutions. Apostolicity, in more or less explicit terms, is the culture of the church, its being the "people of God." This culture bears and expresses its missionary witness, confirming the basic nature of cultivation.

The benefit of this position is clear. As a culture, the wider complex of liaisons constitutive of church life becomes necessary to its apostolicity. One cannot intrude on these without also intruding on the church's living culture and so its witness. Culture explains how the church apostolic remains constant while changing through history. It links the message and mission of the gospel with the existence of a historically visible people. Questions of order reemerge,

---

[4]As a general observation, "inculturation" is the term preferred within Catholic literature and "contextualization" within Protestant. These terms are themselves the most recent iterations of conceptual developments from the mid-nineteenth century. They are used here to indicate "the creative and dynamic relationship between the Christian message and a culture or cultures," especially in the context of what that means for the church's structures, institutions, ritual, practices and the importance of such for definitions of apostolicity. Aylward Shorter, *Towards a Theology of Inculturation* (Maryknoll, NY: Orbis Books, 1988), 11.

[5]See *Baptism, Eucharist and Ministry* (Geneva: World Council of Churches, 1982), §§M34-35.

[6]Peter Bouteneff and Alan D. Falconer, *Episkopé and Episcopacy and the Quest for Visible Unity: Two Consultations* (Geneva: World Council of Churches, 1999), 59.

but as secondary and in service to this people, a necessary expression of this particular culture. This at once relativizes the historical and cultural origins of the traditional order while establishing governing controls for "diversity" in relation to the church. Connecting a social account of the Trinity to the nature of the church as koinonia supplies seemingly clear and ecumenically attractive theological supports. Indeed, the move appears to be something of an ecumenical triumph, garnering ranging support across the traditions.

The singular difficulty with this consensus emerges when setting this definition of apostolicity in relation to the cross-cultural transmission and appropriation of the faith, in relation to world Christianity and its pluriformity of expression.

Christianity beyond the cultural spheres of the former *corpus Christianum* has been largely uniform in lamenting the faith's unnecessary "foreignness," the over-identification of the Christian gospel with its European and American cultural expressions. The wider complaint is well known. To cite Richard King, "in a cross-cultural and post-colonial context the 'provinciality' of European ways of understanding the world, is increasingly being highlighted with reference to the historical specificity of their origins and provenance."[7] But what form does this "provinciality" take when conceived in relation to the Christian church? One answer consigns the complaint to some form of "missionary imperialism." Missions via their relationship with the processes of colonization, so the logic goes, come to bear responsibility for the improper alignment of the Christian gospel and wider Western culture. This reading, while the popular one, fails to attend to the actual forms believers charge with being "Western": dress, liturgy, order, architecture and the framing of space, patterns of ministry, hymnology, theological questions and idiom, and even the imported structures of schism. In other words, the "foreignness" of Christianity applies not first to some liaison between the faith and external political structures. It bears some relation to the "total life" of the church. One need only refer to the central terms of identity, history, tradition, memory, visibility, the relationship of the local to the universal and of continuity to discontinuity to appreciate the fundamental connection between apostolicity and the cross-cultural transmission and appropriation of the faith.

---

[7] Richard King, "Cartographies of the Imagination, Legacies of Colonialism: The Discourse of Religion and the Mapping of Indic Tradition," *Evam* 3, nos. 1-2 (2004): 245-46.

To conceive the problem as one of Christian faith's "foreignness" beyond a Western context, however, is only a negative way of stating the point. This approach evaluates world Christianity's diverse forms in terms of some other singular given. It establishes framing expectations for the gospel's appropriation. Notably, the institutional question, apostolicity as structure, provides the filter for developments within world Christianity. Ignored is the possibility that the local response to the gospel might produce different structural expressions and that this difference might be essential to maturity in the faith. One question basic to the discussion of apostolicity is whether and to what extent its standards are "located," that is, reflect a certain historical expression of the faith, and whether these might be applied without remainder to the pluriform expressions found in world Christianity. Alternately stated, is not world Christianity itself a development within the catholic faith, positively informing the church's recognition of its own apostolicity? Might apostolicity be defined in terms of, and not in contest with, the diverse expressions of world Christianity? In this approach apostolicity would cease to be an issue of how these communions correspond to a supposedly "timeless" gospel expressed through the given language and institution of the church universal and become one of how they proclaim the gospel in vernacular word, deed and structure. A theology of apostolicity, in other words, should approach the positive expressions of Christianity now evident in multiple centers around the world not as potential threats to the continuity of the faith but as embodying the very nature of that continuity.

A basic contest develops when conceiving apostolicity in cultural terms. The range of necessary qualifications notwithstanding, the church apostolic relates to other geographical locations through a process of replication and opposes the polycentrism and pluriformity of expression characteristic of world Christianity. Formulated in these stark terms, the claim is a big one and requires demonstration. Such is the task through the first half of the work. But to accomplish this, it is necessary to forestall an interpretive assumption. Conceiving apostolicity through the lens of world Christianity resists reading the Protestant/Catholic schism as the primary interpretive framework. This study contests the variety of binary oppositions (those of institution against charisma and of missionary flexibility against settled structure) that follow when schism determines apostolicity's constructive definition. Whatever implications follow for this ecumenical question, they are secondary to the positive form of apostolicity that world Christianity suggests. To shift the debate from its expected ecumenical location, we begin with the opposition of the communication against the cultivation of the faith and its determinative effect for apostolicity.

1.2 THE COMMUNICATION OF THE FAITH

The communication of the faith, in that it must speak in a comprehensible manner within a variety of languages and locations, expects a certain contingency of expression. Context, to a varying extent, informs the method and content of the faith's communication. Insofar as mission remained a mediating task external to the church, such circumstantial flexibility received theological sanction. At least in theory, however, to cite John Paul II, mission is no longer "a marginal task for the Church but is situated at the center of her life, as a fundamental commitment of the whole People of God."[8] While this may sound commendable, much of the theological suspicion attached to the missionary communication of the faith focuses on this issue of flexibility, the supposed freedom of form and its consequence for ecclesiology. The contest is obvious. Mission, in that it draws cultural difference into the church, intrudes on the range of institutions, structures, artifacts, symbols and gestures considered basic to Christian koinonia, to the cultivation of the community and to its visible continuity. Cross-cultural transmission is often perceived as a source for disunity and may, as such, dilute Christian witness. Given this, it is worth considering how this now axiomatic drawing of mission into the church is understood in relation to the structures considered basic to apostolicity.

1.2.1 Missionary flexibility. As it developed in the twentieth century, the notion of a missionary church has a rather specific genealogy. The supposed "maturation" of the former "missions" (a recognition of their becoming independent church bodies), combined with the recognition of colonization as a problem for local Christian identity, prompted a radical redefinition of missionary method and act. Mission could no longer be something simply external to the church. The church itself became the mission. As one theological consequence, the absence of mission from traditional accounts of the

---

[8]John Paul II, *Redemptoris Missio: On the Permanent Validity of the Church's Missionary Mandate* (Washington, DC: United States Catholic Conference, 1990), §32.3.

church, as evidenced by the need for volunteer mission structures, indicated a deficit within sophisticated, established ecclesiologies. To quote Lesslie Newbigin, "the very general belief of Christians in most Churches that the Church can exist without being a mission involves a radical contradiction of the Church's being."[9] The critical development of a missionary church, so ran the logic, entails a range of structural changes to the form of the church as received through the tradition. To continue with Newbigin, if mission were accepted as the "raison d'être of the whole body . . . there would be a profound transformation in the accepted patterns of congregational life, of ministry, of Christian action in the world."[10]

In concrete terms, arguments for the repatriation of mission into the church stressed, first, that the type of mobility perceived as basic to the missionary task now applied to the church. This resulted in a largely critical attitude to established structures. These were deemed to be so sociologically derived and historically located as to inhibit the church's contemporary witness. Shaped by their Christendom context, they embodied a form of social cohesion based in stability and immutability. Renowned ecumenist Willem Visser 't Hooft, for example, argued that the merger of ecclesial and partisan political interests during Christendom produced "institutional forms which are characterized by a desire for permanence. It has made the cathedral rather than the tent its outward expression."[11] This applied particularly to the parish structure, which now struggled under the conditions of modern mass society.

Second, recognizing the church's missionary nature meant acknowledging that the local congregation itself lacks structures sufficient for mission. Or, to use Newbigin's emphatic summary, "the very forms of congregational life were a major hindrance to the Church's evangelism."[12] Mission could no longer be defined as the special reserve of individuals, nor as something geographically determined. It described the action of the whole people of God in each place.

---

[9]J. E. Lesslie Newbigin, *The Household of God: Lectures on the Nature of the Church* (London: SCM Press, 1953), 148.

[10]J. E. Lesslie Newbigin, *One Body, One Gospel, One World: The Christian Mission Today* (London: International Missionary Council, 1958), 16.

[11]W. A. Visser 't Hooft, "The Threefold Christian Calling," *Student World* 54, nos. 1-2 (1961): 31.

[12]J. E. Lesslie Newbigin, "Which Way for 'Faith and Order'?," in *What Unity Implies: Six Essays After Uppsala*, ed. Reinhard Groscurth (Geneva: World Council of Churches, 1969), 116-17.

The congregation, in its very ordering, should promote and support local missionary witness. Central to this was the "lay apostolate" and the revision of existing structures so as to promote the ministry of this body. An example of this logic appeared in the 1961 WCC New Delhi report on "witness." Under the heading "Reshaping the Witnessing Community," it affirmed that the task of witness belonged to the "Laos, that is, the whole People of God in the world," and questioned whether church "practices and structures," insofar as they establish a relationship of active clergy to passive recipients, "prevent the message of the Gospel from challenging the world."[13] Context supplies the criterion by which these judgments were to be made: structural changes and different approaches to the pastoral task depended on specific situations. One proposal envisioned the creation of cell or local Christian community groups for an identifiable collective, such as "a handful of typists and salesgirls in a big store, a dozen or so workers on the various floors of a factory."[14]

In both cases, the underlying principle was clear. To cite Visser 't Hooft, "the whole Church must recognize that her divine mission calls for the most dynamic and costly flexibility." This "Pilgrim Church" should not be "afraid to leave behind the securities of its conventional structures" but be "glad to dwell in the tent of perpetual adaptation."[15] The incorporation of mission into the church meant a purposeful freedom in relation to established struc-

---

[13]W. A. Visser 't Hooft, ed., *The New Delhi Report: Third Assembly of the World Council of Churches* (London: SCM Press, 1962), 88, 89. See also Hans J. Margull, "Strukturfragen werden wichtig: Anmerkung zur 'Laien'—Arbeit und zur missionarischen Verkündigung," *Ökumenische Rundschau* 11 (1962): 18.

[14]Visser 't Hooft, *The New Delhi Report*, 89.

[15]Ibid., 90. If the issue of authentic missionary witness were as simple as a focus on the preaching of the Word and the administration of the sacraments and with a latitude for the development of visible forms, then it is conceivable that the Protestant churches of the West should have made more progress on the question of "missionary churches" than is currently the case. Hans Margull, for example, lays great stock in the potential of Reformed theology to develop a robust missionary ecclesiology because of the theoretical freedom it has to revise its shape according to the task of witness. The Reformation account of church structure grants that (1) it is "*always open to change*"; (2) as church structure serves the gospel, so its shape "must be formed in such a way that it *guarantees* and *furthers* witness in each place and situation"; (3) the church's structure is always "*provisional*," meaning that "no structure is fixed for ever, no structure is eternal or sacred." Hans J. Margull, "We Stand in Our Own Way," *Ecumenical Review* 17, no. 4 (1965): 331. None of this, however, guarantees structures will be "missionary," nor, after the passage of some fifty years, is there even a minimal agreement concerning the nature and form of such missionary structures. Flexibility, as such, is not the single criterion the application of which makes the answer any clearer. Indeed, the idea that mission might be promoted and sustained through the simple modification of structures appears now to be both superficial and naive.

tures for the sake of Christian witness within especially Western societies.

As it appeared within this mid-twentieth-century ecumenical discussion, apostolicity referred to the church's missionary sending. Matters of historic continuity held no focus. This is not to suggest a simple jettisoning of traditional emphases. Rather, the two approaches appear as isolated discussions. The aforementioned WCC report on witness prefaces its constructive proposals with an affirmation that Scripture, the Spirit-filled church, the sacraments of baptism and the eucharist, preaching and "the very existence of the Church" constitute the "long tradition of the Church's witness having its origin in God himself, repeating itself constantly in the life of the Church."[16] As to how the charge of a missionary deficit might attach to these definitive practices, matters remain vague. Such an observation seems typical of the wider debate. A strange bifurcation exists between the restatement of traditional formulas and radical suggestions concerning the church's basic organization and forms of ministry. Those institutional aspects associated with the church's apostolicity appear reified and isolated from the seemingly more mundane and situated missionary critiques.

1.2.2 Mission, the church and the replication of cultural structures. In terms of theological reception, mission cautions against the church becoming an "end in itself." The church points beyond itself to the kingdom of God. Its catholicity refers to a proper universality beyond the confines of any particular cultural form. A church concerned "only with itself," so runs the general consensus, is one unaware that its normative institutions are, in actuality, particular cultural instantiations of the gospel. Even Orthodox theologian John Meyendorff supports this characterization. Because the church is apostolic, mission belongs to its "very nature." Like the apostles, it is sent into the world to witness to the resurrection. With this responsibility, any "Church which ceases to be missionary, which limits itself to an introverted self-sustaining existence or, even worse, places ethnic, racial, political, social, or geographic limitations upon the message of Christ, ceases to be authentically 'the Church of Christ.'"[17] Though this rhetoric is common, its actual implications are less than clear. It is never addressed, for example, to

---

[16]Visser 't Hooft, *The New Delhi Report*, 79-80.
[17]John Meyendorff, "The Orthodox Church and Mission: Past and Present Perspectives," *St. Vladimir's Theological Quarterly* 16, no. 2 (1972): 62.

established church identities and especially not to traditions that regard
episcopal order as a sign, if not a guarantee, of the church's apostolic fidelity.
It functions much more as a polemic against other traditions.

Despite this evident lack of application to the actual ordering of the
church—to the liturgical and pastoral forms that might encourage this orientation—the intent is worth pursuing. It is today commonly recognized
that during the colonial period churches of every tradition were guilty of
transporting culturally located forms of Christian expression. These were,
to a greater or lesser degree, presented as normative and necessary to the
gospel and, as such, did set cultural limits on the gospel, its transmission
and appropriation. Though this observation often functions as simple polemic, it raises legitimate questions concerning the potential link between
the processes of colonization and traditional church order.

The so-called 1951 Rolle Statement on "The Calling of the Church to
Mission and to Unity" issued by the Central Committee of the WCC illustrates well the stated concerns. The separation of mission from the church
resulted in "an unconscious confusion of the unchanging Gospel with the
particular cultural, economic and institutional forms of the older Churches."[18]
A replication of Western structures followed, and this inserted "an element
of cultural domination," producing churches that, "though technically independent," remained dependent because of the foreignness of the inherited
form and its distance from the local context.[19] The detachment of mission
from the church produced a model whereby mission replicated the form of
the sending church in another place. While this is clearly an issue, Rolle focused on the common attribution of this problem to cross-cultural mission
alone and the concomitant absolution applied to the sending churches. Assigning the more deleterious consequences of colonization to mission allowed the now generalized problem of intercultural relationship to be re-
framed in terms of ecumenical "unity" and the reconciliation of now
independent identities. Within this schema, priority attached to churches
with an established history and associated claim to apostolic continuity, and
the onus fell on the "younger" churches to demonstrate how they met the
standards of this wider tradition. Rolle opposed this general logic by rejecting

---

[18]"The Calling of the Church to Mission and Unity," *The Ecumenical Review* 4, no. 1 (1951): 71.
[19]Ibid., 70.

the easy identification between mission and colonization. As mission was itself a task of the church, so the problems derived from the "defects of the Churches from which the mission went forth."[20] By implication, the problem of Christian colonization revealed a defect in established ecclesiologies.[21]

David Bosch summarizes the problem thusly: the "West has often domesticated the gospel in its own culture while making it unnecessarily foreign to other cultures."[22] No culture-free gospel exists, so the main concern is not

---

[20]Ibid. As one example of this widely held position, for Margull, when mission is considered a derivative of the church, then it aims at the church's propagation. "Consequently, as practical experience shows, missions then turn into a process of transplanting churches in their historical particularity." Missions "are then actually perverted into expansion of the culture and civilization of those countries in which the churches have a wide penetration and in which they have shared in the creation of culture and civilization. . . . The message is *de facto* identified with the precipitate of the message in a definite historical, that is, conjointly sociological form of the church." Hans J. Margull, *Hope in Action: The Church's Task in the World,* trans. Eugene Peters (Philadelphia: Muhlenberg Press, 1962), 66.

[21]As Rolle addressed especially the Protestant churches, so it included those with the greatest possibility for structural flexibility. One negative critique of such flexibility holds that without creating a dogmatic space for the Christian community, such ecclesiologies lack a sufficient theological basis to protect against an undue identification with Western culture. Missionary imperialism can be seen as a natural outworking of this primary theological problem. Contrary to this judgment, however, the simple fact of a catholic order was not itself sufficient to exempt an ecclesial body from the ties of colonialization.

Writing with reference to the impact of world Christianity upon the church, Karl Rahner observes that "the actual concrete activity of the Church in its relation to the world outside of Europe was in fact (if you will pardon the expression) the activity of an export firm which exported a European religion as a commodity it did not really want to change but sent throughout the world together with the rest of the culture and civilization it considered superior." Karl Rahner, "Towards a Fundamental Theological Interpretation of Vatican II," *Theological Studies* 40, no. 4 (1979): 717. This leads him, among other things, to question whether the "centralized bureaucracy" of the Roman church lays such claim to a knowledge of the kingdom of God that it makes its decisions according to "the mentality of Rome or Italy in a frighteningly naive way as a self-standard" (717-18). He notes that the shift from a European to a world Christianity will involve not only a break of a cultural and historical character but a theological one as well. This "theological break in Church history still lacks conceptual clarity and can scarcely be compared with anything except the transition from Jewish to Gentile Christianity" (727). By way of concrete examples, Rahner envisions the development of "a significant pluralism with respect to canon law (and other ecclesial praxis as well)" (725) and holds that "a world Church simply cannot be ruled with the sort of Roman centralism that was customary in the period of Piuses" (726). While one might question Rahner's account of church history, and so the radicality with which he depicts the contemporary developments, his comparison of the rise of world Christianity with the transition from a Jewish to a Gentile Christianity is more significant than it may at first appear. Many arguments for apostolicity regard the transition from Jewish to Gentile Christianity as singular and normative for the establishment of church order. Any later development occurs in relation to the church as established. To understand the reception of tradition within the context of the cross-cultural appropriation of the gospel, by contrast, presents a challenge to these established accounts of the church's apostolicity.

[22]David J. Bosch, *Transforming Mission: Paradigm Shifts in Theology of Mission* (Maryknoll, NY: Orbis Books, 1991), 455.

the gospel's cultural embodiment. It stems, rather, from the recognition that the local appropriation of the gospel is itself a necessary component of the gospel's communication.[23] Such is the case precisely because the proclamation and so appropriation of the gospel takes the form of a community. This is the missionary lesson of the colonial period: because mission and community belong together, any failure to reference the local community results in the importation of replacement structures. Those importing these structures are themselves blinded to their foreignness because of, first, the persistence of those structures through time in a way that suggests a certain cultural dislocation and, second, the direction of their importation, to quote Kondothra George, from "a dominant culture to various cultural contexts with no power or very little. These so-called particular contexts are, in fact, culturally in the orbit of the dominant culture."[24] The initial globalization of Western culture during the colonial period reinforced the apparent "internationalism" of church structures. Or, even more strongly from George, a "local cultural expression of the faith now claims universal application."[25] It is at this point that difficulties with apostolicity arise.

William Burrows, former Society of the Divine Word (SVD) missionary to Papua New Guinea, addresses the challenge of forming mature communities in a non-Western context. Here, the precipitating difficulty is that "the European past of the church is still being made absolute and normative for

---

[23]Mission theorists, drawing on developments in historiography, note the impossibility of a pure distinction between mission and community. Stanley Skreslet observes how the old approach drew on an idea of "missionary initiative followed by indigenous response." Stanley H. Skreslet, "Thinking Missiologically About the History of Mission," *International Bulletin of Missionary Research* 31, no. 2 (2007): 60. The missionary is the agent, and what characterizes that agency and so defines mission is the initial transference between possession and need. This position no longer holds. No such "first contact" encounter survives "unless indigenous enterprise asserts itself as more than just a reaction to what other, more fully self-aware subjects are doing" (60). This recognition of "indigenous agency" means that the appropriation of the message belongs to the act of proclamation itself.

[24]Kondothra M. George, "Cross-Cultural Interpretation: Some Paradigms from the Early Church," *International Review of Mission* 85 (1996): 220. George argues that the rise of Islam encouraged "defensiveness and parochialism among the eastern Christian communities [which] through the celebration of the liturgy, faithfulness to the apostolic faith and practice of ascetic and monastic spirituality maintained their catholicity. In the west, the collapse of the empire gave rise to an ecclesiastical structure centred in Rome with an absolutist monarchical and mono-cultural ecclesiology" (223). This became conceived in universal terms and then, with colonization, became interpreted in geographical terms.

[25]Ibid., 223.

nonwestern peoples."[26] The church has erected "its own ethnocentric edifice."[27] It assumes the normativety of the "European experience" and attempts to "exercise control" over non-Western appropriations of the gospel through the insistence on "the binding character of [the Western church's] formulation of the meaning of the Christian fact and Euro-American patterns of fellowship and worship."[28] In other words, while inculturation is affirmed as basic, it occurs within the limits prescribed by the assumed normative institutional model, the very formality of which disguises the complexity of its cultural liaisons.[29] Against this, theology must account for the reality that "a church which has long thought of itself in terms of universal values stands accused of imposing its own relative cultural perspectives on the young churches."[30] A solution is not as simple as applying theological controls against mistaken cultural excesses, for the concerns extend to the shape of the controls themselves. "Western canons of acceptability and what would count for 'culture' were rooted in Greco-Roman standards and norms. It was the demand that the converts adhere to those canons that led to the failure of the church in the highly developed and self-confident cultures of China, India and Japan."[31] Not only does the normative theological tradition include values that alienate the Christian message from other cultural settings, it assumes an account of culture itself and so of the artifacts and practices basic to this culture, such as the structuring and interpretation of authorities, the manner of the identification and expression of mores, and a conception of education and of maturity. By way of example, it is necessary for an indigenous person to attain a form and level of

---

[26]William R. Burrows, *New Ministries: The Global Context* (Maryknoll, NY: Orbis Books, 1980), 25.

[27]Ibid., 31.

[28]Ibid., 32.

[29]José Comblin, for example, observes that "after 1960, decolonization began to affect the Catholic church. . . . The term 'inculturation' began to be heard. For more or less thirty years . . . inculturation is said to be a primary objective, or at least a first condition for evangelization. The pope and the Roman curia have adopted the vocabulary, but nothing more than that, because Catholic inculturation has very strict limits: nothing can be changed in the catechism, or canon law, or the liturgical books (except through a very complicated procedure in the case of the later). Inculturation must accept the entire legacy of the Christendom of Western Europe. Support cannot be sought in the Eastern tradition, not even in the oldest black African church, the Ethiopian church." José Comblin, *Called for Freedom: The Changing Context of Liberation Theology* (Maryknoll, NY: Orbis Books, 1998), 13.

[30]Burrows, *New Ministries*, 25.

[31]Ibid., 26.

education only achievable by a minority in the West before he (and often in this context it is only a "he") may serve as a minister in his own local context.

Burrows's own reformulation begins with the ideological use of apostolicity. Specifically, he identifies an "apologist mentality" that succeeded in reading received "orthodox" structures into the primary biblical text. The evident pluralism of office in the early church became treated as "a sort of confusion that was later corrected when the popes were able to bring aberrant church orders into line."[32] While developments in the understanding of early church history no longer support this orthodoxy, at the level of polity the church proceeds "as if the present shape of ministry is the only one warranted."[33] Burrows grants that a normative apostolic tradition exists but finds the approach, which amounts to an interpretive apology for a particular ecclesiastical tradition, unfounded both methodologically and historically.[34] That which might be regarded as the "authentic common denominator," Burrows argues, "is not the complex of Euro-American ways of responding to the challenge of Jesus, for Christian institutions are merely the shape which fellowship takes when men and women have the experience of converting to Christ."[35] Burrows is not here suggesting that form is without theological significance, that as structures have developed in history so they are "merely human," reducible to sociological mechanics.[36] Because the canon testifies to the development of structures, "development" is normative for the establishment of theological institutions.[37]

To further his argument, Burrows turns to Edward Schillebeeckx. As Jesus did not institute any offices prior to his ascension, so the early church could decide on the forms reflective of the message they had received. Burrows rejects the notion that the development of institution was a deformation of an otherwise unburdened apostolic church because "what is really at stake is the church's ability in *every* age to adapt itself to circumstances."[38] This principle

---

[32]Ibid., 79-80.

[33]Ibid., 80.

[34]With reference to the Jerusalem Council in Acts 15, "uniformity, either in forms of office or community life, is not required for being fully church." Ibid., 83. Indeed, Burrows maintains that "there is no theological warrant for uniformity in church structure, for the basic mission of the church lies much deeper than visible models" (48).

[35]Ibid., 48.

[36]Ibid., 84.

[37]Ibid., 80.

[38]Ibid., 85.

of apostolic development presents the church as "first and foremost a communion of local churches, each with a right to its own forms and life-styles."[39] These local churches must be in communion with one another, but this occurs through a process of wrestling between Scripture, tradition and the local culture, not through the imposition of an external unity. Inculturation, insofar as it occurs under the controls of given church structures, fails to permit the type of appropriation of the gospel basic to its hearing; that is, it militates against the formation of local community structures. "It is not enough to give a notional assent to the need to adapt liturgical and institutional forms in external matters. More important is the need to find ways of life in community which allow and encourage nonwestern Christians to express what their encounter with Christ means to them."[40] Given that the community is itself the central organ of missionary witness, structural limitations exert a limiting effect over Christian witness to the gospel and maturity in the faith.

While theologians outside the Western cultural sphere constitute no monolithic other, their voices appear unified and unequivocal in affirming that the institutions regarded as basic to the visible continuity of the church are, in fact, derived from Western culture and that these origins affect the growth of the church in other contexts. As one example, Teresa Okure states, without qualification, that the forms of the Catholic church, its hierarchical structure and linguistic and cultural heritage, all derive from the Roman Empire.[41] The Western church, she avers, needs to remember

> that what has come to be defined as church in terms raised here (structures, symbols, ritual, law of governance), were taken from the pagan Greco-Roman cultures, the matrix from which the western European culture emerged, not primarily from the Gospel of Jesus Christ. Consequently it is a cultural imposition on peoples of other cultural matrix to have to embrace these Eurocentric modes of being church to the detriment of their cultural heritage.[42]

Without acknowledging that culture has informed even this basic structural level, the possibilities for inculturation remain limited. Taking this position seriously will "substantially affect the current church structures, [the] understanding

---

[39]Ibid., 86.
[40]Ibid., 24.
[41]Okure, "Church in the World," 406-7.
[42]Ibid., 425.

of sacraments, canon law and all the other ways of being church inherited or originating from the negative influences of the Empire."[43] While Okure does not employ the terminology, it is clear that she extends this cultural critique to the institutions associated with the church's apostolicity.

Nor is it simply possible to detach apostolic structures from culture, for ecclesial governance is "attitudinal and architectural. The very way in which our churches and sacred places are structured exercise a powerful influence on the way we think, act and relate to one another when we assemble as church."[44] Okure's critique, in other words, includes the framing of space because this too manifests a cultural way of seeing the world. She, by way of illustration, contrasts the received pattern to a more communal model, drawing on African villages built around circular huts. Okure agrees that Christian belief should help shape our social worlds. Her complaint is that the Western forms, if not themselves sullied by their over-identification with this cultural location, impose problematic restrictions on the Christian ordering of the world. Reference to the local culture, by contrast,

> may offer better or more gospel-based forms of being church and living the gospel than the inherited western referents. A key example is the essentially communitarian culture of Africa, with its high premium on hospitality, its strong sense of community that embraces the living, the dead (who are never really dead) and those yet to be born. It promotes a sense of corporate responsibility for the growth and survival of the "clan" and respect for nature.[45]

As the community is itself the proper form of missionary witness, so reducing Christian order to forms derived from the West constitutes a premature closing of that witness.

Okure and Burrows both assume a relationship between an improper imposition of Western culture on churches of other cultural heritage and the normative theological claims of apostolicity. Though they write as Catholics and interpret the matter guided by certain assumptions, this connection between received church structures and culture applies equally to the Protestant churches. While Protestantism, with the axioms of *sola scriptura* and *ecclesia semper reformanda*, may be more open to structural

---

[43]Ibid., 424.
[44]Ibid.
[45]Ibid., 425.

freedom, the testing of this theory in a cross-cultural context demonstrates the difficulties in implementation. This is evident in the confusions and controls applied to ordination during the period of Western missionary expansion.[46] These, first, would not permit missionaries to be ordained (and so they lacked the authority to baptize) until they were in charge of something identifiable as a congregation (for which baptism is basic) and, second, imposed a variety of barriers to the development of indigenous leadership. Protestantism's canonical approach to apostolicity and its minimalist marks of the preaching of the Word and the administration of the sacraments, it might be suggested, may only be sufficient for a context where some relationship already exists between the local culture and the Christian faith.[47] Where this does not exist, where the existence of a living Christian community is at a premium, the submerged cultural shape of the originating church becomes readily apparent. This is evident in the swiftness with which some Protestant missionaries applied the charge of syncretism, of an identifiable discontinuity in the faith, to local attempts to formulate theology in response to their cultural heritage. Mission threatens a notion of continuity based in the replication of structures, be those in institutional or creedal form, because such "continuity" shares all the hallmarks of a cultural residue and is challenged as such in the context of cross-cultural encounter.

It is a peculiarity of the attempt to set mission in relation to the church that it has avoided discussion of the church's apostolicity. Any potential connections between the church's apostolic continuity, the replication of cultural forms and the encouragement or hindrance of the church's mission remain unstated. Whether a particular structure, such as episcopal order, can simply be detached from any discussion of its historical and cultural origin in such a way that it becomes applicable across historical and cultural barriers is a question to be asked. But the issue is wrongly construed if limited to this single issue. An obvious question, for example, is the extent

---

[46]See Klaus Detlev Schulz, "The Lutheran Debate over a Missionary Office," *Lutheran Quarterly* 19, no. 3 (2005): 276-301.

[47]Christopher Moody notes how Protestants are more "likely to put the emphasis on the teaching of the Church rather than on its historical continuity as the focus of its apostolicity." The approach is not culturally benign, for guarding the deposit of the faith expands to include a range of interpretive measures, meaning that "all messages, if they are to be heard at all, must be intelligible within their own culture and context, and that the priorities of one age are not necessarily those of another." Christopher Moody, "Apostolicity and the Call of the Kingdom," *Theology* 94 (1991): 87.

to which accounts of the church's "historical continuity" assume a particular conception of time and history that imposes a range of expectations unachievable in other cultural contexts.[48] As a community, the church will properly maintain a historical social trajectory. But as a community of "Jew and Gentile," it is perhaps reasonable to assume that this trajectory will include the type of disruptions and discontinuities that are part of any boundary-crossing endeavor. At the very least, it appears to be a matter properly addressed to theologies of apostolicity.

EXCURSUS: STEPHEN NEILL ON THE RELATIONSHIP OF CHURCH AND MISSION

In this context, it is worth referring to Bishop Stephen Neill's oft-cited dictum, "If everything is mission, nothing is mission."[49] This reflects a concern that if the term "mission" was applied too broadly, as was occurring within the ecumenical discussion of the church's missionary nature, then it would lose any meaning. "Mission," Neill argues, should be reserved for the specific task of introducing the gospel to those who have not yet heard it.

It is often the case, however, that those who cite this position fail to appreciate Neill's continuing argument. While the dilution of mission is a problem, it is a derivative and revealing one. "A correct theology of the *Church* would include everything that we now regard as the special and separate problems of 'missions' and a correct theology of *ministry* would include everything that now perplexes us as the special problem of the 'foreign' missionary."[50] The potential overemphasis on mission results from an inadequate doctrine of the church and its ministry. Neill expounds his point through an extended treatment of the problematic separation of missionary institutions from the church, and especially the absurdity of a mis-

---

[48]For a brief examination of this issue, see Theo Sundermeier, "Missio Dei Today: On the Identity of Christian Mission," *International Review of Mission* 92, no. 4 (2003): 569-71. Kosuke Koyama too expresses a good deal of circumspection in identifying "a purposeful linear history" with the Christian faith because to do so is to identify the Christian faith with Western civilization. Kosuke Koyama, "New World—New Creation: Mission in Power and Faith," *Mission Studies* 10, nos. 1-2 (1993): 73. He does not deny the "purposefulness of history" but maintains that "the image of straight line, the image of efficiency, and that of the Biblical *hesed*, steadfast love, cannot go together" (73).

[49]Stephen Neill, *Creative Tension* (London: Edinburgh House Press, 1959), 81.

[50]Ibid., 82.

sionary or missionary society seeking to serve a growing Christian community but without the authority either to ordain or to administer the Word and sacraments. Even in a pioneer context, he argues, "a Church must be complete from the start. Completeness includes the *protestas ordinandi*, authority to ordain, in order that the Church may be assured from without of its own continuity, without dependence on any outside authority."[51] That this does not occur reflects "a failure of the Churches to develop a missionary sense," a failure embodied in an ambiguous church order that isolates missionaries from the church and leads to a range of theologically indefensible aberrations.[52] Neill seeks not some simple flexibility in church order. His concern has a much greater force.

> All our ecclesiologies are inadequate and out of date. Nearly all of them have been constructed in the light of a static concept of the Church as something given, something which already exists. Much attention has been concentrated on external "marks of the Church." As far as I know, no one has yet set to work to think out the theology of the Church in terms of the one thing for which it exists.[53]

Neill's concern is clear: the problem encountered by the missionary endeavor lies with an inadequate doctrine of the church, and the radical shift initiated by the inclusion of mission entails a significant revision of even basic church structures and associated doctrines.

Part of the difficulty lies in the concrete implications of such a position, especially as it applies to such a cornerstone theological concept as apostolicity. In a chapter titled "The Unfinished Church," Neill raises the issue of the church's historicity, which includes both unrepeatable achievements, such as the canon and the creeds, and their necessary historical location, which prohibits simple repetition. He notes that "the ground plan of the Church, in its doctrine, its worship, and its organization, is already discernible in the New Testament."[54] This observation he conditions by way of a lament. Instead of using the whole scope afforded by the New Testament, emphasis fell "mainly on the givenness of the Church, on what we have received from the past, and far less on the other

---

[51]Ibid., 92.
[52]Ibid., 84.
[53]Ibid., 111.
[54]Stephen Neill, *The Unfinished Task* (London: Edinburgh House Press, 1957), 16.

aspect of creative development."[55] A contrast formed between the "static" and "dynamic" areas of the church's life, which Neill develops in terms of understanding the church either as an "existing worshiping society, or in terms of its possible missionary outreach."[56] The Reformers, even while reacting to Catholic order, chose to define the church as an existing society—as the visible body where the Word is preached and the sacraments administered. Neill does not deny the validity of such, but it emphasizes what "is fixed, stable, and unchanging; and it is these elements which most naturally find their expression in a fixed and unchanging organization. For this reason, controversies between the Churches tend to find their centre in the question of the ministry and the order of the Church, and of the validity of the Sacraments which are dependent on such ministries."[57] The churches have the "inveterate tendency" to "settle down" to the extent that they "have not merely appeared unconscious of the missionary outreach, but have gloried in their repudiation of it, maintaining that the Church has nothing to do but attend respectably to its local responsibilities."[58] However, against an overemphasis on missionary mobility to the deficit of institution, for Neill, these two elements resist distortion only by being held together. Part of the answer rests in understanding the church as a provisional body moving toward its eschatological future. "In its own dispensation it is all-important, but that importance is derived not from what it is in itself, but from that for which it prepares the way."[59]

Though Neill advocates a basic "catholic" structure, this must itself develop because of the church's missionary witness through history. Thus the question remains as to the concrete implications for church order when considered in a missionary light. Herein lies the difficulty. The church's apostolicity appears isolated from reference to mission, and given that the concept immediately informs the ministry and the sacraments, this withdraws much of the "church" from the critical discussion. For example, a rather notorious apology for the apostolic ministry from a Church of England perspective appeared in *The Apostolic Ministry: Essays on the History and the Doctrine of*

---

[55]Ibid., 17.
[56]Ibid., 18.
[57]Ibid., 19.
[58]Ibid., 19-20.
[59]Ibid., 32.

Episcopacy.[60] In response, Neill collected a range of reviews and wrote an introductory essay for a text published as *The Ministry of the Church: A Review by Various Authors of a Book Entitled "The Apostolic Ministry."*[61] Though this text appears ten years prior to the works referenced above, Neill already had two decades of missionary experience, including experience with the establishment of the Church of South India, to which he makes reference. While he stands opposed to the conclusions drawn in *Apostolic Ministry*, his lack of reference to mission as a theological category informing apostolicity is noteworthy. Neill rejects the outlined position using the same texts and in the same manner as the objectionable argument. This text is, of course, a critical review rather than a constructive text. Nevertheless, it is this capacity to isolate the two discussions even while advocating their rapprochement that is a curiosity characteristic of the wider debate.

1.3 THE CULTIVATION OF THE FAITH

The assumed division of the cultivation from the proclamation of the faith does not result in two equally weighted options: the distinction includes a relative ordering. Cultivation is considered basic for, and thus prior to, the act of communication; the pastoral, the nurturing of a common spiritual life, because it is formative, becomes primary and distinct from a secondary and external mission.[62] Insofar as the contingencies necessary to the communication of the

---

[60]Kenneth E. Kirk and Cecilia M. Ady, eds., *The Apostolic Ministry: Essays on the History and the Doctrine of Episcopacy* (London: Hodder & Stoughton, 1946).

[61]Stephen Neill, *The Ministry of the Church: A Review by Various Authors of a Book Entitled "The Apostolic Ministry"* (London: Canterbury Press, 1947).

[62]As an example, see George Vandervelde's discussion of the 1996 report from the WCC study on ecclesiology and ethics titled *Costly Obedience: Towards an Ecumenical Communion of Moral Witnessing* (published in Thomas F. Best and Martin Robra, *Ecclesiology and Ethics: Ecumenical Ethical Engagement, Moral Formation and the Nature of the Church* [Geneva: World Council of Churches, 1997], 50-90). The report, first, notes how in modern societies a "multiplicity of culturally formative powers" exist that do not simply contrast with the church's power but make the church captive to different cultural interpretations of the faith. George Vandervelde, "Costly Communion: Mission Between Ecclesiology and Ethics," *Ecumenical Review* 49, no. 1 (1997): 47, 48. Second, the report affirms the "formative significance of the liturgy" and "the encompassing nature of worship as the 'enactment' of the story of God's way with the human race'" (48). The liturgy is to be "lived out morally" in such a way that "makes us participants in the Christian story" (50, quoting the report). Vandervelde then observes how the study ignored "the generative matrix of the entire contemporary ecumenical movement, namely mission" (50). To offset this weakness, he draws mission statements into the discussion and concludes that mission gives a "disclosure dimension." Yet, in a confusing reversal, he grants that *Costly Obedience* already includes such a dimension because it regards liturgy as a "disclosure" and a "life-forming event" (53). Vandervelde illustrates, in other words, how reference to the church's

faith appear erosive of the stabilities necessary to its cultivation, mission appears to disrupt the church's community life and so witness. Though mission is valued as perhaps even a necessary "task," it is such at a secondary distance from those institutions deemed constitutive of the church itself: the liturgy, the preaching of the Word, the administration of the sacraments and the ministry. Claims of the church's "missionary nature" become subject to this ordering that now identifies the pastoral with the church and its structures, and mission with a specific action occurring beyond the local congregation and the preserve of especially called individuals.

1.3.1 The institutional divorce of church and mission. The ordering that establishes a primary pastoral "mission" over a secondary and external movement is notoriously present, for example, in *Ad Gentes*.[63] Such inconsistency is common. Without addressing the implications for structures and their replication entailed by such a mission method, *Redemptoris Missio* reinforces the same logic.[64] It describes mission as "a single but complex reality" (RM, §41), thereby permitting an encompassing vision of mission while confining the specific act to an activity on the church's periphery undertaken by those with a corresponding vocation. When it comes to the question of structures, "the early Church experiences her mission as a community task, while acknowledging in her midst certain 'special envoys' or 'missionaries devoted to the Gentiles,' such as Paul and Barnabas" (RM, §61). Mission is first the life of the community alongside which specific mission organs develop and with a flexibility of form that, by this reading, do not attach to the community itself. This external missionary act remains ecclesiologically significant, however, for "without the mission *ad gentes*, the Church's very missionary dimension would be deprived of its essential meaning and of the very activity that exemplifies it" (RM, §34). Thus "mission" serves as a theological predicate of the church in its historical existence, while the mobility acknowledged as necessary to missionary engagement becomes detached from the

---

liturgical life assumes a comprehensive responsibility for the cultivation of the faith, how reference to mission is not itself critically necessary to the formative capacity of the church and how when mission does appear its contribution is already sufficiently stated by reference to the liturgy.

[63] Austin Flannery, ed., *Vatican Council II: The Conciliar and Post Conciliar Documents* (Northport, NY: Costello, 1996), 813-56.

[64] See Eugene Hillman, "Ministry: Missionary and/or Pastoral," *New Theology Review* 14, no. 2 (2001): 76-79.

church's dogmatic substance. Mission, in this latter sense, gains theological gravitas through reminding the church that it is missionary.

Neither this priority given to the church in its mundane historical existence as the form of mission, nor the compartmentalization between an internal missionary dimension and an external act, is a peculiarly Catholic problem. Protestant mission theory, with justification, has argued in a similar vein. In 1958 Lesslie Newbigin held that the "Church *is* a mission."[65] Jesus Christ entrusted his mission to his church, not according to human capacity, but by participation in the mission of the Holy Spirit. The Spirit brings about a "new being" that is

> the common life (*koinonia*) in the Church. . . . This new reality—namely the active presence of the Holy Spirit among [human beings]—is the primary witness, anterior to all specific acts whether of service or of preaching. These different acts have their relation to one another not in any logical scheme, but in the fact that they spring out of the one new reality. This is the city set on a hill which cannot be hid.[66]

While mission is itself determinative for the nature of the community, the community is itself the mission. "The whole life of the Church, rightly understood, is thus the visible means through which the Holy Spirit carries on His mission to the world, and the whole of it thus partakes of the character of witness."[67] The church in the act of worship is already a witnessing community. While the intention behind this argument, in the words of Visser 't Hooft, was not one of "churchifying mission but of mobilizing the Church for its mission," its wider appropriation differed in surprising ways.[68] On the one hand, it politicized mission, linking it to movements of "revolutionary" social change and to a structural mobility whereby the church formed itself in correspondence to these "worldly" developments. On the other, it placed mission within the realm of ethics, and this tended to affirm traditional church structures as themselves basic to Christian "witness," that is, to "maturity" in the faith. Both approaches

---

[65]Newbigin, *One Body, One Gospel, One World*, 17.

[66]Ibid., 20.

[67]Ibid., 21.

[68]As cited by Newbigin from a comment made by Visser 't Hooft during a 1956 preparatory meeting for the integration of the WCC and the IMC. J. E. Lesslie Newbigin, "Mission to Six Continents," in *The Ecumenical Advance: A History of the Ecumenical Movement, 1948-1968*, ed. Harold E. Fey (London: SPCK, 1970), 183.

minimized the more classical definitions of mission, which were by now under sustained attack from the charges of colonialism and "cultural imperialism."

With this priority given to the community, Newbigin introduced a distinction between the church's missionary *dimension* and its missionary *intention*.[69] "Because the Church is the mission there is a missionary dimension to everything that the Church does."[70] This dimension Newbigin describes as the "Church's worship, the perpetual liturgy in which she is joined to the worship of the heavenly hosts . . . directed wholly to God for His glory." In circumstances that prohibit overt proclamation this may "be in fact the most powerful possible form of witness."[71] The missionary intention, by comparison, Newbigin leaves curiously undefined, but it refers to the specific missionary act, which he depicts as *"the crossing of the frontier between faith in Christ as Lord and unbelief."*[72] In similar tone to *Redemptoris Missio*, this act serves the church because "unless there is in the life of the Church a point of concentration for the missionary intention, the missionary dimension which is proper to the whole life of the Church will be lost."[73] An external mission is necessary for reminding the church of its own eccentric existence. But it remains unclear what this process of reminding accomplishes in concrete terms, especially as this pertains to the potential identification and revision of the supposedly "mission-retarding" traditional structures, about which Newbigin himself laments.

This basic pattern, which identifies mission with the church in its mundane existence and which advocates a particular missionary concentration that somehow embodies and reminds the church of its missionary essence, remains dominant across the traditions. At issue is the way in which mission becomes repackaged in terms of the given structures considered constitutive of the church, and the way this insulates church structures from the challenges natural to cross-cultural engagement. The "essential" mission of the church consists of those elements basic to the cultivation of the faith. Chief here is a community capable of sustaining a coherent social trajectory and the range of artifacts basic to such: order, practices, texts, traditions, etc. Mis-

---

[69]Newbigin, *One Body, One Gospel, One World*, 21.
[70]Ibid., 43.
[71]Ibid., 21.
[72]Ibid., 29.
[73]Ibid., 43.

sionary mobility facilitates the transition of new believers into the ordered community of faith, but the development of Christian identity is contingent on stability and the structures—ministerial, liturgical and sacramental—that undergird maturation in the Christian *habitus*. In this sense, the church claims the sacraments and ministry as its own while mission is reduced to a practice beside these other ministries. Historic missions revealed the impossibility of separating the missionary act from baptism, the Lord's Supper and, by extension, issues of ordination with supporting liturgical forms and accompanying concerns related to forming Christian communities. Though this may reflect the actual state of missionary transmission, however, it fails to intrude on the neat division between church and mission. If the operative notion of stability included a better sense of integration with local cultural structures, this position might seem, at least in principle, acceptable for those concerned about the importation of Western structures. But that is precisely the issue: to what extent can the historical continuity considered basic to this account of the church as mission accommodate the challenges posed by the gospel's cross-cultural transmission and appropriation?

1.3.2 Cultivation as culture. Jean Daniélou's 1953 text *Essai sur le Mystère de l'Historie* provides an entryway into the question. Daniélou sets the role of structure in relation to cross-cultural transmission and local appropriation by considering the entrance of Christianity into non-Western contexts via the missionary endeavor. His discussion begins by noting the complaints against Western hegemony, the identification of comparable non-Western "civilizations," the entrance of Christianity into these civilizations as "a foreign import" and the associated call for the "re-incarnation of Christianity in the form of these resurgent civilizations."[74] Against his backdrop Daniélou notes how, in comparison to the christianization of the West, other "cultural traditions . . . remain intrinsically and homogeneously pagan." In relation to these, "Christianity can only be a foreign body: as it has engendered no native cultural monument of any value, it has no place in the tradition of the people."[75] Missionary endeavors, as they will have no effect over individuals at the political center, become restricted to individuals located

---

[74]Jean Daniélou, *The Lord of History: Reflections on the Inner Meaning of History* (London: Longmans, 1958), 35.
[75]Ibid., 35.

on the social margins, and any "conversion will inevitably be regarded as an act of treason against the national way of life." These cultures require an extended process of christianization before the political leaders convert, and it is the conversion of these leaders that is "an essential precondition of any lasting establishment of Christianity."[76] Daniélou's central concern, in other words, is with the missionary act and the establishment of the Christian faith within each civilizational identity.

Daniélou rejects the idea that Christianity can be linked to one particular culture, warns that a too close identification of Christianity with Europe leaves no room for mission and advocates for its translation into other civilizations.[77] Such translation, however, takes centuries as these other cultures first require a "purge" of their idolatrous "dross" before they can be "absorbed" into Christianity.[78] It is necessary then that the Christian idioms normative for the proclamation of the gospel are grounded in Western patterns of thought and language. The faith has been so "deeply rooted" in Western culture that it borrows from this culture "its theological and liturgical terminology and its social patterns" to the extent that it now "seems impossible to disentangle them."[79] Although Christianity does not result from Western culture, from this culture derive the dominant forms by which Christianity enters a non-Western setting.

While not made explicit by Daniélou, this approach explains the perceived cultural foreignness of Christianity in terms of a necessary discontinuity from the idolatrous forms embedded within these non-Western civilizations. Such does not apply to contemporary Western culture because the long process of purification in relation to its pagan Greek heritage has already been completed. It is the continuity of this refined heritage within a non-Western setting that establishes the proper theological distance of a Christian people from its local culture. Christian foreignness becomes a consequence of a proper difference, one in which a local convert abandons his or her traditions and the "paganism they enshrined" in favor of the Christian faith as the convert "finds it, from the West. He would be shocked

---

[76]Ibid., 56.
[77]See his rejection of Karl Theime's position. Ibid., 38-39.
[78]Ibid., 36.
[79]Ibid., 37.

to think of building a Christian church to look like a temple, or singing hymns to our Lady with melodies taken from the repertory of heathen incarnations."[80] While this is an obviously complex issue, defining Christian difference in terms of the importing of foreign cultural structures while, over a period of centuries, the local "dross" is "purged away" seems fundamentally to misconstrue its nature.[81] That it occurs seems to be a necessary consequence of juxtaposing a Christian with a pagan culture and making that conflict basic to the missionary task.

There is a possible inconsistency here. Daniélou, on the one hand, acknowledges the entanglement of Western culture with the liturgical and social structures of the church and, on the other hand, promotes those same structures as theologically normative in a way that detaches them from any cultural location. The church's structures can be coincidentally culturally located and detached, he argues, because of Christianity's translatability. As Christianity began in an Aramaic cultural setting and "absorbed in time the culture of the Hellenes and finally the social structure of Rome," so it is able to absorb other cultural patterns. The church belongs to no particular culture and can derive "an imperishable enrichment from each of the cultures with which it is united." What this oft-stated enrichment looks like in concrete terms, given, for example, Daniélou's rejection of alternate architectural forms as reflective of pagan dross, is unclear. Nevertheless, as the church passes through history, so it incorporates "every variety of human civilization." It becomes "a robe of rich embroidery" (Ps 45:14), an independent entity that has absorbed all the cultures of the world. Thus, China can welcome Catholicism and let it take root in Chinese culture "without repudiating the capital value of its existing investment in Latin forms, which would indeed be a ridiculous act of xenophobic self-impoverishment."[82]

Such translatability depends on a prioritization of certain cultural forms. Daniélou notes the Semitic origins of the faith but enlists Hellenism as normative because of the church's "ineradicable connexions with the Latin

---

[80]Ibid., 36.
[81]Ibid., 37.
[82]Ibid., 41.

culture, and with the historical circumstances of Petrine Rome."[83] He quotes
Georges Florovsky to the effect that Hellenism is "an integral component,
being in fact a permanent category of Christianity."[84] Such an affirmation is
not to be ethnically or geographically limited. It concerns the nature of
spirituality itself and the practical impossibility for appreciating "the in-
wardness of liturgical praxis without some initiation into the mystique of
Hellenism." One must, in some sense, become Hellene to experience fully
the worship of God, for Hellenism is determinative of the church's basic
structures—the liturgy, baptism and the eucharist—and in the "permanent
structure of Christian theology."[85] Other cultures receive the church through
this culture, for the "spirit of Hellenism in the heart of the Roman church"
is the key to its catholicity and unity. Reference to Hellenism supposedly
distances Christianity from its Western embodiment, and this creates space
for the rooting of the faith in other cultures.

The church embodies an international culture unified around a Hellenistic and, by extension, Latin core. All necessary authority for this position,
according to Daniélou, rests in the church's historical origins and the persistence of the associated forms to the contemporary period. What he leaves
unexamined is the extent to which the observed entanglement of Western
culture with the social patterns of the church might, in fact, be revised given
that mission mediates this cultural heritage to other cultures. The open possibility of a non-Western contribution seems difficult to quantify. Daniélou
readily acknowledges the diversity of the church as a theological imperative
along with the vague possibility of future changes, but such changes remain
Limited by the permanence of the Hellenistic cultural norm that Daniélou
deems necessary to the experience of, and maturity in, the faith.

A Protestant version of this argument will appear in a later chapter. Here
it is worth continuing with Pope Benedict XVI, who, drawing on a more
sophisticated theory of cultures and their interaction, has made explicit the
link between a supposed international culture of faith and the corresponding

---

[83]Ibid., 41.
[84]Ibid. Daniélou fails to reference the Florovosky text from which this citation is drawn, but for a
    development along these lines, see Brandon Gallaher, "'Waiting for the Barbarians': Identity and
    Polemicism in the Neo-Patristic Synthesis of Georges Florovsky," *Modern Theology* 27, no. 4
    (2011): 659-91.
[85]Daniélou, *Lord of History*, 42.

impossibility of inculturation. In a 1993 address, Benedict frames the encounter between the Christian faith and culture in terms of the church's "universal mission."[86] His argument begins by defining culture as "the historically developed common form of expression of the insights and values which characterize the life of a community." A number of related observations follow. First, religion is the "determining core" of any culture, and culture is an interpretation of the world according to its understanding of the divine. Second, culture takes up the "common subject" in a way that conserves and develops its insights and permits the individual to transcend himself or herself through participation in this "larger social subject." One's cultural heritage, in other words, is necessary to full human maturity. Third, history leads to the transformation of culture through the encounter with other cultures. Based on this, Benedict rejects the language of "inculturation" in favor of "inter-culturality." Because of, first, the incommensurable religious visions basic to each culture; second, the way in which culture is necessary to the "unity and wholeness" of the individual; and, third, the progress of culture through historical encounter, no "practical universality" exists that would preserve the integrity of both the message and the culture it encounters. Given that this integrity is basic to authentic inculturation, inculturation is itself an impossibility.

Benedict's positive argument for "inter-culturality" maintains that "faith is itself culture. . . . Faith is its own subject, a living and cultural community we call the 'people of God,'" one that has "matured through a long history and through intercultural mingling." This use of "people of God" language, drawing as it does on *Lumen Gentium* §9, seeks to decouple questions of church order from the charge that they are Western in form. As the church is itself a culture, so it is necessarily distinguished from the cultural entity of the West. "This cultural subject Church, People of God, does not coincide with any of the individual historic subjects even in times of apparently full Christianization as one thought one had attained in Europe." As to how they relate, Benedict argues that it is special to the

---

[86]This 1993 address, delivered in Hong Kong to the presidents of the Asian bishops' conferences and the chairmen of their doctrinal commissions, was titled "Christ, Faith and the Challenge of Cultures." It was later published as Joseph Ratzinger, "In the Encounter of Christianity and Religions, Syncretism Is Not the Goal," *L'Osservatore Romano*, April 26, 1995, 5-8. Quotations in this and the following paragraphs come from pages 5 and 6 of this text.

particular "people of God" culture that it overlaps with other cultural entities, maintaining "[the church's] own overarching form" in the encounter.
It is not, as such, merely one culture among others, the joining of which
means the leaving of another culture.[87] "The cultural subject 'people of
God' differs from the classical cultures which are defined by tribe, people
or the boundaries of a common region insofar as the people of God exists
in different cultures which for their part, even as far as the Christian is
concerned, do not cease to be the first and unmediated culture. Even as a
Christian, one remains a Frenchman, a German, an American, an Indian,
etc." Thus, while Benedict constructed his argument for the independence
of the culture of faith through a generalized account of "culture" and its
ongoing transformation through the encounter with other cultures in
history, the "people of God" culture is not finally comparable to the form
of culture described by this generalized depiction.

Nevertheless, Benedict argues that the nature of this overarching
culture was in place during the New Testament period. Christianity bears
Israel's "entire cultural history," and the manner in which Israel "con-
fronted," "adopted" and "transformed" the Egyptian, Hittite, Sumerian,
Babylonian, Persian and Greek cultures becomes paradigmatic for the way
in which the church maintains its cultural identity while purifying the
cultures it encounters "to their own lasting fulfilment." While one might
inquire how the church now displays the fulfillment of, for example, Hittite
culture, Benedict's point is that the church, as it is, is already this overarching culture. While the church may become an "even purer vessel" in
its engagement with other cultures, it is those cultures that experience a
"break" with their own "antecedent history." That a different cultural people
come to accept Israel's history as its own is a key element in the local appropriation of the gospel. The question is whether this engrafting into
Israel is transferable to some notion of the church catholic such that the
necessary cultural break includes an acceptance of the church as it has
developed through its Western trajectory.

Elsewhere Benedict addresses the situation of the so-called younger
churches and their "urgent task of a fruitful encounter with the history and

---

[87]Though he does argue that converts enter "a cultural subject with its own historically developed
and multi-tiered inter-culturality." Ratzinger, "Encounter of Christianity and Religions," 7.

culture of their own peoples and also with their religious tradition," an encounter that will "naturally have profound counter-effects upon the whole
church."[88] As part of this, Benedict recognizes that "the church has not fully
'arrived' as long as it remains a mere Western import," that the "faith can be
identified with no form of culture" and that it needs to be "translated anew."
What this means in terms of effect, however, is not so clear. Translation,
Benedict continues, "means identity in essentials," and these never appear
in "pure form, but always only in historical forms," an observation true of
both the incarnation and the first witnesses. Insofar as this is the case,
Benedict asks, "what in this accidental aspect has become necessity by virtue
of the eternal significance of Jesus Christ? How far must we all, in order to
be Christians, become Jews and Greeks?" If it is then possible for accidental
cultural elements—even broad ones like "Jew and Greek"—to become necessary, the same question applies to central theological affirmations like
"Christological titles," to the "liturgy" and to the "proper order of the liturgical year." Further reference to the incarnation reinforces this circumspection regarding the actuality of inculturation. As the "incarnation does
not come to us in a unilinear way, but only brokenly, through death and
resurrection," so the "first appropriation of the Christian message in the
earliest church" establishes a normative model. The Jewish and Greek cultures were subject to "a certain crucifixion: existing concepts and forms were
broken up and so brought to a new fruitfulness." Benedict's point seems to
be that the church itself is the result of this crucifixion and so is itself the
model of the gospel's appropriation.

Benedict, in his 2006 Regensburg address, privileged Hellenism and, by
extension, Europe in relation to this "culture." Hellenism, through the development of the Septuagint, had an early and formative encounter with the
biblical faith, and the resulting "inner rapprochement between Biblical faith
and Greek philosophical inquiry" led to Christianity taking on "its historically decisive character in Europe." Moreover, "this convergence, with the
subsequent addition of the Roman heritage, created Europe."[89] Such an

---

[88]Joseph Ratzinger, "Culture, Identity and Church Unity," *Ecumenical Review* 57, no. 3 (2005): 358.
    Quotations in this paragraph come from pages 358 and 359 of this text.
[89]Benedict XVI, "Faith, Reason and the University: Memories and Reflections," *Islamic Studies* 45,
    no. 4 (2006): 600.

observation leaves much unsaid, but the main point is that Greek meta-physics is itself basic to the biblical text and that, by extension, Hellenism is, to whatever degree, itself basic to the faith. By comparison, opposition to "the thesis that the critically purified Greek heritage forms an integral part of Christian faith" leads to calls for the "dehellenization of Christianity."[90] Benedict understands this happening in three stages, the first of which was the Reformation and the setting of *sola scriptura* against a perceived extra-biblical metaphysics. The second stage occurred in the liberal theology of the nineteenth and twentieth centuries and its attempt, represented by Adolf von Harnack, to reconcile the faith with science. The third stage, Benedict argues, is occurring now in the encounter between cultures. To quote,

> It is often said nowadays that the synthesis with Hellenism achieved in the early Church was an initial inculturation which ought not to be binding on other cultures. The latter are said to have the right to return to the simple message of the New Testament prior to that inculturation, in order to incul-turate it anew in their own particular milieux. This thesis is not simply false, but it is coarse and lacking in precision.[91]

In sum, while the "people of God" is an overarching culture, it takes the particular form of Hellenism, which, in relation to Rome, created Europe itself and gave Christianity its decisive character. As inculturation presumes that each culture is capable of bearing the Christian message, so it calls into question the claims to this special "overarching" culture. To do so, even in the context of world Christianity, is to deny the faith.

Inculturation, Benedict concludes, is not biblical. The very notion of in-culturation, as it builds on an improper assumption of the commonality of cultures, feeds the charge of cultural relativism. This "dogma of relativism" is responsible for misconstruing the "Christian universalism concretely carried out in mission." Mission ceases to be viewed as "the dutiful passing on of a good, namely, truth and love intended for everyone," becoming in-stead "the arrogant presumption of a culture which thinks itself superior to the others and so would deprive them of what is good and proper to them."[92]

---

[90]Ibid.

[91]Ibid., 602.

[92]Ratzinger, "Encounter of Christianity and Religions," 7. For more on this as it pertains to Bene-dict XVI's interpretation of Europe, see the bibliography in Pablo Blanco, "The Theology of

Benedict objects not to the characterization of the church as a culture but to how the theory of inculturation rejects the necessity of this cultural form and deems its replication improper.[93]

Whether and in what way "culture" might be a category applied to the church needs to be examined. That such a connection is made and invested with such significant theological weight owes much to a particular conception of the church's apostolicity, its historical continuity and the related notion of witness. Culture is proposed as a necessary basis to the church's mission because of the aforementioned ordering of the cultivation of the faith above its communication and the related cordoning of mission from the ecclesial center. Emphasizing the cultivation of the faith to the marginalization of mission privileges culture as the mode of the church's continuity through time and thus privileges established structures and artifacts deemed basic to this culture. This explains the curious inconsistency whereby Benedict validates European culture while refusing to acknowledge the structures of the church as themselves derivative of the Western experience.

To claim apostolicity is to validate a particular lived expression of the gospel. Though this is not of itself a problem, it becomes problematic when that particular expression assumes a certain priority and so becomes the standard against which other expressions appear derivative and secondary. Such a caution neither denies that the community is itself the primary missionary form, nor mandates an unlimited freedom in relation to structures, nor ensures an extreme form of cultural relativism in relation to theological affirmations. It affirms that "apostolicity" is the proper place to find governing theological controls.

Joseph Ratzinger: Nuclear Ideas," *Theology Today* 68, no. 2 (2011): 169n21.

[93]For David Toolan, Ratzinger draws on a "formidable, essentially classicist theological vision" with "the ideas of a re-Christianized Europe as *the* normative culture and a highly lyrical, 'organic' sense of the church—which, though it allegedly bears no resemblance to any political model, corporation, or bureaucracy, attends scrupulously to the Code of Canon Law." David Toolan, "The Catholic Taboo Against Schism: Strained but Holding," *Religion and Intellectual Life* 7, no. 1 (1989): 44. More explicitly, Aylward Shorter describes Ratzinger's position as a "two-culture theory of evangelisation." Aylward Shorter, "Faith, Culture and the Global Village," *South Pacific Journal of Mission Studies* 16 (1996): 34. This "bizarre development of the monocultural or Eurocentric paradigm" welcomes "Euro-American world culture . . . without any apology, as the universal vehicle of missionary evangelisation. All other cultures are subordinated to, or *fused with* this monolithic world culture" (34). Shorter continues: "With its advocation of a double cultural membership in the Church, it canonizes the alienation and cultural parallelism of the *status quo*, bemoaned so loudly by the thinkers and theologians of the Third World" (35).

Nor does this discussion contrast established Catholic structure to Protestant flexibility; the priority of the cultivation of faith over its communication, identified here as the problem of apostolicity, is basic to both traditions. Setting apostolicity under the horizon of schism, in other words, obscures the determinative significance of cultural continuity for the church's apostolicity.

EXCURSUS: GEORGE LINDBECK AND THE MISSION OF A PEOPLE

For a similar Protestant example, one can refer to the work of Lutheran theologian George Lindbeck. In a text simply titled "The Church," Lindbeck finds in a "people of God" ecclesiology the means for advancing the ecumenical discussion.[94] Describing the church thusly makes the narrative of the Christian story prior to any secondary formulations; "church" refers to "concrete groups of people" and "not to something transempirical" (183). This helps explain the unity of the early church, for, if its diversity were examined in a more systematic fashion, it would "fragment into distinct and perhaps incompatible ecclesiologies" (186). Reference to the "identity and mission of the messianic pilgrim people of God" provides a model for dealing with such fragmentation, including the "intractable" questions of "the institutionalization of church order" (191).

Drawing on the language of "continuity," Lindbeck demonstrates how the "encoded historical data vary, and so do the descriptive results, but the identifying code is the same and therefore also the identified people" (192). He identifies four different aspects of the "referential force of this narrative code": first, it is God's act of election and not of human faithfulness; second, these elect communities have "objective marks" such as the sacraments; third, election is communal; fourth, "the primary mission of this chosen people is to witness to God" (193). Mission becomes conceived as something that occurs "above all by the character of its communal life" (194). As such, while the church needs a diversity of peoples, the addition of people may threaten its witness. This produces a particular mission method. The churches should "follow the practice that prevailed in the first centuries of

---

[94]George A. Lindbeck, "The Church," in *Keeping the Faith: Essays to Mark the Centenary of Lux Mundi*, ed. G. Wainwright (Philadelphia: Fortress, 1988), 178-208. Subsequent references are provided parenthetically within the text.

prolonged catechesis. The primary Christian mission, in short, is not to save souls but to be a faithfully witnessing people" (195). Thus, "once the traditional understanding of mission as the saving of souls is abandoned, the task of witnessing tends to become indistinguishable from that socially responsible righteousness, that commitment to peace, justice and freedom, to which all human beings are called" (194). But because the act of witness rests in this communal life, "Christians are responsible first of all for their own communities, not for the wider society" (195). As now the form of "missionary witness to the world," the churches are to display a mutual concern for each other's worship, faith, fellowship and action (195).

Having removed the occasion of external movement as necessary to the church's mission, that is, as basic to its description as a people, Lindbeck seeks to balance "functionalist" Protestant and "structuralist" Catholic approaches. Or, with cultivation the assumed point of agreement, the Protestant/Catholic schism emerges as definitive for a positive concept of apostolicity. First, the witness of especially the Old Testament permits the change in leadership structures to meet new circumstances (195). Second, the very continuity of Israel demonstrates that structures are not a matter of "simple adiaphoron." This caution derives from the nature of the church's communal witness. "Long-surviving institutions, like long-surviving species, can incorporate in their genetic code a wealth of evolutionary wisdom unmatchable by conscious calculation. Or . . . the symbolic weight acquired by durable structures can be incomparably more powerful (for good as well as ill) than anything devised de novo to fit contemporary needs" (196). Third, as it is God who orders the common life of his people, these structures "have his authorization and are not to be lightly discarded" (197). Note here how the reduction of mission to the community itself permits a total neglect of the question of culture even while the issue of the church's historical structures takes on greater significance.

Building on these axiomatic observations, Lindbeck addresses the historic episcopate. He notes how "under the pressure of historical evidence, providentially guided development has now generally replaced dominical or apostolic institution" (198). However, even while the traditional justifications fail, the episcopacy remains the proper order because this was "the most successful institutional expression and support in Christian history of that mutual responsibility which we have seen to be at the heart of the church's mission" (198). The establishment of this culture, this "institution-alization of mutual accountability," explains the missionary advances of the early churches (199). Grounded in this pragmatic rationale, the historic epis-copacy becomes the "only ministry that exists to promote the unity and mutual responsibility of the world wide church" (200). Though Lindbeck's clear intention is for ecumenical unity, it does not seem accidental that such unity is made easier through a retraction of missionary witness into a com-munity with a concentration on its own purity of form. Once the entire issue of the church's engagement with culture is deemed unessential to the church's missionary witness, unity becomes a matter of reestablishing his-toric structures. Christian witness rests in the continuity of its structures quite simply because these structures objectively identify the people of God in the movement of history. The structures are part of the narrative, and so the culture of this people, and are necessary to the cultivation in the faith deemed constitutive of Christian witness and beside which an external witness becomes secondary.

1.4 The Limits of Schism as the Determinative Problem

Formulating the main problem of apostolicity in terms of a contest between the cultivation and the proclamation of the faith fails to follow the tradi-tional diagnosis. Although surveys of the concept admit to a variety of usage, the ecumenical discussion of apostolicity undergoes a swift narrowing be-cause of its framing by the Protestant/Catholic contest.[95] Johannes von Lüpke illustrates the basic ecumenical concern using the language of "sub-sists." According to Lumen Gentium §8, "the church of Jesus Christ is re-alized ('subsists') in the visible Catholic Church led by the Pope and the bishops."[96] The churches of the Reformation, by comparison, drawing on Luther's own language, hold that "the word of God is the living ground of

---

[95]On the variety of usage, see George Vandervelde, "The Meaning of 'Apostolic Faith' in World Council of Churches' Documents," in Apostolic Faith in America, ed. Thaddeus Daniel Horgan (Grand Rapids: Eerdmans, 1988), 22-25.

[96]Johannes von Lüpke, "Was macht die Kirche zur Kirche? Grundlagen evangelischen Kirchen-verständnisses," in Kirche—dem Evangelium Strukturen geben, ed. Hellmut Zschoch (Neukirch-ener-Vluyn: Neukirchener Verlag, 2009), 41.

the church. It 'subsists' in the Word."[97] Defined in this way, apostolicity concerns the extent to which visible institutions might identify the church, and specifically the extent to which episcopal order is not simply a "sign" of but "guarantees" the church's historical continuity.[98] With the Catholic position, the form, because it is the creation of the Spirit, identifies the church. With the Protestant position, apart from the "true preaching of the word and the right administration of the sacraments," form does not of itself identify the church. Apostolic continuity rests in the canon.[99]

Schism determines the ecumenical treatment of apostolicity. But the very clarity of the above division distorts the issue. Specifically, it submerges lines of agreement concerning the priority of cultivation over that of communication. As counterintuitive as this claim may first appear, it is based on the recognition of a "missionary imperialism" that applied to Protestant and Catholic communions alike. The either-or binary signaled by the ecumenical discussion ignores the actual problems encountered in the processes of missionary transmission. Moreover, the proposed solution to the ecumenical problem, one that describes apostolicity first in cultural terms, finds agreement across the ecumenical spectrum, being generally accepted by both episcopal and non-episcopal traditions.

One potential reason for neglect of the cultural element of apostolicity rests in treating the Reformation as a flat theological problem, not as itself an event of cultural appropriation.[100] For Herbert Neve, by way of example,

---

[97]Ibid., 40.

[98]See the Roman Catholic Church's response to *Baptism, Eucharist and Ministry* in Max Thurian, *Churches Respond to BEM: Official Responses to the "Baptism, Eucharist and Ministry" Text* (Geneva: World Council of Churches, 1987), 33, and the corresponding formulation by the Anglican Church, *Apostolicity and Succession: House of Bishops Occasional Paper* (London: Church House Publishing, 1994), §§62-63.

[99]This positive affirmation includes the critical position evident in the Leuenberg treatment of Protestant ecclesiology. "The apostolicity of the church is according to the understanding of the Reformation not guaranteed by the historical continuity in the episcopal ministry of the church. The revelation of God in Christ which is the foundation of the church is not a deposit conferred upon the ecclesial ministry or even being at its disposal." Wilhelm Hüffmeier, ed., *The Church of Jesus Christ: The Contribution of the Reformation Towards Ecumenical Dialogue on Church Unity* (Frankfurt am Main: Verlag Otto Lembeck, 1995), §1.2.3.

[100]Kenneth Scott Latourette could state in 1925 that "no one yet has carefully examined the interesting suggestion that Protestantism is the reaction of the Teutonic mind upon Christianity." Kenneth Scott Latourette, "The Study of the History of Missions," *International Review of Mission* 14, no. 1 (1925): 113. It could, in other words, be possible to read the Reformation as an instance of the local appropriation of the gospel.

the type of religio-cultural unity that persisted through the period of the Reformation permitted the schism to "be debated strictly in terms of theology, and church institutions could claim authenticity on that basis. The social and cultural influences on the development of the institutions [were] not yet sufficiently admitted."[101] The problem of structure, given the claims for divine origins, was presented as detached from cultural considerations. When it came to the rediscovery of ecumenical unity, this assumption had methodological consequences: "if the theologians worked hard enough with their traditional methods, the understanding of the church's unity would emerge."[102] Combined with the "inability of churches at the international level to consider other ecclesiologies than those developed in the West as being valid," this methodology permitted the "economic, political and social assumptions of the Western World [to] lie hidden (or even denied) in the background of the various ecclesiologies under consideration."[103] Neve links, in other words, the contemporary ecumenical treatment of unity and its inability to recognize the cultural form of otherwise supposedly normative ecclesiologies to the Reformation discussion that posits the problem of structures and their authenticity abstracted from culture. This blindness to the cultural location of ecclesiologies normative within the ecumenical discussion of apostolicity, it is argued here, is a symptom of treating cultivation as basic to apostolicity and in contrast to missionary communication.

While diversity might be cherished, the Reformation and the issues framing the Protestant/Catholic schism become paradigmatic for all later considerations of structural change, including the processes of the gospel's appropriation within world Christianity. World Christianity by this measure becomes interpreted as a derivative instance of the Reformation problem. Rather than permitting the actual plurality of Christian expression to inform the nature of unity, such diversity is contrasted with a form of unity perceived to have existed prior to and within the narrow cultural confines of the schism of the Reformation. Treating the problem of apostolicity as first reflective of the Protestant/Catholic schism hinders a positive description of the community that meets the demands of the

---

[101]Herbert T. Neve, "The Diversity of Unity," *International Review of Mission* 60 (1971): 339.
[102]Ibid., 340.
[103]Ibid.

cross-cultural communication of, and local response to, the gospel for which the establishment of witnessing communities is basic.

1.5 SETTING APOSTOLICITY IN THE CONTEXT OF WORLD CHRISTIANITY

A particular contest determines contemporary ecumenical theologies of apostolicity. Apostolicity refers first to cultivation of the faith over its proclamation, a determinative decision supported across the ecumenical divide. Consequences follow, including a hard distinction between a pastoral and an external mission, one which proves unable to accommodate the type of flexibility of form basic to missionary witness across cultural boundaries. The reception of world Christianity with its pluriformity of expression becomes governed by this duality. Rather than being first a positive expression of God's love for creation and the human response of every tribe, tongue and nation, it intrudes, to a greater or lesser degree, on the church's historical continuity and witness—its apostolicity. This study offers a constructive re-definition of apostolicity. It rejects the normative assumption of the church's being a visible and historically continuous society against the cross-cultural transmission and appropriation of the faith. Taking its positive cues from the concrete and living reality of world Christianity, the church as a visible society in the event of cross-cultural transmission is basic to any definition of apostolicity.

Dominant accounts of apostolicity employ culture as the mode of the church's historical continuity. The second chapter examines this strong claim by reference to ecumenical treatments expressed within recent bilateral and multilateral documents. It is here evident not only that apostolicity is framed by the Protestant/Catholic schism but that this framing problem with its specific challenges determines the nature of the solution. To avoid the contentious issue of episcopal order, focus falls on the mission of the church as a community. Apostolicity describes first this body. As the life of the community itself witnesses to the kingdom of God, so those elements basic to this life, its cultivation and maintenance, come into focus. The chapter notes the gifts given the church, including that of leadership, allowing the *episkopé* to reemerge as necessary to, and responsible for, this culture because of its special responsibility for ordering such things as communion and diversity. This approach relativizes questions of structure while giving it wider ecumenical support, but accomplishes this by building on a clear assumption: the church is historically continuous as a culture. Nor is this benign. It includes a particular definition and legitimation of diversity in Christian expression and conceives cross-cultural transmission in terms set by the form of historical continuity that belongs to a culture.

Much of the ecumenical discussion operates at a formal level, framed by specific theological language and with recourse to the tradition. This tends to submerge the overt cultural rationale basic to the ecumenical proposal. To make the connection explicit, the third chapter turns to the work of Lutheran theologian Robert Jenson, who forges a clear connection between the formal ecumenical problem of apostolicity and the church's being a culture. This relationship satisfies the range of theological concerns regarding the church's "visibility" while charting its contingent movement through history. It equally mandates a form of cross-cultural missionary expression: one of cultural contest and replication. Converts enter the church and mature in the faith through a process of enculturation.

This raises a clear critical point, namely, that apostolicity so conceived mandates a mission method historically termed "colonization." Though a contentious charge, the fourth chapter examines the wider utility of apostolicity as cultural continuity in discussions concerned with the role of the church in the secular West and the challenge presented by globalization. If apostolicity shapes the church as a culture, and if this is basic to the church's catholicity, to the processes of identity and community formation sufficient to offset the erosive forces of globalization, then it mandates a form of cross-cultural relationship that relies on the replication of the "catholic" structures and the enculturation of members into this identity. But if this describes the positive theological position, then what is the objection to colonization? To address this question, the chapter introduces the contemporary anthropological discussion concerning the relationship between Western missions and the processes of colonization, along with the reported experience of "non-Western" Christianity. However much missions might have contributed to the problem, non-Western believers tend not to identify Christian imperialism with missionary institutions (voluntary mission societies) or with economic exploitation. Their concern centers on the institutions of the church and the accompanying interpretive measures, such as liturgy, orders of ministry, theological systems, the structures of schism and the associated framing of cultural expectations. To name colonization is not to name the entrance of good news concerning Jesus Christ and him crucified but to name the range of interpretive measures and structures often deemed necessary to the message.

For a contrary approach, chapter five turns to Johannes Hoekendijk and his subjugation of apostolicity to the apostolate. Beginning with a critical evaluation of the mission methods associated with colonization, Hoekendijk moves backwards to the ecclesiologies of the sending church and to the theological supports that conceive the church in "territorial" terms as an entity defined by its geographical and cultural location. Reference to the apostolate, for Hoekendijk, detaches the church from this territorial conception and replaces a definition of mission based in territory with one based in history. Though a significant advance, none of his critics note the point. For them, to attack the residential ground of the church, as well as its concomitant mission method of propaganda, is to deny the church a body. The problem is a real one: how might the church be conceived as non-residential while remaining embodied? Only with reference to theoretical developments within world Christianity does Hoekendijk's critical contribution receive wider support.

To move beyond this entrenched problem, chapter six turns to "world Christianity" and the form of historical continuity this suggests. Though the formal language of apostolicity is nowhere present, theorists of world Christianity depict the church's historical continuity in terms of its movement across cultural boundaries. Christian history includes both accession and recession, and the church has been continuous only because of its cross-cultural engagement and its being translated into the history and religious heritage of these people. The present pluriformity of world Christianity mirrors the continuity of the Christian faith through history and is evident in the New Testament witness. In similar manner to Hoekendijk, mission becomes defined first in terms of history. It is the process of conversion and so the turning of all things to Christ. The community's identity as Christian includes this conversion of the cultural and religious past. When conceived in this context, the binaries otherwise determinative of apostolicity no longer hold. None of this undoes structure, the nature of the church as a body or the significance of maturity in the faith and the institutions supportive of such, but it ties such to the processes of the faith's appropriation, to conversion. The cross-cultural transmission and local appropriation of the gospel must result in structural expression because such is basic to the embodiment of the faith. This demonstrates the vital significance of structures, institutions, order, liturgy, hymnology and historical continuity—all the elements constitutive of apostolicity. It does, however, preclude conceiving Christianity in terms of a singular historical course and so the church in terms of a singular cultural form.

To extend these findings, the study concludes with an examination of the New Testament witness. Though this study presents a complex picture of the nature and work of an apostle, reading the interests of schism into the text exacerbates the difficulties. These interests direct the discussion away from the unity existent in the New Testament witness while limiting the investigation to institutional concerns. This interpolation submerges the role of the apostle in grounding communities with different cultural heritage and character. As to the unity of the New Testament description of the apostle, this is clear: the ground, calling and function of the apostle is Jesus Christ and him crucified. This controls all that follows. Whatever differences in the Pauline and Lukan image of the apostle, their shared christological ground sets conditions for the visibility of the apostolic ministry, for the possibility and form of the gospel's movement across cultural boundaries, for the nature of the appropriation of the gospel within these settings and so for a definition of mission as first a movement in relation to the history of a people. The movement from the apostle to apostolicity lies in this same ground. The identity of the church lies not in itself but beyond it in Jesus Christ, and the church participates in this history only in the power of the Spirit. The New Testament, in other words, reflects more the insights derived from world Christianity than the expectations of schism.

2

....

Apostolicity Under the Horizon of Schism

> *The church as a whole may be compared to a system of*
> *communication, no part of which is strictly irrelevant*
> *to the conveying of coherent meaning.*

THE ANGLICAN/LUTHERAN "NIAGARA" REPORT, 1987[1]

2.1 THE DETERMINING QUESTION

Polemical overtones notwithstanding, the burden of contemporary literature dealing with apostolicity serves the cause of Christian unity. Schism
is the initating problem, and the proposed solutions are subject to the
complex agendas of established theological traditions and ecclesial identities. Attention focuses on the historical instant of rupture, the immediate
calcifying aftermath and the resulting defensive apologies. Although certain
strategies have developed, such as broadening the "apostolic tradition" to
include a range of ecclesial practices, the forms of ministry and especially
that of episcopal order constitute the biggest hurdle to unity. Insofar as this
is the case, however, the question trades on a particular evaluation of the
Reformation. To quote Walter Kasper, as the early Reformers sought not to
break from the order of apostolic succession, so the ecumenical concern is
now "whether this Protestant position only arose out of an ongoing emergency situation or whether the emergency order developed at that time

---

[1]"Episcope, Niagara Falls, September 1987," in *Growth in Agreement II: Reports and Agreed Statements of Ecumenical Conversations on a World Level, 1982–1998*, ed. Jeffrey Gros, Harding Meyer
and William G. Rusch (Geneva: World Council of Churches, 2000), §16.

possesses a principle and constitutive character."[2] Whatever the ecumenical benefit of so construing the problem, it illustrates the assumed determinative significance of the Protestant/Catholic binary for understanding structural difference as such. The emergence of any later difference, including the burgeoning diversity of theological and institutional (and non-institutional) expression in world Christianity, appears somehow continuous with this prior schism, rehearsing the contest of visible structural continuity against the freedom of structural change.[3] World Christian expressions of the faith do not themselves inform the church's apostolic identity. Structural differentiation is not first a positive consequence of the lived appropriation of and witness to the gospel by identifiable Christian communities in different historical and cultural settings but rather the negative result of division. As this wider diversity is related to the Protestant/Catholic divide, so it is a problem to be solved at its root. The European Reformation sets the terms of reference. "Diversity" is offset with "division," and the solution to division through the reconciliation of ministries includes the means to regulate and control diversity.

It is, of course, doubtful that ecumenical descriptions of apostolicity accord with the actual practice of the various traditions in their diverse contexts. Nevertheless, missing from the discussion is the possibility that apostolicity itself promotes a plurality in the human reception of the gospel. We can illustrate this omission in four ways. First, the ecumenical discussion progressively expunges reference to the historical and cultural origins of structures, promoting a sterilized account of a now universalized conception of office and *episkopé*. Second, though reference to mission increases through documentation, it refers to the primary "pastoral" mission of the church. This mission alerts the church to its being a culture and legitimizes those structures deemed basic to the particular culture the church is. Third, "diversity" becomes defined in relation to this culture as a diversity of gifts

---

[2] Walter Kasper, "Die apostolische Sukzession als ökumenisches Problem," in *Lehrverurteilungen—kirchentrennend?*, ed. Karl Lehmann and Wolfhart Pannenberg (Göttingen: Vandenhoeck & Ruprecht, 1986), 342.

[3] Stated from the opposite perspective, Herbert T. Neve observes that "ecumenical debates so far have not given attention to the church-in-mission in relation to the increasing process of diversification in the modern world. Especially from a theological standpoint, churches have been viewed more or less as sociologically the same." Herbert T. Neve, "The Diversity of Unity," *International Review of Mission* 60 (1971): 339.

(the variety of callings within the church, including that of the ordained ministry). Cultural difference, by contrast, threatens the "unity" of the church, that is, its apostolic identity. Fourth, as received structures limit and order diversity, so they stand isolated from the hermeneutical principles applied even to the canon and the sacraments.

This occurs, it is argued here, because the ecumenical discussion posits apostolic continuity first in terms of cultural continuity. As historical continuity assumes a cultural mode, so apostolic identity forms at odds with the cross-cultural transmission and appropriation of the gospel. Absent through the ecumenical discussion is even the merest acknowledgment that missionary engagement and the incorporation of new questions into the life of the church might raise questions concerning the church's structures and ministries, and this in a way that cannot be determined a priori, the richness of the Christian tradition notwithstanding. Ironically, the more that attention is paid to world Christianity and to the place of culture in hermeneutics and theological method, the less that cultural issues have informed formal accounts of apostolicity. It is much more the case that ecumenical advances trade on a progressive elimination of cultural diversity from the definition of apostolicity. Before developing these points, however, the chapter begins with an early approach to apostolicity that understood historical continuity in terms of missionary change.

2.2 AN EARLY ESCHATOLOGICAL TONE: "CATHOLICITY AND APOSTOLICITY," 1971 (LOUVAIN)

While it may seem hasty to chide the ecumenical discussion for a reductionist approach to cross-cultural continuity, the latitude found within its first attempts prompts such an evaluation. Though the earliest of the Faith and Order conferences recognized the challenge that different forms of ministry presented to unity, this was not initially posited in terms of apostolicity. Nor when apostolicity became a focus soon after the inception of the WCC was it bound to the issue of ministry. For Konrad Raiser, these early statements set apostolicity in relation to "foreign missions," especially as the consequences of mission became viewed as a threat to the church's unity.[4] Relating apostolicity to mission provided some theological rationale for the missionary impetus and cautioned the churches of the West against reducing missionary concerns to a matter of ecumenical difference, and so one where established structures held the priority. More generally, these early documents shared an eschatological tone, which, in Raiser's estimation, opened space for the question of continuity in missionary engagement. This eschatological perspective highlighted the challenge mission posed to established notions of church structure and order, but it did not direct attention to a rehearsed Protestant argument for institutional freedom against a Catholic notion of a visible structured society. It affirmed, rather, that the eschatological future rendered every present form of the Christian community provisional. This observation had a positive intention: the church is called to missionary witness. Furthermore, mission in both idea and history became viewed as a tool to help elucidate the nature of apostolic continuity in apostolic change.

Exemplary here is the 1971 study document from the Joint Working Group of the Roman Catholic Church and the WCC titled "Catholicity and Apostolicity" (Louvain).[5] It begins in a way now standard in later ecumenical statements—by grounding apostolicity in mission.

> The Church is apostolic because it is "sent," constituted by *the gift of the mission* which the Father entrusted to His Son, which Jesus Christ accomplished once for all and which the Holy Spirit completes in the last times (cf. Jn. 20: 21f.). . . . It is therefore in virtue of its *participation in the mission* of Christ in the mission of the disciples that the Church is apostolic. For the Holy Spirit manifests this mission, realizes it and communicates it in a community "consecrated and sent" like Christ (cf. Jn. 17: 18f.). (Louvain, §4)

The church is apostolic insofar as it participates, being both consecrated and sent, in Christ's mission. Whereas later statements limit this mission in a specific manner (a point to which we shall turn), Louvain links apostolic announcement to the eschatological future (Louvain, §5) while

---

[4]Konrad Raiser, "Festes Fundament? Die Apostolizität der Kirche im ökumenischen Gespräch," *Ökumenische Rundschau* 60, no. 1 (2011): 80-94.

[5]"Catholicity and Apostolicity," in *Faith and Order, Louvain 1971: Study Reports and Documents* (Geneva: World Council of Churches, 1971), 133-68. Where not indicated by paragraph marks, subsequent references are provided parenthetically within the text. A number of the preparatory documents achieved "classic" status and were reprinted in a special issue of *One in Christ* 6 (1970).

referencing the memory of the church that "embraces all the past" (Louvain, §6). Mission, in other words, sets the church within this wide temporal scope of promise and memory. Louvain notes the "great diversity of forms in the ministries accomplished in the Spirit" and the "permanent responsibility" these ministries have in transmitting "the living testimony of the apostles" (Louvain, §7). None of this minimizes the key divisions between the communions, yet this "broader view of apostolic succession" raises "new possibilities" for developing a "consensus between the Churches" (Louvain, §§8-9).

The statement is itself brief and generous in tone, and its implications for the issue of structure become evident only by reference to its seven appendices.[6] These highlight fundamental questions concerning the place of proper structural diversity, the cultural origins of structures, the tension between fidelity to the tradition and missionary flexibility, and an evaluation of existing forms. One finds here, in sharp distinction to later treatments, a frank assessment of the church's historicity: even the "traditional norms for understanding the faith—Scripture, Creed, the magisterium of bishops in the apostolic succession—have themselves undergone changes in the course of history."[7] Because of the community's constitutive eschatological sending, recognizing such changes does not threaten the apostolic identity and continuity of the church. "From this sending the idea of a transformation of both the world and the Church appears to necessarily emanate. . . . For the mission of the Apostles develops in the Church beyond what the Apostles themselves did and is directed to a fulfillment which the Church and all [hu]mankind is still traveling towards."[8] Mission includes "an element of historical change" because this mission is directed to Christ's return and "surely points to a change which, far from disintegrating the reality of Christ, is directed on the contrary to its fulfillment."[9] This line of thinking concludes with an open question: "Do we not have to understand historical changes

---

[6]These proposed "areas of further research" include the following: "Apostle" in the New Testament; Identity, Change and Norm; Ministry and Episcope; Sacramental Aspect of Apostolicity; Conciliarity and Primacy; Unity and Plurality; The Local Church and the Universal Church. See ibid., 141-58.

[7]Ibid., 144.

[8]Ibid., 144.

[9]Ibid., 145. It further states that changes that occur in the church because of this movement through history reflect the same "tension which underlies the dynamic of the Church's mission."

and plurality of forms of Christian faith and life as essential marks of Christ's presence as the one Saviour of the multitude in the time between His first coming and His *parousia*?"[10] Though this does not address the problem of evaluating such plurality, linking this to the acting of Jesus Christ himself advances the discussion.

Mission reenters at this point. The statement finds in mission "a criterion by which to distinguish between changes in line with the valedictory of the Risen Lord and those which deviate from the Christian mission and so obscure this mandate and nature of the Church."[11] Applied to the divisive issues of the episcopacy and differences in order, the study notes that each tradition validates its form of ministry with "a more or less explicit reference to the fundamental *mission* of the Apostles by Christ. . . . It is therefore by starting from this mission and considering the way in which the Church should fulfil it in order to meet the needs of each period and of each place that an ecumenical study of the ministry seems to become possible."[12] Mission constitutes a positive criterion for historical change, for discerning the fidelity of such change and for drawing the church forward in a unity of missionary confession served by a plurality of form.

Louvain does not stand alone in its concern for historicity and the potential consequences of such for church structures, but it was unique in the connections it formed between missionary engagement, the diversity of forms and the nature of Christian unity, and the church's passage through time and across cultural boundaries. Though the study envisioned no necessary conflict between its proposals and traditional emphases, its attempt at reconfiguring apostolic continuity through missionary change found no support moving forward. Why this occurred, apart from a perceived departure from the established lines of the debate, can only be a matter of conjecture. The direction taken by later studies, however, suggests that the narrowing of focus protects a conception of historical continuity in cultural form.

---

[10]Ibid., 145.

[11]Ibid., 144. This was an idea in its infancy, and the study acknowledged that it remained "necessary to verify the extent to which the idea of mission does justice to the actual changes which have taken place in the course of history."

[12]Ibid., 148.

2.3 ADVANCE THROUGH STERILIZATION: *BAPTISM, EUCHARIST AND MINISTRY*, 1982

Louvain, because of the active Roman Catholic participation, is considered a significant stage leading to the development of the 1982 consensus document *Baptism, Eucharist and Ministry* (BEM).[13] In actuality, BEM represents a major departure from Louvain in that it eliminates reference to mission and affirms the *episkopé* within an account of historical development. None of this is to deny BEM's contribution. Framed in the terms demanded by schism, BEM is an elegant advance on many of the most pressing issues. Its key affirmation that "the primary manifestation of apostolic succession is to be found in the apostolic tradition of the Church as a whole" (BEM, §M34) enables a distinction between the "apostolic tradition" and "apostolic succession."[14] This broadens the *episkopé* so as to establish a general norm of oversight (BEM, §M23) while, by way of presenting the threefold ministry in terms of a normative historical framework, giving episcopal order some degree of primacy as a means to unity (BEM, §§M48, M53b).

BEM achieves these advances, however, by focusing on practices while promoting a methodological sterilization of historical and cultural texture. No reference is made to the threefold ministry's potential historical or cultural origins. Only the supposed early and continuous nature of this order receives any attention. Apostolicity flattens to the possibility of accepting this now "historically" validated order. Certain qualifications certainly appear. BEM acknowledges the adaption of "ministries to contextual needs" (BEM, §M21) and that the ongoing contextualization of the forms of the ministry are themselves "blessed" by the Spirit (BEM, §M22). Nevertheless, any diversity of ministry recorded by the New Testament witness becomes subject and secondary to the authoritative observation that "certain elements from this early variety were further developed and became settled into a more universal pattern of ministry" (BEM, §M19). The New Testament, on the structure question, reflects a stage of ferment and transition

---

[13]William G. Rusch, "Introduction," in *Episkopé and Episcopacy and the Quest for Visible Unity: Two Consultations*, ed. Peter Bouteneff and Alan D. Falconer (Geneva: World Council of Churches, 1999), 5. For the text of BEM, see *Baptism, Eucharist and Ministry*, Faith and Order Paper no. 111 (Geneva: WCC Publications, 1982).

[14]Alan D. Falconer, "En Route to Santiago: The Work of the Faith and Order Commission from Montreal 1963 to Santiago de Compostela 1993," *Ecumenical Review* 45, no. 1 (1993): 48.

and is not, in this sense, authoritative. Ignatius emerges as the key figure for confirming the pattern of ministry accepted by the early church. If note is made of the radical changes in function and responsibility to this order through the church's history, no theological value attaches to such. Nor do the significant shifts in theological rationale in support of episcopal order merit attention. Nor does such change warrant the possibility of alternate structural developments. Instead, the postbiblical development of a "threefold ministry of bishop, presbyter and deacon" becomes the possible "expression of the unity we seek and also as a means for achieving it" (BEM, §M22). The determining significance of the Protestant/Catholic schism for the definition of apostolicity is evident at this point.

BEM's method corresponds to its nature as a "consensus" document. Any description of structure that refers to particular historical or cultural origins risks both the relativization of order unacceptable to exponents of a catholic tradition and an attribution of causality whereby the churches of the Reformation are deemed responsible for destroying the unity of the church. Once established, this method has become normative for subsequent statements through the use of a "case law" approach and because of the vested interest in the historic episcopate. Certain considerations, such as the relationship between the episcopacy and a sacramental understanding of the church, remain unstated, even while the focus on the forms of "ministry" and visible unity sidelines accounts of apostolicity located in the canon.

Furthermore, this approach creates the impression of a broad ecumenical engagement and global application even while withdrawing the discussion from the very lived diversity of Christian expression. Comparing BEM to the 1982 Commission on World Mission and Evangelism (CWME) text "Mission and Evangelism," Paul Löffler makes the obvious point that the "aspects of intercultural and inter-religious witness are almost entirely missing from BEM." Nevertheless, he draws the perplexing conclusion that BEM "heavily underscores the transcultural and universal dimensions of the Christian faith."[15] BEM makes no argument in support of this "transcultural" approach.[16] Nor does it

---

[15]Paul Löffler, "The BEM Document from a CWME Perspective," *Ecumenical Review* 39, no. 3 (1987): 330.

[16]The way in which formal mission responses to BEM and the wider ecumenical debate avoid reference to apostolicity is a curiosity not easily explained. Indian Jesuit Samuel Rayan gives one interesting example of the issue. In terms of baptism, Rayan notes how for "the majority of Indians . . . and

devote any attention to forming communities across cultural barriers and the potential "alienness" of imported structures. The rightness of flattening the issue to a defined period of development shorn of any cultural reference passes unquestioned as the most viable means to achieve visible unity.

We could further this concern by reference to the 1992 "Porvoo Common Statement" (Porvoo).[17] As an agreement between Nordic, Baltic and Anglo churches, the statement acknowledges the "geographical separation" and "wide diversity of language, culture and historical development" in the participating churches. Nevertheless, these churches retain "much common history" (Porvoo, §8) and a remarkable similarity in structure. Henrik Roelvink puts it in stronger terms: the project had many "natural grounds. . . . The geographical, historical and cultural similarities of the countries seem to be greater than the apparent differences."[18] Most are national churches, all are Protestant and all affirm some form of the historic episcopacy. Without denying the complexity of historical and cultural diversity belonging to world

---

perhaps for a majority of Asians, too, baptism as a rite is a thing of horror. . . . Baptism is associated in the minds of millions of people with colonialism, religious and political aggression, western dominance, European culture, denationalization, spiritual uprooting of people, a break with the people's history, a more than implicit condemnation of religious insights and experiences that have given meaning and direction and a sense of transcendence to more people over a longer span of time than the Christian tradition has done." Samuel Rayan, "The Lima Text and Mission," *International Review of Mission* 72 (1983): 200. Equally strong language appears in his treatment of the eucharist. "A celebration that incorporates social classes and power structures, that creates hierarchies in the eucharistic assembly, that incorporates bourgeois values and insists on upper-class clothes for presiding persons, and is manifestly sexist in language and in the exclusion of women from major active roles, contradicts the newness and radicalness of the eucharist and nullifies much of its potential for mission in the modern world. Where foreign cultural elements are imposed and the liturgical creativity of the worshipping congregations is curbed or crushed, the celebration becomes anti-mission" (204-5). Rayan writes as a Jesuit and so is governed by certain assumptions, but this seems to be precisely the point. That baptism and the Lord's Supper constitute the two sacraments of the Christian tradition given by Jesus Christ and are thus "nonnegotiable" is affirmed by the dominant majority of communions. Rayan's indication of the consequences of certain cultural baggage associated with these events is offset by a total absence of any critique of the Ministry section within BEM. He is satisfied with the original grounding of the church in mission and with locating ordination within the wider community. Rayan's exemption of ministry from his sustained cultural critique, including his reproach for requiring believers to wear "upper-class clothes," is difficult to understand. It perhaps illustrates a prior commitment to structure even above that of the sacraments. Or, better, it is structure that grounds and makes permissible this hermeneutical approach to the sacraments.

[17] *Together in Mission and Ministry: The Porvoo Common Statement with Essays on Church and Ministry in Northern Europe; Conversations Between the British and Irish Anglican Churches and the Nordic and Baltic Lutheran Churches* (London: Church House Publishing, 1993).

[18] Henrik Roelvink, "The Apostolic Succession in the Porvoo Statement," *One in Christ* 30 (1994), 344-45.

Christianity (indeed, the reality of such is the point), the Porvoo churches inhabit a narrow band of difference. These churches achieve in real terms the cultural limits proposed by the BEM methodology. Porvoo presents, in other words, a maximized opportunity for the achievement of full, visible unity by means of a shared ministry.

In his evaluation of Porvoo, Roelvink remarks that "the differences between Anglicans and Lutherans are now reduced to geographical, historical and spiritual, that is, non-theological features."[19] Given that arguments for historical succession often draw on the geographical, the historical and the spiritual, Roelvink's identification of what accounts as "non-theological" appears to be a value judgment contingent on prior commitments.[20] John Toy, nevertheless, works with a similar assumption. After recording Porvoo's "ground-breaking investigations into the actual meaning of 'Apostolic Succession,'" sufficient to include churches that have maintained episcopal order but perhaps not a historic succession, Toy outlines the practical limits of the agreement.[21] These include differences in the consecration of female bishops, the cross-cultural exchange of priests, the role of canon law and local political circumstances. Toy then notes the role of language and especially the challenges English-speaking clergy have with Nordic languages. With respect to the history of the churches, notably those from the former Soviet Union, he indicates "the kind of culture gap that can only be bridged by learning the language and the 'soul' of the country."[22] He even includes a caution concerning the "greater prevalence of 'political correctness' in church affairs over there," that is, in Scandinavia, and how there "are certain 'sacred' themes, such as the notion of 'democracy' and 'equal opportunity' about which one must be particularly careful."[23] The central point should be obvious: even within the restricted cultural and ecclesial band represented by Porvoo, the "non-theological" factors lead to a range of confusions and

---

[19]Ibid., 350.

[20]For José Míguez Bonino, this terminology promotes a certain agenda. "The questions of race, sex, class, are . . . not extraneous elements 'ideologically' introduced in the discussion of unity, but the necessary disruption of our 'premature' unities which have incorporated 'the form of the world.'" José Míguez Bonino, "A 'Third World' Perspective on the Ecumenical Movement," *Ecumenical Review* 34, no. 2 (1982): 123.

[21]John Toy, "Is Porvoo Working?," *Theology* 104 (2001): 3.

[22]Ibid., 13.

[23]Ibid., 12.

indeed to differing interpretations and implementations of "theological" factors, including church structure and order.

Recognizing these very real difficulties in reconciling Western communions, with all the underlying continuities, indicates something of the challenges posed by the cultural gulf between Anglo-European communions and those in the wider world. But it is exactly the lack of cultural modesty implicit within the method made normative by BEM that leads Tore Furberg, one of Porvoo's co-chairs, to comment how "the perspective was broadening: the 'world' in [Porvoo] is not just Northern Europe. Porvoo clearly takes a worldwide perspective."[24] This discussion, which notes its own geographical, historical, cultural and structural location, is conceived as applying to the "whole inhabited earth" without attending to how this European development might appear in other settings. Such continuity, it is assumed, resides in the order itself, for that order encompasses, maintains and supports the church's primary pastoral mission.

On this point, Porvoo's opening chapter is overt, to quote Roelvink, in developing "a missionary theology for the evangelization of Europe."[25] This provides a criterion for evaluating the success of Porvoo: how and to what extent has this twenty-year-old agreement on episcopal order renewed the local witness of the Porvoo member churches? Given that much of the argument for apostolic continuity resides in promoting the mission of the church and its advancement through the visible unity of a shared ministry and a common eucharistic communion, an analysis of that mission might prove ecumenically instructive. This is especially the case given the apparent cross-cultural normativity of the proposed ecumenical solution.

2.4 THE FUNCTION OF MISSION LANGUAGE: "EPISCOPE," 1987 (NIAGARA)

The flattening of historical and cultural texture discussed in the previous sections finds confirmation in how "mission" functions through the discussion. It is perhaps not an overstatement to posit mission as the decisive concept within ecumenical treatments of apostolicity. As the single agreed

---

[24]Tore Furberg, "The Sending and Mission of the Church in the Porvoo Common Statement," in *Apostolicity and Unity* (Grand Rapids: Eerdmans, 2002), 206.
[25]Roelvink, "Apostolic Succession," 345.

basis in the New Testament definition, apostolic "sending" constitutes a point at which the various traditions can meet. It equally provides a conceptual framework for the transition between the New Testament witness and the creation of the church, that is, for the normative nature of the postbiblical historical development of structures. Though the irony should be clear, this use of mission distances cross-cultural engagement from the issue of church structures and ministerial order. The approach is so widespread that one can develop a systematic pattern of how mission functions within this ecumenical documentation. The 1987 Anglican-Lutheran study "Episcope" (Niagara), because of the clarity of its approach, its dependence on earlier studies and its appropriation by later ones, illustrates well the logic.[26]

Niagara's preface identifies the episcope as "the chief remaining obstacle to full communion between Anglicans and Lutherans." This problem makes it necessary to locate a beginning point, a foundation on which agreement might be constructed. Such is found in the clear link between apostolicity and mission, or, more specifically, it is located in the twofold recognition of the church's apostolic grounding and its continuing apostolic task.[27] As the church received the apostolic mantle, so "the whole Christian church . . . has been sent on its mission and been given the necessary gifts" (Niagara, §15). This is the first step in the logic. As both ground and task, the apostolic sending means that mission takes the form of a community living according to the promises of God (Niagara, §31). Reference is then made to BEM (§§M1-6) and its setting mission within the calling of the whole church

---

[26]"Episcope, Niagara Falls, September 1987," in *Growth in Agreement II: Reports and Agreed Statements of Ecumenical Conversations on a World Level, 1982–1998*, ed. Jeffrey Gros, Harding Meyer and William G. Rusch (Geneva: WCC Publications, 2000), 11-37.

[27]The 1994 Anglican statement "Apostolicity and Succession" (AS) defines apostolicity in simple missionary terms: "The apostolicity of the Church may be defined by reference either to its origin or to its continuous task. . . . It has to be pointed out that in either sense the primary reference is to mission" (AS, §18). Because it is a matter of foundation, task and even eschatological goal, AS sets this mission in historical terms alone: "The Church can be described as apostolic in two principal senses: on the one hand, it is historically founded and still rests upon the apostles Jesus sent and their witness to him. On the other hand, it is itself 'apostled' or 'sent' in every generation. This means that it is dynamic in its mission and that its continuity through time is filled with God's purpose for the world and looks beyond history to eternity, the *eschaton*. But in every generation it is historically particular and must meet the changing needs of the world and preserve its life in the contingencies of history" (AS, §26). Apart from this historical concern, no reference is made to the type of immediate challenges offered to the church by its movement across cultural borders, nor is there any hint as to how this "dynamic" mission might find expression.

(Niagara, §17). Every member is necessary to the church's witness and is to be an active participant in this witness according to the gift and calling each has received. Witness, in other words, is a type of gestalt, dependent on the proper life of this body.

> In this sense the church as a whole may be compared to a system of communication, no part of which is strictly irrelevant to the conveying of coherent meaning. When human beings communicate with one another it is important, if one is to avoid confusion, that words, gestures, facial expressions and symbolic gifts should not contradict each other. Similarly when the church wishes to be heard in a given culture, it is important that the whole of its "language" be coherently inter-related so that its message makes sense. (Niagara, §16)

As the church's witness consists of these non-rule-governed gestures—its language irrespective of the cultural setting—so it is the witness of a culture. These gestures are fragile and are sustained only through their continual rehearsal by the community's members. Each member is to be enculturated into this language and its subtleties of aesthetic and expression. Moreover, though witness characterizes the whole community, certain individuals are gifted and called to positions of authority to facilitate and direct this mission. Herein lies the rationale for traditional structures as themselves part of the church's language and essential to its mission.

The second step in the logic acknowledges the reality of early divisions within the church but reduces "division" to a flat genus. The tensions occasioned by the early cross-cultural appropriation of the gospel become conceived in the negative terms of a continuum, with diversity at one end and division at the other. No suggestion is made that such tension might advance the mission of the church. The opposite is the case. Division threatened the "coherence of the Christian mission, and the related search for discipline and unity for the sake of mission and witness" (Niagara, §18). The evident solution, given the cultural definition of witness, rests in appropriate structure. Though the New Testament presents no "uniform structure of government inherited directly from or transmitted by the apostles," it is clear that "the mission of the church required the coherence of its witness in every aspect of its life, and that this coherence required supervision" (Niagara, §20). By reference to the church's mission and the related necessity of a unity set in contrast to even the cross-cultural appropriation of the gospel, apostolicity becomes associated with the unifying function of church ministry.

The next step sets this assumed identification of ecclesial being and mission within a historical framework. "Mission indeed comes to special expression in the church's apostolicity. For apostolicity means that the church is sent by Jesus to *be* for the world, to participate in his mission and therefore in the mission of the One who sent Jesus, to participate in the mission of the Father and the Son through the dynamic of the Holy Spirit" (Niagara, §21). This merger of mission and ontological language is, through reference to the kingdom of God, placed within the "over-arching theme of history." Because of this movement through history, the "church's mission is to witness to that reign by its words and rites (proclamation and sacraments), by its structures and governance (Mark 10:35-45, esp. 43), by its *being* as well as its doing" (Niagara, §24). Via the language of "sending," continuity with the apostles occurs in the establishment of the ministry. Missionary sending becomes identical with the church's being, that is, with its internal practices and structures as the means by which the church maintains the integrity of its witness in its historical course.

This leads, fourth, to a description of those elements deemed necessary to this mission of the community in its passage through history. As its mission is primarily ontological, so it is received as a "gift." God gives gifts in their fullness. This establishes a backwards reference to what belongs to the church with its constitution. "In order to *be* such a church it becomes conscious that certain things are required of it" (Niagara, §16). Chief here is doxology, the worship of the Trinity, and the reception of baptism and "the meal" (Niagara, §27). This common use of mundane language to describe the sacraments reinforces the cultural structure of the community. As to the particular elements required of the church, they serve the further requirement of "continuity," which is itself "grounded in God's faithfulness and continuity" (Niagara, §29). Given this divine source, the church can "cherish" the "symbols of continuity," which include the gamut of elements promoted by each tradition: the canon, baptism and the eucharist, orthodox confession, and bishops and presbyters. Niagara acknowledges that these symbols "need constantly to be interpreted afresh" and that the church "only remains what it is through change and adjustment" (Niagara, §30). Such acquiescence to the realities of the historical passage of any culture never-theless remains subject to the continuity that expresses the church's mission. Anything interfering with this continuity interferes with its mission. Given this link, focus falls on the maturation of this community, "its disciplined life together, its activity of nurture and its sense of goal and direction" (Niagara, §41). Simply absent, by this stage of the logic, is the idea of mission as the community engaged in movement across cultural boundaries as well as the potential consequences of this for the church's own celebration of reconciliation and its associated structures and practices. That the absence of mission occurs seems to be a correlate of the division between the being and the doing; that is, space exists for an external mission, but as secondary and without fundamental consequence for the pastoral mission of the church—its culture and attendant structures.

The crowning stage of the logic consists of a special apology for episcopal order, one grounded in two arguments: one from history and one based on the special responsibility this office has for both the mission and the unity of the church. Episcopal office "developed" out of the diversity of the apostolic period, especially as the church came to use "political or quasi political terminology" to express its sense of "identity" (Niagara, §46). As the church became "a *polis*" and "a single 'people,'" so the bishop became the "leader and principal officer in each locality" (Niagara, §46). More expressly, each of the local "churches, in becoming discrete cultures within cultures, constituted a system of belief" (Niagara, §48). As a result, questions emerged as to churches' interrelation and unity. With the bishop elected by "the whole people," and given that bishops from other areas participated in the act of consecration, "the bishop embodied in his office the tension between locality and universality" (Niagara, §49). This cultural setting would later be bolstered by reference to the church's historical continuity, so that "the symbolic position occupied by the bishop had two dimensions, the spatial and the temporal. The connections between the local and the universal, the present and the past, are both aspects of the one *koinonia* or communion" (Niagara, §52). Such a position should not be misconstrued as a simple repetition of established arguments for episcopal order. Niagara includes some hesitation regarding an actual lineal historical succession and understands its own position as opening the way for a mutual recognition of continuity in the apostolic faith. It accomplishes this precisely by positing the church as a culture and the associated "intention to preserve continuity with traditional church structures" (Niagara, §52).

Reference to this pastorally construed "mission" promotes the church as a given culture and the practices and structures that shape and maintain the identity of the church in its historical passage. This includes the necessary structures for ordering the diversity of local churches in relation to the church universal. In this sense, the church's "mission" forms in some contrast to the actual processes of cross-cultural transmission and local appropriation of the gospel.

2.5 DELIMITING DIVERSITY

To observe that ecumenical treatments of apostolicity include only a flat account of diversity is to observe that the reality of "world" Christianity fails to inform discussions concerning the structures of the church and the nature of visible unity. As an account of historical continuity, any structures of more recent vintage, including the past two hundred years of Christianity's global expansion, assume importance only in relation to their "mediated" connection to the apostolic roots of the church, that is, through the Western church. This is not to suggest that the ecumenical discussion ignores the issue. It is rather that apostolicity orders diversity and does so in two related ways. First, as the mission of the church is above all pastoral, so diversity is understood in relation to a particular conception of Christian maturity, the means to achieve it and the structures necessary to such. This does not neglect diversity; it sets the conditions of its legitimation—diversity is first and above all the diversity of gifts. Within the church as a human community structured by the Spirit, each Christian contributes to that life through his or her Spirit-given gifts, and this is constitutive of the community's diversity. Such gifts include those of leadership and office, and it is office itself, especially the episcopal office, that orders this "local" diversity and mediates between it and the church "universal." Second, a distinction forms between diachronic (across time) and synchronic (across space) diversity. Although no firm rule exists, ecumenical documentation tends to align apostolicity with the diachronic and catholicity with the synchronic.

2.5.1 Diversity, koinonia and pastoral order. In terms of the pastoral ordering of diversity, Rowan Williams, offering an amended translation to the Leuenberg statement of Protestant ecclesiology, *The Church of Jesus Christ*, states:

> "In the context of a pluralist society, to experience the Church must be to experience a coherent system of ordered structures in which the 'inner life' of a human being may grow." What this formulation states is that the pastoral care offered by the Church of Christ is . . . part of a continuing and consistent common life whose purpose is to nurture human beings towards spiritual maturity. Structures in the Church exist not only to secure coherence and continuity, but to make possible such growth; coherence and continuity are important only because they are understood as enabling growth.[28]

Christian maturity into the likeness of Christ, by this account, shares in a general anthropological account of human growth. Permissible diversity, by this measure, becomes defined relative to this vision of maturity and the structures basic to such. As the primary mission of the church is pastoral, so diversity is valid insofar as it serves this mission. The "primary obligation of the Church [is] to be a *holy place*, an environment where people may find room for them to mature into the likeness of Christ."[29] Out of this Christians can then "connect with the needs, the hunger, of our wider environment."[30] The objection to this "cultivational" definition, it must be reiterated, lies neither in its concern with community nor in the importance it attributes to structures. It rests in the self-reference of this community, the logical priority that attaches to the creation of a seemingly static holy culture and the formation of a derivative "externality," one contingent on, unnecessary to and occasionally threatening for the primary pastoral mission. In the ecumenical discussion, this basic logic defines the nature of Christian koinonia.

Such is the contemporary focus on koinonia and communion ecclesiologies, of which space precludes even a modest treatment, but the approach's

---

[28]Rowan Williams, "Ways Forward from Meissen: What Kind of Unity in Witness and Mission?," in *Einheit bezeugen: Zehn Jahre nach der Meissener Erklärung: Beiträge zu den theologischen Konferenzen von Springe und Cheltenham zwischen der EKD und der Kirche von England*, ed. Ingolf Dalferth and Paul Oppenheim (Frankfurt am Main: Verlag Otto Lembeck, 2003), 486.
[29]Ibid., 492.
[30]Ibid.

ecumenical attractiveness is clear.[31] Koinonia, as developed within the ecumenical discussion, trades on a neat connection between the communion of
the triune Being, the life of the Christian community and the eucharistic celebration of communion. This theological ground emphasizes "participation"
and so provides a generic platform on which the Orthodox, Roman Catholic
and Protestant traditions can stand. Each can promote the agreed pastoral
nature of the church's mission without the immediate acceptance or denial of
episcopal order and the church's sacramentality. In terms of the Roman
Catholic/Protestant schism, reference to koinonia permits a collegial alternative
to a juridically defined and maintained form of unity while, from the Protestant
side, creating space for a theological account for the church as a community.

   Koinonia, in this discussion, serves as the key theological mechanism
used to affirm the lived diversity of the church.[32] It draws attention to the
local churches and how these "participate in the diversity of historical, cultural and racial situations," supporting a description of the church as "a
communion (*communio*) subsisting in a network of local churches."[33]
However, while diversity is so championed, the language of koinonia includes a clear ordering. Whatever reference is made to the diverse and local,
koinonia privileges unity and its visibility in shared ministerial order and so
eucharistic fellowship. By way of representative example, the 1997 Faith and
Order study report titled "Communal, Collegial, Personal" states: "Being
concretely realized in local churches, from really different races, conditions,
cultures, traditions, histories, often separated by real ethnic or national interests, the church will be held together in a single *koinonia* by different

---

[31]See here the comprehensive Lorelei F. Fuchs, *Koinonia and the Quest for an Ecumenical Ecclesiology: From Foundations Through Dialogue to Symbolic Competence for Communionality* (Grand
Rapids: Eerdmans, 2008).

[32]See, for example, "Some Aspects of the Church Understood as Communion," *Origins* 22 (1992):
108-12. This document from the Congregation of the Doctrine of the Faith notes how the "universality of the Church" includes "a *plurality* and a *diversification*" and that this "diversification
confers the character of communion." Such plurality it applies to "the diversity of ministries,
charisms, and forms of life and apostolate within each particular Church, and to the diversity
of traditions in liturgy and culture among the various particular Churches" (§15). On the reception and interpretation of this position, especially as it is seen to accent the "universal" church
over against the "local" church, see Kilian McDonnell, "The Ratzinger/Kasper Debate: The Universal Church and Local Churches," *Theological Studies* 63, no. 2 (2002): 227-50.

[33]"Facing Unity, Rome, Italy, 3 March 1984," in *Growth in Agreement II: Reports and Agreed Statements of Ecumenical Conversations on a World Level, 1982-1998*, ed. Jeffrey Gros, Harding Meyer
and William G. Rusch (Geneva: World Council of Churches, 2000), §5.

means, among which ministries in common have a specific role."[34] Koinonia provides the order by which difference might be reconciled, and this occurs in the sacraments and, given the structural conditions framing the eucharist, with special importance attaching to the office of the bishop.[35] Diversity itself becomes defined by these limits and the coordinated interests of relationality and participation. In short, the reference to diversity included within communion ecclesiologies serves as an apology for the necessary unifying role of a ministry of oversight as the bond between the local and the universal, beside which diversity adds a confirming color but no critical substance, a mute and confirming diversity.

The essay in which John Willebrands describes communion ecclesiology as "a central insight for the future development of ecumenism" provides a clear outline of these structural assumptions.[36] Koinonia is foremost "a sharing in one reality held in common," the "reality" being the communion of God himself. This communion, Willebrands continues, must be expressed in a community, and the community is the context in which communion develops.[37] Community is so central because via the "economy of the incarnation" God enters into communion with human beings "through the mediation of human realities."[38] Chief here is the "apostolic witness within the community of believers," along with the continuity of this community through each "succeeding Christian generation" and the aligned account of unity and witness.[39] The "marks" of the communion of the Christian

---

[34]"Communal, Collegial, Personal: Report of Group I," in *Episkopé and Episcopacy and the Quest for Visible Unity: Two Consultations*, ed. Peter Bouteneff and Alan D. Falconer (Geneva: World Council of Churches, 1999), 49. One might examine this document further for a concise snapshot of the how koinonia references a diversity that becomes narrowed to "gifts" and governed by the office of bishop.

[35]According to Alan Falconer, the approach to koinonia found in the Faith and Order study *The Nature and Mission of the Church* (NMC) "emphasizes the importance of understanding the church as a community that exhibits diverse expressions and experiences, a community that seeks to express koinonia in a variety of diverse cultural circumstances and geographical locations." Alan D. Falconer, "The Church: God's Gift to the World—On the Nature and Purpose of the Church," *International Review of Mission* 90, no. 359 (2001): 395. Such koinonia, however, sits under certain structures. "God bestows on the church apostolic faith, baptism and eucharist as means of grace to create and sustain the koinonia, and this koinonia is furthered by structures of ministry, oversight and conciliarity" (395).

[36]John Willebrands, "The Future of Ecumenism," *One in Christ* 11 (1975): 313.

[37]Ibid., 313.

[38]Ibid., 315.

[39]Ibid., 315.

community are, first, faithfulness to the teaching of the apostles, which is not simply listening to the Word but includes the celebration of the "one liturgy"; second, baptism as establishing communion between the believer and Christ and his or her brothers and sisters in Christ; third, and most important, the "privileged moment of the eucharistic celebration," with the eucharist as the "great sacrament of communion with Christ and, in consequence, of communion between the faith."[40] Reference to the eucharist directs attention to those entrusted with its administration. "The Christian community is gathered together for a life of holiness by those and around those who continue to exercise in its midst the mission which the apostles received from the Lord, so far as this mission was to be continued through time."[41] The office of bishop, as giving oversight to the eucharist, draws the community together and grounds its pastoral mission. Communion consists of participation in the "mediations willed by the Lord for the establishment of his community and its growth until he comes" at the local level.[42] As each local church participates in the same apostolic marks of communion, so "a visible, ecclesial communion is formed between them."[43] Citing Colossians 2:19, the bishop serves as "the bond of this communion" by "opening" the local church to the universal and by "representing" the universal church to the local.[44] This establishes precise limits for any discussion of structural diversity. Though "conciliarity" has taken different forms through the history of the church, any changes have "only been able to take shape and bear fruit within this conciliarity of the universal Church grouped around the first of the bishops."[45] It could be argued that Willebrands's Catholic commitments shape his schematic depiction, and when filtered through different theological lenses, koinonia might assume a different ecclesial character. In ecumenical treatments of apostolicity, however, it is not the case. Koinonia corresponds to this basic pattern.

2.5.2 *The diachronic control of synchronic continuity.* If identifying the episcopal office as the necessary mediating point between the local and

---

[40]Ibid., 316.
[41]Ibid., 317.
[42]Ibid., 317.
[43]Ibid., 317-18.
[44]Ibid., 318.
[45]Ibid., 320.

universal dimensions of the church constitutes one method of isolating cultural diversity from apostolicity, a second rests in a distinction between two types of diversity: diachronic and synchronic. For Paul Avis, "apostolicity is primarily diachronic: it refers to the calling of the Church to be faithful to the mission of the Apostles and particularly to the apostolic faith in its ongoing mission. Catholicity is primarily synchronic: it points to the universal scope of the salvation that is offered to the world through the mission of the Church."[46] Apostolicity is a question of historical continuity, whereas catholicity encompasses the "universal" scope of the faith and governs cross-cultural diversity through this lens. Though ecumenical treatments of apostolicity avoid describing the difference in such stark terms, by assigning cultural diversity to catholicity, apostolicity becomes isolated from any cultural interrogation.

By way of example, the 1998 Anglican/Roman Catholic International Commission (ARCIC) document *The Gift of Authority III* (GAIII) posits apostolicity as tradition.[47] "Tradition is a dynamic process, communicating to each generation what was delivered once for all to the apostolic community" (GAIII, §14). Using tradition in this way helps affirm consistency "in many varied circumstances and continually changing times" (GAIII, §16) while calling for the church to order its life according to the tradition it has received (GAIII, §17). Apostolicity indicates the continuity of what has already been received, and this process of continuity occurs by way of traditioning. Or, more specifically, "tradition makes the witness of the apostolic community present in the Church today through its corporate *memory*" (GAIII, §18). Memory, as that which is both borne by and the product of tradition, is internal to the tradition itself, and it is the community's responsibility to maintain this memory as the contemporary form of the apostolic witness. While "the witness of proclamation, sacrament and life in communion" (GAIII, §18) constitutes the tradition, memory demands no externality as necessary to the church's mission. It is without reference to the potential consequences of the gospel's cross-cultural transmission and local appropriation for understanding the

---

[46]Paul D. L. Avis, "Rethinking Ecumenical Theology," in *Paths to Unity: Explorations in Ecumenical Method*, ed. Paul D. L. Avis (London: Church House Publishing, 2004), 93.
[47]*The Gift of Authority: Authority in the Church III* (Toronto: Anglican Book Centre, 1999).

nature and form of the apostolic continuity. Apostolicity, so conceived, does not permit this range of considerations.

It is only with reference to the church's catholicity that some notion of diversity emerges. "There are two dimensions to communion in the apostolic Tradition: diachronic and synchronic. The process of tradition clearly entails the transmission of the gospel from one generation to another (diachronic). If the church is to remain united in the truth, it must also entail the communion of the churches in all places in that one gospel (synchronic)" (GAIII, §26). Synchronic diversity belongs to creation itself, meaning that "the Church's fidelity and identity require not uniformity of expression and formulation at all levels in all situations, but rather catholic diversity within the unity of communion" (GAIII, §27). Though affirmed in principle, the concrete form of such diversity remains vague and undeveloped. The discussion's specifics all direct attention back to the *episkopé*: the "charism and function of *episcope* are specifically connected to the *ministry of memory*" (GAIII, §30). Any potential diversity is subject to the fidelity of memory and the structures responsible for safeguarding the historical passage of what has been received.

All necessary authority for this diachronic priority—for Tradition, memory and structure, as should by now be familiar—rests in mission. Jesus bestowed the authority for mission on the disciples and empowered them "to spread the gospel to the whole world" (GAIII, §32). As such,

> the exercise of ministerial authority within the Church, not least by those entrusted with the ministry of *episcope*, has a radically missionary dimension. Authority is exercised within the Church for the sake of those outside it, that the Gospel may be proclaimed "in power and in the Holy Spirit and with full conviction" (1 Thess. 1:5). This authority enables the whole Church to embody the Gospel and become the missionary and prophetic servant of the Lord. (GAIII, §32)

Even while apostolicity means mission, setting the cultural diversity of the church under the mark of catholicity isolates such diversity from apostolicity and thus from the question of governing structures. The mission of the church is the exercise of this authority in maintaining the structures essential to the pastoral witness.

2.6 Maintained in Isolation: *The Nature and Mission of the Church*, 2005

The 2005 Faith and Order study on ecclesiology, *The Nature and Mission of the Church* (NMC), combines well these aforementioned trajectories in a single document.[48] Given the now set nature of the ecumenical position, the study's contribution may be swiftly summarized.

The apostolicity of the church includes, first, the affirmation that mission belongs to its very being (NMC, §53). As to its definition, the "mission of the Church" (NMC, §§34-42) is developed at a secondary distance from "the nature of the Church" (NMC, §§9-33). Mission becomes the persistence of the church in those things by which it receives its identity (preaching, the call to repentance, faith, baptism and diakonia). By these means, the church "signifies, participates in, and anticipates the new humanity God wants, and also serves to proclaim God's grace in human situations and needs until Christ comes in glory (cf. Mt 25:31)" (NMC, §39). This position, in other words, simply rehearses the standard assumptions concerning the primary pastoral form of Christian witness.

Second, in terms of the church's passage through history, apostolicity refers back to the "many ways in which the Church, under the guidance of the Holy Spirit, has been faithful to the testimony of the apostles concerning Jesus Christ" (NMC, §56). As the church returns to this apostolic truth, so it is "renewed in its worship and mission stemming from its apostolic origin (cf. Acts 2:42-47). By doing so it makes visible, and does justice to, the apostolic Gospel which is already given to it and works in it in the Spirit, making it the Church" (NMC, §56). With this backwards referring account of historical continuity, cross-cultural continuity becomes set within the familiar framework of "communion and diversity" (NMC, §§60-63).[49] In its early sections, the document describes diversity as a necessary aspect of "catholicity" (NMC, §16), at least hinting at a wider contextual consideration. As

---

[48] *The Nature and Mission of the Church: A Stage on the Way to a Common Statement* (Geneva: World Council of Churches, 2005).

[49] For an examination of NMC's inattention to the issue of sociocultural identity for ecclesiology, or, more specifically, the inattention to the various models for relating church to nation, people or ethnic group, see Eduardus A. J. G. Van der Borght, "No Longer Strangers or Pilgrims in the Church? Socio-cultural Identities in the Faith and Order Document: Nature and Mission of the Church," in *Strangers and Pilgrims on Earth: Essays in Honour of Abraham van de Beek*, ed. Eduardus A. J. G. Van der Borght and P. van Geest (Leiden: Brill, 2011), 431-44.

it turns to a more direct consideration of apostolic order, diversity becomes the Spirit's giving of "diverse and complementary gifts" (NMC, §60). This sifting of diversity, according to an assumed priority of a non-cultural, historical continuity, determines even its welcome recognition of differences in "Christian life and witness born out of the diversity of cultural and historical context" and the positive ground of this difference in the need of the gospel "to be rooted and lived authentically in each and every place" (NMC, §61). As a correlate of this position, it cautions against the claim of any singular culture to be the normative form of the gospel and the coordinated imposition of this particular form as the gospel's "only authentic expression." It also notes the lack of grace when one culture refuses to recognize the gospel "being faithfully proclaimed in another culture" (NMC, §61). Unfortunately, while this appears a tacit reference to the concerns of colonization in the communication of the gospel and to the freedom of local expressions, no attempt is made to define the form of "culture" in question. Insofar as a "culture" claims to be the normative expression of the gospel, it seemingly follows that this "culture" must have some ecclesial form. Yet no correlation is drawn between this cultural caution and church structures and ministries. What does appear is reference to koinonia ecclesiology and to its structuring of the universal church as a communion of local churches. And though it notes how "local" assumes different meanings in different traditions, with a "communion" ecclesiology uniting these local churches, the step to the mediating function of a ministry of oversight is not a large one.

Third, when it turns to specific ministerial forms under the heading of "The Life of Communion in and for the World," the study mirrors received ecumenical thinking.[50] Apart from a generic reference to the "mission" of the church, no reference is made to any externality that might properly belong to the description of the church's nature and its ministries (including even the earlier recognition of its "pilgrim" nature). The document repeats the standard lines of argumentation. Diversity is a matter of different gifts and ministries. While the New Testament contains "no single pattern" of

---

[50]The study includes an account of the "apostolic faith" (NMC, §§68-73), echoing the wider attempt of Faith and Order to develop such a position. See Hans-Georg Link, *Apostolic Faith Today: A Handbook for Study* (Geneva: World Council of Churches, 1985). When it comes to describing the "continuity in the permanent characteristics of the Church of the apostles," the text simply replicates BEM, §34 (NMC, §71).

ministry, by the third century the "threefold ministry" became standard (NMC, §87). During this period, local congregations moved toward an institutional form of unity, and although the structures of the *episkopé* developed in different ways in different regions, the task of oversight includes "maintaining continuity in apostolic truth and unity of life" (NMC, §92). Though variously interpreted and implemented in different times and places, this persisted until the time of the Reformation. In this breach, alternate approaches to oversight developed (NMC, §93). Without necessarily advocating an episcopal order, the study continues with a description of the personal, communal and collegial facets of the ministry of oversight before turning to the issues of conciliarity and primacy.

On the issue of apostolicity, NMC repeats the ecumenical consensus. It is of interest here, however, for two reasons. First, it was published in 2005. Whereas earlier documents might be excused for not being fully cognizant of the "world" nature of Christianity, by 2005 it is a matter of popular discourse.[51] The document should, precisely as an attempt to describe an ecclesiology for the *oikoumene*, show some signs of taking this into account. It does not. The mission element, which was added on the basis of responses to the 1998 iteration titled "The Nature and Purpose of the Church," makes no substantive contribution except to extend established assumptions concerning the pastoral shape of the mission.[52] Wolfgang Vondey, by way of example, observes that while NMC understands "evangelism" to be the "foremost task of the church" (NMC, §110), "the lack of any further definition of this task reveals the underlying assumption that evangelization is largely synonymous with the ministry of service and proclamation advocated throughout NMC."[53] Gerrit Noort too states that "Faith and Order's intention to reach a common statement about the nature and mission of the one universal Church overrides

---

[51] Though it was recognized generally by the late 1970s within mission studies, it entered the wider theological imagination with the 2002 popularizing work of Philip Jenkins. See Philip Jenkins, *The Next Christendom: The Coming of Global Christianity* (New York: Oxford University Press, 2002); Philip Jenkins, "The Next Christianity," *The Atlantic* 290, no. 3 (2002): 53-68.

[52] *The Nature and Purpose of the Church: A Stage on the Way to a Common Statement* (Geneva: World Council of Churches, 1998).

[53] Wolfgang Vondey, "Pentecostal Perspectives on The Nature and Mission of the Church: Challenges and Opportunities for Ecumenical Transformation," in *Receiving "The Nature and Mission of the Church": Ecclesial Reality and Ecumenical Horizons for the Twenty-First Century*, ed. Paul M. Collins and Michael A. Fahey (London: Continuum, 2008), 59.

the contextual diversity of local Christian communities engaged in mission."[54] While this assessment is correct, the suppression of contextual diversity results from the assumed mode of historical continuity underlying apostolicity and its advocacy of a normative "pastoral" mission. This overrules any potential contribution by world Christianity, concrete and visible.

Second, NMC is a stage toward a "common statement" on ecclesiology. The allegiance demanded by formal accounts of apostolicity issuing from especially bilateral dialogues conditions the possibility of criticism. These documents need to remain faithful to the tradition from which they issue. As a wider ecumenical ecclesiology, NMC demands no such particular allegiance and by this measure exposes a number of underlying methodological assumptions even as these derive from other bilateral and multilateral dialogues (NMC, §6). The reaction to NMC, in other words, rebounds upon these otherwise insulated ecclesial statements.

One critique focused on the irreducibly "Western" inclination of the ecclesiology proposed. Aikaterini Pekridou, reporting on a 2009 Faith and Order plenary discussion of the text, observes that "rather than presenting a common ecclesiology, NMC appears to approach ecclesiology with a specific idea of the church already in mind."[55] A question was raised, he continues, as to "whether the very structure of the project and the formation of its central questions are inherently Northern and therefore largely irrelevant to the lived faith of Christians within the global south." Illustrative of this problem was the lack of attention given to "the way that definitions of culture, experiences of discrimination and marginalization (e.g., the Dalit experience), and the experience of women fit into ecclesiology, especially when the issue of power is present."[56] Moreover, though "koinonia" appears now to be an ecumenical given, Pekridou suggests that the concept is not simply translatable in other settings (e.g., in a caste-based society).

---

[54]Gerrit Noort, "Emerging Migrant Churches in the Netherlands: Missiological Challenges and Mission Frontiers," *International Review of Mission* 100, no. 1 (2011): 14.

[55]Aikaterini Pekridou, "The Plenary Discussion on the Ecclesiology Study of Faith and Order, The Nature and Mission of the Church: The Meeting and its Process," *The Ecumenical Review* 62, no. 3 (2010): 263. Primary documents from the Faith and Order Plenary Commission meeting, October 7-13, 2009, Crete, Greece, are available online at www.oikoumene.org/en/resources /documents/wcc-commissions/faith-and-order-commission/x-other-documents-from -conferences-and-meetings/plenary-commission-meeting-crete-2009.html.

[56]Ibid., 264.

It is tempting to dismiss these observations as primarily political, not applicable without translation for the issue of apostolicity, but they reflect wider observations regarding the possibility of world Christianity's contribution to fundamental theology. Though the plenary discussion was constituted with the intention of garnering such opinion, for Pekridou, it expected

> that global South regions would present differences linked to geography rather than other factors. A key question focused on how far ecclesiological convictions are shared even within communions when expressed in different contexts, and the extent to which theology "comes out of the soil." A further answer would take account of the complex ways that ecclesiology shapes church in a particular context, and how context shapes ecclesiology.[57]

The prescribed limits of diversity result in a methodological paternalism, expectant only of a diversity in color and flavor, not one of theological difference and of challenge to assumed patterns. It is this gulf between the assertion of apostolicity and the inability to connect with expressions of the Christian faith not issuing from the geographical North that suggests a fundamental inadequacy within ecumenical treatments of the issue.

EXCURSUS: *THE CHURCH: TOWARDS A COMMON VISION*, 2013

The third and final development of the "convergence" document as presented in 2013 at the Busan WCC assembly, titled *The Church: Towards a Common Vision* (CTCV), takes the ecumenical position even further down this line of thinking.[58] The document begins with the affirmation that "the Christian community finds its origin in the mission of God for the saving transformation of the world. The Church is essentially missionary, and unity is essentially related to this mission" (CTCV, p. 2). Koinonia emerges in §1 as the key interpretive category. Human beings as created in God's image bear "an inherent capacity for communion (in Greek *koinonia*) with God and with one another" (CTCV, §1). God's own triune being is the source of koinonia, and "the dynamic history of God's restoration of *koinonia* found its irreversible achievement in the incarnation and paschal mystery of Jesus Christ" (CTCV, §1). Koinonia, in other words, establishes the point of

---

[57]Ibid., 264.
[58]*The Church: Towards a Common Vision* (Geneva: World Council of Churches, 2013).

connection between the being of God, the mission of the church and the whole of the created order. Mission is tied to creation, meaning that mission is tied to the location of koinonia: the church. The document observes how each of the four Gospels closes with a mission command (CTCV, §2), and each locates this command within a community context: a community of witness (proclamation), a community of worship (baptism) and a community of discipleship (word, baptism, eucharist). Following this (CTCV, §3) occurs a minimal reference to the grounding of mission in the doctrine of the Trinity, one inconsequential for the remainder of the document, before, in §4, identifying the mission of the church with the nature of the church as a body and the practices attendant to such.

Turning to the question of proclaiming the gospel in different cultural contexts, the document acknowledges the experience of the early church. It recognizes the problem of colonization but, as usual, forms no clear relationship between the forms of the church and the experience of such; that is, the document offers no picture of what colonization in the context of the church looks like. Responsibility for the phenomenon of colonization lies with "those engaging in evangelization" (CTCV, §6). Cultural suppression is conceived not in relation to the church but in relation to some external and vaguely related action. The greater concern with culture rests in Christian unity. Though CTCV acknowledges that "some early writers" treated "diversity within the unity of the one Christian community . . . as an expression of the beauty which Scripture attributes to the bride of Christ" (CTCV, §6), it continues with the now standard ecumenical contrast between unity and "tensions" that "threatened to create divisions" resulting from the Gentile mission (CTCV, §8). Whatever the New Testament experience, this soon gives way to defining "visible unity" in relation to "the Creed of Nicaea-Constantinople" and its description of the "one, holy, catholic, apostolic Church" (CTCV, §9). In short, the document's argument suffers from a fundamental lack of clarity on the issue of cultural diversity and the problem of dictating particular cultural forms in the church. It contains no acknowledgment of the type of complaint issued by world Christian voices concerning the cultural imposition of historic church structures, nor does it mention the contemporary significance of the type of cultural and structural diversity evident in the early church. Instead, the document affirms the primary importance of unity, a concept it leaves undefined, beside which the diversity associated with mission trends toward division.

CTCV's first chapter sought to define the church through mission. The second chapter defines it as the "church of the triune God." Though the "New Testament provides no systematic ecclesiology" (CTCV, §11) and can embrace a "plurality," its importance lies in not denying "limits to legitimate diversity" (CTCV, §12). Before considering how the document defines "legitimate diversity," of note is the role limits play in describing the permissible range of unity. Koinonia establishes the a priori governing framework. "As a divinely established communion, the Church belongs to God and does not exist for itself. It is by its very nature missionary, called and sent to witness in its own life to that communion which God intends for all humanity and for all creation in the kingdom" (CTCV, §13). Leaving aside the absence of divine agency characteristic of the document as a whole, this given koinonia exhausts the church's missionary dynamic. The qualification that it does not "exist for itself," along with its "being sent," concentrates the focus on its "witnessing in its own life" to the form of community it already has and which is intended for the whole of creation. With koinonia basic to creation itself and so the given form of continuity between the church and the world, mission becomes the church in a wholly self-referential existence.

Eucharistic fellowship, with its accompanying hierarchy, follows as a necessary consequence of koinonia as the basic framework. With this groundwork in place, CTCV uses the term "mission" only in relation to forms of ministry. Following the formulation found in BEM (§M9), §20 links the mission command of Matthew 28 to the "eleven" and the related form of a "ministry of word, sacrament and oversight given by Christ to the Church to be carried out by some of its members for the good of all. This triple function of the ministry equips the Church for its mission in the world." Its conception of apostolicity develops a lineage whereby the Father sends the Son and the Son "chose and sent apostles and prophets" who were endowed with the gifts of the Holy Spirit. These men were called to serve as the church's "foundation and to oversee its mission" (CTCV, §22), meaning that the apostolic succession in ministry serves the apostolic faithfulness of the church.

Revisiting its affirmation of "legitimate diversity," the statement describes this as a "gift from the Lord," acknowledges the contribution of "cultural and

historical factors" and cautions against the dominance of one particular cultural expression of the gospel (CTCV, §28). The proper institution for controlling this diversity is the "pastoral ministry" (CTCV, §29). As to the diversity
occasioned by the Gentile mission, the statement looks to "the letter addressed
from the meeting in Jerusalem to the Christians in Antioch" as developing "a
fundamental principle governing unity and diversity"—the imposition of "essentials" (CTCV, §30). The strangely formulated language seems to suggest a
central form of governance (meeting in Jerusalem) and its capacity to discern
and "impose essentials" on a local Christian group. The statement views these
essentials as being expanded at Nicaea 325, where the "bishops clearly taught
that communion in faith required the affirmation of the divinity of Christ," and
as evident today in the condemnation of apartheid (CTCV, §30). What this
means in terms of who bears responsibility today for identifying and imposing
these essentials is nowhere developed. Nevertheless, the document sets these
essentials in relation to "legitimate diversity" and its limits. On the one hand,
referring to the WCC statement "The Unity of the Church as *Koinonia*: Gift
and Calling," illegitimate diversity "makes impossible the common confession
of Jesus Christ as God and Saviour the same yesterday, today and forever (Heb.
13:8)" (CTCV, §30n14). Unity, on the other hand, following the Anglican-
Orthodox 2006 Cyprus statement, is preserved "as long as their witness to the
one faith remains unimpaired" (CTCV, §30). The implications of this position
are by no means clear. From one perspective, it would seem possible to make
common confession without reference to such things as apostolic succession;
that is, alternate forms of order could be recognized as part of the church's legitimate diversity. This is self-evidently far from the statement's intent—and
that is the point. The "limits" of diversity are simply assumed. As CTCV §37
makes explicit, the "attributes" that "serve as a necessary framework for maintaining unity in legitimate diversity" include "communion in the fullness of
apostolic faith; in sacramental life; in a truly one and mutually recognized
ministry; in structures of conciliar relations and decision-making; and in
common witness and service in the world."[59] Transgress this, including its internal definition of the church's mission and the associated interpretation of the
ministry, and one stands outside the "gift of unity."

---

[59]Here citing "The Church: Local and Universal" (1990), §25.

The remainder of the text simply expounds on the church's internal structures. "Faith" becomes the category determinative of Scripture because of the importance of tradition and a wider "ecclesial interpretation" (CTCV, §37). The biblical witness is subordinated to the "Tradition," a move that corresponds to the general absence of a Protestant understanding of apostolicity. This is followed by a treatment of the sacraments, the ordained ministry, authority in ministry, the ministry of oversight and the authority of the ecumenical councils, including the language of primacy and reference to a universal ministry of unity.

In one sense, CTCV does not follow the contest of apostolicity examined in this work simply because it eliminates every reference to any external mission. CTCV constrains mission, if it might be formulated in this way, to the essence of the church because of its strong ontology of koinonia: if koinonia is God's own being, it follows that the church's witness consists of being this body of communion. Koinonia links the being of God, creation, the sacraments, the ministry and the body. This reifies the culture of the church and secures "creation," and so cultural diversity, under above all a pastoral ministry of oversight and the associated structures and interpretive measures. Scripture and the ministry of the Word become subordinated to this koinonia with its accompanying structures as the church's missionary message. Nothing exists beyond the church. With creation subsumed to the ontological category of koinonia, reconciliation loses its theological and social force. Reference to the Trinity and the work of Jesus Christ and the Spirit (which blows where it wills) seems to be exhausted in God's creation of the ministry, historic church structures and the "living Tradition." The persons of the Trinity appear without agency—the livingness of God is less than clear—and in no measure external to the church, leading it beyond itself. An external mission is mentioned only in relation to the problem of diversity/division and prompts the reassertion of "limits." Mission, because the church is finally coterminous with creation, is positively and exhaustively formulated as the church *incurvatus in se*.

2.7 Structure Without Interpretation: *A Treasure in Earthen Vessels*, 1998

Following the proposal to take "context" seriously, the same 2009 Faith and Order plenary discussion questioned how "greater hermeneutical sensitivity to different settings [might] be encouraged in the ecclesiological study."[60] Considering ecumenical accounts of apostolicity, the answer seems obvious—it cannot. Because of the perceived manner of historical continuity and its link to Christian "identity," apostolicity is the determinative concept for any ecumenical treatment of the church. Historical continuity means the abstraction of the structural, discursive, ritual and symbolic elements constitutive of apostolicity from their particular historical and cultural location. This prevailing assumption informs the methodological approach and precludes any such hermeneutical sensitivity.

One might elucidate this isolation of structure by reference to Faith and Order's instrument for ecumenical reflection on hermeneutics, A Treasure in Earthen Vessels (TEV).[61] This document, at least in terms of its framing concerns, appears to support a measure of cultural sensitivity. It sets continuity within the context of both history and culture (TEV, §1), identifies the church as itself a hermeneutical community (TEV, §7), affirms that this is in service to Christian unity (TEV, §5) and holds that the "hermeneutical task undertaken by the Church, with the guidance of the Holy Spirit, is a condition for apostolic mission in and for the world" (TEV, §49). In addition, the text identifies a range of ecclesial elements as instances of hermeneutical endeavor: the textual and oral tradition; the "meaning conveyed through non-verbal symbols: Christian art and music, liturgical gestures or colors, icons, the creation and use of sacred space and time"; Christian practices; and the interpretation of baptism and the eucharist (TEV, §35).

Much is to be commended, such as the stated concern for the local appropriation of the faith. However, it is also at this point that the document's major failing becomes evident. No connection forms between these elements and the ordering of the believing community. Nowhere do office and structure emerge as themselves possible interpretations of the gospel. Instead, a normative account of apostolicity and the derivative decisions concerning the proper ordering of diversity sets the hermeneutical process under an established structure. This structure, as determining the hermeneutical process, is not itself subject to it.

---

[60]Pekridou, "Plenary Discussion," 260.
[61]A Treasure in Earthen Vessels: An Instrument for an Ecumenical Reflection on Hermeneutics (Geneva: World Council of Churches, 1998).

A number of familiar ecumenical devices achieve this relegation of diversity. The first is setting the "one Tradition," defined as the "redeeming presence of the resurrected Christ from generation to generation abiding in the community of faith," in distinction to the "many traditions," defined as "particular modes and manifestations of that presence" (TEV, §45). This seemingly small step establishes a basic hierarchy whereby particular expressions of the gospel (cultural diversity) derive from the cohesive generational transmission of the gospel (historical continuity).[62] As to the relationship between the unity and the diversity of the church, the instrument places "contextuality" in relation to "catholicity." Catholicity refers to both cultural and temporal universality and establishes the means by which contextual expressions remain in unity with the church catholic. "Collegial and conciliar structures" (TEV, §45) and the associated celebration of the eucharist express "the communion of the local church" with churches across time and cultures. So framed, catholicity subjects contextuality to the limits imposed by received accounts of the church's apostolicity. The hermeneutical process and the related task of missionary witness are not necessary to formation in the faith. Formation occurs at some distance from contextual expressions, being "embedded in the life of worship and . . . nurtured by conciliar teaching, the writings of the early church, and the witness of saints and martyrs" (TEV, §51). Explicit reference to the church's apostolicity acknowledges that "churches have developed in their histories specific and differentiated ministerial structures," but this simply affirms given accounts of the function of oversight (TEV, §54). The now familiar entry point of describing the church as a "communion of co-responsible persons" shifts the focus to the *episkopé* as itself bearing the "hermeneutical function" to help the people to "recognize and

---

[62]For a discussion of the development of this position in the 1961 Faith and Order report "The Renewal of the Christian Tradition" as a reaction to the perceived problem of "historical relativism," see Dale T. Irvin, *Hearing Many Voices: Dialogue and Diversity in the Ecumenical Movement* (Lanham, MD: University Press of America, 1994), 51-58. The operative logic Irvin highlights concerns the manner in which the "Western historical past is implicitly the privileged vehicle for the deposit of the apostolic faith. While the history of the churches of the West was not said to be synonymous with the one Tradition, that Tradition was located in the history of these churches" (53). Warnings against the identification of the faith with its Western expression include the overriding reference to the necessary continuity of the church through the ages (53). One finds this pattern repeated through contemporary ecumenical statements.

actualize" their "gifts" (TEV, §55). Then follows an unchallenged account of the responsibility of the *episkopé* for the unity of the local church, the safeguarding of its apostolicity and catholicity, and the enabling of the church in its mission. At this stage of the text, all reference to the hermeneutical process falls away because it is itself derivative of the given structures and the arrangement of diversity to unity.

As one further observation, this official instrument imposes controls over the earlier studies on which it draws. Of particular relevance is the 1995 WCC consultation "On Intercultural Hermeneutics."[63] This document, while not really departing from the received wisdom, includes a richer description of the embodied nature of the Christian faith and, by extension, the problems with receiving an apparently normative Western form of that faith.

As the gospel engages a culture, so it interacts with the stories of that culture, and "although some cultural forms may hinder the gospel, stories from diverse cultural settings also help to convey the meaning of the gospel to illumine its truth and depth more completely."[64] This basic observation, by relating diversity not first to division but to the expansion in the human understanding of and witness to the gospel, moves the text in an alternate direction. By reference to the New Testament and the difficulties the early church had "keeping up with the Spirit as the gospel crosses cultural boundaries and elicits new cultural forms," the document opens space for a positive assessment of the formation of Christian communities outside a Western cultural sphere.[65] Included here are wider systemic issues stemming from the alternate perspectives for social ordering within different cultures.

> Throughout its history Christianity has shown an amazing capacity for integration. In the West the church integrated itself into Jewish, Hellenistic, Roman and Germanic elements. Elsewhere, older Christian traditions integrated Indian, Ethiopian, Syrian and Chaldean elements—to name but a few. Although this is a continuous process in the history of Christianity, it has become a controversial issue in recent centuries as newer churches in the

---

[63]"On Intercultural Hermeneutics: Report of a WCC Consultation, Jerusalem, December 1995," *International Review of Mission* 85 (1996): 241-52.
[64]Ibid., 243.
[65]Ibid., 244.

Third World have sought to integrate religious and cultural elements from their traditional ways of life. Many traditions do not see culture and religion as two separate or even separable entities, and many languages do not have a specific word for "religion." Christians from different cultural backgrounds strive to live integrated lives, in which being Christian does not imply alienation from the cultural community into which one was born. Where culture and religion cannot be separated, this means that Christians strive to integrate their religio-cultural bonds and memories within their Christian identity.[66]

The language of "alienation," of course, reflects the contemporary lived experience of many Christians outside Europe and North America. Not only are they often accused of a form of cultural betrayal, but they equally suffer from a type of spiritual bifurcation. The failure to allow Christianity to answer the local questions arising from the prior religious and cultural context often means that traditional practices remain alongside Christian rituals. This is not to deny a necessary difference as basic to the witness of a local Christian community, but it is to reject an account of that difference located in the importation of structures identifiable with Western culture and history.

It is at this juncture that an understanding of apostolic continuity through a determined cultural form and the manner in which this establishes precise limits on "diversity" emerges as problematic. Even though the ecumenical debate submerges the cultural claims basic to apostolicity via a de-particularized treatment of ministry, the problem of culture reappears when considering the appropriation of the gospel in other cultural settings. This is evident, to continue with the study, in how "some Christians in older centers of power, especially in the North, find it unsettling when people in other contexts—in the South and among minorities and other excluded groups—insist on their right to speak and respond to the Christian story in ways integral to their own contexts and different from those dictated by historically dominant cultures and churches."[67] Whatever theoretical allowance is granted to the local appropriation of the gospel, when it comes to discerning the "authenticity" of these lived expressions of the gospel, active appropriation does not emerge as a criterion. Reflective of this basic fear is the common binary argument that sets the pole of tradition against

---

[66]Ibid., 251.
[67]Ibid., 244.

the pole of local culture. A zero-sum game results: to take the context seriously is to regard elements of the tradition as dispensable. Such an argument, it might be suggested, reflects more the tacit cultural assumptions within the tradition than the actual intention and practice of world Christian communities.

Alternately, the freedom of all Christians to express their faith—including the structuring of communities basic to such—rests in a very basic theological affirmation.

> Whenever the Scriptures are translated into a new language, the gospel assumes a new cultural form. Even so, the church believes that what is being remembered, interpreted and lived in these many different ways is still the same story, the same gospel. But discerning this "sameness" is difficult, for there is no "pure" gospel that can be understood apart from the various forms in which it is embodied in culture and language.[68]

Limiting cultural factors to the interpretation of doctrine alone is a confounding element of this debate. There is an odd privileging given to structures, especially if the argument holds that the institutions are themselves necessary to maturity in the faith. As no disembodied gospel exists, the very structuring of the church itself reflects an interpretation of the gospel in its local context. One of the key arguments for "catholic" structures is that these are themselves evangelical expressions of the gospel. It seems—as an argument for some form of catholic order—entirely legitimate to understand that order as a necessary expression of a proper missionary hermeneutic.

2.8 HISTORICAL CONTINUITY AS CULTURAL PROPAGATION

If a possible rationale for a "catholic" order lies in its being a hermeneutic of the gospel, this, as Michael Fahey suggests, may require the "demythologization" of reified structures.[69] Nor are the theological warrants for such an

---

[68]Ibid., 243.

[69]Michael A. Fahey, "Continuity in the Church Amid Structural Changes," *Theological Studies* 35, no. 3 (1974): 427. On describing the church as the "hermeneutic of the gospel," see J. E. Lesslie Newbigin, *The Gospel in a Pluralist Society* (Geneva: World Council of Churches, 1989), 222-33; John G. Flett, "What Does It Mean for a Congregation to Be a Hermeneutic?," in *The Gospel and Pluralism Today: Reassessing Lesslie Newbigin in the 21st Century*, ed. Scott W. Sunquist and Amos Yong (Downers Grove, IL: IVP Academic, 2015), 195-213.

approach too difficult to find. If, as the common ecumenical position holds, de-particularized church structures are ratified under the same conditions as the creation of the canon, then, at minimum, these should be subject to the same hermeneutical considerations that apply to the text. A "vernacularization" of structures should be possible. Christoph Schwöbel, by way of illustration, advocates a "theological contextualization" of questions of ministry and office. This, in his estimation, does not render such questions unimportant. It succeeds, rather, in denying their claim "to absolute and abstract validity" while relating them "to the foundational theological-reference points in such a way that their theological significance becomes clear."[70] Necessary to this proposal, however, is some capacity to take culture and context seriously as informing the structures basic to the interpretation of the gospel in any local setting. Yet, as is clear from ecumenical renderings of apostolicity, contemporary methodological approaches preclude such investigation. The question is why.

Reference to the work of Dale Irvin helps illustrate the issue. Irvin observes how, while much is made of the contemporary cultural plurality of the Christian faith, such plurality applies not to history. Here "Christianity remains captive to a grand narrative that situates Christianity during its first two millennia almost exclusively within a 'European' or 'Western' historical context."[71] Only with the modern era does this continuous narrative expand to

> encompass the multiplicity of human experiences and cultures across the face of the globe. The history of Christianity is configured as a mushroom: a long, continuous narrative stem that widens at last (at the end of almost nineteen centuries) when Christianity becomes a global religion. The diverse non-European Christian cultural experiences and theologies of the present appear to have at most one or two centuries of a history of their own before they must be traced back to the stream of European church history.[72]

---

[70]Christoph Schwöbel, "'The Church of Jesus Christ': The Leuenberg Study on the Church and Its Significance for the Ways Forward from Meissen," in *Einheit bezeugen: Zehn Jahre nach der Meissener Erklärung: Beiträge zu den theologischen Konferenzen von Springe und Cheltenham zwischen der EKD und der Kirche von England*, ed. Ingolf Dalferth and Paul Oppenheim (Frankfurt am Main: Verlag Otto Lembeck, 2003), 437.

[71]Dale T. Irvin, "From One Story to Many: An Ecumenical Reappraisal of Church History," *Journal of Ecumenical Studies* 28, no. 4 (1991): 537.

[72]Ibid., 537-38.

Contemporary diversity in world Christianity, by this narrative, is derivative, coming from the Western experience and its presumed lineal
historical continuity that leads back to the cross. The objectionable element in this thesis, for Irvin, lies in the divorce of history from culture,
on which it trades.

Though the warnings against a simple replication of Western Christianity are clear (albeit with an uncritical consignment of this problem to
"missionary practice" and without any reflection on what is being im-
properly replicated), separating history from culture achieves something
of the same end. Any claim to cultural diversity runs aground on the priority of European history. Non-Western churches have no history of their
own, and this "confines non-European contextual theologies to reshaping
what is a European cultural religion." As such, the diverse cultural expressions of Christianity "can only be additions to or modifications of what is
essentially a European or Western religious meta-narrative."[73] They are but
variations on a set theme.

This has a determinative effect for interpreting the nature of the
church's apostolicity. Though divergent in notable areas, the Protestant
and Roman Catholic traditions nevertheless agree that the apostolic tradition includes this singular historical line that links Palestine to world
Christianity by way of Europe.[74] The Christian faith expanded from
Europe via Western missions. This inscribed a paternalism into the global
Christian narrative, for the churches outside the West possess no claim
to the Christian tradition or to "an immediate relationship to the sources
of Christian faith," except as they are also heirs of the West's cultural and
historical heritage.[75] This means that "the universal reference for European churches—their direct cultural and institutional continuity with
the ancient churches and through them with resurrection appearances—
negatively constitutes the universal reference for the history of the Third
World and for churches of the Third World." By way of a tradition, which
has been "constructed culturally and historically," the churches of Europe
"have an unmediated relationship to the resurrection," with the churches

---

[73]Ibid., 539.
[74]Ibid., 540.
[75]Ibid., 541.

of the non-Western world linked to the resurrection by the mediating event of Christian missions.[76]

One might add that, even while apostolicity includes claims to authority and the associated right to "recognize" other traditions, formal ecumenical statements are without reference to power and the resulting shaping of history or to a religious economy analogous in the realm of ecclesiology to the institutional capital built up by the West during the colonialist period. On this latter point, Irvin rejects the very notion of a cohesive and lineal Christian history. Notable communities, with long Christian heritages, exist in non-Western lands. Even where Islamic rule claimed once Christian lands, Christian communities remain. Within Europe itself, Christianity benefited from external influences, and diverse centers of Christianity contested the universalizing claims of the dominant churches, being persecuted as a consequence. "Even in Europe, there has not been one church history or one historical essence of Christianity."[77] Regarding unifying statements like the early creeds, Irvin notes that "the cultural-linguistic and political-ecclesial particularities of the ancient councils precluded any possibility that they spoke for all Christians of the world. Many Christian communities and believers remained outside the 'orthodox' consensus forged through successive ecumenical councils."[78] The unified past is, from this perspective, a retroactive warrant. With the assistance of José Míguez Bonino, Irvin notes how in defining the "*oikoumene* an alliance was struck between segments of Protestant and Orthodox Christendom which sought to reconstruct the mythical unity of one 'Holy Catholic Church.' A concrete historical past for this universal church was asserted at the cost of defining away dissent and resistance as heresy." This mythos of a "unified *Corpus Christianum*," however, ensured a "powerful ideological justification for efforts to achieve the unity of the churches on idealistic theological grounds,"

---

[76]Ibid., 542.

[77]Ibid., 544.

[78]Dale T. Irvin, "Towards a Hermeneutics of Difference at the Crossroads of Ecumenics," *Ecumenical Review* 47, no. 4 (1995): 498. While the temptation may be to categorize this position as issuing from the ecumenical margins, Irvin observes a similar concern within official documentation. He cites the 1967 Faith and Order report titled "The Importance of the Conciliar Process in the Ancient Church for the Ecumenical Movement," to the effect that "churches which lay outside the boundaries of the empire or which were in opposition with the empire rejected the imperial councils for political, as well as theological and religious, reasons." Irvin, *Hearing Many Voices*, 56.

with the range of "concrete cultural and socio-political factors" basic to the churches eliminated from consideration for being "non-theological."[79] Yet it is this division along cultural and linguistic lines that informs the account of historical continuity underlying the theoretical formation of apostolicity.

In short, to continue with Irvin, the mythos of a "Western" lineage through Greece to Rome to feudal Christian Europe to the modern world distorts history in a way that serves and is reinforced by an ideology of Eurocentrism.[80] This equally influences the ecumenical movement because the key breach in Christian unity becomes not that of the Great Schism in 1054 but that of the European Reformation, and the key issue is presented as one of theologically grounded institutions at some distance from issues of culture. So the ecumenical quest for unity "has become a Eurocentric quest for tradition. Suppressed by this ecumenical quest is the richness and variety of the many traditions of Christianity, of the multiplicity of Christian histories."[81] Reference to ecumenical statements on apostolicity bears this conclusion out.

Irvin's critical agenda builds on two positive findings. The first, in reference to Amilcar Cabral, holds that "culture is the manifestation of history, and history is the manifestation of culture."[82] The point is an obvious one, and ecumenical arguments for apostolic continuity and structure build on such a rationale. The question is whether the forms of the church understood as basic to its culture and to its visible continuity through history can be so easily distanced from their particular cultural location. Irvin's second finding suggests no. While much within nineteenth-century mission method might be rightly criticized, it is the very reality of ecclesial colonization that leads to the deterritorialization of the "cultural-bound forms of Western

---

[79]Irvin, "Towards a Hermeneutics of Difference," 497.

[80]Irvin, "From One Story to Many," 546. Irvin is here citing Samir Amin, *Eurocentrism* (New York: Monthly Review Press, 1989), 89-90. He further states that "eurocentrism is an ideology that distorts even European history, similar to other distorting ideologies such as racism and patriarchy, which appear today to have hindered the historical understanding of churches in Western Europe and North America." Irvin, "From One Story to Many," 553.

[81]Ibid., 547. For Irvin, most of the hermeneutical models employed within the ecumenical movement "have been adapted from Western philosophical systems that have extolled uniformity or singularity of meaning," and have been "characterized by the 'metaphysics of presence' that mark the Western onto-philosophical project. This philosophical tradition, according to its critics, 'consists in suppressing or reducing all forms of otherness by transmitting their alterity into the Same.'" Irvin, "Towards a Hermeneutics of Difference," 492.

[82]Irvin, "From One Story to Many," 538. Irvin is here citing Amilcar Cabral, *Return to the Source: Selected Speeches* (New York: Monthly Review Press, 1974), 59.

Christianity" and to the recognition that "Western Christian forms of faith do not provide the final standard of Christian identity and practice."[83] Irvin's critical reflections simply draw out the implications of this deterritorialization thesis for Christian historiography. That is, missionary imperialism demonstrated the necessary connection between the historic forms of the church and their particular Western location. While Western theology admits and rejects the connection to colonization, the necessary relationship between culture and history means that the assertion of a lineal historical continuity through Europe constitutes a return to such cultural propaganda.[84] In short, the claims for proper cultural diversity necessitate a correlative historical diversity.[85]

Clear implications follow for received notions of apostolicity, including how we can "think of Christianity as a non-territorial religion which is not at the same time a non-material or a non-embodied form."[86] While this is a matter to be considered, the key suggestion here is that, despite the apparent celebration of diverse expressions of the Christian faith, the account of historical continuity that underlies ecumenical treatments of apostolicity amounts to an ecclesial imperialism in another guise. The isolation of structure from the hermeneutic discussion represents merely one aspect of a much wider problem.

2.9 Viewing Communion Through the Lens of Schism and Against Its Reality

The emerging ecumenical consensus concerning apostolicity has a simple genius. Given the historic difficulties in beginning with structure and office, the focus has shifted to the nature of the church's apostolic sending and witness. This, it is argued, is a consequence of the life of the Christian community itself. Witness is the act of the whole community, with each member living according to his or her gifts. This beginning point finds support across

---

[83]Dale T. Irvin, "Ecumenical Dislodgings," *Mission Studies* 22, no. 2 (2005): 198-99.

[84]Summarizing the work of Emmanuel Ayandele, Irvin states that "the churches most often studied by historians of African Christianity were those that most resembled Western churches, while the history of the indigenous churches had been presented as aberrant and outside the boundaries of legitimate Christianity. This form of church historiography has perpetuated forms of ecclesial colonialism through missions and cannot comprehend the actual growth of Christianity in Africa." Irvin, "From One Story to Many," 552.

[85]Ibid., 539.

[86]Irvin, "Ecumenical Dislodgings," 199.

the traditions, helps explain the almost nonexistent reference to traditional Protestant treatments of apostolicity and illustrates the unchallenged equation of apostolicity with ministry and structure in ecumenical statements. The logic continues that as every community needs institutions, so the structures necessary to the Christian community themselves need to be an expression of, and need to express, the gospel. To talk of a people is, at once, to talk of their organization. By this circulatory path the discussion arrives back at the issues of office and episcopal order and of the manner in which this order maintains the church's historical continuity and governs diversity. Here the process of Christian formation and sanctification take center stage, with "witness" the natural overflow of this proper inward action of upbuilding the Christian koinonia. The nature of Christian witness becomes contingent on this culture insofar as witness is itself contingent on maturity in the faith and its ground in the processes of enculturation. "Apostolicity" encompasses the range of structures, practices and artifacts deemed necessary to the creation of a Christian culture. And while a strong sense of apostolic succession might not itself guarantee historical continuity, it is validated by the proper evangelical ordering of the community, including that of the local to the universal.

Though many find the logic convincing, it depends on a range of assumptions that beg for closer examination. Key here are the underlying account of history, the related conception of historical continuity, the flattening of cultural origins, the consequences for the cross-cultural continuity of the church, and above all the definition of "ecumenical" and its determination for the whole debate.[87] The problem of apostolicity is, so it appears, the problem of Protestant/Catholic schism. One, however, needs to ask whether this limit itself hampers the constructive development of apostolicity and, with this, its ability to address the problem of Christian unity.

Common ecumenical methods, by way of illustration, do not seem as suited to the challenge of apostolicity as they are to finding agreement on doctrinal issues. While "differentiated consensus" proved successful in

---

[87] As to this presumed capacity to flatten cultural origins, one should ask with Peter Brown after the manner in which power, contest, production, forgetting and the refinement of history all play their part. See Peter Brown, *Through the Eye of a Needle: Wealth, the Fall of Rome, and the Making of Christianity in the West, 350–550 AD* (Princeton, NJ: Princeton University Press, 2012).

developing the *Joint Declaration on the Doctrine of Justification*, it has failed to find traction when applied to the issue of church structure. For Pieter De Witte, the strength of this method in relation to doctrinal issues, even those as highly contested as the doctrine of justification, rested in its capacity to conceive different traditions as "different languages of faith" resulting from "different cultural-linguistic backgrounds." This contextual observation allowed each tradition to "recognize" that the other tradition adequately expressed the wider concern of the doctrine. Applying a method of "differentiated participation" to the issue of structure and the forms of ministry, by contrast, "because of its stronger extra-linguistic component, is more difficult to explain in terms of a (mental) act of recognition."[88] The very theological import invested in territorial and experiential considerations of apostolicity, in other words, prohibits an acknowledgment of their contextual character. Harding Meyer extends the point. Whereas doctrinal differences might be resolved by reference to the contribution of context to their formulation, the same does not apply to structural diversity. This is a problem of "*differences reinforced for ecclesial conditions and realities.*"[89] To construe the problem using ecumenical terminology, the method of differentiated consensus worked because it permitted the doctrinal problem to be identified in synchronic terms, in terms of basic continuity within cultural difference. Questions of structure differ because the claims of diachronic continuity applied to structures do not permit the relativization of particular forms associated with synchronic difference. Simply stated, while it is possible to apply a hermeneutic to doctrine, the same is not true for structure.

It is precisely these difficulties with the Christian church's lived reality that illustrate the underlying problem. Understanding apostolicity in terms of cultural continuity excludes the experiences of world Christianity from the solution. After his overview of ecumenical statements dealing with apostolicity, Konrad Raiser identifies the discussion as occurring between the historical churches of the European tradition. As to

---

[88]Pieter De Witte, "'The Apostolicity of the Church' in Light of the Lutheran-Roman Catholic Consensus on Justification," *Ecclesiology* 7, no. 3 (2011): 322.

[89]Harding Meyer, "Differentiated Participation: The Possibility of Protestant Sharing in the Historic Office of Bishop," *Ecumenical Trends* 34, no. 9 (2005): 11.

whether this understanding of apostolicity can also serve as a "firm foundation" for fellowship with the churches in other regions formed as a result of missionary expansion must remain open. Most of these would prioritize the sending commission as a dimension of the church's apostolicity before the backwards link to their apostolic origin, and would view their independent expressions of faith, doctrine and church structure as the fruit of the Holy Spirit's work.[90]

Issued by such a senior ecumenical figure, the observation proves revealing. One might question the very possibility of Raiser's contrast between a Western and non-Western approach within studies intended for the *oikoumene*, for the whole inhabited world. Nevertheless, it is clear that such derives from the assumed nature of the question, that is, the Catholic/Protestant schism. Inasmuch as this is the case, it becomes possible to match a division within the interpretation of apostolicity with a divide between Western and "world" Christianity. There may well be historical grounds for this, but such attribution suggests not only that the different approaches reflect alternate experiences but also that claims of continuity privilege established traditions and their concomitant geographical and cultural locations. Treated as a result of Western missions (and thus historically derivative), formulations of apostolicity identifiable within Southern Christianity become relativized as reflecting particular historical and cultural settings. They cannot, in this sense, be universal.

   One should not interpret the wider complex of problems indicated by the ecumenical approach as a binary contest of missionary freedom against established institutions. If mission theory, building on developments within historiography, understands the local reception of the gospel as basic to its transmission—its interpretation in the Spirit as basic to the conversion of a local community, a culture and its history—then the structuring of the community belongs also to the process of conversion. As arguments for inculturation make clear, an ordered community is itself necessary to its visibility (i.e., its witness) and to its continuity. Lived visibility cannot be something imposed on other local settings. Visibility, identifiability and a historical trajectory remain centrally important because a reconciled and reconciling community is the primary witness to a gospel of reconciliation. However,

---

[90]Raiser, "Festes Fundament?," 94.

isolating the discussion of apostolicity from cross-cultural engagement permits an abstraction of ecclesiology from the concrete conditions of the church even while grounding the apology for that abstraction within an account of the church as a continuous, visible social reality. A fundamental inconsistency is at play here. The logic of the livedness of the church community, if rigorously applied, needs to account for the richness of structures evident in world Christianity and, by extension, their richness through Christian history. Yet, as culture has become basic to apostolic continuity, so the apostolic identity of the church is set, at a most basic level, in opposition to the gospel's cross-cultural transmission and appropriation.

3
· ·

Culture as the Nature of Apostolic Continuity

The church is *a culture.*

Robert Jenson[1]

3.1 Culture as the Solution to the Problem of Apostolicity

The genius of the contemporary ecumenical approach to apostolicity lies in the implied link it draws between the church as a visible and historically continuous community and its being a particular culture. Though a clear strategy, ecumenical documentation with its formal theological language and its framing of the problem in terms of the Protestant/Catholic schism often leaves the relationship between apostolicity and culture implied. Making these links overt is the task of this chapter. It identifies the logic by which the ecumenical discussion finds its conclusion in a contemporary anthropological account of culture. We will accomplish this by reference to the work of American Lutheran theologian Robert Jenson.

Though he is not alone in making the type of connections under consideration, Jenson is explicit in beginning with the ecumenical problem of apostolicity. His proposed solution draws express connections between even the earliest church traditions and the church's being a culture. It is throughout theological. Though the "wrack of 'Christendom'" (STI, 5) informs his sensibilities, his own position does not depend on a precise account of economic, political and social calamity.[2] Jenson interprets these failings more in cosmic

---

[1]Robert W. Jenson, "Election and Culture: From Babylon to Jerusalem," in *Public Theology in Cultural Engagement*, ed. Stephen R. Holmes (Milton Keynes, UK: Paternoster, 2008), 48.
[2]Citations from Robert W. Jenson, *Systematic Theology I: The Triune God* (New York: Oxford

terms, as confirmation of the inevitable end toward which sin leads and which the triune God opposes. Nor, though he has clear sympathies in this direction, is he necessarily beholden to a philosophical substratum associated with the so-called linguistic turn. His own positive theological developments depend not on the rightness or wrongness of a particular genealogy of the current historio-cultural context. Whereas Stanley Hauerwas and John Milbank have been subject to ranging criticisms concerning the cultural location of their positions, Jenson, perhaps because of his claimed ground in the tradition, has been largely isolated from such.[3] As he approaches the issue through established dogmatic problems and by way of theological idiom, so his formulation of culture presents itself as a natural extension of the tradition, albeit in contemporary language. Given that it is basic to his theological project, criticism at this point amounts to a criticism of the whole. This is, of course, the main point: Jenson's use of culture amounts to an intact and inviolate system, one which includes a presumed distance between its normative theological claims and the type of interruptions and disruptions occasioned in the event of missionary transmission.

This chapter traces the logic by which Jenson begins with the ecumenical problem and ends with identifying the church as a culture. His launching point names the flaw shared by both Catholics and Protestants alike: the problem of an "unbaptized" God and the insertion of Hellenistic assumptions concerning divinity into the nature of the Christian God. Addressing this problem creates an alternate path for the church's historical continuity, one for which the church's being a culture is the nature of God's own objectivity for us. "Culture" does not reflect a backwards-oriented form of conservatism but develops continuity in terms of historical and even future contingencies. The advantages of this position are clear, but so are the consequences. The vision of cultural continuity with which Jenson solves the ecumenical problem mandates a particular method of cross-cultural transmission: mission becomes the process of enculturating peoples into the

---

University Press, 1997) and *Systematic Theology II: The Works of God* (New York: Oxford University Press, 1999), will take the form of STI and STII.

[3] See Gloria Albrecht's sharp observation that Hauerwas occupies a position of "class violence masked by a theology of nonviolence rooted in a hierarchical model of truth that denies the politics of its location." Gloria H. Albrecht, *The Character of Our Communities: Toward an Ethic of Liberation for the Church* (Nashville: Abingdon, 1995), 119.

church's culture. Notwithstanding the range of theological caveats Jenson applies to this position, his mandated mission method bears great similarities to the lamented occasion and methods of colonization. Such is the logical end when conceiving apostolicity in terms of cultural continuity.

3.2 THE SHARED FLAW

At the outset, it is worth noting Jenson's broad Catholic sympathies. He supports a communio-ecclesiology and its account of the church "*essentially* as *koinonia*."[4] The historic episcopacy he regards as constituted by a "divine right" and "cannot be challenged by any principle of the Reformation."[5] Following as a necessary correlate, Jenson affirms a broader Catholic interpretation of the local and universal, including its logical terminus in the Roman primacy. For him, "the unity of the church cannot in fact now be restored except with a universal pastor located in Rome" (STII, 247). Jenson, in other words, draws the threads of koinonia, eucharist and episcope together to affirm the church's instrumental or mediatory role.

While these general sympathies direct Jenson's interest in the nature and form of the tradition's continuity, the reality of schism means that he begins with a position critical of both Protestant and Catholic churches. Schism becomes the initiating question, and Jenson suggests, on the basis of already

---

[4]Robert W. Jenson, *Unbaptized God: The Basic Flaw in Ecumenical Theology* (Minneapolis: Fortress, 1992), 66. For a summary statement of his communio-ecclesiology, see Robert W. Jenson, "The Church as Communio," in *The Catholicity of the Reformation*, ed. Carl E. Braaten (Grand Rapids: Eerdmans, 1996), 1-12.

[5]Jenson, *Unbaptized God*, 71. Jenson rejects a "distinguishing of norms" and describes as an "oxymoron" a concept of *sola scriptura* that means "apart from creed, teaching office, or authoritative liturgy" (STI, 28). For him, the "famous threesome of canon, creed, and episcopate emerged simultaneously, in joint response to a single crisis in the life of the church, and were in their origin mutually interdependent aspects of one historical structure. If any one of the three is to be regarded as the result of a reversible development, so must the other two." Jenson, *Unbaptized God*, 71. To question the episcopate is, by extension, to threaten the status of both creed and Scripture.

Though this general approach has proven popular, Michael McGuckian develops an interesting response to a similar argument found in Francis A. Sullivan, *From Apostles to Bishops: The Development of the Episcopacy in the Early Church* (Mahwah, NJ: Paulist Press, 2001). According to Sullivan, though Jesus did not himself mandate a particular order, the Holy Spirit guided its development through the first few centuries of the church's existence in a manner similar to the formation of the canon. McGuckian counters that this position lacks "historical plausibility. . . . The fact that the Church had a decision to make in regard to the Scriptures is documented and clear. Of the corresponding process of canonization of the episcopate, there is, on [the] other hand, no trace whatever." Michael C. McGuckian, "The Apostolic Succession: A Reply to Francis A. Sullivan," *New Blackfriars* 86 (2005): 88.

received ecumenical documentation, that the problem of unity is "not located in any of the theological loci officially in dispute."[6] It resides in "a *shared* basic *flaw.*"[7] In the contest over "apostolic succession" and in the binary opposition of "event" and "institution," how the church remains itself through time occupies much of the ecumenical discussion. This, Jenson agrees, is a problem, but a derivative one. It stems from a doctrine of God not fully conformed to the gospel. The contest of time and continuity resides in the shared assumption, drawn from Greek culture, that there can be no time in God "because timelessness is what makes he or she or it be God. Our shared false construal of temporality reflects the culture-deity of Western civilization."[8] With this "unbaptized God" of the Greeks, eternity becomes timelessness and so "*immunity to time's opportunities,*" and being becomes simple "*persistence.*"[9]

Jenson traces this claim through the development of the doctrine of the Trinity, as itself a confrontation with Hellenistic assumptions concerning the nature of divinity, and into Christology. Insofar as divinity is timelessness, so it is not subject to the accidents of time; it cannot suffer. Impassibility, by extension, frames the christological controversies by inserting a problematic distance between humanity and God in Christ. Protestant ecclesiology, for Jenson, works out this separation through its "ever-repeated dialectical cancellation of the church's structures of historical perpetuity."[10] Catholic ecclesiology, by comparison, attempts to "*make up* for" this separation through a "too-simple identification of Christ with the church," thereby reducing the continuities that maintain the church's self-identity through time to those true of any historical event.[11] A juridical understanding of office results.

Given the bifurcation of apostolicity central to this study, a further point is worthy of note. Though he resists setting them within a general account of historical perdurance, Jenson nevertheless understands given structures as being "plainly necessary to there now being any church at all" (STI, 24). More than a simple observation concerning the relation of institution to historical existence, this concerns the transition from the apostolic to the

---

[6]Jenson, *Unbaptized God*, 107.
[7]Ibid., 108.
[8]Ibid., 118.
[9]Ibid., 138.
[10]Ibid., 115.
[11]Ibid., 125.

post-apostolic period. Acknowledging certain Protestant hesitancies, Jenson notes the eschatological immediacy of the gospel as recorded in the New Testament, beside which "provisions for perpetuity" appear "problematic." Nevertheless, the corresponding Protestant temptation is to regard only the first generation of disciples as normative, forgetting that the absence of "provision for institutional historical continuity" was a consequence of their anticipation of the "immediate coming of the kingdom."[12] A switch occurs, in other words, from the missionary eschatology of the New Testament to the advent of the church. "Bluntly stated, God institutes the church by *not* letting Jesus' Resurrection be itself the End, by appointing the 'delay of the Parousia'" (STII, 170). The church is, as such, "an eschatological *detour*" (STII, 171). For mission the point is quite decisive. The ferment evident of the New Testament, as we shall see, matches the cross-cultural transmission of the gospel through history. To describe the church as an eschatological detour is to set the institution apart from its missionary movement. Mission and the related issue of cross-cultural continuity become unessential because they characterize the parousia detoured by the church.

Framing the problem in terms of the Protestant/Catholic divide is here decisive. By establishing the shift as one from the eschatology basic to the cross-cultural missionary encounter to the institution of the church, the issue becomes first one of diachronic continuity, continuity through time. Interpretive priority attaches to the diachronic over the range of synchronic challenges that occupy the attention of the New Testament. Such an assumption precludes the possibility, by way of example, that the relative absence of biblically mandated institutional forms suggests not a period lacking in institution but the freedom of institutional interpretation in the occasion of the gospel's cross-cultural transmission, that is, in its continuity.

Jenson's use of institutional language to describe the post-apostolic transition illustrates well the issue. He develops a logic of continuity by working backwards from the answer supplied by the early church—canon, creed and office. Jenson begins here because this was the moment of the church's own self-awareness, of its existence as a historically mediated self-identity, a tradition. The perpetuation of this tradition, so continues the logic, demands

---

[12]Ibid., 114.

institutions (STI, 24). Institutions were at first not necessary because "the apostolate itself was an office, that is, a role and position subsisting independently of the individualities of those occupying it" (STI, 25). The original apostles, in that they were "a presupposition of the church," were unique and unrepeatable. But, by understanding office in terms of an institutional position and detaching that from the particular persons, it was possible for the church itself to institute those offices and so to continue the function of the original apostolate. One such function, already in effect during the apostolic period, was a collective exercise "in response to problems that affected fellowship between local churches and so the reality of the one church" (STI, 23). The missionary endeavors of the first apostles become institutionalized as the essential ministry of the church through apostolic succession (STII, 233-34). Jenson cites with appreciation *Lumen Gentium*: "That divine mission, which was committed by Christ to the apostles, is destined to last until the end of the world . . . since the gospel, which they were charged to hand on, is for the church the principle of life for all time" (LG, §20).[13] For this mission, for this handing on of the gospel, "there must always be pastors and . . . they must pass on their office in succession" (STII, 234). None of this is to suggest that Jenson retreats to an account of institutional persistence, but, in terms of dogmatic description, the apostolic mission becomes identified with an institutionally located historical continuity.

3.3 ANTICIPATION AS CONTINUITY

If an "incompletely christianized interpretation of God" constitutes the shared flaw basic to the ecumenical dilemma, Jenson addresses that flaw through the doctrines of the Trinity and the Spirit. Taking up the Orthodox complaint, Catholicism and Protestantism alike share a deficient trinitarianism as expressed in their failure to regard the church's institution "as a charismatic work of the Spirit."[14] Both approach the institution as though it were a "human structure," with the effect that Protestantism detaches the institution from the event of salvation and Catholicism maintains the

---

[13]See Austin Flannery, ed., *Vatican Council II: The Conciliar and Post Conciliar Documents* (Northport, NY: Costello, 1996), 350-426.

[14]Jenson, *Unbaptized God*, 133. Jenson is here citing Nikos A. Nissiotis, *Die Theologie der Ostkirche im ökumenischen Dialog* (Stuttgart: Evangelisches Verlagswerk, 1968), 71.

institution by means of juridical perdurance. The Orthodox alternative holds charism and office together. Charism liberates office from the historically given, from nature. Jenson's own treatment of this decisive move is brief, functioning more as signpost to its development within Orthodoxy. The intent, however, is clear: though the "church's fundamental institutionalization was the creation of the apostolate," such was possible only through the coming of the Spirit.[15] It is the proper work of the Spirit to link the historical event of the resurrection with the present existence of the church. The Spirit, as the founder who is continually present in the church and who works to create community, molds the institutions of the church's common life.[16] In this sense, "the entire institutional life of the church is institutional divine *life*, charism. The Spirit unites the risen One with the church and does so by the way in which he structures the church in its reality as a historically actual community."[17] This, for Jenson, results in a "specifically theological understanding of temporal continuity"; namely, the Spirit's shaping of the church's institutions constitutes the continuity of the present body with the historically past event of the incarnation. For this reason Jenson prefers the Orthodox definition of tradition and its inclusion of "dogmatic teaching, liturgical worship, canonical discipline, and spiritual life," a wider vision that will receive confirmation with Jenson's introduction of culture language.[18]

Alongside his work in linking the historic event of the resurrection with the present life of the Christian community, the Spirit is "God as the power of the future, God as his own and our transforming outcome" (STII, 26). As the Spirit's work is eschatological, so the church's historical continuity pertains not simply to its origins in a historical *past*. A full account of the Spirit's work will recognize that the "church is founded in what is not yet historical event, in a last *future*."[19] The self-identity of the church, its continuity through time, is also an eschatological continuity, an agreement of the church with its end in the Trinity.

A question to be noted is how this identification of the eschatological work of the Spirit with the institutionally configured self-identity of the

---

[15]Jenson, *Unbaptized God*, 135.
[16]Ibid., 136.
[17]Ibid., 135.
[18]Ibid., 136.
[19]Ibid., 137.

church relates to the work of the Spirit in cross-cultural missionary movement that is central to the New Testament narrative. Nevertheless, the payoff for Jenson is clear: the Holy Spirit works by way of anticipation. In contrast to the Hellenistic equation of eternity with timelessness, by accounting for the Spirit's proper divinity,

> eternity would be apprehended as the dramatic mutuality of Father and Spirit, of God as God's origin and God as God's goal, and therefore not as immunity to change but as *faithfulness* in action. Being would accordingly be apprehended not as persistence in what is but as *anticipation* of what is not yet. The church would know herself as the temporal mission not of resistance to time but of faithful change in time, and know her own continuity in that mission not as hanging on to what is already there but rather as receiving what must come.[20]

Anticipation as a category of divine ontology addresses both the ontological relationship between God and humanity (the christological problem of impassibility) and the development and continuity within the church's historical course (the temporal problem of being as persistence). Historical change itself belongs to the witness to the gospel. Compared to the timeless god of the Greeks, the God of Israel "is identified by contingencies" (STI, 64). As God can be "identified by narrative," so "his hypostatic being, his self-identity, is constituted in *dramatic coherence*" (STI, 64).[21] Jenson defines "dramatic coherence" by reference to Aristotle and his conception of story as "one in which events occur 'unexpectedly but on account of each other,' so that before each decisive event we cannot predict it, but afterwards see it was just what had to happen" (STI, 64). So it is with historical development within the church. However, whereas the Greek Aristotle understood such contingency to be an ontological lack, Jenson understands "commitment in a history" to be "an ontological *perfection*" (STI, 64). This creates something of a problem, for "dramatic coherence requires closure if it is to constitute identity" (STI, 65). Anticipation reenters at this point. God's essential actuality, his "self-identity . . . constituted in dramatic coherence . . . is established not from the beginning but from the end, not at birth but at death, not in *persistence* but in *anticipation*" (STI, 66). This anticipation of the end in history is God's eternality.

---

[20]Ibid., 138.

[21]For a treatment of Jenson's approach, which she terms "story Thomism," see Francesca Aran Murphy, *God Is Not a Story: Realism Revisited* (Oxford: Oxford University Press, 2007), 16-22.

One should further note that as anticipation is ontologically basic, that is, as it is true first of God, so it describes the "fundamental metaphysical structure" of creaturely being.[22] Anticpation as an analogy of being means that as the church embodies this metaphysical structure, so its apostolic continuity cannot be understood in terms of general history. Instead, "the church *is* the world's historical continuity."[23] Historical continuity itself derives from the church and the nature of its anticipatory existence.

The significance of this pneumatological point for the issue of apostolicity becomes evident when Jenson applies it to the ecumenical problem of episcopal order. In correspondence to this work of the Spirit and so God's own being, the "classic structure of churchly office is the result of a long series of postapostolic contingencies" (STII, 237). Though Jenson supports an early catholicity in the Pastoral Epistles, historical scholarship's success in disproving the existence of the episcopate at or before Pentecost has undermined the traditional rationale for episcopal order. By implication, Jenson notes, if it were possible to be the church without an episcopal order, then such an order, while it might be of pragmatic benefit, would follow human rather than divine law, being *iure humano* and not *iure divino*. Acknowledging the wider difficulties this line of argument presents— that is, "since every phenomenon of the church's historically developed life can hardly be divinely mandated" (STII, 237)—Jenson redefines *iure divino* according to his revised notion of divine ontology.

This need for what might elsewhere be termed a contextual hermeneutic examines how "'historically relative and conditioned' institutions" might be considered "divinely instituted" (STII, 237). Two conditions are needed for historical contingencies to meet this standard. First, they must be "*dramatically* necessary in the church's history, not mechanically determined beforehand but nevertheless once there the very thing that had to happen" (STII, 237). Second, though historically relative and conditioned, their development within the life of the church must be "irreversible." An irreversible decision is one in which the church so determines its future self-identity that "if the choice were faithless to the gospel there would be no

[22]Robert W. Jenson, "Christ as Culture 3: Christ as Drama," *International Journal of Systematic Theology* 6, no. 2 (2004): 199.
[23]Jenson, *Unbaptized God*, 145.

church thereafter extant to reverse it" (STII, 239). Such evaluations occur only in hindsight: "dramatic necessity can be perceived only when the event is there" (STII, 239). Applying this principle to the church, Jenson affirms that the "narrative hangs together by anticipations of its conclusion. The church is what she is as anticipation of her transformation into God" (STII, 239). Through the promises of God, the vision of the gospel's final fulfillment, it is possible to discern which past decisions were due to the Spirit, including those that "prohibit certain paths" (STII, 240).

As anticipation expects contingent structural development, so such change becomes the necessary leading of the Spirit and, as such, *iure divino*. One can acknowledge the historical and cultural origins of the episcopacy while declaring that order to be divinely constituted and so irreversible for the church. This, in Jenson's estimation, undoes Protestant complaints. With the Spirit structuring the historically actual community, the past irreversible decision for episcopal order determines Protestantism's alternate structures to be against the work of the Spirit. The advent of episcopal order "prohibited" the Protestant path vis-à-vis church structure.

3.4 THE OBJECTIVITY AND AVAILABILITY OF CHRIST'S BODY

Though Jenson regards institution as necessary to continuity, the mere historical course of those institutions cannot guarantee such, a point he illustrates by reference to the children's game of whispering a story around a circle and comparing the first and last versions (STI, 25). Nevertheless, based on his pneumatological commitments, Jenson holds that "*God* uses the church's communal structures to preserve the gospel's temporal self-identity and so also the temporal self-identity of the gospel's community" (STI, 25). God the Spirit can so use these structures because, now shorn of the problem of impassibility and so of any improper distance inserted between the divine and the human, "our Lord's present embodiment, his present availability to us, is the historically concrete body called the church."[24] Jenson places a christological account of "objectivity" alongside his pneumatological development of anticipation. In comparison to the respective Protestant and Catholic temptations to set "the church's agency over against God" or to

---

[24]Ibid., 126.

"identify the church with God," the church as the body of Christ means that God is our "object" and in this way is "available" to us.[25] This objectivity becomes a central pillar in Jenson's approach to the church's witness.

The gospel can be something human beings can see and hear only if God makes himself object for us. This summarizes Jenson's trinitarian ontology and his understanding of the resurrection: "the gospel's God can be an object for us if and only if God is so identified *by* the risen Jesus and his community as to be identified *with* them" (STI, 13). In concrete terms, for Jenson, "the loaf and cup, the bath, and the rest of the gospel's factual churchly embodiment" are God's "own objectivity" (STI, 13). Historical continuity is not temporal perdurance; it is faithful witness to the original and unique event of the resurrection. This is possible only insofar as God acts to unite these structures with their founder, which is the proper work of the Spirit. Witness, by this definition, belongs to the church in its concrete historical reality, in its being an "object in the world," in its "availability" and so in its visibility (STII, 213). The very objectivity of God for us, the witness to the resurrection, rests in the range of historical contingencies that constitute the work of the Spirit in molding the common life.

Noteworthy is the mundane language Jenson uses to describe the eucharist and baptism—loaf and cup and the bath. This language places these sacramental practices in relation to the range of other concrete artifacts that constitute the "gospel's factual churchly embodiment." All those cultural and historical elements that belong to any identifiable community properly belong to the church and are necessary to its witness since the church becomes "available" through this complexity. Precisely as the body of Christ, the church is "a personal availability constituted in a myriad of fundamentally *historical* factors, of perceptible familial, social, and national inclusions and manifestations, of interwoven personal narratives, even of such things as clothing and housing."[26] Moreover, though this visibility is essential to both the method and the content of the church's witness, because it is the visibility of a common *life*, it is not of itself translatable. There exist

---

[25]Ibid., 127.

[26]Ibid., 126. See also his description of the "body," whereby, for the church to be the body of Christ, it is "the object in the world as which the risen Christ is an object for the world, an available something as which Christ is there to be addressed and grasped. . . . Where does the risen Christ turn to find himself? To the sacramental gathering of believers" (STII, 213, 214).

many and powerful signs that are not items of a language, that are not so rule-governed as to be disposable by translation: processions, handshakes, loving-cups, the blood of slaughtered beasts, images, sexual caresses, and so on. They are seen, felt, tasted, smelled, and indeed also heard. Their common feature is their sheer givenness, their irreplaceability as objects in their own right, and that is to say, their otherness over against us, their *spatiality*. . . . Thus at baptism, the verbalized blessings enter the consciousness of participants without remainder; the body of water cannot so accommodate itself and persists in externality. (STII, 60)

While a hermeneutic of history is necessary to the church's continuity, the tactile objectivity of the church is not available to translation.[27] Maintaining a proper objectivity is vital, for it is the objectivity of Christ—the spatiality of its cultural artifacts—which sets the body in an attitude of reception. "When the church is understood with ontological seriousness as the risen Christ's body, an appropriate dialectic of identity and difference between God and the church must result."[28] Jenson describes this distinction as one of a *community*, which is "not another agent than God," against that of an *association*, a "multitude of

---

[27]Robert Wilken draws a similar conclusion regarding the church as a culture and the impossibility of translation. To begin, the "Church is a culture in its own right. Christ does not simply infiltrate a culture; Christ creates culture by forming another city, another sovereignty with its own social and political life." Robert L. Wilken, "The Church as Culture," *First Things*, no. 142 (2004): 32. The distinctive marks of this culture differ from other communities in that, following the *Epistle to Diognetus*, Christians are not identifiable by "nationality, [by] language or by custom" (32). This statement, however, appears only true until the third century, for by this time such a distinction undergoes some revision: the Christians began to shape their space, their time and their language, with the aim "not to communicate the gospel to an alien culture but to nurture the Church's inner life" (33). For example, the liturgical calendar functioned as "a kind of spiritual metronome helping communal life to move in concord with the mysteries of the faith" (34). These developments, Wilken continues, have become indispensable "for a mature spiritual life. Religious rituals carry a resonance of human feeling accumulated over the centuries" (34). As this applies also to the "distinctly Christian language," so "we must be wary of translation" (35). Indeed, it is more "urgent" for the church "to tell itself its own story and to nurture its own life, the culture of the city of God, the Christian republic," than it is "to convince the alternative culture in which we live of the truth of Christ" (36). On the particular issue of a Christian language and the negative possibilities of translation, Wilken elsewhere states that "without the distinctive Christian language there can be no full Christian life, no faithful handing on of the faith to the next generation. For that reason, the words that embody what we believe and practice—words given us by those in whom Christ was present—cannot be frivolously tampered with, translated into another idiom, or discarded." Robert L. Wilken, "The Church's Way of Speaking," *First Things*, no. 155 (2005): 29. Translation of the Christian gospel, which includes here the wide gamut of supporting institutional and symbolic interpretive means into other languages and so cultural forms, retards the possibility of Christian maturity.

[28]Jenson, *Unbaptized God*, 128.

believers," whose agency is that "of the saved and not of the saving."[29] The Christian, in other words, stands under and is disciplined into the culture that is God's own agency. Translation, by contrast, intrudes on the necessary connection between the community and its culture. It undoes the spatiality necessary to Christian growth by promoting association as the primary mode of belonging. It disembodies the church, removing the mechanisms necessary to Christian maturity and to the historical transmission of the faith.

With this account of God's objectivity and availability to the human, the step to using "culture" to narrate this dynamic is not a large one. In terms of positive benefit, this position reinforces notions of the church as a concrete and visible society and of its mediating function. As this "structured continuing community" is "the 'objectivity' of the gospel's truth *pro nobis*," so it is "in its structured temporal and spatial extension . . . the *Bedingung der Möglichkeit* [the condition of the possibility] of faith."[30] The danger, to which we shall turn, is the possibility that this claim regarding *God's* objectivity, itself basic to the church's witness and historical continuity, enshrines relative historical and cultural artifacts as essential to Christian identity, to apostolicity. Such a claim at once isolates (because of its link with divine ontology and the action of the Spirit in lifting the historical above the natural) this contingent cultural location from criticisms issuing from other cultural locations while rendering it essential to salvation for all Christian peoples. As the "condition of the possibility of faith," such objectivities become necessary to faith as such, and so fundamental in the event of cross-cultural transmission.

3.5 The Church Does Not Have a Culture—It *Is* a Culture

Anticipation and objectivity, with their assumed trinitarian ontology, constitute the theological underpinnings of Jenson's description of the church as culture. Anticipation validates as belonging to the church *iure divino* otherwise historically and culturally relative decisions, including those which, by virtue of historical development, may be seen to supersede central biblical themes (a central example being the assumed transition of the missionary activity and associated structural ferment of the apostles into the settled ministry of the church). These decisions direct future developments by being "irreversible." As

---

[29]Ibid., 127-28.
[30]Robert W. Jenson, "You Wonder Where the Spirit Went," *Pro Ecclesia* 2, no. 3 (1993): 303.

Christ's own body, historical contingency is proper to the church and basic to its objectivity and availability.[31] Availability indicates an externality that, within Jenson's schema, is necessary to the dialectic of God's own identity with, and distinction from, the church. Such externality rests in the range of non-rule-governed signs, the tactile and aesthetic, which are not available to translation.

Before turning to his definition of culture, a further formal step is worthy of note. Jenson enters the question of culture through the language of "polity." The church, as a "*people* united in a common *spirit*, that is, a people who have become a community, is a *polity*" (STII, 204).[32] As the "polity of God," the church, in critical opposition to contemporary forms of gathering, cannot be a voluntary association "like a club or an interest group," even if that association is based on a common commitment to Christ (STII, 222). A communio-ecclesiology, by contrast, based as it is on "perichoretic communion," is a "doctrine of church polity drawn from the nature of the church herself, rather than by imitation of the worldly collectives around her" (STII, 223). With church structures both expressing and cultivating a people united in a common spirit, changing structure through imitation amounts to the reshaping of the church to embody another message. When these structures embody the contemporary political zeitgeist, the church serves this master and proclaims it as truth.

Jenson's grounding of his positive construction in the language of polity includes a couple of ancillary consequences. First, it frames whatever might be said of "culture" more generally by making basic the range of theological predicates associated with polity (i.e., communion, office and hierarchy). Polity provides this transition point between the traditional theological language of office and structure and a contemporary anthropological under-

---

[31] Working backwards from the assertion that the church is a culture, "if the church is the body of Christ, i.e., if the church is the availability of Christ in and for the world, and if this body of Christ, the church, is a culture, it follows that Christ is a culture." Robert W. Jenson, "Christ as Culture 1: Christ as Polity," *International Journal of Systematic Theology* 5, no. 3 (2003): 325. The manner in which a culture can be said to be external seems itself to govern the nature of Christ's identity and distinction from his body. It belongs uniquely to Christ that he lived a "life that could and did empty itself by death into a community of disciples without therefore vanishing into the community" (325).

[32] For a study on this aspect of Jenson's thought, see David S. Yeago, "The Church as Polity? The Lutheran Context of Robert W. Jenson's Ecclesiology," in *Trinity, Time, and Church: A Response to the Theology of Robert W. Jenson*, ed. Colin E. Gunton (Grand Rapids: Eerdmans, 2000), 201-37. For the links Jenson creates between the concepts of body, polity and culture, see Jenson, "Christ as Polity," 325-26.

standing of culture. Or, as Jenson understands religion to be the heart of culture itself, so each culture is already a polity and structured according to its religious vision.[33] "Insofar as a culture is a polity, it will be shaped and moved by the political form of self-worship, which Augustine called the *libido dominandi*; insofar as it makes artifacts, it makes graven images, protecting its own lusted-after divinity; insofar as it builds, it builds ziggurats, etc."[34] As all such entities are polities, so this determines the church's relationship to the world: it is "a polity *now*, and just so *in conflict with* other polities, with . . . the polities of this age as a class."[35] Nor does Jenson avoid the political implications of such a position. "If we are in Christ . . . we must expect other polities to make war against us, as China does and as most Islamic societies do, and as do the liberal democracies, in certain ways."[36] The church relates to the world through a clash of cultures, for each culture is a polity and so a competing theological entity populated with artifacts formed as graven images.

With the above theological assumptions, Jenson turns to describe the church as a culture using what he regards as a standard social theory definition: culture "is all that part of a human group's mutual or cooperative behaviour, whose diachronic community is achieved by teaching and not by biological inheritance."[37] To this Jenson adds a secondary definition: culture is "a mutually determining system of signs" capable of being "observed" and "abstracted from" the "whole of a human group's mutual or cooperative behaviour."[38] The two definitions receive an asymmetrical ordering. The latter approach, though "illuminating," is deficient in that "it abstracts to the semiotic structure observable at a momentary state of a culture. . . . Cultures no more than persons exist momentarily; they exist only diachronically."[39] While one might observe in passing how a cultural definition of necessity focuses on "diachronic community" and renders nonsensical any discussion of "synchronic community," two points follow.

---

[33]Jenson, "Election and Culture," 57.

[34]Ibid., 58.

[35]Jenson, "Christ as Polity," 329.

[36]Ibid. Jenson reinforces this position by putting it in christological terms. As Christ is the culture of Israel, so "a relation between, say, Christ and Chinese culture is in itself a relation between Jewish culture and Chinese culture" (323).

[37]Jenson, "Election and Culture," 48. See also Jenson, "Christ as Polity," 323-24.

[38]Jenson, "Election and Culture," 48.

[39]Jenson, "Christ as Drama," 198.

First, this twofold definition is, for Jenson, exhaustive. Nothing more need be said, for even by this minimal standard it is clear that the church is a culture.

> With nothing more than these vague definitions before us, it is already apparent: the community we call the church *has* a culture, or indeed and equivalently, the church *is* a culture. No anthropologist coming across the church as a new discovery, would delay the judgment for a moment. Eucharist, baptism, the ceaseless repetition of certain texts and forms of words, the ten commandments, and the creeds, the idiosyncratic structure and legitimation of her leadership, the shape of her buildings, the eschewing of infanticide and euthanasia—all these, and a thousand things more, are the very sorts of doings and artifacts which persist only by teaching and, in their systematic relationship to each other, constitute a culture. Culture simply as such can be no problem for the elect community, in that this community is itself a culture.[40]

One may question whether it is so possible to claim the authority of the social sciences. Jenson's assertion at this point appears much more in service to this grand theologial substratum of anticipation, objectivity and availability than of acceptance to anthropology as such. Of immediate interest is the swift and undifferentiated movement Jenson makes from what might be described as theologically central practices, that is, baptism and the Lord's Supper, to the "hundred other distinctive gestures" of unknown origin.[41] He develops no criterion for a relative evaluation of these "practices" and "artifacts." All are necessary because all properly belong to the objectivity and externality basic to the culture named church. Of course, not all of these historical decisions attain the status of "irreversible," of being *iure divino*. Yet,

> if the church is a culture of her own, she, like any community, is responsible to cultivate her culture, and can lose her identity if she does not. Arguments about music, discipline, language, ministerial style, architecture and the like are not *in their ensemble* about "matters indifferent," though usually no one such decision is by itself fatal.[42]

---

[40]Jenson, "Election and Culture," 49.

[41]Robert W. Jenson, "Christian Civilization," in *God, Truth, and Witness: Engaging Stanley Hauerwas,* ed. L. Gregory Jones, Reinhard Hütter and C. Rosalee Velloso da Silva (Grand Rapids: Brazos, 2005), 155.

[42]Jenson, "Christ as Polity," 324.

The identity of the church is located within the complex of practices and artifacts that make up a culture. Because it is a complex, and because contingency belongs to its being object for us, small and perhaps over time significant interpretative shifts are possible. But because the church is only historically continuous and available in its being a culture, the full range of interpretive practices are necessary to its being and identity.

Second, the identification of a semiotic system is, for Jenson, only a secondary element in defining a culture because it depends on an abstraction—culture in a frozen "moment." A mode of historical continuity, Jenson counters, itself belongs to the definition of a culture. In the case of the Christian culture (the church), this mode he identifies as "teaching." "Since teaching is always interpretation, the diachronic reality of culture is a tissue of choices that could have been made otherwise: a culture is a particular realm of creaturely freedom."[43] Interpretation itself creates and belongs to the fabric of culture, opening and closing future possibilities. Notable here, again, is the stress on interpretation over translation. As historical continuity itself belongs to the definition of culture, continuity is primarily and exhaustively treated in diachronic terms. The question of synchronic continuity features nowhere, or, better, it features as a consequence of historical contingency. Jenson certainly understands that the church engages with and learns from cultures different from itself, the classical example being the development of the doctrine of the Trinity in reaction to Greek metaphysics (STI, 16). Synchronic continuity occurs, in other words, through the absorption of other cultural elements into the church's own singular culture. Teaching is the process of enculturation, of drawing all into the culture the church is.

Nor is this just any culture. The benefit of naming the church as a culture rests in its thickness. Jenson has in mind a "specific identifiable culture," the culture of Israel.[44] "The church's cultural identity simply is Israel; to see what is our culture as church, we can only read the Old Testament."[45] Reference to Israel, and specifically to the giving of the law, illustrates the form of teaching basic to diachronic continuity: the repetition of "those same words" that were "to be handed on in the archetypical cultural process." As these

---

[43]Jenson, "Election and Culture," 57.
[44]Jenson, "Christ as Polity," 323.
[45]Jenson, "Election and Culture," 59.

words, the Torah, were culturally embodied, so with the giving of the law God "taught Israel architecture"—that is, the design of the tabernacle and later the temple, including specific details of even "the kinds of fabrics to be used."[46] The whole life of Israel as a people, with its "dietary laws, banking practices, leisure-time provisions, and restrictions, etc." declared the nature of the God it served.[47] Teaching as historical continuity and the specific reality of culture go hand in hand. This is so because, in Jenson's estimation, the connection is both the command and the act of God. Israel is the example case even in the manner in which the church comes into being, exemplifying both the necessary relationship between teaching and culture and historical change as interpretation. "The teaching by which a culture is maintained is always interpretation and so is not itself mere repetition. Moreover, the church is Israel only by way of a great *continuity*: the crucifixion, the destruction of the temple and the opening to the Gentiles."[48] Only by way of anticipation can these cultural ruptures be understood in terms of continuity, but this is precisely how the church changes and remains the same through its historical passage.[49]

Culture, so understood, serves as the point of connection between Israel/ the church and the wider world. As culture is a creation of God, so "the *Spirit* agitates every culture, luring it towards the kingdom."[50] The Spirit can so act because with "culture" describing also the being of God, it becomes a form of *analogia entis*, a continuum between God, the church and the world, constituting both the manner of distinction and the nature of con-

---

[46]Ibid., 53.

[47]Ibid., 53-54.

[48]Ibid., 59. For what this process of continuity/discontinuity means in terms of the development of the Scriptures, see STI, 64.

[49]Jenson does acknowledge "discontinuities with canonical Israel," or practices that diverge from the culture given by the law even while that law retains priority. Jenson, "Election and Culture," 60. In these cases, "the burden of proof always lies with the argument for discontinuity." By reference to Levitical dietary and purity requirements, Jenson suggests that it is incumbent on Gentile believers to demonstrate how they may "continue in their dietary ways," that is, how they may be exempt from Jewish purity laws. Nowhere does he address the wider range of cultural implications derived from his chosen example, even when much of the New Testament might be read as addressing this particular problem. Nor does he intimate the wider role of culture in relation to the missionary expansion of the church among the Gentiles. This omission itself illustrates the thickness of the culture Jenson has in mind and the relation of this culture to the speaking of God, divine availability, and to the hearing and learning of God's community, their catechetical enculturation.

[50]Jenson, "Election and Culture," 57.

nection. On the one hand, reference to election elevates the Christian culture above mundane intercultural relationship. The emphasis throughout falls on the form of historical continuity as established by anticipation and so on the charism of the Spirit detaching the historical from the natural and in reference to its end in God. This becomes doubly necessary in Jenson's estimation. Without an elect and "specific christological culture, for which the Spirit takes what is Christ's as the content of his culture-constituting teaching . . . humankind's entire cultural enterprise would rush back into God, to possess him."[51] The elect culture serves as a middle point between God's own life and that of culture as such.

On the other hand, this continuum, especially as part of the Spirit's work, makes it possible for the elect culture to draw from other cultures. Jenson describes this as the "phenomenon of cultural overlap," which is illustrated by the commonality of the temple's floor plan, meaning that "Israel-as-culture is in these formalities like other national cultures, even though every defining feature of that culture is specified by the Lord's electing call."[52] One should note Jenson's reluctance to apply this same logic to matters of structure and order, especially in relation to his caution against imitating the neighbor "worldly collectives." Nevertheless, as part of a general phenomenon, Jenson grants some space for cultural diversity within the church. Such is evident in "the great cultural diversity between the Eastern and Western churches—or between Anglicans and dissenters."[53] The examples are themselves telling. Jenson needs to account for the ongoing reality of the Great Schism and for some continuity between Anglo-Catholicism and the eventual shape the Christian religion assumed in the Americas. But equally evident is the absence of reference to contemporary Christian cultural diversity as developing outside of a Western context.

These same rules of continuity and difference govern entry into this thick Christian culture. In this process, converts "will not cease to be Zulu or Norwegian-American," nor, in opposition to a good deal of social theory, will they

---

[51]Ibid., 58. For a more detailed development of his account of creation that makes such a possession of God possible, see Robert W. Jenson, "Creator and Creature," *International Journal of Systematic Theology* 4, no. 2 (2002): 216-21.

[52]Jenson, "Election and Culture," 54.

[53]Ibid., 49.

cease to be "middle-class or working-class."[54] Jenson grants such cultural difference some benefit. First, each convert brings elements of his or her culture into the church's culture with the possibility of enlarging that new culture. Second, this provides a wider missionary point of connection: "wherever the mission carries the church, she will have an immediate relation to other cultures."[55] But these benefits appear secondary inasmuch as the church's own culture remains prior, determinative and regulatory in the interaction with any other culture. Jenson illustrates this by reference to the church's missionary nature. The gospel must speak to the hopes and fears of its hearers, to the antecedent morality of the people toward which the gospel moves (STII, 209-10). It accomplishes this, however, through the process of interpretation, answering every human hope in its own reality as the objectivity of the coming kingdom and its expression now in the anticipatory act of the eucharist. The hearer's own culture is not determinative of the gospel's reception; it is as one moves into the church that one's antecedent hopes are met.[56]

With this priority of the church's culture, the presence of the "old culture" within the convert stimulates both "Spirit-worked harmony" and "deadly conflicts" between this "previous culture and the church's culture."[57] As with the death-match struggle between polities, so as a culture the church must "expect, as a regular feature of her cultural history, life-and-death conflict between her culture and those from which her converts come."[58] Jenson does not conceive this combat in terms of an inward spiritual event; surmounting any distance between an invisible faith and its outward structure is fundamental to Jenson's project.[59] The non-translatable externality of the culture that the church is cannot be so internalized. As it remains necessarily an object, so the "life-and-death conflict" takes place between visible historical, cultural entities, with entry into the Christian culture experienced

---

[54]Ibid., 50.
[55]Ibid., 60.
[56]Ibid., 50-51.
[57]Ibid., 61.
[58]Ibid., 60.
[59]To cite David Yeago on this point: Jenson is "massively opposed to any account of the social-political and eschatological aspects of the church's life as features located on different ontological planes, such that the 'outward' life of the church as polity would be seen as only the vehicle or concomitant of a more fundamental 'inward' and spiritual life." Yeago, "The Church as Polity?," 203.

as a "wrench."[60] Jenson variously describes the process of "integrating" those from an "alien culture" into the church as a "shock and a puzzlement" (STII, 305), "a nearly unsustainable strain,"[61] with the potential to be "a fatal shock to the moral system, unless carefully overseen."[62]

The solution to this cultural wrench, Jenson argues, lies precisely in the processes of historical continuity—in teaching. "One cannot be born into the church; one can only be inducted into it. Therefore the convert has no antecedent access to the culture she is taking on: a whole new and at many points far from obvious system of signs must be conveyed by sheer teaching."[63] For Jenson, the early church confirms this normative approach. "After a bit of time had passed in which to have experience," which seems to mean after the initial missionary encounter and the instituting of the church, it became apparent that "baptism and subsequent life in the liturgical and moral life of the church, if granted immediately upon hearing and affirming the gospel, were too great a shock for spiritual health. Life in the church was just too different from life out of the church, for people to tolerate the transfer without some preparation."[64] Catechetical instruction became necessary and included, first, "liturgics," that is, the cultivation of new and different "habits and tastes," supplying the convert with the necessary tools of interpretation. This was followed, second, by the imposition of a moral code under the care of "watchful moral disciplinarians." Third came the cognitive task of learning doctrine and the history of the church, for only this would enable them to "resist their culturally ingrained inclusivism and relativism."[65] In short, only "serious catechesis" could "save the Gentile convert."[66] Catechesis enculturates the convert into the body of Christ, placing the convert within the church's prior cultural history and supplying an aesthetic lens through which one can reinterpret the world. By extension, one characteristic of the Christian culture's universalism, its catholicity, is this potential to assimilate all peoples through an extended and observed process.

---

[60]Jenson, "Election and Culture," 50.
[61]Robert W. Jenson, "Catechesis for Our Time," in *Marks of the Body of Christ*, ed. Carl E. Braaten and Robert W. Jenson (Grand Rapids: Eerdmans, 1999), 142.
[62]Jenson, "Christ as Polity," 325.
[63]Jenson, "Christian Civilization," 159.
[64]Jenson, "Catechesis for Our Time," 138-39.
[65]Ibid., 139-40.
[66]Jenson, "Election and Culture," 61.

3.6 High Culture and the Triune God

Given the relationship between Jenson's trinitarian ontology and historical contingency, the church's culture develops through its historical course. For Jenson, as the church's history has matched that of Western civilization, so its culture has assumed a Western semblance. Moreover, the particular artifacts he identifies with that culture come from "high culture," from art, drama, music and architecture.

Apart from the continuities he creates between the culture of Israel and that of the church, in a text titled "Christian Civilization" Jenson traces its particular origins to the church's emergence out of the Roman catacombs. Freed from persecution, the church found time and space to develop "a new and distinctive dramaturgy" for which the "plates and cups and books and identifying costumes and processions were *cultivated*." Architectural forms came into being, ranging from Constantine's use of the basilica, "the utilitarian Roman meeting space," as the basis for a church to how "Christians took over abandoned pagan temples and filled in between the columns of the outermost row to make an enclosed space." Nor should one overlook the developments within the areas of "jurisprudence and medicine and civic ceremonial."[67] This side-by-side development (the Christian use of Roman cultural forms) continued until the invasion by and conversion of the barbarians. As the barbarians, Jenson suggests, were without any prior civilization, so "there came to be not only a Christian culture within the remains of the old civilized empire, but a Christian civilization."[68] Christianity became the originator and patron of cultural creation. "Holy" described the empire built by Charlemagne. Jenson even affirms that the church "created the civilization of Europe and its descendent cultures."[69] It assumed responsibility for cultural creation in a way that was true both of itself and of a surrounding people.

Following these halcyon days, however, Jenson laments an extended period of cultural entropy. After the first "twelve centuries of Christian painting and sculpture" came brief moments of brilliance in "modern and

---

[67]Jenson, "Christian Civilization," 156.
[68]Ibid., 157.
[69]Robert W. Jenson, "The Church's Responsibility for the World," in *The Two Cities of God: The Church's Responsibility for the Earthly City*, ed. Carl E. Braaten and Robert W. Jenson (Grand Rapids: Eerdmans, 1997), 5.

then of modernist art, followed by nothing."[70] To describe this present moment, Jenson echoes Alasdair MacIntyre's famous metaphor: "Barbarians have this time come from within, so that they are not civilized by what they destroy; they are barbarians not by lack of the good things but by 'nostalgia for the muck.'"[71] This "post-modern" period appears, in Jenson's estimation, devoid of merit, a degenerate celebration of humanity's baser instincts.

At this point, the lack of distinction between the church's own culture and that of Western civilization inserts a degree of ambiguity. It is often not clear before which door Jenson lays his charges. He certainly regards the contemporary Western church as being captive to its neighbor culture.[72] As to the identity of the aforementioned "barbarians," Jenson expresses dissatisfaction with the destructive consequences of insufficiently enculturated members within the contemporary church.[73] This improper alliance prompts a distinction between the church and the local culture or civilization. "When the church is one culture and the surrounding civilization is another, the cultural difference is a part of the distinction between church and world; and since cultural differences are not easily overlooked, neither is the difference between church and civilization."[74] Culture itself helps distinguish the church from the local civilization (the world). But this raises an issue in need of clarification. Jenson notes that "Christian civilization" consisted of the "sharing of high churchly culture with a civilization that, however wrapped up with the church, was not the church." The church is able to so share its high culture because it "is a *polity*, and a civilization is not. The church is the segment for this age of the single and unitary city of God, whereas a civilization may encompass dozens of polities or none at all."[75] Whereas a polity is a culture, with the example that China is a polity that confronts Christianity as an opposing culture, the West is a civilization that is not a polity and so presumably without the graven images (cultural artifacts) characteristic of other polities. This civilization does not confront Christianity as an opposing culture even while the church and the West are to be distinguished

---

[70]Jenson, "Christian Civilization," 155n2.
[71]Ibid., 157.
[72]Jenson, "Christ as Drama," 200.
[73]Jenson, "Catechesis for Our Time," 143.
[74]Jenson, "Christian Civilization," 158.
[75]Ibid., 162.

as separate cultural entities. Moreover, the church has a particular duty to share its "cultural treasures" with this civilization as a way of developing and maintaining that civilization's high culture. Indeed, for Jenson, "the West's current revolt against its high culture is an epiphenomenon of its revolt against God."[76] This ambiguity, in other words, seems to validate Western civilization because of its Christian roots in a way that cannot be said of other entities such as the civilizations of Asia. These reduce to polities engaged in a life-and-death struggle, also on the geopolitical stage, with the Christian polity.

Whatever the case, there came a point when the church became culturally captive to this civilization, a fact Jenson laments via the term "inculturation." Whereas anticipation validates historical and culturally relative developments within the church, inculturation appears as its opposite. "Since the church is a culture, there are limits on 'inculturation.' With any culture, there are some elements of other cultures that it can assimilate and others that it cannot without self-destruction."[77] Jenson illustrates this point by reference to the "disruptive" effect of Catholic baroque décor and music when "appropriated" by the church and to the "polar barrenness of a great many Protestant churches, built according to intrinsically rationalistic standards of beauty."[78] Without denying the existence of proper limits, Jenson's use of inculturation is always and only cautionary. Insofar as his evaluation restricts itself to the artifacts of high Western culture and to their despoiling, these examples illustrate the strict limits within which Jenson conceives the church's culture and the possibility of its cross-cultural transmission. Apart from these limits, the church risks its own self-destruction.

As to Jenson's merging of inculturation with aesthetic judgment, this essential focus on high culture itself derives from trinitarian ontology. The gospel, Jenson notes, does not make the creation of civilization "*mandatory*"—an observation based on the absence of such in the early history

---

[76]Ibid., 161.

[77]Jenson, "Christ as Polity," 324.

[78]Ibid. This is illustrative of the main problem because John Milbank, who maintains a similar type of cultural argument, argues for the essential expressive beauty of baroque architecture and music. John Milbank, *Theology and Social Theory: Beyond Secular Reason* (Oxford: Basil Blackwell, 2006), 437. Locating the truth of the gospel and the objectivity of God for us in the aesthetic end of a Christian "high" culture depends a great deal on a subjective judgment detached from either the tradition or Scripture.

of the Western church and because, in his estimation, "nothing comparable has yet happened in Africa or Asia."[79] He argues, however, for its possibility by adding a third element to his definition of culture: "a culture is what a group does with nature as presented to it."[80] This general intention to cultivate becomes "high" culture when "one version of a group's culture . . . has been *carried further*; it is that culture intensified."[81] The failure to develop a high culture, as seen in "lower versions of a church's culture," results from simple neglect and manifests "too little longing for the ultimate cultural action of new creation."[82] Jenson makes no mention of conditions that may be necessary for the creation of high culture, nor of conditions that might limit such: no account of poverty, the reality of being a religious minority, of persecution or of the gospel's spread through the culturally marginalized, such as refugees and migrants. Nevertheless, as the culture develops to a higher level, so a more involved system of signs will "have syntax and semantic possibilities that make a more complicated web of mutual reference and deference."[83] This, in turn, will take longer to teach. Jenson invokes Paul at this point, arguing that converts were to be educated into "a structure of mysteries" understandable "only step by long and arduous step, under continuous training."[84] One might, of course, question the extent to which this description corresponds to the image of Paul's ministry presented in the New Testament.[85] Nevertheless, for Jenson, the convert is to be "inducted" into the "new culture of the church," a culture to which "the convert has no antecedent access" and which stands before him or her "like a mountain."[86]

---

[79]Jenson, "Christian Civilization," 157. Jenson's assertion that the churches in Asia and Africa are without a high Christian culture is simply false. The richness of church music alone should disabuse anyone of this notion. One could further add poetry (see Christina Afua Gyan [Afua Kuma] as but one example), architectural forms or, in the case of New Zealand, woodcarvings. Of the many examples of Christian art, a good starting place is Theo Sundermeier and Volker Küster, *Die Bilder und das Wort: Zum Verstehen christlicher Kunst in Afrika und Asien* (Göttingen: Vandenhoeck & Ruprecht, 1999). That Jenson makes such an assertion may reflect a certain conception of what constitutes "high culture" and that directed by a certain aesthetic associated with Western cultural forms.

[80]Jenson, "Christian Civilization," 158.

[81]Ibid.

[82]Ibid., 160.

[83]Jenson, "Christian Civilization," 159.

[84]Ibid.

[85]As a counter illustration, one concerned with the freedom Paul gave to his communities, see Roland Allen, *Missionary Methods: St. Paul's or Ours?* (London: Robert Scott, 1912).

[86]Jenson, "Christian Civilization," 159.

A mature Christian is one better enculturated into the central mysteries of the complex Christian high culture. It is, moreover, the church's responsibility to cultivate its own specific culture to better embody the new creation.

The ground for such claims Jenson locates in God's own being. With remarkable similarity to his short summary of the Trinity in his *Systematic Theology* (STII, 173), Jenson states that

> what it is to be God is given in the Father's eternal begetting of the Son and enlivening through the Spirit, in the Spirit's eternal liberating of the Father and the Son for one another, in the Son's eternal self-giving to the Father in the Spirit. Thus the triune God is nothing *but* culture, and just so is infinite culture, culture setting nature and transforming it and just so setting nature and so on in an eternal act.[87]

As a culture is a web of signs, so the "person" of the triune God is a "subsistent relation" in which "there is nothing to any one of the three prior to or apart from his special reference to the other two, apart from 'begetting' or 'being begotten' or 'proceeding.'"[88] Since God is a culture, culture expresses the continuity between God and the community. Given that the perfection of the church rests in its absorption into this culture, the church is "*mandated*" and "*commanded*" to cultivate its own high culture so that "its language and visible artifacts and music and choreography . . . suggest the richness and subtlety of the sign-system that God is."[89] At this point, Jenson contradicts his own distinction between mandate and possibility, one developed with the seeming intent not to prioritize Christianity's Western stream over against the church in Africa and Asia. Such processes he now deems necessary to maturation in the Christian faith. If God in Godself is high culture, then a high culture is mandated. Where no such culture exists, so it might be surmised, God is less present as "object" and the church's members less mature in their faith and less capable of accessing its mysteries. It is difficult not to escape the conclusion that, insofar as Jenson sees no Christian high culture as yet existing in Africa and Asia, the possibility of full Christian maturity exists nowhere apart from the church in its Western course.

---

[87]Ibid., 160-61.
[88]Ibid., 161.
[89]Ibid. (italics mine).

3.7 The Method and Goal of Missionary Transmission

Mission, as is typically the case, is the point at which all these elements find pointed expression, rendering concrete what the formal theological language leaves more abstract. Jenson does not divide mission into an internal versus external aspect. Mission is the church itself because, as a culture, it is God's own objectivity. One might note how this position develops in overt contrast to the direction ecumenical mission theory took during the middle of the twentieth century. Compared to the approach that looked "around the world to see where God is at work and jump in to work with him," Jenson states that "if we are to speak of God's *location*, of the place in the world *from* which he is at work in it, then the church is herself that location. The point is, after all, theologically elementary: *Christ* is God's located presence in the world; to be located he has to have a *body*; the church, says the New Testament, is that body of Christ."[90] The church, as the availability of God, is the mediator of the faith. Mission takes form within these limits. "The church as it is determined by the Father's triune role is above all a *koinonia* of *prayer*. The church gathers with the Son and in the Spirit, to petition and adore the Father."[91] It follows, for Jenson, that "if the church's christological and pneumatological realities can be comprehended as its mission, so the church's specific reality vis-à-vis the Father is its *intercession*."[92] Such is the "pattern" of the church's calling in the world: it offers petition and praise to the Father on behalf of the whole of creation. Its vocation is "priestly" and its service "sacrificial."[93] Mission is the church in its embodied attitude of prayer and worship, in the church's being the "visible word," in its being a culture. Everything else follows from this point.

As missionary transmission rests in this culture, so Christianity "invades," to use Jenson's own language, different "geographical" regions.[94] This preference for the term "geographical" as opposed to "cultural" indicates the nature of missionary encounter. The church enters an area and encounters a competing culture, meaning that "the real question is always about the

---

[90]Jenson, "Church's Responsibility for the World," 5.
[91]Jenson, "Church as Communio," 8.
[92]Ibid.
[93]Ibid.
[94]Robert W. Jenson, "God's Time, Our Time: An Interview with Robert W. Jenson," *Christian Century* 123, no. 9 (2007): 33. For the same language, see STI, 16 and STII, 210.

relation of the church culture to some other culture with which the church's mission involves it at a time and place."[95] Christianity is, in this sense, a culture foreign to this location, but given that the triune God is in and for Godself high culture and the source of all human culture, a continuity remains in the work of the Spirit. "The expectation of the church must anyway be to seek and find the ways in which a culture, any culture, is a creature of the Spirit of her Lord."[96] The church will need to address the new questions raised by this alternate religious culture (polity) and weigh "the liturgical and cultural practices to be adopted, adapted or rejected."[97] This is accomplished through interpretation, the key example being the post-apostolic trinitarian and christological developments within the early Mediterranean church.[98] In this engagement of two cultures, the church learns and changes but does so by means of the established rules governing cultural continuity.

These commitments, in Jenson's estimation, allow for the possibility that a form of the church will emerge as different as that found between the first and fourth centuries. How such a possibility might appear with his evaluation of the *iure divino* is a question, but it remains a simple possibility because it is "too soon . . . to know in what ways the churches of Africa or India or China will be specifically African or Indian or Chinese a century or so from now."[99] The extent to which this ignores developments within these localities, the result of there being long-established Christian communities, seems to suggest that the possibility is contingent on a lineal and singular church history/culture, one in which irreversible decisions determine the legitimacy of any subsequent form, rendering any local development dependent on the entrance of the Western church. It ignores the variety of strictures often placed on second-generation Christians, strictures issuing from established ecclesiastical expectations and applied against such things as the incorporation of local architecture, dress and music styles (drums), and the controls imposed on the "faith." It relativizes what might be recognized as African or Asian in

---

[95]Jenson, "God's Time, Our Time," 35.
[96]Jenson, "Election and Culture," 60.
[97]Jenson, "God's Time, Our Time," 34.
[98]Somewhat telling is the single treatment Jenson cites in support of this otherwise complex question: Gerhard Ebeling, "Das hermeneutische Ort der Gotteslehre bei Petrus Lombardus und Thomas von Aquin," *Zeitschrift für Theologie und Kirche* 61 (1964): 281-326.
[99]Jenson, "God's Time, Our Time," 34.

form through a prior demand for institutional/cultural continuity. One might also inquire after the relation between the church being a culture and the possibility of the church having overlapping cultural aspects. Though Jenson permits this in theory, he equally affirms the ongoing significance of Western cultural artifacts: "the church should simply rejoice when African communal solidarity or Roman basilicas so wonderfully enable her life."[100] Nowhere does he address the charge that the Western form of the church hinders the reception of the gospel in other localities, or how this African communal solidarity might find structural and visible expression.

Nor does the question of cultural diversity appear to be a matter of formal theological importance.[101] The church is a culture; that is, it is a historically continuous entity that picks up cultural elements through its contingent historical course. By establishing culture as the ground of the church's relationship with the world, it equally establishes the church's distinction from the world: the particularity of one culture (even as the elect culture) against that of another. In this schema of opposing cultures, the gospel does not enter a culture and convert that culture to Christ such that the gospel takes on another or even multiple particular cultural forms. Jenson interprets the argument that the church "could be or have any culture at all" to mean that "the gospel can be as well 'inculturated' in the form of a Hindu sect as in the culture named by the phrase 'one . . . catholic church.'"[102] The very lack of nuance in this contrast, its reductionist approach to the wider inculturation discussion, illustrates well the determinative influence of Jenson's decisions. These preclude the possibility of cultural pluralism in the church, for to "interfere with the rich tapestry of the church culture built up over many centuries constitutes a moment of possible self-betrayal."[103] Mission, in short, is the question of the church as the elect culture in relation to other cultures.

One should note here the decisive framing of such questions by the Protestant/Catholic schism. This establishes a binary opposition in which community structure becomes an either-or in relation to the gospel. To suggest,

---

[100]Jenson, "Election and Culture," 60.

[101]The only time Jenson refers to Galatians 3:28 in his *Systematic Theology* is in the context of discussing how Hellenistic freedom and Jewish anthropology both found confirmation in the new Christian community (STII, 58).

[102]Jenson, "Election and Culture," 51.

[103]Jenson, "Christian Civilization," 161-62.

in other words, that the gospel not just can but must be expressed in multiple cultural forms contrasts with key tenets of the church's historical continuity, its apostolicity. According to Yeago, Jenson's formal approach to church order rejects any implication "that the whole outward ordering of the church's life is simply irrelevant to the church's theological identity. If no form of behavior or organization is theologically 'better' than any other, then the identity of the church as eschatological community has no implications whatever for the ordering of its public, 'visible' life together."[104] This determinative opposition, however, needs to be called into question, especially when assumed normative for the world church. If the gospel is capable of assuming manifold cultural forms with corresponding manifold orders, it does not necessarily follow that the gospel is neutral regarding polity, nor that outward visible ordering is irrelevant to the church's identity. The debate surrounding the terms "inculturation" and "contextualization" focuses on the necessity of the community's structure. This can neither be a foreign import hindering the gospel from growing sustainable roots nor simply be continuous with the previous local religio-cultural history. It must be the gospel of Christ proclaimed and embodied in this local language and related structural elements.

Given his identification of mission with the church's being a culture, Jenson nowhere addresses mission as a distinct locus. But this is the point: his entire system mandates a clear, if unexamined, mission method. It is no accident that his most forthright engagement with mission occurs within an article titled "Catechesis for Our Time."[105] One finds here the gamut of Jenson's basic theological decisions on display. His logic is as follows: with the delay in Jesus' return, God gifted institutions to the church by which its historical continuity might be maintained. These included canon, creed, episcopal office and teaching. Given the sheer difference of the church's culture from those of its neighbors, catechism became necessary to oversee the shock of the converts' entrance into this culture. The catechetical process included learning a new liturgics (retraining in "habits and tastes" and thus the capacity for right interpretation), a new morality and a new set of doctrines.[106] Furthermore, in catechesis, the convert is initiated into God because it is initiation into God's

---

[104]Yeago, "Church as Polity?," 206.
[105]Jenson, "Catechesis for Our Time," 137-49.
[106]Ibid., 140.

community. With the "Constantinian settlement," a great influx of converts over time eroded the catechumenate and, with this, the cultural difference between the civilization and the church.

This foreground logic produces a precise mission method. In response to the specific post-Christendom context, the church, in both the Protestant and Catholic manifestations, "has tried to maintain its cultural position by minimizing the differences, that is, by minimizing its own character as church."[107] Such minimization is evident in the use of "popular music" during worship and in homilies "on 'love' or some other favorite delusion of the culture."[108] This, in Jenson's estimation, will not do, for it is simple disobedience before God. In this missionary situation, reinstating the catechumenate and the cultural otherness of the church is the necessary response.

> The church, like every living community, has her own interior culture, built up during the centuries of her history. That is, the acts of proclamation and baptism and eucharist are in fact embedded in a continuous tradition of ritual and diction and music and iconography and interpretation, which constitutes a churchly culture in fact thicker and more specific than any national or ethnic culture.
>
> Now of course this tradition might have been different than it is. If the church's first missionary successes had taken her more south than west, her music and architecture and diction and so on would surely have developed differently. And in the next century, when the center of the church's life will probably indeed be south of its *original* concentration, the church's culture will continue to develop, and in ways that cannot now be predicted. But within Christianity, what might have been is beside the point; contingency is for Christianity the very principle of meaning; it is what in fact has happened—that might not have happened—that is God's history with us, and so the very reality of God and of us.
>
> We are not, therefore, permitted simply to shuck off chant and chorale, or the crucifix, or architecture that encloses us in biblical story, or ministerial clothing that recalls that of ancient Rome and Constantinople, or so on and on. Would-be participants will indeed find some of this off-putting; people will indeed drift into our services, not grasp the proceedings, and drift out again. We will be tempted to respond by dressing in t-shirts and hiring an almost-rock group—not, of course, a real one—and getting rid of the grim crucifixes.

---

[107]Ibid., 142.
[108]Ibid., 143.

Then we will indeed need less catechesis to adapt would-be participants to the church, because we will be much less church. If instead we are aware of the mission, and of the mission's situation in our particular time, we will not try to adapt the church's culture to seekers, but seekers to the church's culture.[109]

Such is Jenson's mission method, all the elements of which are both familiar and attached to his account of apostolicity. First, the church is a specific culture, and one "thicker" than other identifiable cultural identities. Its chief practices of proclamation and the sacraments are themselves "embedded" in, and therefore contingent on, this culture, at least for their right interpretation and administration. A loss of culture means a loss of identity and, with this, the authenticity of the Christian expression. Catechesis means enculturation into the Christian aesthetic, "music training and art appreciation and language instruction, for the *church's* music and art and in the language of Canaan."[110] Second, the specificity of this culture, given the church's historical course, is Western in form and artifact. Whatever evident historical criticisms might attach to such a claim, Jenson understands this culture to be normative and universal for the church as evidenced by his locating it within the principle of contingency and juxtaposing it as a present given to a future possibility of Southern Christianity, albeit one conditioned by the church's already established "irreversible" decisions. This confirms, on the one hand, that other cultures will encounter the church as Western in semblance and, on the other, that conversion is into this culture. Third, Jenson reifies this culture by moving it into the triune being of God. The Spirit molds the life of the church in anticipation of the kingdom of God. The church is the body of Christ, and so object and available. Contingency expresses the narrative character of the triune God's own being. This limits the availability of the church's culture to criticism, and especially so in the event of cross-cultural encounter, for this is the encounter of God's own culture with a rival polity. Fourth,

---

[109]Ibid., 144-45 (italics mine).

[110]Ibid., 145. Jenson follows this statement with a warning: "the recommendations of the 'church growth' movement will indeed produce growth, but not of the church." Whatever criticisms might be made against "church growth," Jenson's reference to this is telling on three fronts: first, he understands his position precisely as a mission strategy and one to be compared to other methods; second, it indicates his fundamental resistance to speaking the gospel through local cultural forms; third, the reference is disengaged and dismissive. Jenson has nowhere engaged with the breadth of missionary theory on this question; his proposed dogmatic framework exhausts this line of investigation.

converts enter this culture by way of enculturation, meaning also that the church needs to safeguard its culture against possible dilution.

Jenson's logic of apostolicity, the myriad connections he forms between the tradition and the church as culture, comes together in his mission method. Though it is a question to be asked, this method bears all the hallmarks of the processes of colonialization: mission as cultural replication and conversion and growth in Christian identity by means of enculturation through transplanted structures themselves deemed necessary to the continuity of and maturity in the faith.

3.8 Drawing Connections

Though the very formality of the ecumenical discussion sometimes obscures its cultural thrust, Robert Jenson makes explicit the underlying logic and accompanying end. Though a single voice in a wide-ranging debate, he develops clear theological lines connecting the formal discussion of apostolicity to a contemporary anthropological understanding of culture. Of added benefit, against the likes of Pannenberg, Benedict XVI, Daniélou and Florovsky, Jenson does not merge Christianity's universalism with a single (Hellenistic) culture. The opposite is the case: the ecumenical problem can be traced to an incompletely Christian understanding of God, one which draws too heavily on Greek assumptions of divinity, including that of immutability.[111] By not identifying this culture with the Hellenization of the gospel, Jenson detaches the nature of the church's cultural continuity from worldy processes, from identifying the culture the church is with a particular geographical and historical location. Yet his account of God's own contingency and the nature of God's availability for us in church structures all draw on this fundamental link with culture. Despite his rejection of Hellenism, in other words, Jenson confirms the fundamental assumption espoused by the ecumenical discussion—apostolic continuity follows the mode of cultural continuity.

Jenson's analysis includes a number of benefits. First, framing apostolic continuity in terms of culture supplies a clear account of how the church both

---

[111]One should observe here how Jenson does not apply his identification of Christian theology's "incomplete conversion" to the structures related to these theological positions. That is, if it is possible for significant theological discussions to be, nonetheless, incompletely converted, and if this informs church structures as Jenson ascribes to the shared Catholic/Protestant flaw, is it not possible for such "incomplete conversion" to inform even institution, structure and order?

changes through its historical passage and remains constant, that is, concrete, visible and identifiable. This prioritizes the rules of temporal transmission in the processes of change. Change belongs to the church's witness as the Spirit anticipates the kingdom of God. It permits a future openness while governing the limits of cultural diversity. Change occurs slowly, over time, and by way of interpretation, not translation. Within this, however, the basic catholic order can be understood as bearing the marks of the church's particular historical course while beholding to no singular cultural origin; that is, these theological decisions and accompanying structures can be understood in their contingency as *iure divino* and irreversible. Second, this analysis stresses the objectivity of the culture, the complex range of cultural artifacts and their relationship, relativizing any one particular element (including "the bath and the meal") and rendering all necessary. It gives material shape to the church's "visibility" as the people of God and to the nature of its koinonia. From an ecumenical perspective, this ratifies the historic shape of church structure and order while laying the emphasis not on the order itself but on the culture it serves and, by extension, on the form of Christian witness. Third, culture defines the church's relationship with the world: the church confronts the world as a culture among other cultures, witnessing to the truth of its own way of life. The obverse, fourth, is the nature of the church's distinction within this continuum. The church is the elect culture. This reinforces the cultural rules governing continuity; namely, teaching and not "biological inheritance" constitutes historical transmission. Teaching is itself defined in terms of enculturation and the learning of the Christian cultural aesthetic embodied in structure, liturgy and a range of small accompanying interpretive gestures. As the elect culture, moreover, the church can acknowledge, because of its historical course, its Western character while claiming to be "international," beyond any particular time or place.

As satisfactory as this may appear in terms of the Protestant/Catholic schism and the questions basic to such, when considered from the perspective of cross-cultural missionary encounter, this approach presents difficulties. Though infrequently examined as part of a wider theological system, missionary transmission (its method, content and goal) often gives concrete expression to that system. This is true also of Jenson. His approach to apostolicity mandates a mission method that, following this account of historical transmission as teaching, rests on enculturation. Christian identity (which includes the themes of authenticity and maturity) results from participation in the Christian culture. Though this culture may change, it does so over time and remains singular. Translation is too immediate, intruding on those gestures basic to the Christian aesthetic that are not themselves rule-governed. Mission means transmitting the culture of the church with its full range of gestures and the structures basic to such. Conversion is enculturation into this culture. Yet, despite the centrality given to culture, Jenson's system lacks the mechanisms for handling even simple questions of intercultural relations, unable as it is to acknowledge the pluralism of Christian expression basic to world Christianity. His mandated mission method, in other words, corresponds well to the lamented process of colonization, a comparison that begs the question of his wider system.

Though this may appear a strong charge, two elements are noteworthy. First, Jenson makes his clear cultural claims using formal theological language and method. This very formality seemingly isolates his thick account of church culture from some of the more mundane conclusions regarding the interaction between cultures. Yet it is the very connections Jenson draws between the formal ecumenical discussion and the contemporary anthropological understanding of culture that lead the cultural critique back into the theological system. Second, the main caveat governing this mission method rests in claims for the "international" or "catholic" nature of the Christian culture. One might, of course, argue that Jenson develops his missionary strategy for the particular challenges facing the Western church. No doubt this is the case. However, the strategy follows as a logical correlate of his normative theological claims regarding apostolicity. Though Jenson nowhere considers the non-Western reception of that culture during the colonial period, the judgment made across the denominational divide (Protestant and Catholics alike) is that the gospel entered so wrapped in particular cultural garb as to appear foreign in other contexts. As Christian preaching failed to inform the local cultural roots, so it produced a certain superficiality in the faith. Apostolicity as cultural continuity, in other words, stymies the development of Christian communions in lands with a different cultural heritage than that found in Europe and North America.

4

Apostolicity and Colonization

A Relationship?

With part of himself he [the African] has been compelled to pay lip service to Christianity as understood, expressed and preached by the white man. But with an ever-greater part of himself, a part he has often been ashamed to acknowledge openly and which he has struggled to repress, he has felt that his Africanness was being violated. The white man's largely cerebral religion was hardly touching the depths of his African soul: he was being redeemed of sins he did not believe he had committed; he was given answers, and often splendid answers, to questions he had not asked.

DESMOND TUTU[1]

The Church in Africa came into being with prefabricated theology, liturgies and traditions. In the matter of Christian ethics, the converts found themselves in the position of those early converts before the Council of Jerusalem (Acts 15): "Unless you are circumcised after the custom of Moses, you cannot be saved."

E. BOLAJI IDOWU[2]

To be truly Christian means not to be truly African.

TINYIKO SAM MALULEKE[3]

---

[1]Desmond Tutu, "Whither African Theology," in *Christianity in Independent Africa*, ed. Edward W. Fasholé-Luke et al. (London: Rex Collings, 1978), 366.

[2]E. Bolaji Idowu, "The Predicament of the Church in Africa," in *Christianity in Tropical Africa: Studies Presented and Discussed at the Seventh International African Seminar, University of Ghana, April 1965*, ed. Christian G. Baëta (Oxford: Oxford University Press, 1968), 426.

[3]Tinyiko Sam Maluleke, "Christ in Africa: The Influence of Multi-Culturity on the Experience of Christ," *Journal of Black Theology in South Africa* 8, no. 1 (1994): 53.

4.1 "Global" Christianity as the Normative Model for "World" Christianity

The distinction Lamin Sanneh draws between "global" and "world" Christianity sets well the key consideration of this chapter. For him, the phrase "global Christianity" reflects a concern for "the faithful replication of Christian forms and patterns developed in Europe." Global Christianity becomes interchangeable with Christendom, bearing "vestiges still of that root imperial phase" through enlisting the Christians of the world as "evidence of the economic and political security interests of Europe." Global Christianity carries "connotations of parallels with economic globalization, with the same forces of global trade and the internet revolution fueling the spread of a seamless environment of information and exchange without borders."[4] It paints a vision of the faith tied to Western expansion, rendering Christianity a subset of the Western experience, of value because it draws adherents into a global cultural discourse. "World Christianity," by comparison, is the

> movement of Christianity as it takes form and shape in societies that were previously not Christian, societies that had no bureaucratic tradition with which to domesticate the Gospel. In these societies Christianity was received and expressed through the cultures, customs, and traditions of the people affected. World Christianity is not one thing, but a variety of indigenous responses through more or less effective local idioms, but in any case without necessarily the European Enlightenment frame.[5]

World Christianity is something in and for itself, not reducible to an enlarged Christianity in Western form. It is a development at some distance from that tradition, independent and polycentric. Though one might question the very clarity with which Sanneh draws this distinction, the conceptual opposition of a global to a world Christianity informs this chapter.[6]

---

[4]Lamin O. Sanneh, *Whose Religion Is Christianity? The Gospel Beyond the West* (Grand Rapids: Eerdmans, 2003), 23.

[5]Ibid., 22.

[6]As to validity of this discussion within the field of world Christianity itself, Namsoon Kang has raised some noteworthy questions. Namsoon Kang, "Whose/Which World in World Christianity? Toward World Christianity as Christianity of Worldly-Responsibility," in *A New Day: Essays on World Christianity in Honor of Lamin Sanneh*, ed. Akintunde E. Akinade (New York: Peter Lang, 2010), 31-48. Outside the field and especially in the discussion of globalization, Sanneh's argument appears justified. Kwame Bediako too notes how the terminology of "global" suggests a relocation of power from the West to elsewhere. "It is more helpful, and indeed more accurate,"

As we saw in the previous chapter, Robert Jenson makes explicit the links between the basic theological materials and the cultural end to which they are directed, and these links broaden apostolicity's application beyond the formal ecumenical discussion. Apostolicity as cultural continuity defines the structures essential to the church catholic and, as such, becomes key to witness and identity formation in opposition to the contemporary erosion of culture characteristic, first, of political liberalism and, second, of the exporting of this erosion via the processes of globalization. The cultural argument basic to apostolicity, in other words, remains neither in the rarefied atmosphere of ecumenical dialogue nor in the narrow confines of the church in Europe and North America. It informs the global nature and mission of the church as it combats a cultural decline originating in a particular political and economic history. The movement is from a Western to a global context. This establishes a normative problem, one for which the church catholic appears as its necessary opposite. Insofar as globalization "disciplines the body," insofar as it enculturates, so the church catholic witnesses through an alternate process of enculturation. To demonstrate this point, the chapter considers the form apostolicity takes in service to this picture of the church catholic combating the cultural erosion of political liberalism on a global stage.

Setting the question in these global terms permits a better comparison between apostolicity as cultural continuity and the processes of colonization. Colonization ceases to be consigned to missionary activity and distanced from the church. It becomes something defined in relation to the formation of a culture and its determinative structures, interpretive measures and visible artifacts. In other words, with reference to certain anthropological concerns, the cultural definition of apostolicity as well as the manner of cross-cultural replication this promotes mirrors the processes of colonization. However one evaluates diversity and the future possibility for development, apostolicity, when conceived in these cultural terms, opposes the pluralism and polycentrism inherent to world Christianity. Not only does it isolate the dominant theological tradition from the criticisms of world Christianity

---

he suggests, "to recognize the emergence of a 'world Christianity,' the result of diverse indigenous responses to the Christian faith in various regions of the world, the emergence of a positive polycentrism, in which the many centres have and opportunity to learn from each other." Kwame Bediako, "The Emergence of World Christianity and the Remaking of Theology," *Journal of African Christian Thought* 12, no. 2 (2009): 52.

(namely, that much of the tradition embodies particular cultural themes alienating to Christian peoples with another heritage), it also fails to appreciate the relationship between local appropriation and historical continuity.

Despite this critical work, the intent of this chapter is constructive. Setting theological accounts of apostolicity in relation to the historic problem of colonization helps shift the frame of reference from the West to the local translation and so embodiment of the gospel. Recognizing this is a first step in a positive redefinition of apostolicity.

4.2 CATHOLIC ORDER IN OPPOSITION TO CULTURAL FRAGMENTATION

The general diagnosis begins with a fall: social and cultural fragmentation is endemic within Western societies. Though he was not the first to draw the connection between such cultural dilapidation and capitalism, Alasdair MacIntyre in his 1981 *After Virtue* set the tone by provoking an image of morality's "state of grave disorder."[7] The structures necessary to moral formation have been eroded to the extent that all we possess today are the "fragments of a conceptual scheme, parts which now lack those contexts from which their significance derived."[8] This problem need not be developed in detail. Its importance lies in its urgency, the type of pristine binary such urgency creates and the direction it gives to the positive response.[9] The individualistic "way of life structured by a free market economy" demands the construction of "new forms of community within which the moral life could be sustained so that both morality and civility might survive the coming ages of barbarism and darkness."[10] This description of the problem and its necessary opposite—this relationship between a perceived atomistic individualism responsible for a wider cultural fragmentation and a positive reformulation of communities marked by their capacity to reconstitute the moral life—establishes the framework for all that follows. It sets the West as the key actor. Via the free market,

---

[7]Alasdair MacIntyre, *After Virtue* (Notre Dame, IN: University of Notre Dame Press, 2007), 2. For an earlier account, see Daniel Bell, *The Cultural Contradictions of Capitalism* (New York: Basic Books, 1976).

[8]MacIntyre, *After Virtue*, 2.

[9]For a critical engagement with both the stated problem and the proposed solution, see Jeffrey Stout, *Democracy and Tradition* (Princeton, NJ: Princeton University Press, 2004).

[10]MacIntyre, *After Virtue*, xv, 263.

this Western problem becomes global in scope. A viable solution must be like in scope and cohesive in intent.

MacIntyre's own response draws on a premodern account of rationality, a social knowledge based in a "living tradition," that is, in a "historically extended, socially embodied argument, and an argument precisely in part about the goods which constitute that tradition."[11] Tradition, as a form of language, demands an appreciation of "narrative history" because the intelligibility of the practices basic to the tradition are themselves embedded within a larger history.[12] The body, as itself necessary to agency and "intelligible action," requires discipline and learns such through "practice."[13] Virtue is necessary to achieve the good internal to the practices, meaning that the discipline of practice occurs within a community that shares a common *telos*, a common vision of the character and end of human life, the "way our whole life is constructed."[14] Though the merest sketch of MacIntyre's position, its importance lies in the correspondence between this array of conceptual tools and those found in the contemporary approach to apostolicity. Given MacIntyre's own Thomistic sympathies, his theological interpreters often identify his description of tradition and its relationship to virtue ethics as a description of the church and its necessary catholic structures.[15]

"Tradition," so defined, addresses the West's cultural fragmentation, but the solution is not as easy as returning to the church. The church has itself been injured by the erosive forces of political liberalism. For William Cavanaugh, such injury follows the modern liberal state's restriction of "religion" to a realm of personal conviction, a form of belonging properly separate

---

[11]Ibid., 222.
[12]Ibid.
[13]MacIntyre defines "practice" as "any coherent and complex form of socially established cooperative human activity through which goods internal to that form of activity are realized in the course of trying to achieve those standards of excellence which are appropriate to, and partially definitive of, that form of activity, with the result that human powers to achieve excellence, and human conceptions of the ends and goods involved, are systematically extended." Ibid., 187.
[14]Ibid., 175.
[15]One of John Milbank's points of disagreement with MacIntyre lies in the latter's failure to identify Christianity as the tradition in question. John Milbank, *Theology and Social Theory: Beyond Secular Reason* (Oxford: Basil Blackwell, 2006), 328. The complaint is not against the substance of MacIntyre's position, only against his refusal to name that particular culture as itself the necessary form of the tradition.

from citizenship. Modernity's definition of "religion as a trans-historical phenomenon separate from 'politics'" was "designed to tame the church."[16] Christianity became, in the first instance, "a set of demonstrable moral truths, rather than theological claims and practices which take a particular social form called the Church."[17] A secularization thesis that equates this disembodiment with the banishment of religion fails to understand the point. Religion became instrumentalized and, thereby, at the service of the state.[18] If the justifying rationale of the liberal state lay in its achievement of national unity, then the "transnational Church produces conflict by dividing people's loyalties between sovereign and pontiff."[19] Cavanaugh, in other words, posits the premodern existence of a transnational (global) church, one defined by its connection to Rome, and links the erosion of the church's culture to a politically enforced disruption in this relationship. How world Christianity might be defined in relation to this schema and its particular history is an issue to be addressed. Nevertheless, reconfiguring the church as a religion permitted a more formal relationship of church to state and became a "means of binding the individual to the sovereign."[20] It was, in short, necessary to "domesticate the Body of Christ in order to produce unity."[21] The triumphed religious freedom offered by the modern state is simply myth. The body is split from the soul, with such freedom achieved by "handing the body over to the state."[22]

The state, not the church, disciplines the body, and this follows the trajectories of the liberal state itself, its organization of the public and the private built on certain approaches to production, ownership and commodity. Liberal politics and capitalist economics go hand in hand, and religion becomes simply another commodity governed by the logic of the market. In this, Robert Bellah's 1985 *Habits of the Heart* represents a classic

---

[16]William T. Cavanaugh, *Theopolitical Imagination: Discovering the Liturgy as a Political Act in an Age of Global Consumerism* (London: T&T Clark, 2002), 82.

[17]Ibid., 34.

[18]Nor is this a problem of "religion" alone. "Local social groupings were recast as 'intermediate associations' between state and individual, and such institutions have played an important role in mediating the state project." Ibid., 101.

[19]Ibid., 38.

[20]Ibid.

[21]Ibid., 39.

[22]Ibid., 87.

statement: "the citizen has been swallowed up in the 'economic man,'" with the effect that "the ever increasing, self-interested, consumptive appetite of American culture destroys the very ties necessary to the maintenance of community."[23] This general observation applies also to the church. The liberal state, so runs the logic, produced a mode of belonging mirroring the belonging constitutive of the state itself—the church gathers as a voluntary association of private citizens.[24] Peter Berger's analysis of religious belonging according to a market model represents a logical endpoint of the preceding schema.[25] Membership becomes contract based, indicating the church's being held captive to the capitalist vision of the human good.[26]

With this definition of the problem, the solution becomes clear. Only a vision of the human good embodied in a transnational tradition, one capable of offering an alternate form of discipline, is able to overcome that mandated by the liberal state. And the only tradition with such capacity is the one with premodern historical roots that continues, injured but nonetheless intact, to the present: the church catholic. Its importance lies in its continuity, in its apparent detachment from this present age. The church must become again a community of moral and, by this, cultural formation, and the "already traditioned" church constitutes the means by which this is accomplished.[27] This recovery of the Christian "tradition" is conceived primarily in structural terms, in "the church" as a historically narratable entity that is, in some sense, external to its members. As the person participates in this living tradition, so she or he grows in Christian "identity," becoming a person of virtue. Such is the importance of the church's apostolicity.

---

[23]Robert N. Bellah et al., *Habits of the Heart: Individualism and Commitment in American Life* (Berkeley: University of California Press, 1985), 271.

[24]For the classic statement of this position, see James Gustafson, "The Voluntary Church: A Moral Appraisal," in *Voluntary Associations: A Study of Groups in Free Societies*, ed. D. B. Robertson (Richmond, VA: John Knox Press, 1966), 299-322.

[25]Peter L. Berger, "A Market Model for the Analysis of Ecumenicity," *Social Research* 30, no. 1 (1963): 77-93; Anthony J. Blasi, "A Market Theory of Religion," *Social Compass* 56, no. 2 (2009): 263-72.

[26]A number of examples of this position may be given, but for a clear and concise statement, see Stanley Hauerwas, "Discipleship as a Craft, Church as a Disciplined Community," *Christian Century* 108, no. 27 (1991): 881-84.

[27]Paul Ramsey, in his famed treatment of "Liturgy and Ethics," permits the possibility that "new forms" might develop but maintains that "divine governance in world history and the Holy Spirit who keeps the community indefectible to the end of time compels us once again to manifest 'the church being the church' believing and praying and doing well" in a manner "already traditioned." Paul Ramsey, "Liturgy and Ethics," *Journal of Religious Ethics* 7, no. 2 (1979): 140.

Excursus: Community—A Protestant Deficiency?

We can formulate the argument as follows: if modernity strips the traditions and institutions necessary to the formation of mature human beings and sustainable communities, then the solution rests in the capacity of traditions and institutions to discipline and form communities of memory and meaning. One should note the debt this position owes to the work of Ludwig Wittgenstein and his correlation between language and a form of life, to Victor Turner on ritual and to Pierre Bourdieu on practice and *habitus*, especially as conceived in relation to a liturgical critique of modernity. The accent falls on the formative role of cultural practices in constituting communities.[28] Yet, as much as this is the case, theological authors read these developments through historic arguments for a Catholic order, including a confirming rehearsal of typical Catholic critiques against Protestant ecclesiology. Protestantism, precisely because of its redefinition of apostolicity, bears some responsibility (either by promoting such fragmentation or by being unable to stop it and thereby becoming its unwitting accomplice) for the individualism and voluntarist mode of belonging characteristic of the contemporary Western church.

To swiftly summarize the logic, the Reformers presupposed the social framework of Christendom, its form of relation between church and state, as constitutive of the church's community structure. While this afforded space for a critical theological stance against the hierarchical structures of Catholicism, in effect the Protestant church handed the bodies of its members over to the state. The church's special responsibility rested in caring for the now dislocated spiritual life of its members.[29] While the state remained at least nominally

---

[28]For an example of this logic, see Medi Ann Volpe, *Rethinking Christian Identity: Doctrine and Discipleship* (Malden, MA: Wiley-Blackwell, 2012).

[29]Cavanaugh, following Milbank, is more interested in the development of "religion" as an identifiable category and so understands the development of Protestantism as resulting from a prior political narrative. "The concept of religion being born here is one of domesticated belief systems which are, insofar as it is possible, to be manipulated by the sovereign for the benefit of the state." Cavanaugh, *Theopolitical Imagination*, 35. Luther fell into this trap: though he sought to distinguish between civil and ecclesiastical jurisdictions, he succeeded only in denying "any separate jurisdiction to the church" (24). As a result of this sociopolitical arrangement, the church reduced to "merely a *congregatio fidelium*, a collection of the faithful for the purpose of nourishing the faith. What is left to the Church is increasingly the purely interior government of the souls of its members; their bodies are handed over to the secular authorities" (24). In handing over the "body" to the state, the church became disciplined by the state and powerless to offer an alternative to liberalism. Likewise, for Milbank, "the new, secular dominium could not, according to the totalizing logic of willful occupation which now mediated transcendence in the public realm,

Christian, the consequences of such a division were not immediate. It was, for Reinhard Hütter, only with the "extinction of the Christian state, that is, of a confessionally defined territory," that the "ontological basis of Protestantism" changed.[30] Without state support, the Protestant church found itself incapable of forming alternate Christian communities; it was not itself, nor was it capable of becoming, in Hütter's language, a "public."[31] Its *de facto* placing of the community's constitution within a socio-political framework, and so outside the theological framework of the church, including that of the territorial episcopate, rendered the Protestant church subject to the whims of culture. "This eclipse of the Protestant church as public might be one reason it is susceptible to becoming the bearer of national and other identities and projects."[32] Without apostolic order, the Protestant church proved unable to resist cultural pressures. Central doctrinal developments, notably *sola scriptura*, exacerbated the problem, for these stressed the freedom of individual interpretation against that of instruction through tradition. Each individual could follow his or her conscience regarding the interpretation of Scripture. Such freedom, not being grounded in an established theological structure, took shape in relation to the dominant market forces with their commodification of religion and the development of a volunteer mode of gathering.

In the hands of Stanley Hauerwas, the critique receives sharper focus. "Protestantism remains both theologically and sociologically a parasitical form of the Christian faith."[33] Protestantism survived by consuming the cultural deposit left by the Roman Catholic Church and thus itself contributed to the degradation of Christian symbols and language constitutive of communities capable of moral formation. After devouring this deposit,

---

really tolerate a 'political' Church as a cohabitant. Hence it was first necessary, with Marsiglio and Luther, to produce the paradox of a purely 'suasive' Church which must yet involve external state coercion for its self-government." Milbank, *Theology and Social Theory*, 19.

[30]Reinhard Hütter, "The Church as 'Public': Dogma, Practices and the Holy Spirit," *Pro Ecclesia* 3, no. 3 (1994): 339.

[31]Hütter defines "public" as "a human 'space' which is constituted by binding teachings, principles, and norms; that makes possible a 'coming together' for action and interaction; and that creates a common identity and mutual accountability." Ibid., 336. As to what this means in concrete form, Hütter, like Jenson, turns to the Torah (348).

[32]Reinhard Hütter, *Suffering Divine Things: Theology as Church Practice*, trans. D. Scott (Grand Rapids: Eerdmans, 2000), 11.

[33]Stanley Hauerwas, "The Importance of Being Catholic: Unsolicited Advice from a Protestant Bystander," in *In Good Company* (Notre Dame, IN: University of Notre Dame Press, 1995), 96-97.

parasitical Protestantism relocated to another host, that of liberalism. As it feeds off this host, so it takes on its characteristics. "Protestantism more reflects a culture than creates a culture."[34] Giving this observation precise form, Hauerwas laments how, in employing the volunteer principle, "Protestantism helped to create, but even more, to legitimate, a form of social life that undermined its ability to maintain the kind of disciplined communities necessary to sustain the church's social witness."[35] Belonging based in voluntary commitment forgets that "Christianity is an extended set of skills learned through imitating others, an imitation that is meant to help us make our baptisms our own over a lifetime."[36] These skills become virtues capable of resisting "the powers that would otherwise determine our lives," and such resistance constitutes the nature of Christian witness.[37] Voluntary gathering opposes the basic commitments necessary to the formation of Christian identity. Protestantism, because its fundamental decisions regarding apostolicity oppose the formation of a "culture," is nourished by a way of life the central symbols of which are, at best, incapable of forming people in a Christian identity and, at worst, contrary to that identity.

One might, with justification, express some dissatisfaction with the account of Protestantism as presented, and not simply because this normative judgment of deficit occurs without reference to the grounding of Protestant communities outside the traditional lands of Christendom and the issues of belonging this revealed. Yet John Webster's sober assessment that "much modern Protestant theology and church life has been vitiated by the dualist assumption that the church's social form is simple externality and so indifferent, merely the apparatus for the proclamation of the Word," suggests that the argument should not be dismissed out of hand.[38] Webster's observation

---

[34]Stanley Hauerwas, "In Defense of Cultural Christianity," in *Sanctify Them in the Truth: Holiness Exemplified* (Edinburgh: T&T Clark, 1998), 165n16.

[35]Hauerwas, "Importance of Being Catholic," 99.

[36]Hauerwas, "In Defense of Cultural Christianity," 166.

[37]Ibid., 167. Reference to Gerald Schlabach reinforces the point. Because of Protestantism's ambivalence concerning the salvific role of the church, and the very nature of the "Protestant principle as a self-corroding identity marker," voluntary association "tends to corrode the very commitments needed to sustain community, stripping us of the language we need to articulate the common good that underwrites that commitment." Gerald Schlabach, *Unlearning Protestantism: Sustaining Christian Community in an Unstable Age* (Grand Rapids: Brazos, 2010), 40, 23.

[38]John B. Webster, "On Evangelical Ecclesiology," in *Confessing God: Essays in Christian Dogmatics II* (London: T&T Clark, 2005), 154. He further notes how "among some strands of evangelical

may reflect one variety of ecclesiological consequence stemming from the opposition of mission to church that is endemic to the discussion, a point to which we shall return. But the diagnosis should be heard for two further related reasons. First, positing Protestantism as fundamental to the contemporary Christian problematic makes the proposed alternative clear. For Gerald Schlabach, "if the gospel is to transform the shape of a life in a Christian way, it must take *shape* in a community. To name that shape is to name a culture."[39] Protestantism failed because it located that culture external to the church itself. A better solution, so runs this line of argument, defines the church as itself a culture. This helps explain the relative lack of theological detail in the charges presented against Protestantism. This is due to the long-standing Catholic critique that runs in the background. The ecclesiological diagnosis and its proposed solution, in other words, extend the dynamics played out within ecumenical discussions and the spirit of the proposed solution in apostolicity.

Michael Ramsey's celebrated 1956 essay *The Gospel and the Catholic Church* illustrates well the point. His treatment of the Reformers matches this contemporary diagnosis of Protestantism's failings, and, unsurprisingly for the archbishop of Canterbury, the necessary solution lies in the affirmation of an "evangelical" Catholic order. Ramsey begins with the charge that the Reformers ignored the elements of the New Testament witness concerning the importance of church structures. "The Reformers omitted from their view of Christianity that element which the Apostolate represented by its place in the Body," and "its omission led to the maiming of its witness both to the Church and to the Gospel."[40] One significant difference here with the preceding discussion is the forthright manner in which Ramsey names the origins of the Protestant failing: its neglect of the apostolate. Church structure, including its hierarchy, for Ramsey, secures the dependence of the parts on the whole, and the apostolate expresses that dependence. Whatever the stress laid on the proclamation of the Word, by omitting this structure the churches of the Reformation succeeded in "maiming" the necessary witness to the gospel.

Protestantism, assimilation of the voluntarism and individualism of modern political and philosophical culture has had especially corrosive effects" (155).

[39]Schlabach, *Unlearning Protestantism*, 40.

[40]Michael A. Ramsey, *The Gospel and the Catholic Church* (London: Longmans, Green, 1956), 181.

Luther's key failing, for Ramsey, lay in his inability "to see that in Apostolic Christianity the order of the Church matters supremely, expressing the dependence by which every group and individual learns the full meaning of the life-in-Christ." Without the order by which "the soul, once justified, is led along the road of sanctification," Luther created a "false antithesis between the inward and the outward."[41] Not only, in other words, did Luther remove the conditions necessary for a corporate maturity in the Christian faith; he effectively reduced that faith to a subjective condition. As an immediate consequence of removing this first layer of dependency, Luther missed the "local church's dependence upon one visible and continuous order."[42] Without this concrete order, Luther secured the tasks of preaching the Word and administering the sacraments, in effect, by passing control to the state. The results of this twofold failure, according to Ramsey, became evident during Luther's own lifetime. In terms of church membership, Luther's description of the priesthood of all believers sometimes slipped into the language of the "independent rights of the laity in a manner that is easily 'politicized' and 'individualized.'"[43] Lutheranism "became the handmaid of religious nationalism, and its submission to prevailing political systems bears witness to the defect in Luther's thinking and statesmanship,"[44] though Ramsey does not himself examine whether and to what extent the Church of England, even with its episcopal order, might be described in similar terms, and especially so during the colonial period. As to the relationship of the local church to the church universal, Luther effectively exchanged dependency on the "one historic society," God's "own humanity," for a "solitary Christ."[45] Luther's weakening of the gospel as expressed by his neglect of the apostolic order meant that "the tendencies to individualism and subjectivism . . . could not but increase."[46] The church when conceived as a visible continuous society, by contrast, lifts the horizon of its members beyond their local perceptions. Without this society, the church

---

[41]Ibid., 191.
[42]Ibid., 192.
[43]Ibid., 188.
[44]Ibid., 192.
[45]Ibid.
[46]Ibid., 192-93.

is left alone with its contextual and immediate concerns, unable to rise "above all partial and ephemeral 'isms' and controversies."[47]

Though the language may differ, remarkable parallels exist between this account and the contemporary diagnosis drawn from the ills of political liberalism. The proposed solution is also similar. For Ramsey, without a catholic order, Protestant worship seldom escapes the perils of anthropocentrism and "religious egoism."[48] Worship conducted within a catholic order, by contrast, means participation in the "continuous liturgical action of God," and only within this order is such a liturgy possible. Translating these mechanics into contemporary terminology, a catholic order forms as a culture sufficient to impress people with a Christian identity. We should note the immediate relation of Ramsey's argument regarding apostolicity, and so the church's catholic structure, to the parallel contemporary treatment of ecclesial ethics and the related expectation of a necessary historical continuity. One might further note, given these parallel lines of reasoning, how little influence the more recent popular recognition of world Christianity with all its diversity has had over the analysis and the related solution based on a Christian culture. One reason for this is the worldwide application of this regional analysis via the phenomenon of globalization.

4.3 A Unified Witness Against the Threat of Globalization

Nor does this remain a problem confined to the West. Some argue that, through the processes of globalization, the domestication of the Western church by market forces has emerged as the defining problem of the church catholic, affecting its self-definition and its approach to issues of diversity and structure.[49] Discussing globalization is beyond the scope of this investigation.

---

[47]Ibid., 201.

[48]Ibid., 199.

[49]James K. A. Smith, a Reformed philosopher who owes much to John Milbank and Radical Orthodoxy, establishes the problem by describing the experience at a local American mega-mall using liturgical imagery. His point is that we (our aesthetic and sense of longing) are formed through this liturgical experience. "Because our hearts are oriented primarily by desire, by what we love, and because those desires are shaped and molded by the habit-forming practices in which we participate, it is the rituals and practices of the mall—the liturgies of mall and market—that shape our imaginations and how we orient ourselves to the world. Embedded in them is a common set of assumptions about the shape of human flourishing, which becomes an implicit *telos*, or goal, of our own desires and actions. That is, the visions of the good life embedded in these practices become surreptitiously embedded in us through our participation in the rituals

Within the field of theology alone, the matter is complex, the literature extensive and the proposed responses ranging. Of specific interest is the relation of apostolicity to the account of catholicity deemed to be the necessary opposite of political liberalism and its global spread.

The type of "syncretism" globalization threatens finds its opposite in the church as a historically continuous, visible community.[50] Catholicity becomes the preferred term, not because it assumes priority over apostolicity, but because catholicity refers to the product of apostolicity, to the culture.[51] Avery Dulles, by way of example, assumes a direct connection between apos-

---

and rhythms of these institutions." James K. A. Smith, *Desiring the Kingdom: Worship, Worldview, and Cultural Formation* (Grand Rapids: Baker Academic, 2009), 25. It is an arresting image. A significant part of the problem, however, rests in using the mega-mall (and the immediate connections this forms between consumerism and a liberal capitalist economy) as a metaphor speaking to a wider non-American Christian audience. One might ask after the location of this image and its supposed universalism. Given the collapse of the mall in light of the new online economy, it is doubtful that the image even reflects a dominant contemporary American experience. The attempt to so globalize this narrative reflects a failure to recognize the very geographical and historical locatedness of the American self-narrative. As the problematic liturgy is an American one, so the "necessary" form of liturgical response appears equally situated, despite the attempt to give it a "catholic" validity.

[50]See Bell, *Cultural Contradictions of Capitalism*, 13.

[51]As an interesting example of this point, given that he is explicit in conceiving the church catholic as a "missionary church," see Mark S. Burrows, "Globalization, Pluralism, and Ecumenics: The Old Question of Catholicity in a New Cultural Horizon," *Journal of Ecumenical Studies* 29, no. 3/4 (1992): 346-67. For Burrows, the pluralism evident in globalization mirrors the situation of the early church, a context to which it responded by developing the catholic order. "The eventual emergence from early missionary communities of an institutional church began to clarify the limits of pluralism, while retaining certain features of diversity" (363). It was the creeds, the canon and apostolic authority that became the "consolidating boundaries within which Christian identity could be defined in the midst of the enculturation that was the consequence of cross-cultural missionary expansion" (363-64). Burrows's position is sophisticated and the mission sensibility welcome. As to its meaning, matters become less than clear. Burrows defines "catholicity" first in theological and not structural terms, but the interpretive voices he uses are, in the main, those of Avery Dulles and John Henry Newman; that is, the structural is assumed as basic. For a sample of further texts that view globalization through the lens of catholicity, see William J. Danaher, "Catholicity and Globalization in the Anglican Tradition," *Internationale Kirchliche Zeitschrift* 100 (2010): 147-61; Peter De Mey, "Is the Connection of 'Catholicity' and 'Globalization' Fruitful? An Assessment of Recent Reflections on the Notion of Catholicity," *Bulletin ET* 13 (2002): 169-81; Avery R. Dulles, "The Catholicity of the Church and Globalization," *Seminarium* 40 (2000): 259-68; Richard Marzheuser, "Globalization and Catholicity: Two Expressions of One Ecclesiology?," *Journal of Ecumenical Studies* 32, no. 2 (1995): 179-93; Vincent J. Miller, "Where Is the Church? Globalization and Catholicity," *Theological Studies* 69, no. 2 (2008): 412-32; Robert J. Schreiter, *The New Catholicity: Theology Between the Global and the Local* (Maryknoll, NY: Orbis Books, 1997); Robert J. Schreiter, "Globalization, Postmodernity and the New Catholicity," in *For All People: Global Theologies in Contexts* (Grand Rapids: Eerdmans, 2002), 13-31; John R. Wright, "Catholicity and Globalization: A Perspective from the Episcopal Church," *Internationale Kirchliche Zeitschrift* 100 (2010): 75-89.

tolicity and catholicity because "continuity in the temporal dimension corresponds to the communion in the spatial."[52] This directs how "unity," assumed to take structural form, regulates diversity within the world church. "Now that Christianity is becoming for the first time truly planetary and culturally pluralistic, it is more important than ever to have a central authority that will keep the regional groupings in communion. The *centrifugal* forces of social and cultural diversity must be counterbalanced by the *centripetal* attraction of a symbolic focus of unity."[53] The assumptions that a real cultural diversity pulls communion apart, on the one hand, and that a "symbolic" unity might exert a sufficient power of attraction to counter this cultural pluralism, on the other, presuppose a controlling authority. The power of the authority lies in the structural pattern it mandates.[54] Pluralism in Christian expression, by contrast, reflects the triumph of cultural dislocation over against a proper Christian emphasis on a unifying catholic order.

---

[52] Avery R. Dulles, *The Catholicity of the Church* (Oxford: Clarendon, 1985), 88.

[53] Ibid., 142 (italics mine).

[54] Dulles gives a complete description of the church through the language of catholicity, including separate chapters that deal with the issues of synchronic and diachronic continuity. Much space is given to the essential diversity of the church, the manner in which, to cite Paul VI, "the Church, by virtue of her essential catholicity, cannot be alien to any country of people; she is bound to make herself native to every clime, culture, and race." Ibid., 76. This includes a recognition, referring both to the Great Schism and the Reformation, that "cultural factors . . . contributed to schism" (80). With this, Dulles appears sympathetic to "reconciled diversity" (29, 82). But, again, what it means in concrete terms, especially given the implications that would follow for Roman descriptions of the church, is far from clear. When he turns to diachronic continuity, Dulles avoids apostolicity as this "would raise more specialized questions, such as the succession in the ordained ministry" (87), and, with this, he leaves unaddressed assumptions concerning the culture-shaping nature of church structures and, by extension, the accompanying account of the church's perdurance through time. On his view, it is clear that in the universality and unity of the faith, the church is like a culture. "It is a system of meanings, historically transmitted, embodied in symbols, and instilled into new members of the group so that they are inclined to think, judge, and act in characteristic ways." Avery R. Dulles, "The Emerging World Church: A Theological Reflection," *Proceedings of the Catholic Theological Society of America* 39 (1984): 6. Dulles describes this very universality, understood under the conditions of a representative unity, in terms of a culture and fears that "any disturbance, any change, or any relaxation of the essential structure of the Church would suffice to endanger all spiritual renewal." Avery R. Dulles, "True and False Reform," *First Things*, no. 135 (2003): 17. Within this context, change must be gradual and "inscribed within the framework of apostolicity," for "to give in to revolutionary impulses would impoverish the Church's divinely given legacy and impair her mission to the world" (17). This cultural interpretation permits Dulles to assume a link between even the call for structural revisions and an erosion of Catholic intellectual identity, spiritual and moral. Against this, Dulles calls for a reassertion of given Catholic authority and the recognition, by the laity, that "doctrinal teaching, pastoral governance, and liturgical leadership are tasks ordinarily reserved to persons in holy orders, especially the pope and bishops" (18).

Attending to the structural and cultural changes globalization entails illustrates well the supposed threat diversity poses to catholic order. To continue with Cavanaugh, globalization "is not properly characterized by mere fragmentation, but enacts a universal mapping of space typified by detachment from any particular localities."[55] This complaint applies first to the erosion of the local, for while globalization may appear to cherish the local, it does this only insofar as the local is itself a novel commodity; the consumer must be dis-located and so free to consume multiple particularities.[56] The subject thus becomes "radically decentered, cast adrift in a sea of disjointed and unrelated images. If identity is forged by unifying the past, present, and future into a coherent narrative sequence, the ephemerality and rapid change of images deconstructs this ability."[57] It is important to note the juxtaposition of rapid change to the coherence of narrative and the role of such narrative in identity formation. Without making the connection explicit, the underlying assumption regarding spatial communion parallels the catholic expectation of temporal continuity, an assumption that becomes decisive when considering the cross-cultural transmission of the gospel and the rise of a polycentric Christianity. But the main point here concerns the continuity assumed between the failings of liberalism and the forces of globalization. M. Douglas Meeks is often cited on this point. For him, the "circulation of goods" dilutes the "shared meanings and background practices of community," with the effect that the person now "emptied out as a deracinated 'I' is set adrift from community in a process of individuation and atomization."[58] Mirroring the threat of liberal capitalism, globalization represents a form of discipline that Cavanaugh terms the "discipline of detachment" and that produces fragmented subjects.[59] Globalization results in the atomized individual writ large, magnifying the precipitating "Western" problem through a detachment from place.

If globalization disciplines detachment even in its own proposed form of unity, the alternative demands the relocating or recentering of the Christian

---

[55]Cavanaugh, *Theopolitical Imagination*, 98.

[56]Ibid., 111.

[57]Ibid.

[58]M. Douglas Meeks, "The Future of Theology in a Commodity Society," in *The Future of Theology: Essays in Honor of Jürgen Moltmann*, ed. Miroslav Volf (Grand Rapids: Eerdmans, 1996), 258.

[59]William T. Cavanaugh, "The World in a Wafer: A Geography of the Eucharist as Resistance to Globalization," *Modern Theology* 15, no. 2 (1999): 186.

subject.[60] This process Cavanaugh regards as essential to catholicity. Drawing on Henri de Lubac, he argues that while *universal* indicates "spreading out," *catholic* "suggests the idea of an organic whole, of a cohesion, of a firm

---

[60]Dislocation does not tell the full story, for globalization offers its own narrative of unity. Much of the agreement within theological statements concerning globalization, following the popular formulation of Michael Hardt and Antonio Negri, names this form of unity: empire. Michael Hardt and Antonio Negri, *Empire*, trans. Michael Hardt (Cambridge, MA: Harvard University Press, 2000). By way of illustration, see Moiseraele Prince Dibeela, "Conversion, Evangelism and Market," *International Review of Mission* 97, no. 386/387 (2008): 187-97; Bryan P. Stone, "The Ecclesiality of Mission in the Context of Empire," in *Walk Humbly with the Lord: Church and Mission Engaging Plurality*, ed. Viggo Mortensen and Andreas Østerlund Nielsen (Grand Rapids: Eerdmans, 2011), 105-12. Such language appears in the "Accra Confession, Covenanting for Justice in the Economy and the Earth," adopted by the World Alliance of Reformed Churches (WARC) General Council, August, 2004, and is subsequently developed by the 2010 "Globalisation Project" undertaken by the Evangelisch-reformierte Kirche, Deutschland and the Uniting Reformed Church in South Africa: "Gemeinsam für eine andere Welt: Globalisierung und Gerechtigkeit für Mensch und Erde. Die Herausforderungen des Bekenntnisses von Accra für die Kirchen." See Puleng Lenka Bula, ed., *Choose Life, Act in Hope: African Churches Living Out the Accra Confession. A Study Resource on the Accra Confession: Covenanting for Justice in the Economy and Earth* (Geneva: World Alliance of Reformed Churches, 2009). A further source document in this context is *Alternative Globalization Addressing Peoples and Earth (AGAPE): A Background Document* (Geneva: World Council of Churches, 2005). This general argument has found support within CWME statements on the nature of Christian mission; see "Mission in the Context of Empire: CWM Theology Statement 2010," *International Review of Mission* 100, no. 1 (2011): 128-25; "Mission in the Context of Empire," *International Review of Mission* 101, no. 1 (2012): 195-211.

"In contrast to imperialism," according to Hardt and Negri, "Empire establishes no territorial center of power and does not rely on fixed boundaries or barriers. It is a *decentered* and *deterritorializing* apparatus of rule that progressively incorporates the entire global realm within its open, expanding frontiers. Empire manages hybrid identities, flexible hierarchies, and plural exchanges through modulating networks of command." Hardt and Negri, *Empire*, xii-xiii. Noteworthy is both the similarity of definition and the benefits that accrue to catholicity when set in opposition to "empire." Given the assumed detachment of empire from any particular and contingent origins, so the particular and contingent origins of catholic order cease to be a point of focus. As empire has grown beyond its specifically Western origins, so certain cultural facets, which may or may not be ascribed to a time and place within Christian history, become irrelevant. The importance of catholicity rests in its being likewise defined without a territorial center and draws on a power without fixed boundaries. It is, in other words, the transhistorical and transcultural nature of catholic order that enables it to oppose empire. This encourages a strong definition of a catholic culture that renders it unnecessary to defend against the claim of religious colonization. And, as decentered and deterritorialized become descriptors of empire, so these are already indicators of a community that is "neither Jew nor Gentile," that is, a community that offers a true account of transcultural human unity (as opposed to the perversion of these themes within globalization) even while maintaining the particular location of its members. Catholicity within this ecumenical discourse appears to be the baptizing of empire. With such a position, one suspects that it makes no difference whether an author views globalization as an aid or in opposition to catholicity, for the form of catholicity in question appears to be "not much else than the religious expression of the capitalist global market." Teresa Berger, "A Note on Notions of Catholicity in Ecumenical Reflection," *Studia Liturgica* 26 (1996): 321.

synthesis, of a reality . . . turned toward a center."[61] This center is the eucharist, the "decentered centre" of the church catholic, and Cavanaugh develops its significance via a rehearsal of traditional order. The eucharist succeeds in relating the local to the universal through the office of the bishop. With this structure, the local church in the celebration of the eucharist is a "concentration" of the whole church and accommodates not cultural diversity but, in reference to Galatians 3:28, "natural and social divisions."[62] Through this immediate relation of eucharist to order, Cavanaugh projects the embodying function of structure onto the eucharist itself. Globalization falls down by positing the relation of the local to the universal in geographical terms. The eucharist, by contrast, is no place, but a story, one "not simply told but performed; space is organized by a body in movement, its gestures and practices. As such, the spatial story is not simply descriptive, but prescriptive. Stories give us a way to walk."[63] These key concepts of spatial creation, story, performance, practice and (ethical) direction indicate the centrality of a catholic order for the embodiment of an alternate reality to that offered by globalization. This culture becomes, quite simply, the nature of Christian witness, the proclamation of the truth of the gospel.

Inasmuch as this is the case, however, difficulties emerge when considering the rise of "global Christianity." This appears as a correlate of globalization and negatively considered in relation to the church's proper catholicity.[64] By way of example, Kam Ming Wong, drawing on Cavanaugh, distinguishes catholicity from "globality," understanding the latter as a child of globalization with

---

[61]Cavanaugh, *Theopolitical Imagination*, 113, citing Henri de Lubac, *The Motherhood of the Church: Followed by Particular Churches in the Universal Church* (San Francisco: Ignatius, 1982), 174. Though Cavanaugh does not employ the language of empire to the same extent as some, the same merging of globalization and empire is clear. William T. Cavanaugh, "The Empire of the Empty Shrine: American Imperialism and the Church," *Cultural Encounters* 2, no. 2 (2006): 7-29.

[62]Cavanaugh, "World in a Wafer," 190-91.

[63]Cavanaugh, *Theopolitical Imagination*, 117. Cavanaugh, in like manner to Jenson, traces this logic to Israel and the Torah. The Torah was culture-creating as all the practices of the law combined to "form a distinctive body of people" (87). This observation allows Cavanaugh to draw an immediate connection to a Thomist account of religion (88): "Virtuous actions do not proceed from rational principles separable from the agent's particular history; virtuous persons instead are embedded in communal practices of habituation of body and soul that give their lives direction to the good" (32).

[64]For a strong statement of the need for a catholicity in opposition to the supposed fragmentation resulting from Christian diversity, see David L. Schlindler, "Catholicity and the State of Contemporary Theology: The Need for an Onto-Logic of Holiness," *Communio* 14 (1987): 426-50.

its economy "of detached universalism," "an inauthentic attitude to place" and the juxtaposition of "diverse things and humans from all over the world in the same space-time."[65] Yet more is at stake. Globality presents itself as a challenge to the established means of relating the local to the universal. "As opposed to the term 'global' church, the catholic church must not be conceived as merely an amalgamation of all local churches."[66] This form of religious belonging, perceived as characteristic of especially the Protestant church under the conditions of liberalism, threatens the universalism of the church catholic. To this Wong adds the language of time and continuity. "In the whirlwind of globalization, historical continuity is undermined and place is downgraded. All this is likely to lead to a fluid, fragmented, and disengaged self, incapable of telling a genuinely catholic, coherent narrative or engaging a catholic community."[67] The focus, in direct opposition to globalization, falls on continuity and its determination of place. Thus, while globalization initiates and frames the discussion, the subject of the discussion is the ecclesial community. "The term 'catholic church' cannot equate with the contemporary catchphrase 'global church.'"[68] As to the question of cultural diversity within the church, where this breaches the limits of catholic order, it is a consequence of globalization and a servant of empire.

The treatment given here matches neither the complexity of globalization nor the variety of theological response, but the central concern should be clear. Though catholicity is the preferred nomenclature, it represents the triumph of a certain account of apostolicity: the dynamics of the local and universal, the creation of a particular identity through the discipline of a narrative (tradition), the basic nature of a community of memory, the sense of stability and countercultural witness, and the need to reserve its particular and constitutive practices against the forces of commodification. In that the

---

[65]Kam Ming Wong, "Catholicity and Globality," *Theology Today* 66, no. 4 (2010): 466.

[66]Ibid., 468.

[67]Ibid., 466. Timothy Radcliffe makes a similar point: one "particular fruit of globalization" is that "we do not know where the world is going. We do not have a shared sense of the direction of our history." Timothy Radcliffe, *I Call You Friends* (London: Continuum, 2001), 186. Interestingly, he juxtaposes this to the missionary endeavor linked to the colonialist project. Although missionaries may variously have acted in support of colonial authorities or against these authorities in defense of the local peoples, there existed, nonetheless, "a shared sense of where history was going, towards the Western domination of the world. That gave the context of mission" (187). The observation is a grotesquely honest display of the basic logic.

[68]Wong, "Catholicity and Globality," 474.

fullness of "both Jew and Greek" already characterizes the church's life, catholicity becomes the form of community necessary to oppose the false universalism of globalization, and does so precisely as the geographical extension of apostolicity. This illustrates the wider utility of apostolicity common within contemporary ecumenical statements: the continuity of the church through time and across "geographies" is that of a culture. It equally mandates a form of cross-cultural transmission, one in accordance with the temporal continuity of the faith—the transmission of a culture.

The evident downside of such a position, when considered from the perspective of world Christianity, is the manner in which non-Western voices add nothing of substance.[69] To be sure, the argument for a living tradition includes the openness to future historical contingencies. Nevertheless, the structures of catholicity—given their long historical courses, their irreversibility and the assumed opposition between narrative identity and rapid change—precede and determine any developments within world Christianity. World Christianity and its pluralism of expression, through this lazy linguistic relationship of "global" Christianity to "globalization," better aligns, so it appears, with the novel and the loss of particularity characteristic of globalization and its erosion of belonging, identity and community. According to this line of logic, the church's opposition to the false universalism of globalization depends on the maintenance of its culture and institutions. To propose that the "church" listen to the voices of world Christianity regarding structural concerns amounts to a betrayal of the historic faith and to an erosion of its witness by applying the disciplines of globalization to the body catholic.

EXCURSUS: ROBERT WUTHNOW ON AMERICA'S "BOUNDLESS FAITH"

Despite the wide support for defining apostolicity in cultural terms, I have resisted doing so here, not simply because it proves insufficient in relation to world Christianity, but because in many key respects the approach opposes what apostolicity is supposed to be concerned with, namely, visible and historic Christianity. My central presumption is that world Christianity exists, that it finds expression in the local appropriation of the gospel and thus has a

---

[69]By comparison, see Enrique Dussel, "Beyond Eurocentrism: The World-System and the Limits of Modernity," in *The Cultures of Globalization*, ed. Fredric Jameson and Masao Miyoshi (Durham, NC: Duke University Press, 1998), 3-31.

plurality of form, and that it has sufficient theological merit to inform and challenge settled elements within the received Western tradition. In this regard, it is worth addressing the concerns with world Christianity expressed by respected American sociologist Robert Wuthnow. For Wuthnow, the theory of "global Christianity" (his preferred way of describing the phenomenon) presents a "huge conceptual obstacle" to appreciating the true dynamic of contemporary Christianity: the "globalization of American Christianity."[70] Wuthnow's own positive account of globalization is far removed from the call for a "catholic" Christianity, but his negative evaluation of global Christianity as a theoretical framework makes for interesting reading.

His first objection targets the theory's devotion to demography, and it can be parsed in three ways. First, the numbers are misleading: the "major vitality in the global South may say more about high birth rates than about conversions" (45). A related point, alluded to rather than developed, is the manner in which much of the demographic argument rests in prognosis. The forecast "fact" that in 2025 over 75 percent of Christians will live outside the West should inform our present theological and ecclesiological structures. Second, the demographical perspective is "arbitrary." Wuthnow draws on the guru of Christian statistical analysis David Barrett to argue for an alternate reading, one which includes "greater continuity with the past" and finds no need to "emphasize a global shift or perceive it as the centerpiece of a new era in Christian history" (46). The numbers are open to interpretation. Third, numbers themselves do not speak to significance. Though the demographic center of Christianity might be shifting to the global South, "the organizational and material resources of global Christianity remain heavily concentrated in the more affluent countries of North America and Europe" (94). The North remains the power center of Christianity.

Wuthnow, second, objects to the imprecision of the theory's central concepts and to the terminological difficulties associated with juxtaposing a "Western" or "Northern" Christianity to a "non-Western" or "Southern" Christianity. Such binaries, to extend Wuthnow's point, lack the sophistication to

---

[70]Robert Wuthnow, *Boundless Faith: The Global Outreach of American Churches* (Berkeley: University of California Press, 2009), 32. Subsequent page references are provided parenthetically within the text. For a pro–world Christianity response to Wuthnow, see Mark Shaw, "Robert Wuthnow and World Christianity: A Response to Boundless Faith," *International Bulletin of Missionary Research* 36, no. 4 (2012): 170-84.

recognize the Western cultural identifiers informing the likes of Singapore or South Korea, on the one hand, and the more local cultural elements informing the likes of New Zealand or South Africa on the other. The difficulty here, as suggested by Wuthnow, is that global Christianity appears not as a real entity but as a conceptual counterpart developed for the sake of addressing failings within Western Christianity. "The global South becomes an ambiguous term that does not mean the southern Hemisphere at all but anything that lies south of the United States—or perhaps east or west as well, depending on one's predilections" (41-42). While one might question Wuthnow's assumption that everything needs to be interpreted with the USA at the center, his main point stands: the terminology is not sufficient as a scientific apparatus. It reflects more a subjective construct, one that becomes "data" only in relation to the argument being made.

Wuthnow's third objection rests in the narrative spun around these figures, one that "takes on additional drama" and through which it "becomes more intellectually compelling and emotionally engaging" (36). This narrative follows the mythos of much Christian teaching: "It is a before-and-after story of dramatic change, even of conversion or rebirth, of transition from apparent death to new life, and thus of synergy and hope. The narrative tension in the story moves from despair to salvation" (37). Wuthnow attributes the popularity of global Christianity to this salvific mythos. It is "likely that the new paradigm . . . gained popularity because it resolved—or appeared to resolve—underlying concerns about the fate of Christianity" (47). Specifically, it offers a counterstory to the secularization thesis and the charges of postcolonialism. Global Christianity secures Christianity's future and may, by way of reverse mission, contribute to the re-evangelization of Europe. It also redresses the complaint of colonialism by emphasizing indigenous agency and repudiating the "cultural biases associated with that era" (51).

Wuthnow does not object to the reality of global Christianity understood as some form of simple numerical Christian majority located outside North America. This he accepts. His central concern lies in how reference to global Christianity isolates different expressions of Christianity from one another, whereas "the central logic of the globalization thesis is that different parts of the world are becoming more closely connected" (51). The global Christianity paradigm "seems to imply that Christianity in different parts of the world is simply growing or declining, largely on its own and in its local contexts, without significant cross-national influences, especially from countries that are militarily and economically powerful" (61). The global Christianity paradigm overlooks the nature of the connection between churches and the stimulation this brings. Wuthnow grants local diversity an increasing place within the global church, but "celebrating that diversity should not take the place of considering the flows of resources, information, and people that increasingly bring local expressions of Christianity into contact with other communities, traditions, and influences" (55). Global Christianity, by stressing the relative independence of each local Christian expression, neglects the existing commerce between the churches and fails to appreciate the dominance of the churches issuing from powerful "global player" nations.

As to the form of that unity, it is worth noting the title of the chapter in which Wuthnow deals with this issue: "The Global Christianity Paradigm: From Cultural Connection to Demographic Distance." If much of Wuthnow's critique rests in the perceived "distance" that reference to global Christianity inserts between the churches, his alternate understanding of a "cultural connection" does not receive much attention. Only later in the text does the relationship between globalization and culture become clear. "The cultural crucible in which Christianity is inevitably shaped remains. It cannot be escaped. In subtle ways, the spread of Christianity continues to include the spread of American practices, whether in music or styles of administration" (250). Although, as a sociologist, Wuthnow is more willing than exponents of catholic Christianity to identify the cultural origins of this unifying and connecting Christianity, the basic theory is familiar. Whether identified as a historical culture carried by globalization or a more detached theological culture opposed to globalization, continuity and connection nonetheless reside within a particular and dominant culture that functions as the norm for unity. Likewise, any challenge to this culture through its relativization by the development of a polycentric Christianity amounts to the destruction of a normative connection, and thus the destruction of the given form of unity.

In response, one must question whether the global Christianity paradigm actually neglects the issue of connection in its interest with diversity. It seems more the case that Wuthnow avoids the variety of relationships advanced by proponents of "world Christianity," which is the term preferred by theorists in the field. For example, exponents of world Christianity do not argue, as Wuthnow suggests, that this religious expression is "closer to that of the early church than it had been for a long time" (37). While such assertions may be part of the self-description of local churches (should they understand their belief and ecclesiological structures as a return to "biblical" Christianity), this is not basic to the world Christianity paradigm. Exponents argue, instead, that the variety of cultural expressions of the Christian faith that one sees across the spectrum of world Christianity better align with the properly intercultural nature of the Christian community, a nature evident in the New Testament and in the expansion and recession of the church throughout its history. The proper "connection" between the churches is a consequence of, not a challenge to, this cultural diversity. This insight contrasts quite explicitly with a notion of continuity based in a single cultural pattern. Wuthnow, by contrast, seems to assume that "diversity" reflects a lack of cultural commonality that is essential to the notion of "connection."

His observation that the center of Christian influence and power remains with the West illustrates the point. Exponents of world Christianity are, of course, aware of this dynamic. It is this very power that blinds Christians of the Western cultural and religious tradition to the newness of the questions being asked within Southern Christianity. The problem, for Kwame Bediako, issues not from "a stubborn western intellectual hegemony alone" but from the way Christianity has entered into non-Western cultural realms. "Our knowledge of Christianity, shaped exclusively by the modern intellectual experience of the West, may well not provide adequate preparation for our understanding of its interaction with the events and process that take place in the South."[71] Recognizing this, for Bediako, helps reframe the basic contest. It is a problem of recognizing the positive contribution made by Southern Christianity against the assertion, illustrated by Paul Gifford, that "whatever else it is, Christianity is a cultural product honed in the West over centuries."[72] It is a contest of cultural power in which "an echo of the Eurocentrism of the past" prevents the full appreciation of what is occurring in

---

[71]Kwame Bediako, "Africa and Christianity on the Threshold of the Third Millennium: The Religious Dimension," *African Affairs* 99 (2000): 308.

[72]Paul Gifford, *African Christianity: Its Public Role* (London: C. Hurst, 1998), 322, cited by Bediako, "Africa and Christianity," 310.

African Christianity. Influenced by this expectation of a dominant cultural form, we fail to understand the limited nature of the cultural overlap between the churches of the West and wider world Christianity and recognize relationships based only where a sufficient cultural overlap is perceived.

In addition, it is worth noting the manner in which Wuthnow's own positive argument concerns only one side of the conversation. Christianity's ongoing global significance is based on a characterization of American Christianity as embodying a "transcultural church," which "means being involved in or interested in activities that take place outside of the United States and holding attitudes about such issues as international trade or military intervention that affect people in other countries besides the United States" (30). As one obvious question in response, to what extent must non-Western churches conform to a preexisting image of what a church is—to safeguard against the fear of syncretism—before any relationship with an American church might be forthcoming? Tinyiko Maluleke laments how it is "not possible even to see African forms of Christianity," for "the Western church-type and Western Christendom is the standard of what it means to be Christian. Often, dubious forms of Western 'Christianity' will be tolerated, whereas the slightest 'deviation' from (Western) tradition by African Christians will be looked upon with much suspicion and ridicule."[73] Wuthnow's evaluation of American Christianity's transculturality, in other words, seems to reinforce the cultural priority of America and its interests. There is no measurable account of how the "target audience" in Africa, Asia or Latin America receives that work. Nor does Wuthnow mention the connections that have developed between the non-Western churches, such as Korean missionaries in Indonesia and the reciprocal presence of Indonesian theological students in Korea, satellite Latin American churches in Africa, the ambiguous relationship of Western churches to migrant churches in their geographical midst or the successful church plants of African origin in Western lands. These relationships, it should be noted, also belong to the definition of globalization. Though Wuthnow grants a tempering of North American Christianity as a result of its global contact, the only connection that seems decisive for Wuthnow's vision moves from North America to other global players.

---

[73]Maluleke, "Christ in Africa," 53-54.

Set within the context of our wider discussion, Wuthnow fits the basic template we have seen thus far, which, first, posits the continuity between the churches in cultural terms and, second, understands the discussion of world Christianity as intruding on this continuity. The characteristics of the culture in question naturally differ for Wuthnow from that described by the language of "catholic" Christianity, but the necessary dominance of a culture bearing the hallmarks of Western history remains the same.[74]

4.4 THE CHURCH IN RELATION TO COLONIZATION

A simple claim has been made to this point: the dominant approach to apostolicity conceives the continuity of the church in terms of a culture. Nor is this theological position confined to the rarefied level of ecumenical statements. The valorizing of a catholic order, according to this approach to apostolicity, has other functions, including a critical diagnosis of the cultural fragmentation within Western societies and, thanks to globalization, the universal export of this culture. Witness becomes foremost the simple existence of the church ordered according to its culture and so to the accompanying structures necessary to the cultivation of Christian identity. With Christian identity understood as growth in this culture, the convert is discipled through an enculturating participation in the culture. Mission is then understood as the secondary and external extension of this primary and internal witness, meaning that cross-cultural missionary transmission must take place in accordance with the principles governing historical transmission.

In other words, if the apostolic church is a culture and if missionary transmission amounts to the replication and local appropriation of this culture, then what is the theological problem with colonization?

One should note the oddity of this question. The theological discussion about apostolicity appears largely untroubled by the potential connections between the church (its institutions, liturgies and order) and the historic problem of colonization. When it comes to discussions about Christianity's relationship with colonization, one finds a clean demarcation between "missions" and "church." Missions bear full responsibility, or so it is assumed,

---

[74]For a similar set of concerns, see Chandra Mallampalli, "World Christianity and 'Protestant America': Historical Narratives and the Limits of Christian Pluralism," *International Bulletin of Missionary Research* 30, no. 1 (2006): 8-13.

while the church is isolated from criticism.[75] Missions are identified with the colonial period. By contrast, the ecumenical framework supposedly corrects and normalizes the relationship between Christians from different geographical locations. This is because the account of the church as a culture ostensibly distances the church from its cultural context, thereby affirming the church's own independent identity against the type of improper liaisons evident during the twentieth century. To consider such a constitutive concept as apostolicity in relation to colonization appears, by these standards, to be somewhat anachronistic.

Matters are not nearly so clean, however, as this theological compartmentalization suggests. While historical and anthropological studies on the relation of Christianity to colonialism have tended to focus on the missionaries and not on the institutions of the church and their potential role in the colonial process, this is undergoing revision because of changes in the historiography informing the study of mission and colonialism. The focus has shifted from the economic and political to the cultural and aesthetic. This brings into focus precisely the role of the institutions necessary to the formation of a Christian culture, namely, the church.

4.4.1 Colonization as economic imperialism. Whether and to what extent it is possible to compare accounts of apostolicity on the basis of cultural continuity with the historic problem of colonialism depends on how one conceives of colonization, its processes and its relationship to Christian missions. The basic charge is well known: "The imperialism represented by Christian missions in Africa and other non-European countries is a unilateral process of cultural transmission."[76] Because of its capacity for cultural erosion by way of intruding on local customs, indigenous beliefs and traditional authorities, Christian missions constituted the vanguard of Western colonization. These missions perpetuated a "cultural imperialism" that both paved the way for and was reinforced by political and economic imperialism.[77]

---

[75]As an example, see Timothy J. Gorringe, *Furthering Humanity: A Theology of Culture* (Surrey, UK: Ashgate, 2004), 177-214.

[76]Ako Adjei, "Imperialism and Spiritual Freedom: An African View," *American Journal of Sociology* 50, no. 3 (1944): 190. As a further example, see G. Gordon Brown, "Missions and Cultural Diffusion," *American Journal of Sociology* 50, no. 3 (1944): 214-19.

[77]Horst Gründer provides a good instance of this logic. For him, "mission played a central role

Though such a position may continue to inform popular opinion, recent treatments have acknowledged the problematic influence of the framing question. Investigating the relationship of missions to colonization through the question (to quote John and Jean Comaroff) "Whose side were the missionaries on?" reduced "complex historical dynamics . . . to the crude calculus of interest and intention, and colonialism itself to a caricature."[78] The question directed the conclusion. Though some recognized the contribution made by certain missionaries to the local population over against colonial powers, the final answer prioritized the agency of the missionary and favored the partnership of missions and colonial authorities. Though the language used was that of culture, the chief point of contention concerned the connection between missions, politics and economics. This is a key issue. Recognizing how the initial framing of the question is bound up with a particular political analysis indicates the controlling influence of a materialist (Marxist) historiography.

The influence of a Marxist historiography is hardly accidental. This influence itself developed in service to a certain ideological agenda. Brian Stanley traces its origins to Chinese Communist propaganda and its characterization of Western missions using Marxist-Leninist definitions of imperialism, that is, in terms of a politico-economic system.[79] In service to the Communist agenda, and in conjunction with the "long-standing Chinese cultural tradition of anti-foreignism," Christian missions became identified as the "ideological arm of Western imperial aggression."[80] Key conceptual models, such as cultural impe-

---

within the structures of Western expansionism which has long remained unnoticed: it constituted an integral component of the colonial movement and fulfilled a major function in the colonial organization." Horst Gründer, "Christian Mission and Colonial Expansion: Historical and Structural Connections," *Mission Studies* 12, no. 1 (1995): 25. Christianity was the cultural message that both accompanied and was made persuasive by political, economic and military pressure. During the colonial era, religion was used "to induce a process of religious and cultural transformation, by means of which one's own territory could be extended and secured" (24). Where missionary expansion failed, it was because "the traditional religious and cultural structures were intact and the indigenous identity was unchallenged" (24).

[78]Jean Comaroff and John L. Comaroff, "Christianity and Colonialism in South Africa," *American Ethnologist* 13, no. 1 (1986): 1.

[79]Brian Stanley, *The Bible and the Flag: Protestant Missions and British Imperialism in the Nineteenth and Twentieth Centuries* (Leicester, UK: Apollos, 1990), 14-15. For some of the attendant difficulties in defining "imperialism" in relation to missions, see Andrew N. Porter, "'Cultural Imperialism' and Protestant Missionary Enterprise, 1780–1914," *Journal of Imperial and Commonwealth History* 25, no. 3 (1997): 367-91.

[80]Stanley, *Bible and the Flag*, 15. An interesting example is the story of Nosipho Majeke, *The Role of the Missionaries in Conquest* (Johannesburg: Society of Young Africa, 1953). Majeke was express

rialism, developed within and served this context, and their continued use extends the polemic.[81] In the ferment of nationalization and decolonization, this analysis was transported to and repeated in Africa. By the 1960s, this historiography, albeit better systematized and with greater conceptual sophistication, had become entrenched to the extent that it informed non-Western theological evaluations of the missionary movement.[82] Even during the 1980s, when Marxian historiography had fallen out of favor within other discourses,

---

in rejecting any positive missionary motivation. Missions were identified with Western imperialism, proceeding "from a capitalist Christian civilization and unblushingly found religious sanctions for inequality, as it does to this day, and whose ministers solemnly blessed its wars of aggression" (Majeke, as quoted by Hexham). However, as Hexham suggests, this work "gained credence because it was believed to be authored by a Black South African who was 'writing back' against colonial domination" and was, as such, "taken very seriously because it was believed to reflect a genuinely Black viewpoint." Irving Hexham, "Violating Missionary Culture: The Tyranny of Theology and the Ethics of Historical Research," in *Mission und Gewalt*, ed. Ulrich van der Heyden, Jürgen Becher and Holger Stoecker (Stuttgart: Franz Steiner Verlag, 2000), 196. "Nosipho Majeke," in point of fact, was not black but was a pseudonym for Dora Taylor, the English wife of an economics lecturer at the University of Cape Town. Her position rehearsed the Marxist perspective on missions. Hexham even suggests that the work might have been promoted by the Nationalist government that sought control over the black population by removing missionary interference.

Of course, positive Christian evaluations of the relation between mission and imperialism do exist. Writing in 1902, T. A. Gurney links mission with an "Imperialism of Duty." T. A. Gurney, "Modern Imperialism and Mission," *Church Missionary Intelligencer* 27 (1902): 484. Imperialism bespeaks an interdependence within the empire that "cannot fulfil itself except by a continual bestowment of its blessings upon its more needy parts" (486). One should also note the "theology of imperialism" developed by Max Warren, who, while acknowledging its problems, notes imperialism's providential consequences and its function as "a *preparatio* for God's good will for the world." Max A. Warren, *Caesar, the Beloved Enemy: Three Studies in the Relation of Church and State* (London: SCM Press, 1955), 30-41.

[81]In an extended examination of the favored phrase "cultural imperialism," Ryan Dunch locates its origins in China sometime prior to the Second World War and relates its development to the common polemical caricature of the missionary. Ryan Dunch, "Beyond Cultural Imperialism: Cultural Theory, Christian Missions, and Global Modernity," *History and Theory* 41, no. 3 (2002): 301-25. For him, the concept suffers from three main flaws: "it is intertwined with essentializing discourses of an imagined national or cultural authenticity; it disregards or slights the agency of the 'acted upon'; and, by conceptualizing cultural transitions in terms of coercion, it reduces a complex set of interactions to a dichotomy between actor and acted upon, and skews our gaze too much towards looking for subjugation, collaboration, or resistance, or, even less usefully, towards fruitless debates about motives and unsupportable distinctions between cultural exchange and cultural imposition" (318).

[82]Even the sober voice of Orlando Costas could regard it as self-evident that the "missionary enterprise has been used as a justification and a cover for the domination of people. The interrelation between mission, technology, and imperialism is well known. The expansionistic ambitions of militarily and economically powerful countries have always been accompanied by a missionary interest." Orlando E. Costas, *The Church and Its Mission: A Shattering Critique from the Third World* (Wheaton, IL: Tyndale House, 1974), 245. See further Orlando E. Costas, *Christ Outside the Gate: Mission Beyond Christendom* (Maryknoll, NY: Orbis Books, 1982), 58-69.

the use of this perspective to frame the question within the scholarly discourse concerning missions retained its force. The field of research expanded to include the long-term processes of capitalist expansion, state formation and proletarianization, but, according to Jane Samson, the firm expectation remained that "Christian universalism must be exposed as apologetics for capitalist colonialism."[83] Western power maintained the center, and the missionaries, given their capacity to influence deep structures of belief, remained in service to that power whether consciously or not.[84]

Drawing attention to the Marxist-materialist bias in received accounts of mission does not automatically imply a defense of Christian missions. It highlights, instead, the isolation of the church as an institution from the discussion. With colonialism defined in terms of the imperialism of a politico-economic system, and missions present as its servant, reference to the church intrudes on the clarity of this connection by inserting another institutional authority. On the one hand, the variety of "universalism" that is central to the debate traces elements belonging to Western civilization (e.g., the nation, science and technology, the autonomous individual) without reference to the forms and structures of universalism expressed by the institutions and structures of the church catholic (e.g., order, liturgy, hierarchy, creed). On the other hand, the church as an institution interrupts the direct relationship assumed to exist between individual missionaries and the structures of colonialism. Alternately stated, to quote Ryan Dunch, the debate is restricted "by the long-standing assumption that religion and modernity stand in opposition to each other, with the former belonging to the world of 'tradition,' destined to be superseded by 'modern' rationality, the secular nation-state, and the individual-as-consumer."[85] With tradition identified with the premodern, and with the missionary and missionary

---

[83]Jane Samson, "The Problem of Colonialism in the Western Historiography of Christian Missions," *Religious Studies and Theology* 23, no. 2 (2004): 10.

[84]This position finds its clearest expression in the work of Thomas Beidelman. For example, "missionaries sought to change not only the ways of work and politics of native peoples but their innermost beliefs, feelings, and deepest held values as well; and because of this missionaries may be considered the most ambitious and culturally pervasive of all colonialists, attempting social change and domination in their most radical forms." T. O. Beidelman, "Contradictions Between the Sacred and the Secular Life: The Church Missionary Society in Ukaguru, Tanzania, East Africa, 1876–1914," *Comparative Studies in Society and History* 23, no. 1 (1981): 74.

[85]Dunch, "Beyond Cultural Imperialism," 319.

structures identified with the modern, tradition seemingly remains historically aloof from the processes of nineteenth-century missionary transmission. This general logic certainly dislocates church structures from any identification with the processes of colonization.

4.4.2 The colonization of consciousness. Recent changes in the historiography of missions, however, suggest a comparison with conceptions of apostolicity as cultural continuity. Terence Ranger, writing in 1986, observed the "oddity of much recent historiography of early mission Christianity" in the way it "greatly overplayed the manifest political and economic factors in its expansion" and "greatly underplayed the cultural and religious."[86] Ranger's own interest lies in changing the question from the "imperial political" to the "indigenous cultural," an emphasis to which we shall turn.[87] But it indicates a wider methodological concentration on the cultural, and this is generally associated with the work of John and Jean Comaroff.

Their two-volume work *Of Revelation and Revolution*, in rejecting a narrow politico-economic approach, conceives colonization as foremost a "colonization of consciousness." "The final objective of generations of colonizers has been to colonize [native] consciousness with the axioms and aesthetics of alien culture."[88] It is possible, according to the Comaroffs, for a state of colonization, "a condition of being," to be in place before and apart from a colonial state, "an institutionalized political order."[89] Part of this reorientation includes acknowledging the indeterminate political influence of the missionary. Earlier models granted too much power to the individual missionary in relation to colonial political mechanisms. Nor can the complex processes of colonization be reduced to the binary camps of domination and resistance or explained by "grand models of the politics of imperialism or

---

[86]Terence O. Ranger, "Religious Movements and Politics in Sub-Saharan Africa," *African Studies Review* 29, no. 2 (1986): 32. He would further note that even those "writing from within the missionary societies, have emphasized institutional achievements, the build-up of schools and clinics and have hardly discussed the impact of missionaries and their African catechists on the cultural imagination of Africans" (32).

[87]Terence O. Ranger, "Christianity, Capitalism and Empire: The State of the Debate," *Transformation* 23, no. 2 (2006): 69.

[88]Jean Comaroff and John L. Comaroff, *Of Revelation and Revolution*, vol. 1, *Christianity, Colonialism, and Consciousness in South Africa* (Chicago: University Of Chicago Press, 1991), 4. See also Nathaniel Roberts, "Is Conversion a 'Colonization of Consciousness'?," *Anthropological Theory* 12, no. 3 (2012): 271-94.

[89]Comaroff and Comaroff, *Christianity, Colonialism, and Consciousness*, 5.

the economics of the modern world system."[90] Investigating interactions at the cultural level better accounts for the complexity. Though the Comaroffs name the culture in question—reflective of the ongoing framing of the question in terms of economic, political and military power, as that of European capitalism and Western modernity—the important point concerns the strategies by which this colonization of consciousness takes place.[91]

Colonization happens at the level of practice and habit, with the colonizer seeking to influence the "diffuse terrain of everyday life."[92] Protestant missionaries could achieve this because their "civilizing mission was simultaneously symbolic and practical, theological and temporal."[93] Following Pierre Bourdieu's theory of practice, this involved drawing human subjects into the "natural," which is not reducible to the political narrowly defined but found "in such things as aesthetics and religion, built form and bodily presentation, medical knowledge and the mundane habits of everyday life."[94] Such control over the quotidian occurred not first through violent persuasion. It required "the internalization of a set of values, an ineffable manner of seeing and being."[95] This included, the Comaroffs note, the introduction of Western concepts of time, of property ownership, of architecture and domestic arrangement, of dress, of individual effort, of rationality and the medicalized body, and of the division between religion and politics, to name a few. Though the Comaroffs fail to entertain any distinction between Western culture and the forms particular to Christianity and do not devote any attention to Christian practices as such, they see the above values and structures being instilled by way of practices such as baptism and Bible reading, along with the wider shaping of social space through church buildings, liturgical order and the structures of ministry.[96] Colonization, by this measure,

---

[90]Ibid., 5.

[91]See Samson, "Problem of Colonialism," 11.

[92]Comaroff and Comaroff, *Christianity, Colonialism, and Consciousness*, 5.

[93]Ibid., 9.

[94]Comaroff and Comaroff, "Christianity and Colonialism," 2.

[95]Ibid.

[96]Comaroff and Comaroff, "Christianity and Colonialism," 13-14. Webb Keane is more explicit when he speaks of the "moral impetus" and its embodiment in "everyday practices—the stuff of Michel Foucault's 'capillary power.' Potentially unlimited, these can include learning a creed and catechism, setting out on pilgrimages, reading and discussing scripture, praying, singing hymns, listening to sermons, attending regular church services, undergoing confession, even dairy-keeping and the introspective probing of one's thoughts, desires, and motives." Webb Keane, *Christian Moderns:*

resided not first on the political and economic level but in the "subtle internalization" of the "categories and values" found in "Protestant ideology," in the cultural assumptions embedded in the Protestant liturgical rhythm.[97]

With the process of colonization so defined, it is possible to draw a parallel with the logic underlying apostolic continuity based in cultural continuity. Though articulated using theological language (hierarchy, liturgy, catechism, institution, polity), apostolicity describes the processes of Christian identity formation using social-science categories.[98] Yet, using this same repertoire of conceptual tools, the Comaroffs describe the cultural disruption occasioned by Christian transmission, the mechanisms of which consist of learning the Christian language through catechesis, taking on the Christian aesthetic and framing one's life around its calendar, liturgies, rituals and values. As apostolic continuity consists of the cross-cultural subject taking on the range of subtle cultural artifacts, so it conforms to the Comaroffs' description of the colonization of consciousness. The two arguments share a fundamental identity.

Freedom and Fetish in the Mission Encounter (Berkeley: University of California Press, 2007), 42. As an example from a theological source, William Countryman flirts with a comparison between the acceptance of the historic episcopate and the New Testament discussion of circumcision. He notes how "in the context of modern Christian missions . . . the gospel preached has often looked and sounded suspiciously like a pious version of European or American culture, and where conversion has meant abandoning indigenous culture or even execrating it." L. William Countryman, *The Language of Ordination: Ministry in an Ecumenical Context* (Philadelphia: Trinity Press International, 1992), 14. This common observation he combines with a specific naming of the ecclesial practice involved. With respect to Anglicanism, the "adoption of the historic episcopate is a kind of cultural price tag attached to the gospel. . . . It appears to be another chapter in the long Christian saga of 'We want you among us, but not as you are—only if you will become like us, the people truly acceptable to God'" (15). Interpreted according to the failure to recognize the ministry of other denominations, Countryman continues, "what is worse, it is difficult to deny that these charges have some basis in fact" (15). It is an instance of enforcing religious purity laws in a cultural image. The wider point concerns the shaping effect of church structure through this identification of what needs to be purified (i.e., what lies outside accepted cultural norms) and the processes by which this purification takes place (i.e., structural replacement).

[97] Comaroff and Comaroff, "Christianity and Colonialism," 14.

[98] As a basic illustration, note the similarity between this quote from Bourdieu, which underlies much of the interest in "practices," and the logic for apostolicity found in ecumenical documentation. "In short, the habitus, the product of history, produces individual and collective practices, and hence history, in accordance with the schemes engendered by history. The system of dispositions—a past which survives in the present and tends to perpetuate itself into the future by making itself present in practices structured according to its principles, an internal law relaying the continuous exercise of the law of external necessities (irreducible to immediate conjunctural constraints)—is the principle of the continuity and regularity which objectivism discerns in the social world without being able to give them a rational basis." Pierre Bourdieu, *Outline of a Theory of Practice* (Cambridge: Cambridge University Press, 1977), 82.

We can extend the parallel by looking at the criticisms issued against the Comaroffs. Elizabeth Elbourne focuses her challenge on the range of binaries necessary to the Comaroffs' conception of hegemony, chief of which is their presentation of the interaction between the missionary and the local population as between "two key groups of interlocutors, dependent on the notion of difference."[99] The objection, in other words, centers not on the Comaroffs' cultural concern but on the singularity and simplicity of the agents involved, with the resulting emphasis on the missionaries as the protagonists and the identification of Christianity with the culture and actions of the missionaries. Such an approach, Elbourne argues, fails to account for the

> rapidity with which Christianity was out of the hands of the missionaries and settlers who brought it, the corresponding importance of non-Europeans in the spread of Christianity, the multiplicity of uses to which diverse interest groups of all ethnicities put Christianity as both a language and a practice, and the political and cultural complications of regions with multiple power players.[100]

Acknowledging this complex mixture of forces is necessary to do justice to the entrance and transmission of Christianity in different cultural spheres. Methodologically, it means, to quote Ranger, approaching "Christianity as part of the whole religious history of indigenous peoples."[101] The question of continuity is less about the imposition of an external message than its local indigenous appropriation. Proceeding from this perspective casts suspicion on treating Christianity as a single cultural form—the weakness of the Comaroffs' position—and advances the discussion of Christian identity by taking into account the actuality of cultural plurality.

4.4.3 Appropriation in contrast to colonization. Elbourne's anthropological concern finds confirmation in the work of Christian historian Lamin Sanneh. He, in like manner, objects to the vision of missionaries as servants

---

[99]Elizabeth Elbourne, "Word Made Flesh: Christianity, Modernity, and the Cultural Colonialism in the Work of Jean and John Comaroff," *American Historical Review* 108, no. 2 (2003): 443. For a second critical review, see Paul S. Landau, "Hegemony and History in Jean and John L. Comaroff's *Of Revelation and Revolution,*" *Africa* 70, no. 3 (2000): 501-19.

[100]Elbourne, "Word Made Flesh," 444. Isabel Hofmeyr supports a further historiographical revision based on the observation that "much of the groundwork of proselytisation consequently fell to African evangelists and catechists and much of the success of Christianity in Africa is attributable to the fact that it was spread by Africans." Isabel Hofmeyr, "Studying Missionaries in a Post-National World," *African Studies* 63, no. 1 (2004): 120.

[101]Ranger, "Christianity, Capitalism and Empire," 70.

of Western imperialism because to "fuse the theme of the African religious response with the political theme and annex it as a subplot of the great nationalist cause is to overlook the explicit religious concerns of those concerned."[102] Sanneh counters that the history of Christianity in Africa should be interpreted "by reference to African religious models, with local African agency as an indispensable link in the historical chain of transmission."[103] How the local and diverse appropriation of the gospel might define its historical continuity, in contrast to dominant definitions of apostolicity, is the subject of a later chapter. But it is clear, for Sanneh, "as long as Western Christianity continues to consider itself as the true and sole guardian of the heritage of the Apostles, so long will it continue to appropriate the North African Church as a European phenomenon, with a corresponding repudiation of other manifestations of Christianity."[104] The more immediate interest here lies in the distinction Sanneh posits between cultural pluralism and colonization. Conceiving missions as "instruments of religious and cultural pluralism," he argues, disconnects them from "what has until now been considered as the ideological motive force of mission, namely, Western political and cultural dominance."[105] Recognizing that pluralism is necessary to the vernacular expression of Christianity, and understanding the transmission of Christianity from the perspective of local religious history, decouples Christianity from the singularity of its Western expression and from its perceived service to a Western cultural imperialism. Sanneh, however, does not seek to reestablish the Western missionary as an exotic hero of the gospel. Mission, instead, becomes "a principle for indigenous reconstruction and an integral part of Africa's pluralist heritage."[106] Sanneh's concern is with African agency and the capacity of the gospel to invigorate local cultures, and this promotes pluralism as a key category in understanding the faith's transmission.[107]

---

[102]Lamin O. Sanneh, *West African Christianity: The Religious Impact* (Maryknoll, NY: Orbis Books, 1983), xiii.

[103]Ibid., xiv.

[104]Ibid., xvii.

[105]Lamin O. Sanneh, "Christian Mission in the Pluralist Milieu: The African Experience," *International Review of Mission* 74, no. 294 (1985): 199.

[106]Ibid., 202.

[107]As an interesting caution, Webb Keane notes that while reference to "agency" appears to detach historiography from categories that impose a Western frame of reference on particular narra-

Sanneh illustrates his point by distinguishing between a "hardware" approach, which views what is transmitted as "a complete package put together without reference to the different presuppositions of another culture," and a "software" approach, which is the human agent "responding to the different acoustic space of cross-cultural encounter."[108] Hardware focuses on the materials considered necessary to a Christian identity, including judgments about both the cultural goods accompanying the missionaries and the comparative deficit of local customs and rituals. This approach presents itself as "the normative criterion for God's enduring reality across cultures."[109] Defined in this way, the hardware approach corresponds well to the method of cross-cultural transmission mandated by apostolicity conceived as cultural continuity.

Sanneh locates the software approach, by contrast, in the "vernacular character of Christianity." This "forces some sharp questions about the legitimacy of insisting on the specific Western cultural scaffolding as the accompanying support for the religion."[110] Such a critical stance, it is important to note, results not from a supposed divisive diversity. It results from indigenous resistance to the advance of a cultural homogeneity, to forms and artifacts that the missionary conceives as natural and universal but are received by the gospel's hearers as a Western imposition. This key distinction reveals the debate's parameters. Sanneh devotes no attention to the relationship of diversity to unity; pluralism of vernacular expression presents no threat to unity because such pluralism is essential to the gospel itself. What is at stake is rather the expanding understanding of the gospel in contrast to its premature closure by reference to an existing cultural expression.

We will develop Sanneh's line of argumentation in a subsequent chapter. Our concern here is to see that the relative emphases of the Comaroffs and Sanneh illustrate the potential relationship between apostolicity as cultural continuity and the processes of colonization. One should first note the basic agreement between the Comaroffs and Sanneh: both resist a narrow

---

tives, agency itself speaks to a form of self-consciousness that bears all the hallmarks of the Western intellectual tradition. "The problem is not just a matter of having failed to take into account 'the native point of view' but also follows from the inseparability of people's self-understanding from the historical specificity of the concrete practices and semiotic forms in which their self-understanding is embedded." Keane, *Christian Moderns*, 4.

[108]Sanneh, "Christian Mission," 202.

[109]Ibid., 205.

[110]Ibid., 202.

political-economic definition of colonization. A Marxian historiography does not drive the analysis, and the evaluation of Christian mission cannot be reduced to a simple handmaiden of Western economic imperialism. One needs, instead, to understand how Christianity was transmitted and appropriated at a cultural level.

This agreement, however, reveals the nature of the opposition. Because the Comaroffs identify Christianity with the missionary agent, it remains a singular and foreign cultural import. Colonization is the process by which the Christian faith as a cultural overlay reformulates the *habitus* and practices of the local population through a variety of artifacts and their symbolic range. To be sure, the Comaroffs fail to differentiate between "Western" and "Christian," but that is the point: without considering Christianity's local appropriation—and the pluralism of form this engenders—Christianity enters as a foreign culture and its local acceptance consists of an enculturation into its aesthetic. Sanneh objects. Conversion is not simple "cultural subversion."[111] Because of Christianity's local appropriation, the connection between missionary transmission and colonization fails to hold. The culture in question is that of the indigenous hearers of the gospel. Appropriating the gospel means drawing different cultural frameworks into the institutions of the Christian faith, and this stimulates a proper plurality of form.

Sanneh, in other words, outlines a response to colonization that apostolicity, when construed as cultural continuity, can only oppose. Apostolicity so construed obviates reference to such pluralism by, first, privileging the historical givenness of the culture deemed basic to Christian identity and as such necessary to conversion and shared ecumenical recognition and, second, by attributing pluralism itself to the forces opposing that culture. It is difficult to escape the parallels between this definition of apostolicity and the conception of colonization as developed by the Comaroffs. Apostolicity as cultural continuity promotes the "colonization of the consciousness" (or, to use positive language, catechism into the Christian *habitus*) and considers the pluralism of form occasioned by the local appropriation of the gospel an anathema, a threat to the very catholic structures of the faith.

---

[111]Lamin O. Sanneh, *Disciples of All Nations: Pillars of World Christianity* (Oxford: Oxford University Press, 2007), 138.

4.5 ECCLESIOLOGY AND THE LOSS OF IDENTITY

Given the neglect of church structures within the anthropological discussion, any association of the processes of colonization with the transmission of church structures might seem short on specifics. When read from the perspective of the indigenous receivers of Western ecclesiologies, however, the relationship becomes clear. Bolaji Idowu's 1965 classic, *Towards an Indigenous Church*, exemplifies the logic.[112]

Writing during the period of Nigerian independence, Idowu examines the assumed role of Christianity as a servant of Western imperialism. If Christianity is "a kind of imperialistic witchcraft which has been employed to fetter the souls of Nigerians for the sinister purpose of colonial exploitation, then as colonialism has now had its day and its imperialistic hold upon Nigerians has been released, it means that its spell has been broken."[113] Formulated in this manner, Idowu seeks to address the prevailing criticisms of Christianity in a postcolonial period, a period of cutting imposed ties and reformulating identity. His response denies Christianity's essential foreignness, but he acknowledges the "European structure of the Church in Nigeria" and "the distinctive European complexion of its Christianity."[114] Neither an assertion of imperial power nor a tool for economic exploitation, the problem lay in the manner of presentation; it was a Christianity "heavily tinged with Western culture."[115] So integral did this cultural heritage seem to Christianity that no alternative appeared possible. This Westernness, coupled with the necessary dynamics of conversion, established a range of continuities between the Christian gospel and wider Western civilization, including a positive evaluation of European dress, ethics and language and "a corresponding disdain" Nigerians felt for their own culture.[116] Idowu is not concerned with the Western inculturation of the faith. This he understands to be a necessary phenomenon of church history. Where the faith fails to become local, it perishes. Where it finds local expression, where Christianity does not enslave but liberates, it thrives. Idowu, in other words, does not evaluate the wider relationship of Christianity to colonialism in terms of political or economic

---

[112]E. Bolaji Idowu, *Towards an Indigenous Church* (London: Oxford University Press, 1965).
[113]Ibid., 2.
[114]Ibid.
[115]Ibid., 4.
[116]Ibid., 5.

structures and the amorphous yet determinative power they exert over the religion. He is concerned with the range of cultural artifacts, discursive and symbolic interpretations, and the aesthetic and etiquette deemed necessary to "Christianity" and to the process of becoming Christian. Elsewhere he summarizes the matter thusly:

> The Church in Africa came into being with prefabricated theology, liturgies and traditions. In the matter of Christian ethics, the converts found themselves in the position of those early converts before the Council of Jerusalem (Acts 15): "Unless you are circumcised after the custom of Moses, you cannot be saved"; and that is virtually the position today.[117]

Christian identity, on this account, involved a form of cultural proselytism that clearly paralleled the very problem combated by the early church as it moved across the cultural and religious boundaries between Jew and Gentile.

Notably, Idowu is aware of the central theological challenge with reinterpreting the problem of colonization in terms of Christianity's own cultural packaging. Though he does not use the terminology, it is a problem of apostolic continuity. Using the metaphor of an "organic cell" in a body, Idowu acknowledges that certain characteristics belong to the local church, ones it "shares in various forms as common heredity with other cognate cells." This applies to what might be termed the level of origins, to the "faith once delivered to the saints" (Jude 3), but equally to the level of historical contingency, to "certain inevitable elements which have become in various forms integral marks of the life of the visible Church."[118] Idowu grants the reality of both as necessary and proper to the Christian church in its historical and cross-cultural continuity. Changing his metaphor, the church flows like a living stream through the nations,

> bringing from and depositing in each place something of the chemical wealth of the soils which it encounters on its way, at the same time adapting itself to the shape and features of each locality, taking its colouring from the native soil, while in spite of all these structural adaptations and diversifications its *esse* and its *differentia* are not imperiled but maintained in consequence of the living, ever-replenishing, ever-revitalizing spring which is its source.[119]

---

[117]E. Bolaji Idowu, "Predicament of the Church in Africa," 426.
[118]Idowu, *Towards an Indigenous Church*, 12.
[119]Ibid.

It belongs as a theological necessity to each local church that it maintains its "cherished heritage which runs down the ages." Should it attempt to divest itself of "all 'foreign' elements," the church would succeed only in cutting itself "adrift from the stream of history and end in an eddy," denying itself "the spiritual tonic which 'the Communion of the Saints' affords. In short she will cease to be a living cell within the whole Body."[120] Apostolicity, understood as continuity through history and across cultures, places obligations on the local church that help safeguard it against an undue concern with its own limited cultural form.

Even if we recognize the importance of contingent historical development in the church order, this does not address Idowu's express concerns with a culturally prepackaged Christianity. The problem is exactly that of a church caught in a historical eddy through an "inordinate loyalty to hereditary structure," in which case "structure often becomes an end in itself and thus acquires a quasi-magical virtue in consequence of which it is believed that it must remain intact in the form in which it has been handed down."[121] Though often an abstract theological caution, Idowu's concerns reflect lived experience in a cross-cultural context. The full lordship of Jesus Christ, according to Idowu, is not real to Nigerians because the "authority which must be obeyed is largely that of some 'Oracle' enshrined in the Vatican, in Canterbury, in Scotland, or elsewhere in the United Kingdom or Europe, or of some 'Providence' who dispenses dollars from America."[122] The Nigerian church is an outpost of, variously, the Anglican, Catholic or Baptist churches and constantly under the threat of "punishment, whether that be of excommunication or of cessation of dollars, if she does not do as she is told from abroad."[123] One could interpret Idowu's objection in terms of power and control, yet this is to miss his main point: the need for control stems from the need to maintain the continuity of structures without which the church as such would not exist.

As to what the "European structure" of the church is, Idowu names a number of artifacts that in other hands appear essential to the church's apostolic identity and necessary to its missionary transmission. After ex-

---

[120]Ibid.
[121]Ibid.
[122]Ibid., 13.
[123]Ibid., 14.

amining the range of hermeneutical and methodological concerns encountered in biblical translation, evangelistic preaching and theological formulations, the general discussion of which is familiar today, Idowu turns to liturgy.[124] Far from being a historic message that transcends its particular temporal and geographical location, the Anglican liturgy proves to be spiritually unsuitable because it is "for the English to be used by English worshippers."[125] Acknowledging that its authors composed it following "the heritage of the Church Universal," it remains the case that "its language, its phraseology, its particular references, all proclaim its origin and the end for which it was designed."[126] Nor does Idowu find the solution "in go-as-you-please orders of the 'Evangelical' churches," as these too often betray a lack of preparation and take the form of a concert before that of a service of worship.[127] Both approaches, for Idowu, reflect more a simple desire to preserve foreign traditions than any serious consideration of the spiritual needs of the local worshipers.

With hymnology, Idowu notes that whereas Nigerian songs match words and tune so that the two together convey meaning, the prefabricated liturgies translated into Nigerian languages push "the limit of cultic atrocity."[128] Hymns are either falsely translated or extol the virtues of the "home" nations while condemning the blindness of the heathen for bowing down to wood and stone.[129] With indigenous tunes or instruments not permitted, true worship is seen to depend on an imported pipe organ or a harmonium.

Likewise with dress and vestment, the expectation is that the congregation will be properly attired, that is, dressed as Europeans. Should a worshiper appear in traditional African dress, "he would either be turned back, or he would find himself so out of place and unwelcome that he would never

---

[124] As an example of the influence over theology, see Ogbu U. Kalu, "Unconquered Spiritual Gates: Inculturation Theology in Africa Revisited," *Journal of Inculturation Theology* 1, no. 1 (1994): 25-37.

[125] Idowu, *Towards an Indigenous Church*, 27.

[126] Ibid. Idowu illustrates the problem by reference to the church elder who can "wade through the ritual with the seriousness of one who is reciting an incantation, praying fervently in 1964 for Alexandra the Queen Mother (where an ancient Book of Common Prayer has not yet been rescued from him) quite unconscious that Her Majesty has been dead for years" (28).

[127] Ibid., 28.

[128] Ibid., 32. As a further example, for Felix Nwatu, the "liturgical symbols lack relevance and therefore fail to connect with the community's interpretive symbol-system." Felix Nwatu, "'Colonial' Christianity in Post-Colonial Africa?," *Ecumenical Review* 46, no. 3 (1994): 356.

[129] Idowu, *Towards an Indigenous Church*, 32-33.

dare to do so again!"[130] As to the ministerial vestments, Idowu recognizes the need for continuity within the universal church but cautions that these should also bear some local originality.[131]

Idowu nowhere seeks to detach the Nigerian church from the wider church. He does, however, reject what Bernard Ukwuegbu has termed an "imperialistic ecclesiology" with its expectation "that Black Africans should adopt a culturally conditioned concept of Church that arose in the West."[132] The larger point concerns the identification of church structures, order and liturgies with the process of colonization. As one consequence, the church becomes confined to the space within the church's four walls because only here does the necessary culture exist. To continue with Idowu, the rejection of local culture that often accompanied the entrance of Christianity—the failure to take account of indigenous beliefs and customs and the presentation of Jesus Christ as a "completely new God who had had nothing to do with the past of Africa"—meant that "no proper foundation [was] laid for the Gospel message in the hearts of the people and no bridge between the old and the new."[133] The church came speaking in "strange tongues" and without thought of translation. Christian converts, as a result,

> live ambivalent spiritual lives. Christianity to them is a fashionable religion
> which has the habit of beginning and ending within the walls of a church

---

[130]Ibid., 38.

[131]Though Idowu stops at this point, one could continue the point with John Mbiti and question the manner in which imported Western church architecture structures the world in a certain way. As to the importing of Western church architecture, he states: "If worship is to become meaningful, then the architecture of the churches should be determined by the congregation and not vice versa.... Would, for example, a round or oval church building be more conducive to worship than a rectangular or square one for an African congregation since traditional houses and villages are generally built in a round shape?" John S. Mbiti, "The Ways and Means of Communicating the Gospel," in Baëta, *Christianity in Tropical Africa*, 335. He regards many hymns used in tropical Africa as being "of second-rate quality and often slanted according to denominational allegiance. The fact that nearly all these hymns are translations, and are sung to imported tunes, makes their teaching appear foreign" (334). Given that a "good number of Christian rites were originally borrowed from either Hebrew or pagan sources," he considers it possible for Christians to "baptize" many traditional African rites by giving them "a Christian content and blessing" (344). Much of this has, of course, occurred in the intervening years, though it often remains unrecognized within the Western theological guild with its presupposed expectations of what constitutes a "contextual" theology.

[132]Bernard Ukwuegbu, "'Neither Jew nor Greek': The Church in Africa and the Quest for Self-Understanding in the Light of the Pauline Vision and Today's Context of Cultural Pluralism," *International Journal for the Study of the Christian Church* 8, no. 4 (2008), 311, 307.

[133]Idowu, "Predicament of the Church in Africa," 433.

building; it does not reach those vital areas of the personal needs of Africans. Thus, it is possible for an African to sing lustily in Church, "Other refuge have I none," while still carrying an amulet somewhere on his person, or being able to go out of the Church straight to his diviner, without feeling that he is betraying any principle.[134]

Far from an uncommon observation, the experienced foreignness of Christianity, along with the assertion of this foreignness over against the local appropriation of the gospel, results in a bifurcation within the lives of Christian converts themselves.[135] The ecumenical movement's method of recognizing the cultural and historical origins of a structure while denying its ongoing cultural force often underlies the possibility of apostolicity as cultural continuity. Yet many Christians in Africa, Asia, Latin America and Oceania experience such cultural artifacts as simply Western and a hindrance to the local growth of and witness to the gospel. As Idowu's reference to Acts 15 suggests, it appears that Africans need to take on these culturally specific symbols—they need to become Western to be Christian. It is difficult to shake the conclusion that the dominant ecumenical model for apostolicity, that of cultural continuity, mandates colonization as the method of cross-cultural missionary transmission with all that this entails for uneven power relationships, paternalism, building relationships of dependence and, finally, maintaining a state of Christian infancy.

4.6 World Christianity Confronts Cultural Continuity

As we have seen, apostolicity as cultural continuity informs key strategies in contemporary Christian ethics, particularly with respect to the church's relation to globalization. In this context, a problem identified as being Western in origin assumes a global character and is countered by a catholicity determined by the decisions defining apostolicity. That is, the nature of the church's continuity through time determines the nature of its spatial continuity. This wider application of apostolicity illustrates the material consequences of the formal discussion. With the emphasis on the historical

---

[134]Ibid.
[135]For a further example, this time from Hong Kong, see Archie C. C. Lee, "Cross-textual Hermeneutics and Identity in Multi-scriptural Asia," in *Christian Theology in Asia*, ed. Sebastian C. H. Kim (Cambridge: Cambridge University Press, 2008), 198-99.

extension of a particular form of social embodiment as normative within the global context—framed as an ordered diversity combating a false diversity—it is clear that the ecumenical consensus regarding apostolicity functions as an assumption in this discussion. For example, while ecumenical theory may appear to cherish "diversity," it does so insofar as this illustrates the supposed a priori universality of the church as experienced in the West, an international (i.e., catholic) culture beyond any single instantiation. Andrew Walls complains that the "hidden assumption is that Christianity is essentially a religion of the West, and that the new theological task is to celebrate the achievements, insights and variant formulations of other cultures."[136] Diversity, especially when defined in the narrow terms of gift, is cherished to the extent that it reinforces and does not intrude on the specific Western cultural heritage of the universal church.

In bald terms, apostolicity understood as cultural continuity produces the type of contest feared by Ian Douglas "between an hegemonic, monocultural expression of Western Christianity and an emerging, multicultural global Christian community embodying radical differences."[137] Claims to "apostolicity," of course, include a defense mechanism against these type of charges. Even if they arose in a clearly contingent manner, so it is argued, the structures definitive of apostolicity have sufficient historical distance from these origins and are not simply reducible to "Western" Christianity. Such an argument has merit but ignores the way in which apostolicity establishes a particular understanding of the church and its witness and results in a mission method of cultural replication. The focus, in other words, falls not on the adjective "Western" but on the underlying demands of an assumed cultural form and the conflict this creates with the diversity of expression already found in world Christianity.

Any claims for cultural and historical neutrality become questionable when considered against the backdrop of colonization and the role played by the church and its institutions. Arguments for the international nature of the community do not cohere with the lived experience, which tends to

---

[136]Andrew F. Walls, "Of Ivory Towers and Ashrams: Some Reflections on Theological Scholarship in Africa," *Journal of African Christian Thought* 3, no. 1 (2000): 3.

[137]Ian T. Douglas, "The Clash of Global Christianity: A Review of 'The Next Christendom: The Coming of Global Christianity' by Philip Jenkins," *World & I* 18, no. 2 (2003): 222.

be one of cultural imposition and of the "foreignness" of Christianity. In this cross-cultural engagement, the foreign location of the transmitted "way of life" becomes evident. The social exclusion, the loss of cultural identity and even the accelerated death rates of indigenous peoples prove difficult to reconcile with the rhetoric of nonviolence and growth in ecclesial identity. Linking church structures to the processes of colonization precludes a simple identification of the problem with either the Catholic or Protestant approaches, since both exported Western culture with the Christian gospel. Recognizing the realities of the context of colonization unmasks the assumption that Christianity developed along a singular historical course and created a singular Christian culture, and so criticizes "the hubris of thinking that our own culture is the standard for translating, judging and evaluating whatever we encounter."[138] The colonial account of Christianity grants no determining significance to local agency, for this in no way informs the nature of historical continuity, the structures of which are established well in advance of, and are understood to determine, any local appropriation of the gospel.

Uncomfortable parallels emerge between the variety of criticisms applied generally to Western culture in the context of colonization and those applicable to the positive theological construal of apostolicity as cultural continuity. Recourse to "aesthetic taste" simply pushes this concern into the intangibles of a wider cultural system with its self-referential "common sense."[139] Viewing these cultural factors as simply "natural" undercuts any controls against cultural imposition. Though this concern with aesthetic might appear one step removed from that of concrete structures, it affords an even greater justification for those structures by isolating them from the question of their own authentication. When aligned with such conceptual tools as Bourdieu's approach to *habitus* and practice, we can see connections between the normative dogmatic view of the church and the historic processes of ecclesial imperialism during the colonial period.[140]

---

[138]Richard J. Bernstein, "The Hermeneutics of Cross-Cultural Understanding," in *Cross-Cultural Conversation: Initiation*, ed. Anindita N. Balslev (Atlanta: Scholars Press, 1996), 36.

[139]See Clifford Geertz, "Common Sense as a Cultural System," *Antioch Review* 33, no. 1 (1975): 5-26.

[140]To give a more contemporary example, Claudio Carvalhaes, reflecting on the commemoration of Calvin's five hundredth birthday, notes how faithfulness to the "Calvinist tradition was closely related to order of worship and music that originated in either Europe or the United

A constructive definition of apostolicity needs to account for the local appropriation of the gospel and the pluralism of expression this entails. Though made difficult by schism, the task is not impossible. As Kathryn Tanner observes,

> Christianity is a hybrid formation through and through; nothing need be exempted out of fear that the distinctiveness of Christianity must otherwise be lost. . . . Christian distinctiveness is something that emerges in the very cultural processes occurring at the boundary, processes that construct a distinctive identity for Christian social practices through the distinctive use of cultural materials shared with others.[141]

Cross-cultural transmission and local appropriation are necessary to a theological definition of apostolicity. This, it needs to be reinforced, is a historical point. To quote Retief Müller, the role of Christianity as "a counter-cultural protest movement" is not something it can "play with any degree of legitimacy because of its hybridising tendencies and intercultural entanglements throughout history."[142] Though the ecumenical discussion might generally affirm that the gospel cannot be reduced to one particular cultural expression, this caution is never linked to the church

States. Absent from these services were songs and prayers from the global South." The "proper" tradition was that found in Europe and the United States, while what occurred in other parts of the world was not "tradition but mission and missionary work, merely an addendum to tradition." For Carvalhaes, this "reifies the notion that one set of people holds the proper way, while all others must learn about it to become proper. Everyone who wishes to belong must learn a religious language, an ethical code, a mode of being, a certain cultural category deeply attached to the gospel of Jesus Christ and its ways of belief, prayers and practices." One must, in other words, assume the cultural markers of a particular Christian expression to be recognized as Christian. The Brazilian Carvalhaes applies this caution to the Reformed standard of "decency and order." The question is one of cultural aesthetic judgment: whose decency and order? On one occasion when he, himself a Presbyterian minister and professor of liturgy at an American seminary, came to preach within a local Presbyterian church, the regular minister prepared the congregation with the following words: "Today we have Claudio preaching for us, so we will not have our usual service in decency and order." Though meant as a jest, it equally identified "a foreign presence. . . . The order we do not recognize looks like disorder. The decency that does not come wrapped up in certain moral codes and known religious clothes seems indecent, and thus improper to the faith and, consequently, to our world view. I will always be a foreigner, always a person to be evangelized, until I learn the notion of decency and order." But this is itself impossible. Claudio Carvalhaes, "Communitas: Liturgy and Identity," *International Review of Mission* 100, no. 1 (2011): 40.

[141]Kathryn Tanner, *Theories of Culture: A New Agenda for Theology* (Minneapolis: Fortress, 1997), 114-15.

[142]Retief Müller, "Christianity and Globalisation: An Alternative Ethical Response," *HTS Teologiese Studies / Theological Studies* 67, no. 3 (2011): 7.

and its structures. If we take this line of argument seriously, we must acknowledge that no single theological tradition already possesses an "international" culture, one justifiably so concerned with its own purity to fear the integration of other appropriations of the gospel. It is not possible to be the community of "both Jew and Gentile" apart from the ongoing cross-cultural encounter that this vision demands.

5
. . . .

Subordinating Apostolicity to the Apostolate

The nature of the Church can be sufficiently defined by its function,
i.e. its participation in Christ's apostolic ministry.

JOHANNES CHRISTIAAN HOEKENDIJK[1]

The community (in its entirety) is the unit of proclamation, which,
with its message, devotes itself to every urgent need of its environment,
translating this message into practical service (diakonia). The first and
fundamental service is that the community itself exists in an "exem-
plary way" (Barth) and thus erects a sign of the coming kingdom.

JOHANNES CHRISTIAAN HOEKENDIJK[2]

5.1 THE CHURCH AS INSTRUMENT

If identifying apostolicity with the continuity of a culture represents one side
of the debate, its opposite subordinates the church and its structures to the
apostolate. The church becomes an "instrument" for missionary witness. This
position finds classic expression in the work of Johannes Christiaan Hoekendijk (1912–1975).[3] Working backwards from both the positive demands

---

[1]J. C. Hoekendijk, "The Church in Missionary Thinking," *International Review of Missions* 41 (1952): 334.

[2]J. C. Hoekendijk, *Kirche und Volk in der deutschen Missionswissenschaft* (Munich: Chr. Kaiser Verlag, 1967), 291.

[3]While no biography exists, Hoekendijk develops a short autobiography in a letter written to Gianfranco Coffele. See Gianfranco Coffele, *Johannes Christiaan Hoekendijk: Da una teologia della missione ad una teologia missionaria* (Rome: Universita Gregoriana, 1976), 18-21. Hoekendijk published a spate of articles during the late 1940s and early 1950s but developed no book-length

occasioned by the non-Western appropriation of the gospel and the problem of a mission method he labels "propaganda," Hoekendijk finds fault with established ecclesiologies. When Christian witness is conceived primarily as a function of the church's own internal culture, the focus falls on the structures, rhythms and aesthetics needed for the cultivation of such. These artifacts define the church as a body and produce a territorial conception of mission. Hoekendijk counters this "residential" interpretation of the church with his positive account of the "apostolate," one which builds on terms like "kingdom of God," "people of God," "koinonia" and "shalom." In other words, he uses the apostolate to critique received notions of apostolicity.

The reaction Hoekendijk provokes is often immediate and visceral. According to many commentators, Hoekendijk denies the church a body.[4] He dissolves the church into a dynamic, leading David Bosch to condemn him for articulating "a view that leads to absurdity."[5] The very dismissive reaction is itself noteworthy because commentators engage neither Hoekendijk's diagnosis nor the positive shape he gives the church. Hoekendijk's position has problems—his polemical tone no doubt draws attention away from his substantive position—but the reaction is disproportionate and, for this reason, revealing. The confusion centers on the way commentators are unable to conceive of mission apart from the event of geographical expansion, and this is because they cannot conceive of the body in non-territorial terms. From this perspective, Hoekendijk appears to deny mission its necessary basis in the church even while making that (now groundless) principle the church's critical predicate.

Hoekendijk's critical diagnosis of the "residential" church and its necessary mission method of "propaganda," which constitutes the first part of the chapter, is followed by his constructive definition of the apostolate and

---

treatment of his constructive approach. His singular monograph remains his 1948 dissertation, a German version of which appeared in 1967, titled *Kirche und Volk in der deutschen Missionswissenschaft*. His 1967 text, *The Church Inside Out* (Philadelphia: Westminster, 1966), is a lightly revised collection of his articles. For a bibliography of Hoekendijk's works, see Coffele, *Johannes Christiaan Hoekendijk*, 525-31.

[4]Bert Hoedemaker, a Hoekendijk supporter, observes how "one is struck by a certain stubbornness with which his central theological affirmations were repeated over and over in an aphoristic way, and by the absence of any self-critical dialogue with theological critics." L. A. Hoedemaker, "The Legacy of J. C. Hoekendijk," *International Bulletin of Missionary Research* 19, no. 4 (1995): 170.

[5]David J. Bosch, *Transforming Mission: Paradigm Shifts in Theology of Mission* (Maryknoll, NY: Orbis Books, 1991), 385.

the corresponding shape of the church he envisions. However objectionable to established traditions the ecclesiology he develops might be, Hoekendijk does not forget the church. He does reject defining mission first in geographical terms, and thus he rejects a territorial definition of the church that mandates such a missionary approach. Hoekendijk instead conceives of mission in relation to history, hence his use of the "apostolate." The apostolate is God's faithfulness to his promises, his sending of the promised Messiah and his eschatological calling of all nations to himself. Difficulties certainly emerge in that Hoekendijk subsumes God's own agency into history, but this conceptual move is a significant advance toward a positive definition of apostolicity.

5.2 Dutch Theology of the Apostolate

Hoekendijk's own understanding of the apostolate developed as part of the wider "theology of the apostolate" that emerged in Holland during the first half of the twentieth century.[6] Little secondary reflection is available on the origins of this approach, but it is clear that, while other names bear some relationship to it (Johannes Blauw and Evert Jansen-Schoonhoven), the central voices were those of Hendrik Kraemer, A. A. van Ruler and Hoekendijk. Drawing on these voices, Bert Hoedemaker offers a simple summary of the approach.[7]

First, with assistance from dialectical theology and the German church struggle, the theology of the apostolate drew on the rediscovery of the "independent, critical, anti-religious witness of the gospel over against everything that happens in the world." This was, in Hoedemaker's estimation, Kraemer's particular contribution. Against the backdrop of secularization and the associated threat it posed to cultures and religions, a particular responsibility of missionary preaching was to form communities that might consciously live out of God's revelation and enter dialogically into the religio-cultural context. This intentionality indicates a proper distinction

---

[6]In terms of the concept's genealogy, van Ruler's minimal historical account within a short footnote seems to be the fullest available in English. See A. A. van Ruler, "A Theology of Mission," in *Calvinist Trinitarianism and Theocentric Politics: Essays Toward a Public Theology* (Lewiston, NY: Edwin Mellen, 1989), 199-200n2.

[7]The following summary is derived from L. A. Hoedemaker, "Die Welt als theologisches Problem: Kritischer Rückblick auf die niederländische Theologie des Apostolates," *Zeitschrift für dialektische Theologie* 2, no. 1 (2004): 9-11.

between the church and its cultural location and, with this, a deliberate movement of the church to this location. The second emphasis, one Hoedemaker associates with Hoekendijk's contribution, concerns the relationship between church and mission, especially as it was formulated within ecumenical discussion of the period.[8] Church and mission are not distinct and independent entities; the church is itself missionary in essence. The third emphasis, and probably the most important when thinking of the apostolate within its context, is the Dutch Reformed interest in theocracy as promoted by A. A. van Ruler. This presented a more dogmatic voice and stressed the christianization of culture and society. As a fourth focus, the theology of the apostolate reasserted the significance of Israel for Christian theology. Though a general concern in post-WWII Europe, van Ruler and Hoekendijk both draw from the Old Testament to critique a perceived narrowness in how the church construes itself and its role in the world. Reference to Israel places the work of God in a wider cosmic framework.

Even as a general background, this overview identifies certain interpretive lines often ignored by Hoekendijk's critics. On many fundamental points he is not the idiosyncratic voice the majority of scholars make him out to be. Though he is often charged with radicalizing the theology of the apostolate, historical distance perhaps allows for a greater measure of continuity between Hoekendijk and the wider Dutch approach, as well as for greater clarity concerning the points where he differs.[9] For example, as critical as Hoekendijk is of the church, he lies close to Hendrik Kraemer's development of the apostolate against an improper ecclesial introversion.[10]

---

[8]While self-evidently part of Hoekendijk's thinking, one should observe his ambiguous relationship to this tendency within the ecumenical discussion, especially as it risked reducing mission to a program of an otherwise unaltered church: "Missions will now figure on the official agenda of synod meetings (e.g. as item 47?)." Hoekendijk, "Church in Missionary Thinking," 335.

[9]L. A. Hoedemaker, "Hoekendijk's American Years," *Occasional Bulletin of Missionary Research* 1, no. 2 (1977): 8.

[10]Though the term "apostolate" was already present in Dutch thought in the 1920s, Hendrik Kraemer seemingly bears responsibility for its development owing to a series of shorter texts published in 1936 and for his 1938 text written for the IMC Tambaram conference of that same year, *The Christian Message in a Non-Christian World*. In this text one is struck by the paucity of reference to apostolicity and the apostolate. Positively formulated, Kraemer describes the church's "essential nature" as apostolic, indicating not that "its authority is derived from the apostles" but that "in all its words and actions it ought to be a bearer of witness to God and His decisive creative and redeeming acts and purposes." Hendrik Kraemer, *The Christian Message in a Non-Christian World* (London: Harper and Brothers, 1938), 2. This positive emphasis follows a clear critical background. Though

Insofar as Hoekendijk argues along similar lines on this point, he does not diverge from the norm. One should, instead, read this interpretation of the apostolate against the stress within the Dutch Reformed context on the processes of christianization. As this represented the necessary end of the concrete church, and as this became the practical end toward which the theology of the apostolate flowed, Hoekendijk emerges as a clear opponent of this element within the Dutch theology of the apostolate: to posit christianization as the apostolate's practical end is to reinstate a territorial church. Christianization embodies the cultural emphasis that Hoekendijk diagnoses as basic to the problem of a residential church, against which the apostolate provides the solution. Recognizing this helps us understand a tension within Hoekendijk's thinking: on the one hand, he supports a number of the driving assumptions within the wider Dutch theology of the apostolate; on the other, he rejects its stated conclusion. This exacerbates Hoekendijk's appearance as an idiosyncratic figure.

5.3 BA'AL: THE RESIDENTIAL GOD

In turning to Hoekendijk's specific contribution, it is difficult not to follow his own method of front-loading the critical. One clear danger with this

---

it may seem a small point today, Kraemer broke with the basic theory that conceived of Christendom as necessary to both church life and the missionary enterprise. Kraemer saw in Christendom the triumph of the "pagan ideal of religion," which recognized "the community (or state) as its basic foundation" and which "blended with the Christian idea of the Church" (26-27). Matters of "faith, worship and life" became "expressions of 'custom'" (58). The ends of the church overlapped with those of the world—a point of extreme significance for Hoekendijk. As a consequence of this deficit, the church was reduced to a static and introverted body, something that conceives of itself as "a *possessor* of the truth that God has mercifully revealed" (208). Theological discussion becomes preoccupied with the form of the "true" church, while the church conceives of "itself almost exclusively as a body to conserve values and maintain a once-attained position" (34). To describe the church as apostolic, by contrast, is to describe its purpose. It is "characteristic of this fellowship . . . that it does not exist for its own sake but for the sake of the world" (418-19). The apostolate cannot be separate from the church; the church becomes the church only as it is apostolic, that is, missionary. Only as it is missionary does the church avoid this tendency to cultural domestication. One could, with Hans Margull, observe that while Kraemer used "apostolic church," Hoekendijk used "apostolate," meaning, by implication, that Kraemer retained the priority of the church over the apostolate. Hans J. Margull, *Hope in Action: The Church's Task in the World*, trans. Eugene Peters (Philadelphia: Muhlenberg Press, 1962), 125. But it is equally evident that the intent to disrupt a static relationship between the church and a set cultural form drives both Kraemer and Hoekendijk, who find the means for this disruption in a missionary dynamic. The church becomes the church precisely in the apostolate. Insofar as this describes defining themes of Kraemer's approach to the apostolate, no great theoretical distance separates the two.

approach lies in the negative so consuming the horizon that it obscures any positive alternative. We see evidence of this danger in the way Hoekendijk's critics assume that his criticisms of the church amount to a simple denial of its necessity and reality. This danger notwithstanding, Hoekendijk's constructive advances cannot be understood apart from the connections he forms between mission method and ecclesiology. In other words, mission method is derivative of one's understanding of the church's nature and witness. Though Hoekendijk's critical stance can appear to be wide-ranging, it is possible to summarize his key point using one term: Ba'al. Ba'al indicates a conspiracy present throuhout church history—namely, the tendency "to make [God] again the residential god of a well-defined locality; which may be a continent (corpus christianum?), a nation (Volkskirche?) or a more restricted residential area (parish?)."[11] While his criticisms of the parish attracted the attention of English-language audiences, the first two hold greater importance when interpreting Hoekendijk. Everything follows from his diagnosis of the myth of Christendom, the ideology of Volk and their end in ecclesiocentrism.

5.3.1 Christendom as myth. Though critical appraisals of Christendom are commonplace in contemporary theological discourse, Hoekendijk pioneered this investigation through a unique diagnosis of the relationship between the *corpus Christianum* and mission method. In contrast to the popular focus on Constantine's political decisions, Christendom began when a conception of the church as coextensive with the world came to replace the eschatological mission characterizing the New Testament church. As the church consumed the territorial horizon, pastoral proclamation became the key form of mission. The church—understood as the goal of world history—became the origin and end of every missionary endeavor.

---

[11]J. C. Hoekendijk, "Notes on the Meaning of Mission(-ary)," in *Planning for Mission: Working Papers on the New Quest for Missionary Communities*, ed. Thomas Wieser (New York: U.S. Conference for the World Council of Churches, 1966), 42. On the terms *Volkskirche* and *Volk*, Hoekendijk himself refuses to translate them because *Volk* has a "mythic ring," and translating it would cause the word to lose its "ideological overtone." Hoekendijk, *Kirche und Volk*, 101. He refers to the documentation from the 1937 Life and Work Oxford Conference: "The word 'Volk' is quite untranslatable, because it designates both a sentiment and a body of convictions to which there is no exact, or even approximate, parallel elsewhere" (101n9). I will follow Hoekendijk's lead here and leave both terms untranslated. For a developed examination of the term *Volkskirche*, see Wolfgang Huber and Henning Schröder, "Volkskirche," in *Theologische Realenzyklopädie*, ed. Gerhard Müller (Berlin: Walter de Gruyter, 2003), 35:249-62.

Hoekendijk rejects this assumed relationship. This idea of a "basic unity of the whole of life founded in the Christian faith" was never a "fact, but a very powerful myth."[12] A myth defines rather than interprets a situation. It turns a shared historical experience into a common narrative, giving a group "a firm solidarity."[13] The myth of Christendom informs the mechanics of the "historic" church and its use of received structures to define belonging and identity. Central to this myth's power is its capacity to "canonize," that is, to sanctify moral codes, cultural artifacts, aesthetic vision, confessional lines and ethnic superiorities. These canonized elements are not interpretive but definitive of Christian solidarity. This applies equally to claims of historical continuity. For Hoekendijk, the operative "history" underlying normative ecclesiological claims is shaped in accordance with the basic myth. The "contingencies of a hallowed past are stabilized by elevating them to the dignity of the timeless."[14] Historical elements are appropriated in a way that makes them determinative for the group and necessary to its being. Should these be removed, by extension, the group loses its essence.

This myth reduces the church, Hoekendijk argues, to a "temple." The canonization of historical contingencies withdraws the church from history and imagines it as a holy space with doors capable of being closed to the world. In this space, the church possesses something in and for itself. It becomes a temple, a place within which God might reside, sustained by rituals and institutions that secure an unchangeable circle of life.[15] Christendom becomes a "protective shell of the Church," and in "this well-protected area the Church can have its own style of life, speak its own language, determine its own time."[16] Hoekendijk issues this complaint against no single tradition. Though he understands it as characteristic of the Roman Catholic Church, the Reformation failed to break the same shackles; it simply produced a "reformed temple."[17] This occurred as a result of "a strong conviction of togetherness," a "unity of historical solidarity" shared between the Protestant and Catholic

---

[12]J. C. Hoekendijk, "Christ and the World in the Modern Age," *Student World* 54, no. 1-2 (1961): 76.
[13]Hoekendijk, *Church Inside Out*, 63.
[14]J. C. Hoekendijk, "Mission—a Celebration of Freedom," *Union Seminary Quarterly* 21, no. 2 (1966): 139.
[15]J. C. Hoekendijk, "Kirche," in *Theologie für Nichttheologen II*, ed. Hans Jürgen Schultz (Berlin: Kreuz-Verlag, 1964), 103.
[16]J. C. Hoekendijk, "The Call to Evangelism," *International Review of Missions* 39 (1950): 166.
[17]Hoekendijk, "Kirche," 104.

churches.[18] The conflict Hoekendijk develops, in other words, is not one between Catholics and Protestants. Christendom reduces both traditions to
sects that are defined, to cite Hans-Werner Gensichen's summary, as "not the
one-sided development of an aspect of the gospel message, but the displacement of the gospel from its central position (even a 'Volkskirche' *can,* in
this sense, be a sect!)."[19] Whatever apparent differences they exhibit in terms
of structural expression, both retain the same mythic substructure.

Moreover, insofar as the myth of Christendom uses the gospel to elevate and
support a cultural narrative, it succeeds in domesticating God, in reducing God
to a Ba'al. "This illusion of the temple has been supported for centuries by that
other fiction of a Christian Occident: the historically powerful God of the
exodus, on whom the church is solely dependent, assumed the features of a
European Ba'al—he became the local god in charge around here, captured in
the sacral order which we had built around him."[20] Propaganda follows as the
natural mission method of this god.[21] As he cannot himself go, so it becomes
necessary to replicate his sacral order with its institutions and liturgies in other
locations. Mission, by this definition, represents the attempt to restore "the
Corpus Christianum, as a solid, well-integrated cultural complex, directed and
dominated by the Church."[22] Propaganda is proselytism, a process of enculturation whereby an individual and a people need to assume, first, the wider
supporting cultural milieu, and second, even the smallest details of the corresponding church culture, including its underlying myth, the historical contingencies constituting the church's apparent substance.

---

[18]Hoekendijk, "Christ and the World," 76-77.
[19]Hans-Werner Gensichen, "Grundfragen der Kirchwerdung in der Mission: Zur Gespräch mit
J. C. Hoekendijk," *Evangelische Missions Zeitschrift* 8 (1951): 40.
[20]Hoekendijk, "Kirche," 103-4.
[21]Hoekendijk here enlists a conceptual distinction between mission and propaganda developed by
New Testament scholar Martin Kähler (1835–1912). See Martin Kähler, *Schriften zu Christologie
und Mission: Gesamtausgabe der Schriften zur Mission* (Munich: Chr. Kaiser Verlag, 1971), 108-16.
"Propaganda" results from the identification between the gospel message and the form the message
assumes in any particular context. It occurs when those who "think that in bringing their particular Christianity, they are bringing Christianity itself, and thus the gospel itself" (115). With propaganda it makes no difference if the message is one of "a churchly Christianity, a confessional,
institutional morality, or some non-church modern faith. One just expands what is already one's
own. Here competition with other religions and worldviews automatically results. It is a matter of
human acquisitions and formations only. One proselytizes, that is, makes repetitions of oneself"
(114). For a good English-language summary of Kähler's position, see David J. Bosch, "Systematic
Theology and Mission: The Voice of an Early Pioneer," *Theologia Evangelica* 5, no. 3 (1972): 165-89.
[22]Hoekendijk, "Call to Evangelism," 163.

Mission within Christendom becomes conceived foremost in territorial terms with an associated distinction between an inner (home) and outer (foreign) mission. It takes a different form, in other words, depending on the relation of a particular location to the culture of Christendom. In terms of home missions, Hoekendijk turns to the pioneering work of Johann Hinrich Wichern (1808–1881). By defining the missionary task as winning the lost back to Christendom, Wichern narrowed the term "pagan" to refer to either moral or intellectual deviants. Salvation then became "moral rearmament" or the reception of "wisdom," and the forgiveness of sin amounted to ignoring a "wild past" or overlooking "stupidity."[23] Within Christendom, mission presupposed a people shaped by a Christian cultural milieu but differentiated by certain behaviors and associated classes.

In terms of foreign missions, the myth of Christendom demands the establishment of a Christian culture. Beginning with Gustav Warneck's 1890s definition of missions as "the total activity of Christendom (= all true believers) to plant and organize the Church among Non-Christians," Hoekendijk notes the basic tendency to divide the world into Christian and non-Christian areas. There exists "a 'faith'-locality and an 'unbelief'-locality with a 'frontier' in-between, and missions are then defined as 'the crossing of this frontier between faith and un-belief.'"[24] Conceived as it is in spatial categories, this act of boundary crossing produces a mission method of relocation: a prior cultural form is repeated in a new geographical location. Hoekendijk illustrates this with reference to missions that rejected all cultural work in favor of individual conversion. The Moravian church, for example, soon discovered that its missionaries needed "to build up a form of what they called 'Christian civilization' before they could begin to harvest the individual souls."[25] According to Karl Graul (1814–1864), a missionary to India and the director of the Leipzig Lutheran mission, conversion would not achieve a required depth unless it was accompanied by a process of *Volkschristianisierung*, a christianization of the people/culture. Such missionary assumptions found support even in the work of theologians ranging from Friedrich Schleiermacher to

---

[23]Ibid., 167.
[24]Hoekendijk, "Notes on the Meaning of Mission(-ary)," 40.
[25]Hoekendijk, "Call to Evangelism," 165.

Ernst Troeltsch. They confirmed that "it would be impossible even to think of converting people without the simultaneous expansion of Western so-called Christian civilization."[26] For Hoekendijk, this approach to "foreign missions" understood "conversion" and maturity in the Christian faith in terms of the convert's capacity to take on the Christendom aesthetic, mimicking its patterns of speech, dress, morality, lines of authority and *telos*.

5.3.2 *Volk* as ideology. This myth of Christendom, Hoekendijk argues, underlay the ideology of *Volk*. Ideology relates to myth as interpretation relates to definition. Myth establishes the context, and ideology consists of supporting "patterns of thought" and "rules of speech. It regulates the emotional values of everything and determines what is and what is not important."[27] *Volk* assumed this governing role within German mission theory.

Two clarifying statements are in order. First, the concept of *Volk* is commonly translated as "people" or "nation" and refers to the fullness of culture, language and history. But in the context of mission, as defined by Hoekendijk, it carries an additional set of emphases. *Volk* refers to a certain interpretive approach to other cultures and national identities, one that includes such catastrophic notions as "cultural purity" and determines the appropriate form of the indigenous church and its cultivation. Second, in criticizing the ideology of *Volk*, Hoekendijk is writing against the claim that German missions had a "special charisma." To quote Gustav Warneck (1834–1910), compared to "Europeanization" or "perhaps even worse: Americanization," this charism consists in its "respecting foreign nationalities, its capacity to enter selflessly and with impartial gentleness into the peculiarities of other peoples."[28] German mission theory, in direct contrast to the perceived "internationalism" of the Anglo-American approach—with its perceived concern for a global uniformity modeled after English and American cultural values—sought to preserve and nurture original cultural ties and indigenous local churches.[29]

---

[26]Ibid.

[27]Hoekendijk, *Church Inside Out*, 62.

[28]Gustav Warneck, *Evangelische Missionslehre: Ein missionstheoretischer Versuch* (Gotha: Friedrich Andreas Perthes, 1903), 23n1, cited by Hoekendijk, *Kirche und Volk*, 102. Hoekendijk does not understand this as originating with Warneck; notably, he traces it to the work of Nicolaus Ludwig von Zinzendorf.

[29]Hoekendijk, *Kirche und Volk*, 102-3.

The role of *Volk* within German mission theory occupies Hoekendijk's single book-length work, his 1948 dissertation *Kerk en Volk in de duitse Zendingswetenschap* (*Church and Volk in German Missiology*).[30] Hoekendijk traces the rise of an "ethnopathos" through the early stages of German mission theory, from Nicolaus Zinzendorf (1700–1760) to Warneck. The complex idea of *Volk*—drawn as it was from the German historical and political experience, from theoretical developments linked with "nature" and "community," along with a dose of romanticism, and supported by the biblical concept of *ta ethne* as interpreted by "scientific exegesis"[31]—became, in the words of Hoedemaker, a "pseudotheological category."[32] The consequences were complex and wide-ranging. To begin, this ethnopathos reduced the "ecological differentiation" available to the church; the variety of permissible social forms was narrowed according to the vision of a *Volk*. The stress on local cultures precluded the expectation that they take on German culture, but what counted as "culture" and, by extension, maturity in conversion, stemmed from the German vision. Through notions of "blood and soil," "primal ties" and the "orders of creation," *Volk* sought to "preserve" the past. It ordered "the space of truth which must accompany the message" and delivered the material "constitutive for the building of the church."[33] This included a "pedagogical" approach that nurtured converts toward maturity through the organization of indigenous churches and the wider christianization of society.[34] The "village with its strong social coherence" became the characteristic form.[35] *Volk* defined "the universal," encompassing all aspects of the truth, and what is *Volksgemäß* (appropriate to the *Volk*) determined Christian acting and preaching.[36] As matters progressed, even the Reformation became interpreted as God's sanctification of the German *Volk*, and later, on the basis of this underlying "ethnopathos," German mission

---

[30]For a summary, see Walter J. Hollenweger, "Johannes Christian Hoekendijk: Pluriformität der Kirche," *Reformatio* 16, no. 10 (1967): 663-77.

[31]Hoekendijk, *Kirche und Volk*, 101.

[32]Hoedemaker, "Legacy of J. C. Hoekendijk," 166.

[33]Hoekendijk, *Kirche und Volk*, 105.

[34]J. C. Hoekendijk, "Evangelization of the World in this Generation," *International Review of Mission* 59 (1970): 26.

[35]Hoekendijk, *Kirche und Volk*, 248.

[36]Hoekendijk, *Kirche und Volk*, 102.

theorists could find varying degrees of commonality with the ideology of National Socialism.[37]

The final link with National Socialism shows the significance of the issue, but it could lead one to view the problem of *Volk* as specifically German and not one that has wider theological significance. However, as the Ba'al metaphor suggests, Hoekendijk disagrees. He sees a continuity between the theological identification of Israel as a people and the related use of "people of God" terminology. The cultural concern, Hoekendijk argues, derived from precise theological supports. Theorists drew justification for the assumed relationship between church and *Volk* from the Old Testament. Israel constituted a *Volk* and developed its identity within the variety of cultural processes that correspond to those of *Volkchristianiserung*.[38] One finds here a "life association" (*Lebensverband*) in which the individual stands and must be christianized as a consequence of this cultural organization.[39] Hoekendijk finds this logic directing the wider ecumenical discussion.[40]

While certainly no synonym for the contemporary anthropological definitions of culture, *Volk* is part of a linguistic set including "culture" and "civilization."[41] And while *Volk* refers to the wider "national" or "ethnic" cultural milieu, for Hoekendijk, it builds on the myth of Christendom. The world and the church overlap in such a way as to fill the same horizon. The cultural difference of the church rests in its reification of this wider culture. As itself the interpretive criterion derived from the myth of Christendom, *Volk* determined the nature of conversion, set the standards of Christian maturity, established the methods by which this was achieved, transplanted certain necessary forms (ecclesial, educational, cultural—i.e., the structures

---

[37]Ibid., 133. By way of illustration, see the translation of the 1914 manifesto by twenty-nine theologians and missiologists in support of the military cause of the German *Volk* on the grounds that this would fulfill the missionary task of the 1910 Edinburgh Conference: "Appeal of German Churchmen and Professors to Protestant Christians in Foreign Lands (1914)," in David W. Congdon, *The Mission of Demythologizing: Rudolf Bultmann's Dialectical Theology* (Minneapolis: Fortress, 2015), 837-43. See further Congdon's discussion of the 1933 debate regarding the Aryan paragraph, in which the Erlangen school defended it on the grounds that the church was no longer a missionary church but instead a *Volkskirche*, and Bultmann's counterpoint that the church is always a missionary church, in Congdon, *Mission of Demythologizing*, 431-36.

[38]Hoekendijk, *Kirche und Volk*, 239.

[39]Ibid., 238.

[40]Ibid., 240.

[41]Ibid., 229.

needed for christianization) basic to such and reinforced this with theologies that build a sacral order around this cultural process.

5.3.3 Ecclesiocentrism: the church, alpha and omega. Hoekendijk summarizes the above ideas under the concept of "church-centrism," or "ecclesiocentrism" as it has become known.[42] The myth of Christendom and the interpretive ideology of *Volk* invest all theological significance in the church— or, rather, "the church." Nothing exists beyond it, and all is ordered in relation to it.[43] "The whole space at one's disposal is filled with ecclesiology. . . . The world has disappeared from the horizon."[44] Because it occupies this position, being both the means and the end of Christian witness, the church conceives itself as "God's secure bridgehead in the world . . . a *beatus possidens* which, having what others do not have, distributes its possession to others, until a new company of *possidentes* is formed."[45] The church has the solution already in and for itself and without which it would not be the body of Christ.

Ecclesiocentrism determines the appropriate mission method. The church is the true witness to the kingdom, and mission is "the road from the Church to the Church."[46] According to Hoekendijk's description of this position, "the Church is the ultimate object of the Mission and takes its place."[47] The church's external activities aim at "*churchification.*"[48] Mission, by this

---

[42]Hoekendijk does not himself often use the term "ecclesiocentrism" (Hoekendijk, *Kirche und Volk*, 331), which seems to have been first developed in J. C. Gilhuis, "Ecclesiocentrische aspecten van het zendingswerk met name bij de ontwikkeling daarvan in Indonesië, bijzonder op Midden-Java" (diss., Vrije Universiteit, 1955). Hoekendijk's own criticisms are often conceived as a reaction to the 1938 IMC Tambaram conference. He, for example, plays on the famous Tambaram summary: "How else should we interpret the famous oecumenical slogan 'Let the Church be the Church' than as 'Let the Church be the Mission'?" Hoekendijk, "Church in Missionary Thinking," 335. Tambaram certainly "rediscovered" the church as an entity distinct from the Western cultural milieu, but, for Hoekendijk, the problem was already characteristic of the 1928 IMC Jerusalem conference. Even while this conference "watered" the gospel "down to something like a 'religious message' . . . the Church was discussed at great length, with assured determination and *parrhesia.*" Ibid., 325. Though all other aspects of the gospel might fall away, the church remains. It is its own culture grounded in the myth of Christendom and pursuing the ideology of *Volk* in all its various iterations.

[43]See also Hoedemaker, "Die Welt als theologisches Problem," 9-20.

[44]J. C. Hoekendijk, "Die Welt als Horizont," *Evangelische Theologie* 25 (1965): 79.

[45]Hoekendijk, "Call to Evangelism," 170.

[46]Citing Johannes Dürr, *Sendende und werdende Kirche in der Missionstheologie Gustav Warneck's* (Basel: Basler Missionsbuchhandlung, 1947), 47. See Hoekendijk, "Church in Missionary Thinking," 324.

[47]Hoekendijk, "Church in Missionary Thinking," 326.

[48]Hoekendijk, "Call to Evangelism," 171.

definition, has no significance apart from its capacity to bear a religious culture, "a repetition outside of what happens inside, as an extension or repetition of the pastorate."[49] It consists of relocating established patterns of Christian maturity along with the (pedagogical, liturgical, hierarchical, structural) means by which such maturity is achieved. Mission reduces to proselytism, the demand that converts (and churches) take on a particular cultural form to be recognized as "mature" Christians. For this reason, Hoekendijk cautions against incorporating new members into existing churches because of "the closed and non-receiving character of many Churches which one cannot join unless one has endured a painful cultural circumcision."[50] This is the basis of Hoekendijk's oft-cited conclusion: *"Church-centric missionary thinking is bound to go astray, because it revolves around an illegitimate centre."*[51] To define mission in terms set by a residential understanding of the church is to produce a mission of cultural replication.

Hoekendijk extends this critique using two additional terms: "morphological fundamentalism" and "heretical structures." Defining the former, Hoekendijk states that,

> in its broadest sense, the combination of the term "morphological" and "fundamentalism" indicates a rigid and inflexible attitude toward the morphe (structure, "Gestalt") of the congregation similar to the attitude prevalent in "biblical fundamentalism." Consciously or, more often, unconsciously, the existent forms of the life of the Christian community are taken to be fixed once and for all.[52]

The myth of Christendom expresses itself ecclesially in a fundamentalist attitude toward structures. The structures become sacrosanct, excluded from critique. While theological assertions are allowed to range widely, church structures must conform to a narrow orthodoxy, especially since they are

---

[49]Hoekendijk, "Notes on the Meaning of Mission(-ary)," 45.
[50]Ibid., 46.
[51]Hoekendijk, "Church in Missionary Thinking," 332.
[52]J. C. Hoekendijk, "'Morphological Fundamentalism,'" in *Planning for Mission: Working Papers on the New Quest for Missionary Communities*, ed. Thomas Wieser (New York: U.S. Conference for the World Council of Churches, 1966), 134. According to Margull, the term "morphological fundamentalism" entered the discussion through Hans Schmidt; see Hans J. Margull, *Zeugnis und Dialog: Ausgewählte Schriften* (Ammersbek bei Hamburg: Verlag an der Lottbek, 1992), 110. Hoekendijk, however, notes that the 1958 dissertation of H. Beusekom developed the term six years prior. See Hoekendijk, *Kirche and Volk*, 328n58. Cf. J. H. van Beusekom, *Het experiment der gemeenschap: Een onderzoek naar plaats en functie van de 'orde' in de reformatorische kerken* (The Hague: Voorhoeve, 1958), 161-80.

seen as creating and sustaining Christian identity. Hoekendijk's preferred example is that of the territorial parish. Far from being part of the church's "original" structure, this was a contingent historical invention of the Middle Ages. Hoekendijk even says it was developed to serve "as a missionary structure, namely for the conquest of the countryside."[53] The parish became canonized as part of the myth of Christendom and its sacralizing of certain accidental developments within cultural history. This morphological fundamentalism affirms the necessity of the church's structural development beyond the New Testament, but it arbitrarily canonizes certain developments over against others. The canonization of contingent structures applies only to those that are canonized—the argument is tautological and serves only to exclude any further change. Contemporary developments, insofar as they might conflict with this canon, threaten the defining substance of the church.[54]

If morphological fundamentalism indicates the church securing a familiar cultural zone for itself into which it might retreat, the charge of "heretical structures" relates to the withdrawal of the church from history.[55] Heresy, in this context, does not refer to any inter-church conflict over doctrine. "Heresy is the fundamental refusal to participate in a common history."[56] The culture of the church is a culture of the past, with social structures that fail to speak to those not already enculturated into Christendom.[57] Converts must immigrate into this alternate culture, with the effect that they become lost to their own surroundings.[58] The heresy maintains the logic of the temple. Either the church participates in history or it

---

[53]Hoekendijk, *Church Inside Out*, 97.

[54]Margull notes, with regards to the notion of structural fundamentalism, how the historical development justification of structures does not apply to present developments in history. He describes the approach that "allows historicity for the past but regards with suspicion any historic consideration of the present and future" as a "surprising contradiction." Hans J. Margull, "Structures for Missionary Congregations," *International Review of Mission* 52, no. 4 (1963): 439.

[55]The term "heretical structures" developed within the WCC study titled *Missionary Structure of the Congregation* (MSC), being first mentioned by Roman Catholic sociologist Greinacher; see Margull, *Zeugnis und Dialog*, 114. This is confirmed in Colin W. Williams, *Where in the World? Changing Forms of the Church's Witness* (New York: National Council of the Churches of Christ in the U.S.A., 1963), 82n8. For a fuller development, see Eugene L. Stockwell, *Claimed by God for Mission: The Congregation Seeks New Forms* (New York: World Outlook Press, 1965), 19-34. For its use within the WCC study, see *The Church for Others, and the Church for the World: A Quest for Structures for Missionary Congregations* (Geneva: World Council of Churches, 1967), 19-20.

[56]Hoekendijk, *Kirche und Volk*, 348.

[57]Hoekendijk, "Call to Evangelism," 166.

[58]J. C. Hoekendijk, "Ende und Anfang der Verkündigung," *Quatember* 17, no. 2 (1953): 75.

removes itself and builds a temple structure around a specific cultural period and associated artifacts.

"Ecclesiocentrism" refers to the church defined by a sacralized and theologically codified culture that is closed to everything beyond itself. Its method of connection with what lies beyond its borders is the act of witnessing to the things contained within them. Mission becomes the task of replicating the structures, liturgies and order necessary to the primary witness of the church's culture. The endpoint, for Hoekendijk, is a church turned in on itself, "ecclesia in se incurvata."[59]

5.4 THE MESSIANIC APOSTOLATE

Hoekendijk uses the metaphor of Ba'al, the residential god of a particular location, to refer to a Christian heresy that determines the church's ecclesiology, including the orientation of its sacraments, liturgy and order and the corresponding mission method of propaganda. In Hoekendijk's estimation, this ecclesiology reduces the nature of continuity, including its understanding of authority and authenticity, to the cultural and the sacral order developed to protect this "ethnos." Hoekendijk opposes this residential Ba'al with the God of the exodus.[60] The move is decisive inasmuch as it conceives mission not in terms of geographical expansion but in terms of history. Hoekendijk develops this point with reference to the revision of mission method and theology that took place in response to the problem of colonialism. This reconstruction, he argues, succeeded only in reorganizing the fundamental logic. The attempt to redraw missionary boundaries so that they no longer correspond to continents but, citing Newbigin, to communities in "every land . . . living without the knowledge of Christ" nonetheless ended up defining missions according to "their receiving end; as frontier-crossing-movements towards 'unbelieving' communities."[61] When conceived in spatial terms, mission will remain a secondary concern shaped by and dependent on the replication of cultural territory. With the God of the exodus, by contrast,

---

[59]Hoekendijk, "Die Welt als Horizont," 84.
[60]Hoekendijk, "Mission—a Celebration of Freedom," 141.
[61]Hoekendijk, "Notes on the Meaning of Mission(-ary)," 40, citing J. E. Lesslie Newbigin, *One Body, One Gospel, One World: The Christian Mission Today* (London: International Missionary Council, 1958), 29.

it is essential to recognize *history as the decisive context of the* Mission: the God who is identified and known by His Mission, remains a non-residential God; He is not one of the ba'als. And, strictly speaking, [the person] who is touched by the Mission becomes equally non-residential; he [or she] can live on only as a sojourner and pilgrim: his [or her] land is historized into a "land of promise," his [or her] community into a "people of the promise."[62]

Hoekendijk turns to the apostolate as his primary category precisely because it defines the church's movement through history. It is, as such, one stage in a comprehensive eschatological logic. Though the WCC study *Missionary Structure of the Congregation* (MSC) would make famous the ordering "God–world–church," Hoekendijk prefers what he considers the biblical logic of "kingdom–gospel–apostolate–world."[63] This ordering is not a progression. It identifies different points within a single event: the encounter between the kingdom of God and the world. The church is a notable omission from this logic, appearing only as it is subsumed into the apostolate. Most of Hoekendijk's critics stumble at this point and reinsert a pattern of a historically continuous church with a contingent and geographically defined mission. Hoekendijk's basic concern, however, is conceiving the ground and goal of mission in the setting of history. This comes first from an understanding of Jesus Christ's own messianic apostolate. Christology, in other words, mandates a historical and not a geographical definition of mission.

5.4.1 A sign of the kingdom. Mission is only possible with the fulfillment of the messianic promise. It is "an eschatological *datum* par excellence. (Also literally: *datum* = gift)."[64] To understand what mission is, in other words, one

---

[62]Hoekendijk, "Notes on the Meaning of Mission(-ary)," 42.

[63]Hoekendijk, "Church in Missionary Thinking," 333. This is itself a development on the pattern outlined in his 1948 dissertation: "kingdom–Spirit–community–history." See Hoekendijk, *Kirche and Volk*, 244; J. C. Hoekendijk, "Mission in der Krise," *Evangelische Missions Zeitschrift* 6, no. 3 (1949): 7. He would also use the order "Kingdom–apostolate–oikoumene." Hoekendijk, *Church Inside Out*, 38. Though Hoekendijk nowhere offers a rationale for the change, one might suggest that his emphasis is always on the necessary movement of the community into history; that is, one should not constitute the community at a step removed from history. The "apostolate" indicates the being of the community in its history. As to the order of "God–world–church," according to Margull, it was developed by Georges Casalis. Margull, "Structures for Missionary Congregations," 445. Hoekendijk does, on rare occasion, use this formulation in his later work. Even here, however, the priority of the world over the church consists of the church forsaking any sacral order and developing its structures in relation to those found in the world. See *Kirche and Volk*, 344-45 and *Church Inside Out*, 71. For the MSC formula, see *Church for Others*, 16-17, 69-71.

[64]Hoekendijk, *Church Inside Out*, 165.

204   APOSTOLICITY

must first turn to the Old Testament, its telling of God's promises and the
signs of their presence: in the "fulness of time" the glory of the Lord will be
revealed to all peoples and the nations will turn to YHWH (Is 2:2; 11:10;
25:6-8; 40:5; 42:5; 45:6, 18; 55:5; Jer 16:19; Zech 8:20-23). This, Hoekendijk
maintains, is "nothing less than a messianic miracle, the eschatological acting
of YHWH himself, who comes to judge the nations."[65] Mission does not arise
out of some accidental historical ground such as the power of a particular
nation. It is itself a sign of eschatological expectation and fulfillment.

The New Testament confirms this logic. Mission is a "postulate of
eschatology."[66] It remains an act of God. The coming of the Gentiles to
YHWH cannot, as such, be "described as a progressively developing
universalism."[67] It is no natural possibility to be executed by natural means.
This is evident in Jesus Christ's messianic concentration on the people of
Israel. Only after the cross, resurrection and ascension is the way to the
Gentiles opened, because only then were the messianic promises fulfilled
and the new age a present reality. The command given in Matthew 28, with
its relationship to Daniel 7, confirms, for Hoekendijk, the presence of the
messianic eon and the form of fellowship in the coming kingdom.[68]

> It is the business of the Messiah to announce (gospel) and perform the de-
> cisive redeeming act of God; in the "last" (= decisive) days and in a universal
> context (to all nations, unto the ends of the earth); thus inaugurating the new
> order of the Spirit by establishing the Kingdom, offering "peace and salvation."
> Mission is the inner dynamic of this cluster, relating the different elements in
> a meaningful frame of reference; it is THE messianic event, by which history
> is brought to its destination.[69]

In the book of Acts, Hoekendijk argues, this includes the gift of the Spirit as
the presupposition of the mission to the Gentiles. Mission is inseparable from
Christology and pneumatology and receives its order from the acting of the
Son and the Spirit to establish the reign of God. This applies equally to ecclesiology, which "cannot be more than only one paragraph in christology."[70]

---

[65]Hoekendijk, *Kirche and Volk*, 235.
[66]Ibid., 232.
[67]Hoekendijk, *Church Inside Out*, 36.
[68]Hoekendijk, "Call to Evangelism," 167.
[69]Hoekendijk, "Notes on the Meaning of Mission(-ary)," 41.
[70]J. C. Hoekendijk, "Gesprek onder-weg," *In de Waagschaal* 6 (1951): 350.

Mission begins, in other words, not with some historical phenomena, but with the promises of God, their messianic fulfillment and the resulting signs of the present kingdom, namely, the turning of the Gentiles to the God of Israel.

This messianic context, Hoekendijk argues, establishes the "world" as the necessary correlate of the "kingdom." In contrast to the ecclesiocentric reduction of the "oikoumene" to inter-church relations (and the effect this has over such terms as koinonia), the New Testament defines it as the whole world that stands opposed to the gospel.[71] Hoekendijk conceives the world as a unity, the "living horizon" of God's great acts, the destination of the proclamation of the kingdom (2 Cor 5:19; Jn 3:16; 16:33; Mt 13:38).[72] It has its own existence separate from the church.

To recognize this is to set the church in a particular relationship with the world. Against the territorial reading that treats the world as "a sort of ecclesiastical training-ground," the church as the servant of the kingdom is determined by its service to the world.[73] The church exists within the eschatological relationship between the kingdom and the world. Hoekendijk rejects any notion that the church is either the starting point or the goal of mission. Defined by the context of the kingdom confronting the world, the church is without a "fixed place. . . . It *happens* in so far as it actually proclaims the kingdom to the world."[74] Though this is clearly a critique of the complex problem of ecclesiocentrism, it does not follow that Hoekendijk rejects the church as an entity. It is a positive statement of the church in light of the eschatological fullness that grounds its existence. "The Church has no other existence than *in actu Christi*, that is, *in actu Apostoli*. Consequently it cannot be firmly established but will always remain the *paroikia*, a temporary

---

[71]See, for example, the objections in J. C. Hoekendijk, "Mission und Oekumene," *Evangelisches Mission-magazin* 95 (1951): 145-56; Hoekendijk, "Die Welt als Horizont," 80-84.

[72]Hoekendijk, *Kirche und Volk*, 229.

[73]Hoekendijk, "Church in Missionary Thinking," 324. For an interesting survey on the interpretive issues surrounding "world" as a theological category in especially the theology of the apostolate, see Hoedemaker, "Die Welt als theologisches Problem," 9-20. He states, "One only views the church, and so this theology, correctly when one perceives it within the fundamental relationship of the kingdom of God and the world. Otherwise stated: eschatology precedes ecclesiology. There is a church because the coming kingdom of God exerts pressure over world occurrence [Weltgeschehen]. The first and most important thing which can be said about the church is that it is *sent* (*apostello*)" (9).

[74]Hoekendijk, "Church in Missionary Thinking," 334.

settlement which can never become a permanent home."[75] The church possesses no sacral order that might house a residential god; it exists only in the messianic establishment of the kingdom, and so only in history, in the encounter between the kingdom and the world, and so only in mission.

Hoekendijk illustrates this critical distinction between the church as a body *in actu Christi* and one gathered in service to the residential god by reference to the supposed solution to missionary imperialism, namely, to the development of autochthonous churches, indigenous "people's churches."[76] If a church might become autochthonous, so the logic goes, it follows that the associated mission method and ecclesiology cannot be described in simple imperialistic terms. Cultural conservatism was presumed to be the opposite of an imperial mission method. However, first, the problem of imperialism was exactly that of promoting a form of cultural conservatism, meaning, second, that the local church received space to express itself only as long as it conformed to the pattern embodied by the sending church. This was supposed to be achieved through the use of "allegedly 'universal' patterns," which, in the final reckoning, "are simply 'western.'"[77] The end result maintains the residential procedure of retreating from "history" and into "churchdom." Alternately stated, this approach to autochthony trades on the church forgetting its transitory character. The church has "designed its own history, a reserve into which it might now retreat."[78] Hoekendijk counters that "only in so far as the Church shares in the mission of the Apostles, only in so far as it is on the way towards the ends of the earth and the end of time, does it remain 'autochthonous.'" Autochthony rests in Christ, who is not a "new Moses" but a "second Adam (Rom. 5:12; 1 Cor. 15:22, 45)" who gathers his community as the advent of a new humanity (Eph 2:14ff.).[79] To be autochthonous is to be native to Christ and so concentrated on the gospel's appropriation in the creation of this new humanity.

Defining the church as participant in the eschatological confrontation of the world by the kingdom for the salvation of the *oikoumene* leads Hoekendijk to his now infamous conclusion: "The nature of the Church can be

---

[75]Ibid.
[76]See Hoekendijk, "Church in Missionary Thinking," 328-30.
[77]Ibid., 330.
[78]Hoekendijk, "Die Welt als Horizont," 83.
[79]Hoekendijk, "Church in Missionary Thinking," 334.

sufficiently defined by its *function*, i.e. its participation in Christ's apostolic ministry. To proclaim the gospel of the kingdom throughout the *oikoumene* is the Church's *opus proprium*, in fact, it is not her work at all but *ergon Kyriou*."[80] "Function," in this sense, does not refer to a simple activism. The church's essence and purpose (i.e., its function) rests in and serves the messianic fulfilling of the whole of creation, in the eschatological mission of the kingdom. It is without a (residential) givenness that might become the focus of its message as a thing in itself and that reduces mission to a process of replicating the cultural artifacts constitutive of the church. To follow this path is to interpret *Credo ecclesiam apostolicam* as "I believe in the Church, which has an apostolic function."[81] Hoekendijk reverses the order. The church is "a function of the Apostolate, that is, an instrument of God's redemptive action in this world. . . . It is (nothing more, but also nothing less!) a means in God's hands to establish shalom in this world."[82] God in Christ, in God's acting in and for the world, forms the church as an instrument for God's purposes. Apart from this, the church has neither basis nor reason to exist.

5.4.2 *Apostolicity follows the apostolate.* The fulfillment of the messianic promises, the present eschatological context, establishes the apostolate as the form of human participation in the kingdom. Inasmuch as the kingdom confronts the world, so it is basic to the gospel that it must be proclaimed. It follows, for Hoekendijk, that

> *the Gospel and the Apostolate belong intrinsically together.* Through the apostolate the gospel comes to "fulfilment" (Rom. 15:19; cf. Col. 1:24) and is brought to its destination. In the *apostolate* God continues to struggle with the world for the sake of the world. Its *subject* is "the Apostle Jesus" (Heb. 3:1); the "deeds of Christ" (Matt. 11:2) are continued in the apostolic "works of the Lord" (1 Cor. 15:58; 16:10).[83]

Characterized by and derivative of Christology, the apostolate is bound to the work of the Spirit (Jn 20:12). "The time of the Spirit is the time of the apostolate."[84] The apostolate is, again, nothing other than God's own work.

---

[80]Ibid.

[81]Hoekendijk, "Call to Evangelism," 170.

[82]Ibid.

[83]Hoekendijk, "Church in Missionary Thinking," 334.

[84]Hoekendijk, "Mission in der Krise," 6.

The human response consists of participation in Jesus Christ's apostolic sending. The apostles are themselves "messengers of the eschaton, proclaimers of the near day of the Lord (Isa. 52:1, cited in Rom. 10:13-19), who declare the fulfillment of the messianic promises (Isa. 49:8 cited in 2 Cor. 6:1f.)."[85] They do this only as captives in God's triumphal procession. With God being "apostolic," and with those called by God taking the corresponding form of apostolic service, so the apostolate has both a chronological and theological priority over apostolicity.[86]

Hoekendijk develops the apostolate with only minimal reference to the tradition concerning apostolicity. Apostolicity appears to be a theological control in support of the residential god and the associated heretical withdrawal from history. The "biblical order" (i.e., the eschatological order found in both the Old and New Testaments), Hoekendijk maintains, does not make the apostolate dependent on the church—the church is instead taken up in the apostolate.[87] Any concern for apostolicity, understood as authenticity, must follow this order. The church is the church of this apostolic God only when it lets itself be used in God's missionary movement. "Its apostolicity (in its doctrine as in its church order) must prove itself in the apostolate."[88] This includes the need to think of the church as "an apostolic event before we can even think of it as an institution."[89] Without following the commission given to the apostles, the church cannot understand what they taught. Only as the community "acts *with* the apostles" does it "stand in apostolic succession."[90] Such succession, in other words, is not the reserve of a few especially called individuals—the "*whole* community stands in the apostolate."[91]

---

[85]Hoekendijk, *Kirche und Volk*, 236.

[86]Ibid., 346.

[87]Hoekendijk, "Mission in der Krise," 5.

[88]Hoekendijk, *Kirche und Volk*, 346.

[89]Hoekendijk, "Church in Missionary Thinking," 336.

[90]J. C. Hoekendijk, "Mission—Heute!," in *Mission—Heute! Zeugnisse holländischen Missionsdenkens: Vorgetragen auf einer Tagung des Bruderringes evangelischer Missionsseminare und des Studentenbundes für Mission in Oegstgeest bei Leiden, 23.—28. Mai 1953* (Bethel: Studentenbund für Mission, 1954), 9.

[91]Hoekendijk, "Mission—Heute!," 9. Hoekendijk illustrates this by contrasting the liturgy for confirmands in the "old" churches with that practiced by the Church of South India. With the former, the bishop lays hands on the confirmand and gives them the mission command to go into all the world. With the latter, the confirmand lay his or her own hands on the head and states, "Woe to me if I do not preach the gospel" (9-10).

As to the form of the apostolate, because the Messiah makes the Gentile mission possible, so the form of mission must correspond to the life of the Messiah. It must follow the *"Messianic life-pattern"* of election, witness, service, self-identification and suffering. As the "apostolate is participation in the apostleship of Jesus Christ," so it occurs by adopting "the pattern of the life of the servant."[92] Nor is this a mere possibility that may or may not be actualized. The apostolate has an involuntary and absolute character. Following Philippians 2:5-11, kenosis shapes Hoekendijk's positive account of missionary practice.[93] When the church claims something for itself, it begins to exist in and for itself. This departs from the Messiah's own form of existence—he neither claimed equality with God for himself nor withheld part of himself from his mission. Likewise, the church cannot "only be *partly* circumscribed by the 'Apostolate.'"[94] The church exists for the world. Fashioning its own life after the messianic pattern means that it "will have to *empty* itself, to practice kenosis . . . mortifying its ecclesial stature and status, in order that it may 'bear human likeness and be revealed in human shape.'"[95] In other words, Hoekendijk applies kenosis also to structures. The apostolate, the encounter between the kingdom and the world, determines the church as a body shaped for service.

---

[92]Hoekendijk, *Church Inside Out*, 88.

[93]Ibid., 71, 89.

[94]Hoekendijk, "Church in Missionary Thinking," 331.

[95]Hoekendijk, "Notes on the Meaning of Mission('-ary)," 44. Donald MacKinnon develops an almost identical argument, applying kenosis to ecclesiology and understanding it as basic to the renewal of mission. He talks of a "fundamentalism" and the ecclesiological and liturgical forms that are "at least as deadly" as the biblical variety. Donald M. MacKinnon, "Kenosis and Establishment," in *The Stripping of the Altars* (London: Collins, 1969), 19. With reference to Kirk's *The Apostolic Ministry*, MacKinnon states that "the deadly evils which characterized the Anglo-Catholicism of the early forties . . . are of course part of the built-in inheritance of the Constantinian Church, the Church whose status is guaranteed and which allows the manner of that guarantee (the exercise by the civil power of a measure of external compulsive activity) to invade the substance of her life" (25). He cautions against "the cultivation of the status of invulnerability, issuing in a devotion to the structures that preserve it" (33). MacKinnon is unconvinced by the apologetic that finds the "public confirmation of Christ's victory . . . in the stabilities of a so-called Christian order" (36-37), and he counters by calling for "the radical application of the law of *kenosis* to the evaluation of its present institutional life" (28) and an accompanying "demythologization of the highly questionable myth of apostolic succession" (29). His concluding position bears all the hallmarks of Hoekendijk's own: the Christian is to live in the world today an "exposed life; [one] stripped of the kind of security that tradition, whether ecclesiological or institutional, easily bestows" (34). See further Timothy G. Connor, *The Kenotic Trajectory of the Church in Donald MacKinnon's Theology: From Galilee to Jerusalem to Galilee* (London: T&T Clark, 2011).

This emptying, Hoekendijk continues, itself takes positive form in relation to the "substance" of the apostolate. Because it takes place within the
oikoumene, it will establish "signs of kingdom-salvation, i.e. *shalom*."[96] Following the definition found in Psalm 85, shalom is more than "personal
salvation," being, at once, "peace, integrity, community, harmony and
justice."[97] So grounded within this Old Testament framework, the form that
mission takes corresponds to what Israel expected of the Messiah—he will
establish shalom. "Shalom is the briefest and, at the same time, the fullest
summary of all the gifts of the messianic era: even the name of the Messiah
can simply be: shalom (Mi. 5:3[-5]; Eph. 2:4); the gospel is a gospel of shalom
(Eph. 6:15) and the God proclaimed in this gospel can often be called the
God of shalom."[98] Shalom, for Hoekendijk, summarizes the New Testament
concept of salvation: the life in the new eon (Jn 14:27), Christian sending (Jn
20:21), the preaching of apostles (Acts 10:36), the calling to be Christ's am-
bassadors and proclaiming the day of shalom (2 Cor 5:20; 6:1-2). "Shalom-
ization," which Hoekendijk prefers to "humanization," is a social event undertaken with co-humanity.[99] By extension, it cannot "be reduced to a
simple formula, to be applied in all occurring instances: it must be found
and worked out in actual situations."[100] This is, of course, the point at which
a number of complaints develop. Hoekendijk appears to sacrifice the concrete, visible and historical church to an amorphous missionary movement.
If shalom is the substance of the apostolate, how does he conceive the church
as a living, gathered community?

EXCURSUS: LUDWIG RÜTTI ON THE RELATIONSHIP OF ECCLESIOCENTRISM TO APOSTOLICITY

For all the emphasis he places on the apostolate, Hoekendijk simply avoids the
wider tradition concerning apostolicity. For an application of Hoekendijk's
theology of the apostolate to apostolicity, one turns to the work of Catholic
theologian Ludwig Rütti. Rütti, writing in 1972, finds immediate correspondences between the problem of ecclesiocentrism and its concomitant mission

---

[96]Hoekendijk, "Church in Missionary Thinking," 334.
[97]Hoekendijk, "Call to Evangelism," 168.
[98]Hoekendijk, "Notes on the Meaning of Mission(-ary)," 43.
[99]Hoekendijk, *Kirche und Volk*, 346-47.
[100]Hoekendijk, "Notes on the Meaning of Mission(-ary)," 43.

method and developments within twentieth century Catholic theology. His entry point is Pierre Charles (1883–1954), professor of dogmatics and missiology at Löwen in Belgium, and Charles's "plantation" theory of mission.[101] This approach, Charles himself suggests, is the logical culmination of various Catholic assumptions concerning the nature of the church.[102] The church is itself the true witness and the bearer of salvation. The missionary task, by extension, consists of "erecting the church there where it is not yet present, and, with this, to always further extend its area of effect."[103] Since the visible church is defined in juridical-institutional terms, what is erected includes "gathering rooms, chapels, shrines, monasteries, manses, religious objects, cemeteries. It must be securely grounded in the soil. A nomadic church is without duration."[104] The church's future depends on the continuity and visibility of these given structures. Mission consists of "planting" these structures, for, once established in another geographical setting, they constitute a lasting entrance for all people to receive the Word and the sacraments.

According to Rütti, this approach reflects an underlying assumption in Catholic theology. Even while Vatican II spoke of the church as the "people of God" and a community before jurdically defined institution, Vatican II failed to address the fundamental problem of ecclesiocentrism.[105] This occurred, Rütti maintains, because the church is assumed to be an absolute in relation to the world and to history. The church is itself "the divine form of the world," meaning that it already possesses a culture capable of integrating the world.[106] "As the 'family of God' and the 'body of Christ' it is a fellowship which, going back to its very origins, transcends all other human groupings, and for that very reason can represent a universal and new people, whose boundaries

---

[101]See also Giancarlo Collet, *Das Missionsverständnis der Kirche in der gegenwärtigen Diskussion* (Mainz: Matthias-Grünewald-Verlag, 1984), 101-3. For a consideration of Charles's theory in relation to that of Joseph Schmidlin and its significant for such theorists as Henri de Lubac, see Andreas Seumois, *Auf dem Wege zu einer Definition der Missionstätigkeit* (Möchengladbach: Kühlen, 1948), 9-14. For a positive evaluation of Charles, see Ronan Hoffman, "The Development of Mission Theology in the Twentieth Century," *Theological Studies* 23, no. 3 (1962): 422-24.

[102]Ludwig Rütti, *Zur Theologie der Mission: Kritische Analysen und neue Orientierungen* (Munich: Chr. Kaiser Verlag, 1972), 26.

[103]Rütti, *Zur Theologie der Mission*, 26, citing Pierre Charles, *Dossiers de l'action missionnaire* (Louvain-Bruxelles: Editions de L'Aucam, 1938), no. 35, 4.

[104]Rütti, *Zur Theologie der Mission*, 27, citing Charles, *Dossiers de l'action missionnaire*, no. 35, 2.

[105]Rütti, *Zur Theologie der Mission*, 28.

[106]Ibid., 29, citing Pierre Charles, *Études missiologiques* (Bruges: Desclee de Brouwer, 1956), 37.

should coincide with those of the world."[107] Mission has the single task of exploiting this integrative culture to facilitate "the growth of the church to its full form, until it is identical with the geographical borders of humanity."[108] When it comes to the question of contextualization and the accommodation of cultural diversity within the church, Rütti notes how, first, this is subject to the prior processes of christianization and the establishment of church structures, and second, it takes place within an ordering of a higher Western culture over against the lower cultures found in primitive tribes. The quest for diversity does not challenge the underlying mission method, derived as it is from fundamental theories concerning the nature and order of the church.

Rütti criticizes this ecclesiocentrism in mission theory on three related grounds. First, it is triumphalist. Because it judges everything already in relation to the church, the church and its interests remain at the forefront of all thinking. Second, it slides toward institutionalism. Rütti admits the good that hospitals and schools have done, but he laments the legacy of associating Christian life with the full church apparatus as developed in the lands of *corpus Christianum*. Not only is this beyond the means of the local churches, but Christianity itself is then viewed as the religion of the "white man" and experienced as part of the "authority and in the cultural form of the West."[109] Thus, third, ecclesiocentric mission method implies a Christendom model of the church. Terms like "Christian civilization" and "Christian society" involve an integration of the church with the structures of colonial power. This integration might not be political, but there still exists an assumption of stability and hierarchy, one archetypical for the whole of human society—a wider "theocratic order" so embedded within worldly institutions that it characterizes the political system.[110] In short, Western Christianity, with its historically developed doctrines and systems, is transported to peoples outside the West who need to receive these passively as gifts and who, by extension, have nothing to offer. Ecclesiocentrism, grounded as it is in orthodox "catholic" ecclesiology, determines a mission method otherwise termed colonialization.

---

[107]Rütti, *Zur Theologie der Mission*, 30.
[108]Ibid., 30.
[109]Ibid., 34.
[110]Ibid., 36.

Turning to formal definitions of apostolicity, Rütti examines how these negatively determine the nature and place of mission within the church. While the concept in its original usage coordinated both ecclesiology and mission, with the early church's struggles against gnosticism and movements for reform, it sought to secure the interpretation of the faith and church order against internal disagreements, becoming a theological expression of an inner-church problematic. This, in turn, produced a mission theory that "is nothing other than the extension and extrapolation" of this problematic.[111] According to this missionary method, mission is only concerned with erecting in foreign lands the structures and institutions necessary for guaranteeing the unchanging identity of the church. More than this, this mission method is itself necessary to the church's historical continuity, its "apostolicity." Rütti objects because the New Testament presents neither a unilinear nor a uniform understanding of office or order. No simple path connects the apostle to the bishop, and the development of such an order within the early church is of such historical complexity that it should permit some dogmatic openness toward the diversity of organization evident within the New Testament and in history.

Though Hoekendijk ignores the tradition surrounding apostolicity, Rütti uses it to draw the same connections between ecclesiology, mission method and the processes of colonization. He traces this, furthermore, to the elimination of the mission sensibility from apostolicity, the resulting prioritization of the church as institution and the reduction of continuity to the hierarchical and sacramental elements that developed to support this lopsided emphasis.

5.5 EXODUS: A PLURALITY OF FORM

Though Hoekendijk devotes little attention to apostolicity, his conception of the church within the apostolate mandates its own structural controls. In correspondence to the exodus-God, the exodus, both as liberation and as journey, informs the church's shape in its eschatological and missionary path. "The church begins with the exodus; it begins with a departure from all these fixed attachments, and it can only remain as an exodus community church, constantly ready to collapse its tents in order to remain in the age."[112]

---

[111]Ibid., 46.
[112]Hoekendijk, "Kirche," 103.

Behind this openness to revision remains Hoekendijk's opposition to Ba'al and the problem of the residential god. No positive ecclesiology can be grounded in a "fixed *geo*location."[113] All one can do is "mark a route, a *via*," with all the provisionality this language connotes. A positive ecclesiology could never consist of "something like a recipe book or a set of blueprints."[114] To be sure, Hoekendijk promotes a plurality of form unsatisfactory to many ecclesial traditions, but when considered in light of the criticisms issued against him, he does not neglect the body. He developed a detailed account of the church as guided by its ground in the eschatological apostolate.

5.5.1 Mission, the rule not the exception. Hoekendijk begins his reconstruction at a perhaps surprising point: the "people of God." After dismantling the manner in which the modern and romantic concept of *Volk* traded on a secularized version of the concept, Hoekendijk warns in 1948 against a further misuse in the "new ecclesiological consensus."[115] Based on a presumed "rediscovery of the original Christian concept," this approach sought to purify the church of all things deemed secondary and foreign.[116] By way of illustration, he references how developments within Lutheranism used "people of God" language to prioritize ecclesiology over even the "eschatological context of mission." Such developments conceived the biblical language of the "people of God" as indicating a stage beyond the first missionary movement, a settled and already integrated culture, with the consequence, in Hoekendijk's estimation, that it reflected more a notion of "people" assumed within German culture.[117]

Hoekendijk, in contrast, prefers the "people of God" image because of its eschatological setting and thus its potential "to localize the church within the biblical context of mission."[118] As the people of God, the church is neither a continuation of creation nor identical with a particular people, and so is not bound to any particular sense of community (*Gemeinschaftsgefühl*). In the new covenant, the people of God is gathered as a new community of the messianic age. "The church is a sign of the already inbreaking end, an

---

[113]Hoekendijk, *Kirche und Volk*, 340.
[114]Hoekendijk, *Church Inside Out*, 70.
[115]Hoekendijk, *Kirche und Volk*, 240.
[116]Ibid.
[117]Ibid., 241.
[118]Ibid.

organ of the kingdom of God that has come and is coming, the 'temple of the Spirit,' the messianic *Volk*, and (as such) the 'body of Christ.'"[119] It is, in short, a "sociological impossibility," a novum in which "ethnic, linguistic and national moments" appear only on the periphery.[120] This receives paradigmatic expression, Hoekendijk concludes, in Paul's vision of the church as a community of Jews and Greeks.

Hoekendijk does not conceive mission apart from the life of the community. He can, to be sure, state that the church has "no model of an 'exemplary existence.'"[121] This denial results from his understanding of shalom, which can never be a possession, something associated with a particular locality. But this does not contradict the contrary affirmation that the community, in its wholeness, is "the entity of proclamation [*Verkündigungseinheit*]," and its "first and fundamental service" is to exist "in an 'exemplary way' (Barth)" and by this to erect "a sign of the coming kingdom," that is, shalom.[122] The people of the new covenant are constituted in the fulfillment of the messianic promises, becoming a sociological reality only in the missionary encounter with the world. Because the people of God is a novum of the new creation, its structure depends on the "missionary situation." And, since mission is basic to the Christian gospel, no occasion or location exists that might be characterized as non-missionary. "The gospel presents itself as a missionary message, . . . and we do not possess it in any other way. Wherever the gospel arrives, there a 'mission situation' emerges. Not just here and there, but universally! Not just now and then, but permanently!"[123] Mission is not an occasional endeavor motivated by some external reason, and structure is not a given that exists apart from missionary encounter.

Hoekendijk questions the idea that mission is an exception within church order. "Usually the argument runs somewhat as follows: the mission church has its place in the simple, experimental beginning stage of the church, during which obviously the maximum flexibility must be observed and a definite organization must be delayed."[124] Once this stabilizes into the church, with

---

[119]Ibid., 344.
[120]Ibid., 345, 243.
[121]Hoekendijk, "Notes on the Meaning of Mission(-ary)," 44.
[122]Hoekendijk, *Kirche und Volk*, 291.
[123]Hoekendijk, *Church Inside Out*, 94-95.
[124]Ibid., 96.

Europe the representative example, flexibility is warranted only in "exceptional" circumstances (e.g., with students, prisoners or the military). As to when an exceptional circumstance occurs, the judgment is based on "the clerical devaluation of the term 'mission situation.' . . . [A] situation is meant in which the church does not yet function normally through the offices."[125] A set institutional framework provides the norm beside which all other instances become exceptions, and so excluded from the narrative of historical continuity. Such flexibility of church order determines also the "foreign" missionary context, Hoekendijk continues, based on the perceived immaturity of the hearers. Once a proper level of maturity is attained, it is hoped that the traditional distinctions would become relevant and affirmed. The entire approach trades on conceiving mission in geographical and occasional terms and in relation to an office, the presence or absence of which determines whether something qualifies as an "exception" (i.e., subject to missionary flexibility).

Hoekendijk rejects this arbitrary notion of exception on two grounds. First, the very identification of a situation as an exception presupposes a contrasting rule in the same way that calling something "abnormal" assumes a corresponding "normal." In this case, the rule is a residential account of the church. But this prevents one from seeing the ostensibly "exceptional" situation as perhaps indicative of a different rule altogether. "Events are called 'unique' and so are isolated and kept outside the formulas; all things seem to be lined up to prevent the facts from ever being seen as precedents. The emergency at hand may not be evaluated as a continuum."[126] It is an instance of double bookkeeping used to maintain a certain appearance of continuity. Second, as the church exists in the eschatological encounter between the kingdom and the world, so the missionary gospel determines its life and order. What is "admissible *extra muros* [outside the walls], for the sake of the salvation of the nations, will have to be legitimately possible *intra muros* [within the walls]. . . . What is often admitted as an exception to the rule in a missionary situation (and then often only demurely and with all kinds of ulterior thoughts) should be valid as the normal and acknowledged

---

[125]Ibid.
[126]Ibid., 161.

rule of church order."[127] The diversity that characterizes missionary flexibility, which is often the result of "remarkable differences in cultural background," should also be a general principle of church order.[128]

5.5.2 *The contextual structure of the apostolate.* If we integrate these supposed missionary exceptions into church history, it becomes apparent that structural variety is a normative part of the church's past and present existence. Already "in the New Testament we find different fundamental types of ecclesiology beside one another, which cannot be simply harmonized." This "stunning range of variation" itself expresses the liberation found in Jesus Christ.[129] No sacral order exists. No structure possesses an "ontological status."[130] The church is without a "private sociology."[131] All structures are demonstrable and provisional developments within the history of the church. This does not, however, render them unimportant. The church is placed in history and must find itself here. Structures remain, to use Hoekendijk's language, a "function of hope" and an expression of the "obedience of faith."[132] Precisely as such, they are contingent and situationally variable. The biblical, historical and missionary evidence, according to Hoekendijk, all support a contextual approach to church order.

The contemporary context invites a pluriformity of structure. The church should assume "various—yes, even mutually contrasting—forms."[133] As to where the church might draw its inspiration for its structures, Hoekendijk turns to the "world." He does not advocate an indiscriminate approach. Only insofar as they are "usable," insofar as they are "structures-for-others," should the church take shape according to "available worldly structures."[134] This draws attention to the laity as basic to the apostolate, for only the laity can truly be "worldly." They stand "visible in God's shop-window in the world."[135] Though the language of the apostolate and the associated need to structure the church suggest a certain

---

[127]Ibid., 159.

[128]Ibid., 158. In relation to the reality of church order in other cultural contexts, Hoekendijk observes that "it is nonsense to behave in New Guinea as if one were in the Netherlands. We have accepted this pluralism for a long time" (78).

[129]Hoekendijk, "Kirche," 102.

[130]Hoekendijk, *Kirche und Volk*, 345.

[131]Ibid., 344.

[132]Hoekendijk, "Notes on the Meaning of Mission(-ary)," 46.

[133]Hoekendijk, *Church Inside Out*, 78.

[134]Hoekendijk, *Kirche und Volk*, 346.

[135]Ibid., 349.

energy, "activism" is not an accurate descriptor of Hoekendijk's position. The lay apostolate does not consist of "*something to do*" but is a matter of being present.[136] The church should serve this presence by being an actor in history. It must not withdraw from the cultural milieus it is called to serve by standing still. It is called to be a participant in the economy of "main street."[137] The laity, liberated by the gospel, are the ones who determine the church's structures.

While the language of "presence" lacks precision, Hoekendijk offers a guiding historical model for this approach, namely, the vision of the church developed by August Francke, Nicolaus Zinzendorf and the early John Wesley. It is not their form of piety that interests Hoekendijk but their rediscovery of the kingdom of God and the manner in which this stimulated their emphasis on mission and their functional approach to church structure. "All three agreed on this point: Christ is present and at work in the whole world. We have only to follow him in our universal mission of peace, and this mission can only be fulfilled by small, flexible, mobile groups of dedicated members who live in commitment and disponibilité—availability."[138] Hoekendijk distills this into five aspects: mobility, diversity in approach (with a stress on "presence"), laity, small groups and cooperation.[139]

In one of the only passages where Hoekendijk examines the relationship of apostolicity to the apostolate, he draws this logic together.[140] On no account should a church body seek to return to the time of the apostles. The "historicity of the gospel" renders it impossible to repeat the apostolic witness or to copy the model of the original community. Faithfulness to the apostles means making one's way in the "apostolic situation," which in concrete terms means "participating in the work of the apostles."[141] Wesley emerges as a key representative. His rediscovery of the gospel's missionary context occasioned by his mission to the Americas illustrates how the apostolate is necessary for apostolicity. It is the "hermeneutical key" that opens the scriptural text. This,

---

[136]Hoekendijk, *Church Inside Out*, 125.
[137]One example Hoekendijk gives is the East Harlem Protestant Parish in New York. See Hoekendijk, *Kirche und Volk*, 353-54. While it is, in his estimation, impossible to romanticize this community, turning it into an ideal, it did gather under the express intention to be a missionary community.
[138]Hoekendijk, "Christ and the World," 79.
[139]See Hoekendijk, *Church Inside Out*, 124-25.
[140]Hoekendijk, "Die Welt als Horizont," 74-75.
[141]Ibid., 74.

for Hoekendijk, is of normative significance: something is "apostolic" when it is used by the apostolate, as seen in Wesley's search for inductive and pragmatic structures for his missionary community. Hoekendijk rejects Wesley's later attempt to justify these structures by reference to the early church. Their apostolic justification rests in their functionality and not in any potential identity with the early Christian model. "The 'apostolic church' is found-in-formation, more a task and a commission than a given and a fact."[142] In short, as the apostolate is the way and norm for apostolicity, so history is free for improvisation and experimentation. No "principle" governs apostolicity (including the principle of identity with the apostolic church). Apostolicity is always a contextual matter, determined by its usability in the apostolate.

5.5.3 The house church and its order. As the apostolate first belongs to the laity, so Hoekendijk regards it as a task for the congregation. "The congregation is the bearer of the apostolate, and she will have to make the Word and thus also the apostolate credible through her existence and life, through word and deed."[143] The congregation, which Hoekendijk envisions as a small group, is necessary to the cultivation of a communion strong enough to offset the homogenizing forces of a post-industrial and urban society. Each congregation must itself witness to the kingdom.

Within a context of perpetual change, the most suitable form for such witness is that of the house church. Hoekendijk enlists no lesser an authority than Luther to make his case. In his "Preface to the German Mass," Luther presents the house church as a legitimate ecclesial form, one complete with Word and sacrament, prayer and offering. Hoekendijk acknowledges that these also appear within the established church, but in a house church they take place "in a context where supervision is possible, in a group where everyone knows one another and therefore can admonish one another."[144] Hoekendijk grants that while house churches are subject to their own temptations—because they are less occupied with ritualized accompaniments, such as singing, and allow the sacraments to be celebrated "in a brief and fine way"—they better direct Christian life "toward Word, prayer, and mutual love."[145]

---

[142]Ibid., 75.
[143]Hoekendijk, *Church Inside Out*, 66.
[144]Ibid., 93.
[145]Ibid., 94.

This internal shift should find corresponding architectural expression: from "sacral architecture" to a "fellowship house."[146] While people should be able to "see" the witness of the church, such visibility is not contingent on a "sacral space . . . separate and different from the world." As opposed to the cathedral, which is "symbolic of a stable society, a permanent rest point from which Christ the King stretches his hands out in blessing to all of life," the chapel best expresses the liturgy of diakonia (service). This is a "moveable house, a sort of tabernacle, which in a previous era was carried along into battle. It can easily be dismantled and moved so that it can be where the people are. This is the symbol of an era of mobility!"[147] Hoekendijk opposes neither form nor institution but maintains these as contextual developments directed to the church's service in the world.

The house church structure, in his estimation, lends itself to the development of "categorical churches," churches "which—in distinction from the parish (= territorially determined congregation)—are orientated toward groups in society that do not have to live together in a 'cadastrally defined area.'"[148] These might appear within the armed services, in hospitals, offices, factories or apartment buildings, and should be considered neither "abnormal" nor "interim." Such judgments stem from notions of exception and from the perception that a traditional form of office is necessary. Hoekendijk regards a categorical church as "*a common and completely normal variety of church life.*"[149]

To create space for the categorical church, Hoekendijk addresses the dominance of the parish. Its original development matched the patterns and rhythms of life of its context. From this "incidental pattern it became a normative model; from a historically conditioned phenomenon it became an unchangeable divine institution."[150] Now canonized, contemporary urban

---

[146]Ibid., 82.

[147]Ibid., 83.

[148]Ibid., 197-98n1. With this language, Hoekendijk is again criticizing the idea of defining the church in geographical terms. A related idea to that of "categorical" made famous by the MSC is "Zonal Structures." See *Church for Others*, 31-33; Western European Working Group, "Zonal Structures for the Church," in *Planning for Mission: Working Papers on the New Quest for Missionary Communities*, ed. Thomas Wieser (New York: U.S. Conference for the World Council of Churches, 1966), 208-14.

[149]Hoekendijk, *Church Inside Out*, 96.

[150]Ibid., 98.

congregations are expected to disrupt their normal rhythms—and such disruption becomes codified as a necessary discipling element drawing the individual into the culture of the church. Hoekendijk further charges that the parish presumes a "stable society" and is conceived "*exclusively for the* '*conserving*,' and not for the 'outreaching', ministry."[151] This does not mean that Hoekendijk rejects the parish as a model. He objects to its being the *only* model of the church, beside which other models appear incomplete, less refined. His pluriform approach, which grants multiple and even contradictory forms, permits the existence also of the parish. Nevertheless, within the contemporary urban context, the parish model does not best serve, and may even hinder, the apostolate.

In addition to his well-known criticisms of the parish, Hoekendijk questioned how office itself informs mission.[152] He notes how perhaps the concept of a "mission church (i.e., the lay community in the vanguard)" might be considered "acceptable," but it would be so only as a "forecourt, 'a preliminary form of the church', a halfway house between the world and the church. In order to be and to remain fully the church of Jesus Christ, an additional factor is needed . . . [one] called 'the office.'"[153] Hoekendijk objects, not because he denies office a place, but because, first, the only constitutive office is that of Jesus Christ. "This office is the prerequisite for the church. It is not added to it, but precedes it."[154] Jesus Christ gathers people into his office, making them into a missionary body. This holds true, Hoekendijk argues, also in relation to the Spirit, for where the Spirit gives its gifts, there the church is complete. Second, office should be regulated by the primary apostolic service of the laity. Office serves the laity in their mission and thus needs to be both "concrete and contextual," defined by the location and the demands encountered there.[155]

---

[151]Ibid., 99.

[152]Another example Hoekendijk gives concerns the church calendar. The church did not produce a fifty-two-week, seven-day calendar. It found it in society. Today, according to Hoekendijk, "the calendar of an industrial society has come to look different" (*Church Inside Out*, 82). To retain the old calendar amounts to putting the sabbath before the person, imposing it "upon people to make time for God." As an alternative, Hoekendijk proposes "ten or fifteen 'Christ days' per year, festive occasions, and in between gatherings at times when people are really there." Ibid., 82.

[153]Ibid., 100.

[154]Ibid.

[155]Hoekendijk, *Kirche und Volk*, 350.

In terms of the Lord's Supper, Hoekendijk proposes an "open communion." Drawing on his own experiences within Holland, he questions services that begin by first removing those who are not members.[156] This, in Hoekendijk's estimation, reflects an attempt to detach practices intended for service to the apostolate and to reserve them for a carved-out sphere of the church. Drawing on 1 Corinthians 11, Hoekendijk warns against the "kind of sacramentalists who had staked everything on the Lord's Supper," who celebrated it "frequently and gladly" and perhaps even correctly from a "liturgical point of view" but who reduced it to an "isle of safety on which to withdraw from life—very pious, but a devoutness without hands and feet, which did not make a bit of difference in daily behavior."[157] The sacrament, in other words, ends up supporting the church's turning in on itself. By contrast, the "order" of this common meal, this "eschatological Sacrament of Communion," should be "open-ended" and with a "somewhat provisional and even floating character."[158] The Lord's Supper should become again a "common meal," one that builds fellowship among its participants.[159] The sacrament becomes "not a matter of formulations, but of communion life . . . incarnated in the common things of daily life and there creates community and congregational life."[160]

5.6 Body, Maturity, History and God

Despite Hoekendijk's own claims to an open ecclesiology, his position occupies a rather narrow band of ecclesial experience, one reflective of the Pietist and Anabaptist traditions. However, reference to his clear ecclesiology sets his critics in a peculiar light. The single dominant charge against Hoekendijk concentrates on his supposed categorical denial of the church. Konrad Raiser, in a telling essay titled "Mission oder Bestandssicherung?" (Mission or Securing the Status Quo), delivers the following summary judgment as "the Christian faith never lives without the community of believers, without the gathering of the community," so the "radical subordination of the church to its task of being sent, as proposed by Hoekendijk, causes the community

---

[156]Hoekendijk, "Gesprek onder-weg," 349.
[157]Hoekendijk, Church Inside Out, 106.
[158]Ibid., 168.
[159]Ibid., 107.
[160]Ibid., 108.

and its service of God as the bodily form of the gospel to fall from sight."[161] This is the representative position: Hoekendijk denies the church a body. The very clarity of the conclusion needs to be contested, not in defense of Hoekendijk, but because it exposes certain entrenched assumptions concerning the nature of the body. Because Hoekendijk critiques the residential or territorial definition of the body and its manner of establishing mission, so it follows for his critics that he denies the church both its substance and its necessity. With this as the focus, no engaged attention treats Hoekendijk's positive link between mission and history, the connections he draws between cultural continuity and church structures, or his constructive reading of biblical and theological themes, including for all its notoriety his positive formulation of the apostolate.[162] It is also evident that defenses against

---

[161]Konrad Raiser, "Mission oder Bestandssicherung?," in *Jahrbuch Mission 1987*, ed. Joachim Wietzke (Hamburg: Missionshilfe Verlag, 1987), 17. It is not without a certain merit, given the critical direction ecumenical mission theology took during the late 1960s and early 1970s, and over which Hoekendijk had significant influence. Even here, however, two observations need to be made. First, generally stated, the period itself famously represents a confluence of both social and theological concerns: death of God theology, the emphases on the secular and on revolution, dissatisfaction with colonialism and theological imperialism, the need for the world to set the agenda. It is difficult to attribute this general milieu and its clear influence over the ecumenical discussion to Hoekendijk alone. Second, though one might question Hoekendijk's direct contribution to Uppsala (the official attendance record does not list him as present), the text of the MSC certainly owes much to him. He served as a member of both the Western European and North American Working Groups, and many of his basic insights were taken up and developed by this discussion. For an indication of the depth of his involvement, see Hoedemaker, "Legacy of J. C. Hoekendijk," 168. Conversely, however, these groups included persons suspicious of Hoekendijk's emphasis on the apostolate. Hans Margull, influential apologist for this discussion and one-time executive secretary of the Western European Working Group, rejected Hoekendijk's "one-sided and excessive subtilization of the problem of the church by consistently employing the 'theology of the apostolate.'" Margull, *Hope in Action*, 130. Margull also states, with regard to Hoekendijk's relating of "world" and "kingdom," that "his statements are in part dependent on his enthusiastic personality and often lack sufficient basis" (46). The study was the result of multiple contributions from multiple authors, a collection of which were republished as Thomas Wieser, ed., *Planning for Mission: Working Papers on the New Quest for Missionary Communities* (New York: U.S. Conference for the World Council of Churches, 1966). Hoekendijk's lack of contribution is notable. The independence of the MSC study can be seen in its sparing use of shalom, preferring the language of humanization, and its omission of the "apostolate." There appears to be only one paragraph on the "ex-centric position of the church," which deals with the coordinated ideas of propaganda, shalom and the apostolate (see MSC, 17-18). Hoekendijk was, without doubt, influential, but there is no one-to-one correspondence between his thinking and the final statement. How Hoekendijk conceived God's acting in history and the consequence this has for the church is a valid concern, but sufficient qualification exists to question the simple, immediate and undifferentiated connection drawn between Hoekendijk and these wider developments.

[162]The only commentator who addresses Hoekendijk's criticism of *Volk*, by way of example, is Hans-Werner Gensichen. Though Gensichen grants that the "*volksorganische*" mission thinking

Hoekendijk are driven to exaggerated affirmations of the church and its structures precisely to reinforce a set account of its embodiment.

5.6.1 First the church and then the mission: structure constitutes the body. Though most interlocutors simply dismiss his arguments, the few who engage with Hoekendijk reinforce the priority of a structured and located church beside which mission develops as a secondary and external thing. Two voices will suffice: those of Hendrikus Berkhof and Georg Vicedom.

Berkhof is an interesting respondent because his own sympathies lie with a dynamic account of the church, even to the point of arguing that when the church fails to "understand itself in all its functions as a missionary church [it] lives out of a half distorted and petrified apostolicity."[163] Nevertheless, in an extended "open letter" to Hoekendijk, Berkhof fears that the subordination of the church to the apostolate denies its fundamental mystery and so undoes its substance.[164]

Berkhof grants Hoekendijk's concern that, when ordered in relation to other functions (preaching, liturgy, catechism, pastoral work and diakonia), mission becomes undervalued, a "cinderella." Mission, as the New Testament makes clear, is more than one function of the church among others. According to Berkhof, however, Hoekendijk does not ground his position in theology. He reflects rather the cultural zeitgeist by proposing a "seductive" theory "in line with our modern feeling of life" and unjustified by the New Testament.[165] Whatever the biblical warrant for mission, the church as experienced "on the ground" constitutes the interpretive framework through which the New Testament as a whole is to be read. The church is more than an instrument, Berkhof avers; it is the body of Christ,

---

went astray after the First World War because it followed a questionable theology of order, he denies that this intrudes on the fundamental rightness of the *Volk* approach. Gensichen, "Grundfragen der Kirchwerdung in der Mission," 45. By not attending to this, Hoekendijk supposedly denies the "concrete actuality" of the body as defined in the New Testament. Notable, of course, is the manner in which Gensichen—even in a post-WWII context—reads the concept of *Volk* as basic to the "theological" supports he marshals against Hoekendijk.

[163]Hendrikus Berkhof, "De Apostoliciteit der Kerk," *Nederlandse Theologisch Tijdschrift* 2 (1947): 201.

[164]Hendrikus Berkhof, "Kerk en Zending," *In de Waagschaal* 6 (1951): 260, 264. My gratitude to Tijmen Aukes for his assistance in translating the Dutch-language works consulted throughout this chapter.

[165]Ibid., 260.

placed in the world as itself a prophecy of the new world.[166] Hoekendijk's approach, by contrast, neglects the church's "mystery."[167]

Though Berkhof nowhere examines this supposed conflict between instrument and body, it underlies a necessary distinction he draws between the church and apostolic activity. The church attracts people (the key form of missionary activity) only because it is itself more than this activity. A necessary ordering follows whereby the Lord's Supper is the "speaking sign" at the center of the life and order of the community under the Word. This "stands at the greatest distance from the apostolate."[168] The practices of liturgy, pastoral care and religious life exist as concentric circles radiating out from this center. Each has a meaning independent of the church's apostolic action. Berkhof offers no support for this distinction of the Lord's Supper from mission, but he deems it necessary for the gravitas of the church itself.

After distinguishing between church and mission, Berkhof then examines their reconciliation. He finds this in the reign of Jesus Christ, which is "not a circle with only one middle point, but an ellipse with two foci."[169] Christ's reign is present here and now in Word and sacrament. Its substance, in other words, belongs to the church. Insofar as this reign is hidden in Word and sacrament, insofar as Christ's kingdom is coming, mission takes form alongside the church as a second foci.[170] Though Berkhof regards the second focus as necessary, its significance lies only in relation to the church and does so only negatively: when one overemphasizes the mission focus "everything dissolves in dynamics and eschatology."[171] Mission is not simply insubstantial in relation to the kingdom: to attribute it some degree of theological substance in relation to the church intrudes on the kingdom's present substance.

Georg Vicedom serves as a second example. While most commentators avoid Hoekendijk's treatment of the apostolate, Vicedom makes it central to

---

[166]See also Hendrikus Berkhof, *Christian Faith: An Introduction to the Study of the Faith* (Grand Rapids: Eerdmans, 1986), 413-14.

[167]Berkhof, "Kerk en Zending," 260. Berkhof would later affirm, for example, that "there is no doubt that in the New Testament the apostolary activity is overshadowed by the fact of the church, and where it does not stand out it presupposes and draws its strength from that fact." Berkhof, *Christian Faith*, 415.

[168]Berkhof, "Kerk en Zending," 260.

[169]Ibid., 260.

[170]We must leave aside for the moment the theological implications of this limitation of mission to the pre-eschatological.

[171]Berkhof, "Kerk en Zending," 264.

his critique, appearing as part of his 1958 examination of *missio Dei*. His critique begins by setting the apostles and their work in relation to God's own act of "sending."[172] The apostles were a select group, identified first with the Twelve, into which Paul was included as an isolated act of Jesus Christ for the cause of the Gentiles. Theirs was a special calling from Jesus Christ to proclaim the gospel and gather the faithful into congregations. The apostolic office, by implication, was "unique and basic" and not an office of the church. For the church, the apostles created "a new office . . . and installed, not apostles, but bishops." The gift of neither apostle nor evangelist translated into a "missionary office" (64). Mission is something the church does and depends not on the "transmission of the apostolic office, but on the missionary attitude which the apostolic service awakened and which was transmitted to the church through the apostles" (65). Mission, Vicedom maintains, has no connection, first, to the apostles and, second, to any established church structure.

With these decisions he turns to the "Dutch theology of the apostolate." With nothing more than a straw-man binary, Vicedom reduces the theology of the apostolate either to a confirmation of Luther's priesthood of all believers or to the claim that "today the messengers still have all the gifts and functions of the apostles" (71). The authoritative definition of apostolicity remains the one given at Nicaea, and only as the church and its tradition "rests upon the foundation of the apostles and prophets" can it be apostolic. When it comes to the specifics of Hoekendijk's contribution, Vicedom's treatment is surprisingly minimal. Vicedom concentrates on the link Hoekendijk forms between the apostolate and the sending of the Spirit, and so between the apostolate and the eschatological mission to the Gentiles (66). This mission, because it prepares the world for judgment, "has a history-shaping mandate" (67). Vicedom objects. The "sending" is neither "a fact of the last times" nor linked to the gift of the Spirit (69). It is, Vicedom claims, "based on the operation of the Triune God in His relationship to the world" and "based on the completion of the facts of salvation in the resurrection" (69, 70). To what extent this counters

---

[172]Georg F. Vicedom, *The Mission of God: An Introduction to a Theology of Mission*, trans. Gilbert A. Thiele and Dennis Hilgendorf (St. Louis, MO: Concordia, 1965). Subsequent references are provided parenthetically within the text. Especially for a German audience, Vicedom's work serves as something of a final interpretive word when addressing Hoekendijk. See, for example, Heinrich Balz, *Der Anfang des Glaubens: Theologie der Mission und der jungen Kirchen* (Neuendettelsau: Erlanger Verlag für Mission und Ökumene, 2010), 159-62.

Hoekendijk's own position is a question worth asking, but the purpose of Vicedom's objection is clear: the "objectively established fact" of the apostolic commission sets the "direction of the church." The subsequent work of the Spirit helps the church "execute" its sending, thereby preserving it from "the stagnation of 'churchianity.'" Jesus Christ's mandate and the Spirit's supporting role establish the church's "apostolic character." It becomes "an entity active by [its] very existence as well as through the special sending" (70). The apostolic mission rests not in any particular structure but in the church as structure, beside which exists a secondary and external witness.

Vicedom's constructive alternative focuses on discipleship as the prerequisite of apostolic service. Where one is a disciple, "the urge to witness and therewith apostolic service come spontaneously." This emphasis both makes a congregation necessary and sets an order whereby the "congregation always precedes the mission of the church and takes over the apostolic attitude" (73). Vicedom, in other words, buys into the oppositional and asymmetrical ordering of church over against mission. The church, as defined by its "apostolic" structures (a threefold ordering of James, Peter and Paul, and which does not include any additional missionary office), becomes responsible for bearing Christian witness, and this occurs primarily as a spontaneous expression of its apostolic character through the nurturing of disciples. Discipleship admits to a continuum within the congregation itself. Every church becomes a *Volkskirche* through infant baptism, meaning that disciples are a minority in every church, with even "unfaithful disciples" outnumbered by "nominal members." And because God retains the initiative in calling people to discipleship, it "cannot simply be equated with church" (81). The church is a wider body.

Vicedom makes clear allowances for church members whose Christianity lies in a formal relationship to the church as a social institution. But due to this link between discipleship and witness, "the command to missions will no longer be a special mandate for certain restricted groups, nor a legalistic compulsion for the undecided" (82). This directs mission to given church structures. The church serves the "apostolic ministry" through its institutional support of those who are willing to enter the ministry of "spreading the Gospel." Behind all of Vicedom's normative theological thinking, in other words, stands the actual circumstances and structures of the *Volkskirche*. Because the church is "the result of the apostolate," it is proof that the "Gospel belongs also to the heathen" (82). In being founded by mission, and in the gift of the Spirit, "the church is privileged to act in God's stead even as God sent Himself in His Son. . . . The church performs the sending and thereby the *missio Dei* becomes visible to the world" (83-84). Mission, by this account, is "no independent, arbitrary, optional work of the church," nor is it "determined by circumstances" (83). Mission characterizes the church as an immediate overflow of its faith. How this tallies with Vicedom's own distinction between church member and disciples—that is to say, how might mission emerge as a natural overflow of this body—is not a question he addresses. Nevertheless, as the church needs no "missionary command," so it need not subordinate itself to the apostolate.

This leads Vicedom to the language of the "new people of God" (88). An inherent danger exists that the church will confuse its own life with that of the people, for it is "a fellowship into which a person is born" (89). Such danger exists because the church's missionary sending "takes place not in some dynamic operation of the congregation, but in the concrete transfer of the ministry and in instruction." This institutional ground corresponds to the *missio* through which God "confronts" and "establishes His relationship to the world"; it is God's gift to the church of "the same position which He holds" (88). The two elements are important, for as confrontation means distinction, so it is the form of relating. The danger of cultural confusion is mitigated when the church recognizes its being "loved out" of the world as the new people of God. This equally constitutes its sending: "the congregation in the world must function primarily through her presence" (89). Though disciples are a minority in the church, the church's mission as the people of God lies in its being a contrast community. It depends on "recognizing" and "preserving" its "otherness," and all missionary emphasis falls on the institution and its structures (92).

Discipleship is the standout constructive point in Vicedom's treatment, and its absence in Hoekendijk is a clear weakness. But one might question Vicedom's own development of the theme, for it appears to be nothing more than a conduit to reaffirm a *Volkskirche* structure and its wider supporting edifice. In other words, though "disciple" is a way of indicating the church as a "body" or a "people," Vicedom's focus falls on the structure within which this group (and the wider constitutive elements within a *Volkskirche*) exists.

He says nothing of the church as a reconciled people, nor *can* he say anything, given the small sample of disciples that exists within the body. "Sending" is first the transfer of ministry and instruction. "Witness" is the overflow of the church's life through the visibility of its institutions and the manner of its confrontation with the world. To talk of the church as a people is to talk of the institutions framing this people.

In terms of specifics, Vicedom's contrasting account reaffirms Augsburg Confession VII and the need for both a congregation and an office (86). Vicedom forges links between sacrament, fellowship, maturity and witness, and he affirms the church's proper "global diversity" found in its "ethnic emphasis," a position that falls precariously close to the pre-war *Volk* concerns (86, 95). Hoekendijk, by contrast, owing to his circumspection regarding the established institution, dissolves the church "into an event, into an insensible entity, vanishing continually in the apostolate. . . . Thus visibility is discarded" (85). Whatever the problems in Hoekendijk's account, the contrast is telling. Vicedom regards visibility as the hallmark of mission. To challenge this—that is, to challenge the substratum of structures deemed necessary to this visibility—is to negate the mission of the church. Without this structure, Hoekendijk renders desolate the community under its care.

Berkhof and Vicedom reflect a pattern evident across Hoekendijk's critics: his position is dismissed as simply unwarranted. None engages with the particulars of his position. None examines Hoekendijk's attempt to redefine mission in historical rather than geographical terms. None entertains the continuities Hoekendijk draws between Old Testament promises, New Testament events and their missionary form. None addresses Hoekendijk's critical redefinition of "people of God" or koinonia. None even hints at the constructive shape Hoekendijk gives to church structures. On the contrary, all respond by reasserting the order of church as primary followed by mission as secondary. For the church to be a body, this logic holds, it must be something in and for itself with its liturgies, sacraments, practices and institutions directed to this end. To deny this is to deny the church a sufficiently concrete form.

The inconsistency, however, should be clear. Even though Hoekendijk is deemed to neglect the "body," the counterarguments equate body with the structure—specifically, with the structure detached from any movement beyond itself. This account of the church, despite its appearance of necessity, appears just as abstract as Hoekendijk's. Structure defines the body, the form of maturity, identity and witness. The responses to Hoekendijk, in other words, indicate a wider problem, one which today determines any evaluation of world Christianity and its pluriformity.

5.6.2 God washed out on the tide of history. Apostolicity as cultural continuity produces an account of witness that depends on Christian maturity and the practices deemed necessary to the cultivation of this maturity. Witness corresponds to the aesthetic internal to the culture itself. Beside this occurs an external mission tasked with transplanting the forms, practices and interpretive means that belong to this cultural vision. To claim that historical progress sanctifies these developments only succeeds in further withdrawing the church from history, ever sacralizing the church's residential form. Given how entrenched these assumptions are in the discourse, it is not surprising that Hoekendijk avoided all discussion of Christian maturity.

Hoekendijk, of course, did not deny the church an internal life. Similar to contemporary arguments for the reinstitution of a catholic order, Hoekendijk sought "genuine communion." This was possible, in his estimation, only in small and mobile groups. Only these "closely knit relationships which nevertheless remain open" will be able to hold "out against an overpowering environment that tries to squeeze everything into the same mold."[173] This form of belonging is not voluntarist. Against the "institutionalized indecision" of the *Volkskirche*, "within which the 'religion without decision' is nurtured, upheld, and propagated," these groups, like Paul, stand under the obligation of the apostolate.[174] As Hoedemaker suggests, Hoekendijk's church reflects no "comfortable pluriformity of a consumer society. It makes sense only in combination with the incisive eschatological question of shalom, in which final judgment and final promise are held together."[175] Only in the missionary engagement of kingdom and world does this body find its bonds.

Nor does Hoekendijk advocate a simple return to a New Testament ecclesiology. Hans Margull claims that Hoekendijk's "call to battle against the repose of the church" amounts to "pure dynamism, a call which consists in a

---

[173]Hoekendijk, *Church Inside Out*, 186.
[174]Ibid., 182.
[175]Hoedemaker, "Legacy of J. C. Hoekendijk," 170.

passionate though un-justified return to origins (the first generation)."[176] This is simply incorrect. For Hoekendijk, the very historicity of the church belongs to its witness and so its structure. A return to a New Testament image of the church would amount to a further retreat from history and the development of heretical structures. The apostolic church is the church grounded in the apostolate, grounded in the encounter between the kingdom and the world and so in history. Nor does a missionary emphasis dissolve everything into "dynamics and eschatology."[177] Hoekendijk's justified response questions the necessity of this fear.[178] When read against the New Testament, the apostolic mission grounded communities and stimulated structures.

Hoekendijk did not sacrifice the church on the altar of a phenomenologically defined mission. Mission is grounded in history, not territory, and to define the church as a "function of the apostolate" is to define it as "more than a function of the mission."[179] Aware of the arguments against him, Hoekendijk notes how koinonia is often set in opposition to the apostolate with the intent of disconnecting the church's internal life from its apostolic action. This reduces the church to an end in itself and produces an "endless ecclesiastical self-reflection."[180] He conceives koinonia instead as participation in Christ and so participation in his mission to the world. In so acting, the church "astonishes the world and becomes itself a question."[181] The church is called to point away from itself and to the kingdom, but this, contrary to Berkhof's charge, does not violate its glory. The church's glory and mystery lies in its "self-emptying service."[182] The church's exemplary existence and so its distinction from the world lies in its kenotic service, in excentric existence, in giving its life for the world. This is itself a creative and community-forming movement because it is a participation in God's own promises and their eschatological fulfillment.

Hoekendijk did place the church in a theologically derivative position, a thing of second-order theological reflection, with the intent to relativize its

---

176 Margull, *Hope in Action*, 126.
177 Berkhof, "Kerk en Zending," 261.
178 Hoekendijk, "Gesprek onder-weg," 349.
179 Ibid.
180 Ibid., 350.
181 Ibid.
182 Ibid.

significance. He subsumed it to the apostolate and could even affirm that "the Church's liturgy has no purpose in itself ('mass means *missio!*')."[183] But he did not omit the church. His preferred model is that of a "gathered church" ecclesiology, one conceived after Wesley, Zinzendorf and Francke, with freedom in relation to institutions, a stress on lay leadership and a relativized account of the ordained ministry. Hoedemaker notes how these "evangelical" tendencies were "often mistakenly interpreted as a refusal to take the Church seriously."[184] There is much to this point. One can appreciate the measure of theological dissatisfaction with this position when approached from the ecclesiologies of the Catholic and Reformed alike, but it is a significant step to say that Hoekendijk denies the church.

All this being said, however, one misses certain notes in Hoekendijk's argument. Maturity need not be conceived as enculturation into a residential narrative, but Hoekendijk does need to account for such things as discipleship, conversion and entrance into the Christian community. Despite the pneumatological ground he gives to the apostolate, he devotes no attention to the fruit of the Spirit, to love, joy, peace, forbearance, kindness, goodness, faithfulness, gentleness and self-control (Gal 5:22-25). He touches on these themes through his use of shalom, reconciliation, freedom and hope, but these he orients toward eschatological justice and completeness. While Hoekendijk's position is more than simple social activism, it neglects grace and includes no account of God's own witness shining through Christian weakness and faithlessness. One finds no mention of sin or forgiveness, doubt, suffering and vulnerability.[185] Nor does one find any appreciation for different life phases. Lay witness within the workplace is one thing, but what of the young, the old, caregivers, the disabled, the unemployed, the addicted, the refugee, the migrant and so on? Absent from Hoekendijk's church is a certain human texture.

This is not to reaffirm the critique that Hoekendijk neglects the body. A more credible origin for this abstraction lies in his doctrine of God. Hoek-

---

[183]J. C. Hoekendijk, "Evangelism—The 'Raison d'être' of the Church," *Ecumenical Review* 4, no. 4 (1952): 432.

[184]Hoedemaker, "Hoekendijk's American Years," 8.

[185]See the defense mounted against the charge of social activism by Hoedemaker. L. A. Hoedemaker, "Mission and Unity: The Relevance of Hoekendijk's Vision," in *Changing Partnership of Missionary and Ecumenical Movements: Essays in Honour of Marc Spindler*, ed. Leny Lagerwerf, Karel Steenbrink and F. J. Verstraelen (Leiden-Utrecht: Interuniversity Institute for Missiological and Ecumenical Research, 1995), 33-35.

endijk's whole project refuses any avenue that might secure the church an existence prior to and independent of its missionary witness. Part of his solution rests in relativizing the church. As derivative and secondary to the doctrine of God, ecclesiology can never be more than a paragraph in Christology. But this critical element alone is not enough. Hoekendijk must equally elevate mission, giving it sufficient theological gravitas to offset the ecclesiological losses suffered. He accomplishes this by linking mission to history, which is the key point in his use of the apostolate. It is a significant step, one that needs to be developed as our argument progresses. Hoekendijk, however, overreaches—mission gains this gravitas by pouring God out into history. God's being becomes, through God's own act, somehow secondary to historical process itself.

Though Hoekendijk would later use the formula *missio Dei* to support his position, his earlier work forms similar connections through the eschatological fulfillment of the messianic promises. In Christ, the new eon is now a present reality and the Gentile mission a sign of the promised culmination of all things in God. Hoekendijk interprets this to mean that "as God directed his plan toward the world, so he released it into history."[186] This historical setting establishes the "messianic pattern" as the form of the church's acting in history. Hoekendijk's intent is clear: the church knows this God only insofar as it participates in God's movement to the world. The world is the location of Christ's "real presence."[187] Focus falls on the continuity between God's own life, the calling of the church and its necessary involvement in history as the arena of God's acting. For Hoekendijk, "*apostolate/Mission is a predicate of God.* ... He operates and makes Himself known through an all-encompassing sending economy: sending His angels, prophets, word, Messiah, Son, Spirit, apostles, Church, etc."[188] The difficulty resides in making the apostolate a general category of history and, with this, the sendings of the Son and Spirit no different from the sending of the church. God and the human become determined by the now abstract category of sending, carried along by the tide of history. It is not that Hoekendijk lacks a church. It is more that the strange inhumanity of Hoekendijk's ecclesiology

---

[186]Hoekendijk, *Kirche und Volk*, 345.
[187]Ibid., 347.
[188]Hoekendijk, "Notes on the Meaning of Mission(-ary)," 41.

stems from a corresponding lack in God's own life. It seems better to admonish Hoekendijk using Karl Barth's axiom: "God gives Himself, but He does not give Himself away."[189] A depopulated God leads to a depopulated church. Or, to put it in ironic fashion, Hoekendijk trusted too much in structure. "Sending" and the "messianic pattern" are structuring principles, but without God retaining the initiative they became abstractions filled with a range of historically determined social concerns.[190]

The solution to Hoekendijk's theological problems does not, however, lie in a repeated reassertion of the asymmetrical ordering of the cultivation of the faith over its proclamation. The force of his diagnostic connection between propagandistic mission method and a residential church, and his linking of mission to history, is only increased with reference to developments within world Christianity.

EXCURSUS: A. A. VAN RULER ON CHRISTIANIZATION AS THE END OF THE APOSTOLATE

When considering the difficulties surrounding Hoekendijk's doctrine of God, it is worth addressing A. A. van Ruler's contribution to the theology of the apostolate. The fullest expression of his position is found in the 1954 text "Theologie van het Apostolaat."[191] Here he draws similar connections to Hoekendijk between the kingdom of God, history and mission, but he differs by interpreting the apostolate through the theocratic interests of Dutch Reformed theology.

The church, van Ruler argues, must be viewed "essentially in terms of its mission or 'apostolic' nature and function" (199). It becomes a matter of giving shape to that mission, which van Ruler does by linking the church's apostolic shape to its eschatological calling. The kingdom of God is now

---

[189]Karl Barth, CD IV/1, 185.

[190]José Míguez Bonino observes, with reference to this tendency to identify what God is doing in history, that "once people think they have discovered 'what God is doing,' they quite logically tend to absolutize it and their own actions; they are led to sacralize their own ideology." José Míguez Bonino, "Historical Praxis and Christian Identity," in *Frontiers of Theology in Latin America*, ed. Rosino Gibellini (Maryknoll, NY: Orbis Books, 1979), 275.

[191]Published as A. A. van Ruler, "A Theology of Mission," in *Calvinist Trinitarianism and Theocentric Politics: Essays Toward a Public Theology*, trans. John Bolt (Lewiston, NY: Edwin Mellen, 1989), 199-226. Subsequent references are provided parenthetically within the text. For a wider survey of van Ruler's position, see Allan J. Janssen, *Kingdom, Office, and Church: A Study of A. A. van Ruler's Doctrine of Ecclesiastical Office* (Grand Rapids: Eerdmans, 2006), 81-110.

active "in the complexities of the world-historical process" (203). The "whole of christological salvation-history" is a series of "eschatological events," and it is mission that fills "the gulf" or "forms the bridge" between the two *parousia*. Mission, as a consequence, "cannot be encapsulated entirely in a christological framework" (204). Insofar as mission looks to history, the nations and pneumatology, it "has to do with the gospel of the kingdom, which is not wholly identical with the gospel of Jesus Christ." Likewise, the office of the apostle is not an office of the church; it belongs to the kingdom. The corresponding apostolic vision focuses not only "on Jesus Christ and his church, but behind and around them, on God himself and his world" (205). Attention shifts to the Old Testament as encompassing the New Testament, leading van Ruler to argue for a wider trinitarian (i.e., theocentric) vision aligned with the kingdom of God.

Eschatology refers to a direct relationship between God and the world, and mission serves as mediator between the two. Given this role, mission is restrained from an improper overemphasis only by stressing the agency or "predestination" of God, "the dimension of God who himself acts." God has already had contact with the nations, and mission is the intensification of such contact. This also relativizes the church, which becomes an instrument of God's own acting. "The essence of the church as mission does not reside in the fact that the church goes out, witnesses, and is present in the world. Rather, it is that she is used! The church is an instrument! She is used by God himself in *his* engagement with the world" (207). Apostolicity is thus neither an "attribute" nor a "mandate" of the church. To think in these terms risks so accenting the church's act of witness that it "becomes too much a matter of anthropology." God's work is wider than the church, as he himself participates "in the great drama and the great struggle of the nations as they seek to give political, social, economic, and cultural shape to life." The church exists in the middle of this "great totality of world-history, which may be rightly understood as the drama of God" (208). Mission is the church's placement in the world, not to reproduce itself, but to christianize the wider culture and society through the planting of the law and the telling of the gospel. Nor is this "an accidental by-product of the preaching of the gospel"; it belongs "in an essential way to the scope of mission as such" (225). Mission, under the agency of God's acting in history, is the act of christianization.

Note the relationship between van Ruler and Hoekendijk at this point. At the level of elementary decision, the two are almost identical. Both begin with eschatology and its emphasis on apostolic agency, with the missionary activity of bridging the two *parousia*. They emphasize first the acting of God and the corresponding acting of the church as it becomes an instrument of God working in history and through culture to bring about the kingdom. Both place God's acting within the world and in history, and conceive the church as existing within this encounter. The world lives in its own right and not simply as a type of ecclesial parasite. Most significant is the consequence of such decisions for the doctrine of God. In placing God's acting first in the "world-historical process," van Ruler finds it necessary to set God's trinitarian acting, the presence of the kingdom, at some distance from Christology (203). His "trinitarianism" seems much more categorically aligned with "history" and, as such, evacuated of Christ's own particular agency. Van Ruler famously maintains that both the incarnation of the Son and the indwelling of the Spirit will be "undone," leaving only "two realities": "God himself and the existence of things—the triune God and humanity" (214). This future of God has present effect, with mission becoming "the activity of Christianization [as] the effectuation of the sacrifice of Christ applied to the world" (212).

Hoekendijk's doctrine of God follows similar lines with the same problems of retaining reference to God as the acting subject. It might be suggested, in other words, that many of Hoekendijk's basic moves originate within this wider discussion of Dutch Reformed theology. However, while Hoekendijk shares in this background logic, he rejects the goal of christianization as precisely the problem found in the German emphasis on *Volk*. Christianization is the envisioned end of the residential church, which is definitive of its structuring (the orientation of its liturgies and sacraments) and basic to its mission. Hoekendijk's rejection of this approach amounts to a rejection of the church as such.

Van Ruler's conflict with Hoekendijk centers on ecclesiology. While van Ruler agrees with Hoekendijk's supposed assertion that in the eschaton "the particularity of special revelation" will fall away (a point that Hoekendijk does not himself seem to make, but is a telling assumption from van Ruler), the eschaton is not yet present in its fullness. Because the eschaton does not fully hold sway, the need for particularity remains. "Implicit in this notion of particularity, and thus together with the apostolic conception of mission as such, is the reality of a concrete, particular church. Whether it be pastorally or liturgically oriented, the church is a given concrete reality" (219). Hoekendijk fails on this point, van Ruler suggests, because he treats the "individual" as the primary witness. This van Ruler rejects: "One must be a Christian for that" (219). Likewise, against the notion that salvation must "be translated and transposed into the common forms of existence," van Ruler asserts that this "takes place only partially—they cannot be transformed in their entirety!" (219-20). The church is a reality in itself as the appearance of the kingdom in a particular form.

In short, the positive form of the church that van Ruler formulates in opposition to Hoekendijk, one linked to his understanding of the apostolate, is the express form against which Hoekendijk reacts. For van Ruler, "humanity is ours only in the form of Christianity, and true culture only in its christianized form" (219).[192] This notion of cultural growth in relation to the gospel means that Europe and America can present as "more Christian" over against the "pagan" cultures of especially Africa and Asia. The significance of this becomes clear in the distinction between "home" and "foreign" missions. Despite the contemporary difficulties it presents, van Ruler considers it "an enormous blunder" to view "the entire world as the one great mission field of the church today" (223). He rejects as "neither psychologically nor theologically defensible" the notion of Europe or America inhabiting a "mission situation," because these locations bear a Christian character fundamentally different from the paganism typifying, for example, Asia (200). Such is true because Christians "are more than mere individuals; we also stand in the continuity of the generations." Without a Christian culture built up through the generations, there is no Christian. "The heart is historically formed!" In the pagan context of Asia, by contrast, the "apostolic mission fully has the character of 'being sent.' It is a bringing of the truth to those who live in a complex of lies." To suggest that this method defines the relation of the church to its "surroundings in countries which are historically

---

[192]For an extended treatment of his concept of christianization, see A. A. van Ruler, *Gestaltwerdung Christi in der Welt: Über das Verhältnis von Kirche und Kultur* (Neukirchen Kr. Moers: Verlag der Buchhandlung des Erziehungsvereins, 1956). Van Ruler also defends the notion of *Volkskirche*; see Janssen, *Kingdom, Office, and Church*, 98-101.

Christian . . . does violence both to human beings and to God. . . . Here we find a deep spiritual and theological difference in principle" (224). In van Ruler's reflection on colonization, the logic becomes acute. To quote Johannes Blauw's summary of van Ruler's position:

> Revelation is the presence of God on earth, a presence that has taken shape in the "Christian" culture of Europe and America. Culture can never be neutral before the true God. Even if Euro-American culture may be very secularized, it remains completely different from cultures that have another religious basis. Therefore, one cannot be anti-colonial without denying the presence of God in Western culture. The justification of the colonial system thus finds its origin in the refusal to surrender to secularism and neutrality.[193]

Hoekendijk would identify this overt liaison with colonization as the logical conclusion of christianization and its validation of the church as a thing in itself.[194] If this is the one and only "church," then Hoekendijk certainly opposes it.

This reference to van Ruler illustrates well the impasse basic to Hoekendijk. On the one hand, Hoekendijk shares in outline the connections between the kingdom of God, eschatology, mission, history and the church. On the other hand, he cannot follow van Ruler to the perceived end of christianization, the end definitive of God's own agency, and so he is charged with failing to give the church the type of texturing needed for this end. Hoekendijk's ecclesiological maladies result, at least in part, from holding these assumptions while opposing the established cultural conclusions.

5.7 TURNING TO THE WORLD CHURCH

Even at the discussion's height, Hoekendijk's theory of the apostolate did not gain much penetration. The enduring summary of his position is that his "instrumental" view of the church *eo ipso* denudes the church of its "body."

---

[193]Johannes Blauw, "Das Missionsdenken in den Niederlanden 1945-1955," *Evangelisches Mission-Magazin* 106 (1956): 118, summarizing A. A. van Ruler, "De Kolonie," in *Visie en Vaart* (Amsterdam: Nijkerk, 1947), 128-200.

[194]Though commentators understand van Ruler's later work at some distance from his conception of the apostolate, the difference seems to consist of a strengthening of his ecclesial position. In a later article titled "The Church Is Also an End in Itself," van Ruler reinforces the link between the church and its cultural service of God in the world. A. A. van Ruler, "De kerk is ook doel in zichzelf," in *Verwachtingen Voltooiing: Een bundel theologische opstellen en voordrachten* (Nijkerk: Callenbach, 1978), 53-66.

But with this dismissive approach, Hoekendijk's positive contribution remains largely unexamined: history, not geography, is the context of mission.

Hoekendijk traces the problem of propaganda, the mission method of replicating the sending church, back to the prevailing ecclesiology. It is because the church conceives itself and its end in cultural terms that its external missionary activity transplants the range of structures and theologies basic to the cultivation of this culture. Hoekendijk explores this problem in relation to the influence of *Volk* within German mission theory. His conclusion: despite its claim to cherish local cultures, *Volkstum* ideology established parameters for the indigenous expression of the gospel. Though this emphasis would reach its termination with the Third Reich, Hoekendijk in almost prescient fashion finds the same theological position in the ecumenical appropriation of the "people of God" and "koinonia." The problem of propaganda applies more generally to the identification of the church with a particular historical and cultural location and to its corresponding theologies, liturgies and rituals. Hoekendijk's positive construal of the church within the apostolate attempts precisely to dissolve this connection. The church is a function of the apostolate, and thus it is irreducible to a particular culture or history.

Many of Hoekendijk's themes have an enduring significance. First, as a surprising omission, none of his critics observes Hoekendijk's interest in Israel and the Jews and the development of the apostolate against this background. His own work with Jewish orphans in Holland during WWII and the post-war recalibration of the church's relationship to Israel and the Jewish people, along with his PhD work with the Old Testament, shaped his thinking. Hoekendijk sets the New Testament treatment of the messianic mission, including the sociological impossibility of the people of God, in continuity with the promises of the Old Testament. This forms the basis of his critique against arguments for cultural continuity.

Second, though expressed through his idiosyncratic schema of Ba'al and propaganda, the opposition between proselytism and mission drives a good deal of contemporary mission theory. Hoekendijk describes proselytism as "the very contrast of Mission; the proselyting Church conceives itself as the mediating-centre of salvation and extra ecclesiam nulla salus."[195] On this

---

[195]Hoekendijk, "Notes on the Meaning of Mission(-ary)," 47.

point, his eschatology includes some untapped resources. Hoekendijk's redefinition of mission through his rejection of territorial categories in favor of
history and the apostolate remains a key insight. The distinction he employs
between proselytism and mission corresponds to a concern seen often today:
is it necessary to take on another's history in the process of conversion, or can
one's own history be redeemed? Hoekendijk gives a clear answer: the apostolate characterizes history's own redemption.

This later point unveils a possible path beyond the duality of apostolicity.
To limit the discussion to the normative claims of the ecumenical debate is
to allow a supposedly "concrete" church to dominate the horizon while
leaving mission, insofar as it demands a structural flexibility, to defend itself
against charges that it erodes the "body." The rules of the game determine
the outcome. By turning to world Christianity we are able to shift focus from
the traditional claims regarding what constitutes a concrete church and address a context occupied with questions of mission, continuity and structure.
In contrast to a Christianity defined by cultural and historical closure, we
must examine a Christianity engaged with multiple histories and a diversity
of cultural and structural expressions.

6

Historical Continuity in the Perspective of
World Christianity

> *The question with which we are faced fundamentally is this:*
> *Of the two processes at work, the historical transmission and*
> *the indigenous assimilation, which one is more significant? . . .*
> *Without hesitation it is the latter. For it is within that that*
> *the historical process itself becomes meaningful.*
>
> LAMIN SANNEH[1]

> *The later church has seen many heresies come and go, but the*
> *earliest of them has been by far the most persistent. The essence*
> *of the "Judaizing" tendency is the insistence on imposing our*
> *own religious culture, our own Torah and circumcision.*
>
> ANDREW WALLS[2]

6.1 NON-TERRITORIAL BUT EMBODIED

To claim apostolicity is to claim legitimacy and recognition for a lived experience of the gospel. This underlies the elusiveness of an ecumenical solution,
the attractiveness of the cultural continuity approach and so the tendency to
identify the church in territorial terms. Though often submerged by layers of

---

[1]Lamin O. Sanneh, "The Horizontal and the Vertical in Mission: An African Perspective," *International Bulletin of Missionary Research* 7, no. 4 (1983): 166.

[2]Andrew F. Walls, "Converts or Proselytes? The Crisis over Conversion in the Early Church," *International Bulletin of Missionary Research* 28, no. 1 (2004): 6.

theological tradition, the cultural rationale accompanying such claims becomes evident when the church crosses geographical boundaries. A form of mission develops that bears all the hallmarks of the repudiated processes of colonialization. Herein lies Johannes Hoekendijk's contribution. He worked backwards from the mission problem to its source in the "sending" ecclesiology and its accompanying range of theological supports. Insofar as the "residential" church mandated this mission method, rejecting the method amounted to rejecting the church. Commentators failed to draw this connection and so overlooked Hoekendijk's rather radical redefinition of mission. Hoekendijk's proposed ecclesiology corresponds to few communities existing today or in history. Nor did he raise the theological issues of historical continuity and maturity in the faith. These gaps need to be filled. But Hoekendijk's refusal to reduce mission to a derivative function of a residential church, to the geographical replication of necessary structures, led him to conceive it in terms of history and eschatology. This significant advance finds confirmation in the contemporary discussion of world Christianity.

A positive reconstruction of apostolicity, following Dale Irvin, must account for "Christianity as a non-territorial religion which is not at the same time a non-material or a non-embodied form."[3] This is the challenge Hoekendijk leaves us. To address it we turn to world Christianity and three of its main theoreticians: Andrew Walls, Lamin Sanneh and Kwame Bediako. The suggestion that these theorists advance Hoekendijk's key insight might surprise some, but the connection is worth pursuing. First, they too define mission in terms of history and in critical negation of a territorial approach. Hoekendijk's rejection of "propaganda" in favor of "mission" finds correspondence in Walls's distinction between "proselytism" and "conversion" and that developed by Sanneh between "diffusion" and "translation." Hoekendijk's concern for the redemption of history is basic for these church historians. However, second, where Hoekendijk is at least open to the charge of being somewhat distant from the lived experience, Walls, Sanneh and Bediako describe the church concrete and visible, the church as it exists in various historically and culturally diverse settings. The body defined in the New Testament and as it appears today in world Christianity is the

---

[3]Dale T. Irvin, "Ecumenical Dislodgings," *Mission Studies* 22, no. 2 (2005): 199.

subject of their investigation. The result is a vision of the church both non-territorial and embodied.

World Christianity is often marshaled in support of a negative point: it reveals the Western guise of the church catholic. As one consequence of this position, the Western church retains the focus as the acting subject and sets world Christianity as a critical opposite. The approach in this chapter differs. While reference to world Christianity helps dislocate the entrenched focus on the Protestant/Catholic schism, it provides a positive and material datum for the reconfiguration of apostolicity. In terms of the theological discussions dominant in Latin America, Africa and Asia, one struggles to find any account of apostolicity in the formal terms preferred in the ecumenical movement. One does, however, find strong reference to "continuity" in relation to the local historical, cultural and religious heritage. No doubt exists as to the *Christian* identity of the groups struggling with this question; it is because they are Christian that the question arises. The issue of structure and accompanying interpretive forms develops against this problem of continuity. Nor is this a historically isolated example. Theorists of world Christianity argue that this cluster of concerns embodies a logic generally true of the church's history. Though the formal language of apostolicity does not appear, the church, according to this argument, has been historically continuous *only* because it has moved across cultural borders. The very non-territoriality of the church is the nature of its historical continuity and so the nature of its embodiment.

6.2 GENERATIONAL CONTINUITY AND SERIAL EXPANSION

The oft-made observation with which discussions of world Christianity begin today concerns the shift in the faith's "center of gravity." By way of example, a 2011 report from the Pew Forum on Religion & Public Life, titled *Global Christianity: A Report on the Size and Distribution of the World's Christian Population*, holds that, whereas in 1910 82 percent of all Christians lived in Europe and North America, one hundred years later 60 percent live in the "global south."[4] A quarter of this Christianity, 8.5 percent of the

---

[4]Pew Forum on Religion & Public Life, *Global Christianity: A Report on the Size and Distribution of the World's Christian Population* (Washington, DC: Pew Research Center's Forum on Religion & Public Life, 2011), 14. Though one sees a general acknowledgment of this point during the mid-1970s, the first academic statement of this shift appears to have been made by Andrew Walls in a paper read to the Conference of Scottish University Divinity Faculties at Aberdeen on May 5, 1967. Walls here

world's total population, is Pentecostal or charismatic.[5] One cannot ground theological substance in statistical forecast; however, though many presume a future continuation of this trajectory, the shift is not forecast. The statistics speak to the present shape of the Christian church. For Walls, churches have emerged in Africa that "owe little to Western models of how a church should operate, and much to African readings of Scripture, for which the conditions of African life often provide a hall of echoes."[6] Though this speaks to a certain distance, the point is a positive one. African Christianity—and, by extension, world Christianity—is not derivative of the Western church but itself a positive development in church history. Whether or not one supports Walls's judgment that "what happens within the African churches in the next generation will determine the whole shape of Church history for centuries to come," it is apparent that world Christianity constitutes a significant disruption across a range of fronts to the settled theological tradition.[7]

For the question of apostolicity, two observations present themselves. First, world Christianity is Christianity visible and concrete. Insofar as "visiblity" constitutes a theological legitimation drawn from the lived reality of the church, it should not be selectively shaped to fit the contours of a

argued that the "centre of gravity of the Christian world has changed, and violently. . . . We must get used to the fact that most Christians are going to be Africans, Asians, or Americans, and that fifty years hence, European Christians may be a numerically insignificant and still dwindling minority in the church." The presentation was not published, and my thanks to John Hitchen for the reference and text. For a review of this paper and its importance, see Wilbert R. Shenk, "Challenging the Academy, Breaking Barriers," in *Understanding World Christianity: The Vision and Work of Andrew F. Walls*, ed. William R. Burrows, Mark R. Gornik and Janice A. McLean (Maryknoll, NY: Orbis Books, 2011), 35-50.

The first published treatment is attributed to a 1974 German work by the Franciscan Walbert Bühlmann. Bühlmann observed that the Western church "no longer constitutes the focal point of Christianity," nor is it the "centre of religious cultural unity for the whole of Christianity, a post which derived from the medieval situation." Walbert Bühlmann, *The Coming of the Third Church: An Analysis of the Present and Future of the Church* (Maryknoll, NY: Orbis Books, 1977), 19. Instead, the church's future belongs to the "'Third Church,'" an entity Bühlmann associates with the "new nations" of the Third World (4). Though the value of statistical forecasts is questionable, his assessment that, by the year 2000, 70 percent of the Catholic world population would live in Latin America, Africa and Asia proved broadly accurate.

[5]Pew Forum on Religion & Public Life, *Global Christianity*, 17.

[6]Andrew F. Walls, "A History of the Expansion of Christianity *Reconsidered*: Assessing Christian Progress and Decline," in *The Cross-Cultural Process in Christian History: Studies in the Transmission and Appropriation of Faith* (Maryknoll, NY: Orbis Books, 2002), 17.

[7]Andrew F. Walls, "Towards Understanding Africa's Place in Christian History," in *Religion in a Pluralistic Society: Essays Presented to Professor C. G. Baëta*, ed. J. S. Pobee (Leiden: Brill, 1976), 183.

particular institutional ideal. This church does not correspond to the rules of continuity that governed the European church during the Middle Ages. It is polycentric and pluriform. Second, the numbers challenge the logic of exception. World Christianity is no emergency situation for which a range of accommodations might be made, a unique event detached from the continuum of Christian theology. Quite the opposite is true. World Christianity opens the theological field because it detaches that discourse from a singular concentration on a constricted history and its attendant range of questions. African Christianity will not "mature" into a form corresponding to the Western experience but will continue to develop its own forms corresponding to its own questions.

To read this as a negation of the wider theological tradition is wholly to miss the point. For Walls, "Africa is already revealing the limitations of theology as generally taught in the West. The truth is that Western models of theology are too small for Africa."[8] Established theologies require modification because "the churches of Africa and Asia are being forced to work out some sort of Christian response to situations where Western theology has no answers because it has no questions or relevant experience. . . . Themes are being recognized in the Scriptures that the West never noticed."[9] This particular observation when applied to the whole of Christian history lends itself to a prescriptive conclusion. "Each time the gospel crosses a cultural frontier,

---

[8] Andrew F. Walls, "Globalization and the Study of Christian History," in *Globalizing Theology: Belief and Practice in an Era of World Christianity*, ed. Craig Ott and Harold A. Netland (Grand Rapids: Baker Academic, 2006), 74. Sanneh chides Western academic theologians for "having decided to turn their backs on world Christianity as the offspring of mission's outdated theology of territorial expansionism. . . . However the missionaries may have represented Christianity, goes the theological argument, aboriginal populations could form no adequate concept of Christian doctrine to have embraced the religion correctly. So their profession of Christianity is misguided and mistaken, if not downright corrupted." Lamin O. Sanneh, "World Christianity and the New Historiography: Historical and Global Interconnections," in *Enlarging the Story: Perspectives on Writing World Christian History*, ed. Wilbert R. Shenk (Maryknoll, NY: Orbis Books, 2002), 102.

[9] Andrew F. Walls, "Christianity in the Non-Western World: A Study in the Serial Nature of Christian Expansion," in *The Cross-Cultural Process in Christian History: Studies in the Transmission and Appropriation of Faith* (Maryknoll, NY: Orbis Books, 2002), 46. By way of example, Walls notes how Western theology struggles with "issues involving such things as witchcraft or sorcery, since these do not exist in an Enlightenment universe. Nor can Western theology usefully discuss ancestors, since the West does not have the family structures that raise the questions. Western theology has difficulty coping with principalities and powers, whether in relation to their grip on the universe or to Christ's triumph over them on the cross. The reason is that it is hard for Western consciousness to treat them as other than abstractions." Walls, "Globalization," 76.

a fresh set of intellectual materials is available for the task."[10] The faith itself is enlarged in its cross-cultural transmission; cultural translation is the ground of positive theological construction. Acknowledging this positive point means recognizing some critical distance from received answers as they appear within the tradition. For Kenneth Ross, this entails a "radical shift in approach," one that depicts the Christian faith "not in terms of the transposition of certain denominational forms of the faith from Europe to Africa but rather in terms of the experience of African peoples addressed by the gospel of Jesus Christ and responding to it in various ways."[11] Africans become themselves the agents of theological reflection. Their [African's] material concerns focus less on the institution and the variety of distinctions between religion and public life associated with this approach, and more on the "traditional marriage systems, kinship loyalties, rites of passage, social clubs, traditional medicine, oracles, and festivals" and under the conditions of pluralism characteristic of African (and Asian) society.[12] None of this belongs to the ambiguity of statistical forecast. It describes the current reality of the Christian majority.

As a key tenet within this discussion, the gospel cannot find expression apart from cultural form. For Walls, "all churches are culture churches, including our own."[13] Mathias Mundadan, developing the same historiographical concerns from an Indian perspective, draws an identical conclusion. The gospel is "not identified with cultures but is identified in cultures. It cannot exist apart from a cultural expression."[14] The point concerns the gospel as a living entity, meaning that

---

[10] Andrew F. Walls, "The Rise of Global Theologies," in *Global Theology in Evangelical Perspective: Exploring the Contextual Nature of Theology and Mission*, ed. Jeffrey P. Greenman and Gene L. Green (Downers Grove, IL: IVP Academic, 2012), 26. Drawing correspondences between early Christianity's encounter with a Hellenistic thought world and that presently occurring in Africa, Sanneh notes how "this convergence between Christianity and the lively [African] historical pagan heritage would accrue credit to Christianity—as Aquinas said of the pagan heritage of the early church fathers." Sanneh, "World Christianity," 110.

[11] Kenneth R. Ross, "Doing Theology with a New Historiography," *Journal of Theology for Southern Africa*, no. 99 (1997): 95.

[12] Ibid.

[13] Andrew F. Walls, "Africa and Christian Identity," *Mission Focus* 6 (1978): 12. See also the informative discussion in Anthony J. Gittins, "The Universal in the Local: Power, Piety, and Paradox in the Formation of Missionary Community," in *Mission and Culture: The Louis J. Luzbetak Lectures, 2000–2010*, ed. Stephen B. Bevans (Maryknoll, NY: Orbis Books, 2012), 133-87.

[14] A. Mathias Mundadan, "The Changing Task of Christian History: A View at the Onset of the Third Millennium," in Shenk, *Enlarging the Story*, 24.

the history of Christianity is the history of the encounter of the gospel message of Jesus with different peoples and their ever-newer religious-cultural and sociopolitical contexts. It is the history of the impregnation of these contexts by the gospel, the assimilation of the cultures of the peoples by the gospel and that of the gospel by their cultures, and the history of the consequent changes in the Christian movement and of the cultures of the people.[15]

In other words, the fear of cultural syncretism that so often influences the theological evaluation of developments in world Christianity reflects more a failure to appreciate the depth of the tradition's own cultural limits. This account of Christian history intrudes on any such false identity. A simple binary of continuity and discontinuity, as is often used to validate approaches to succession and institutional continuity, lacks sufficient conceptual sophistication.

As an illustration of this point, Walls contests the definition of schism operative within ecumenical discourse. In similar manner to Hoekendijk, this he conceives along cultural and linguistic lines. Turning to the decisive early ecumenical councils, these for Walls "represented a consensus between those who did their theological thinking in Greek and those who did it in Latin. . . . The century after Chalcedon, as successive emperors sought imperial unity by imposing the formula as the final statement of Christology, brought disaster, the Church split three ways, and broadly along cultural and linguistic lines: Greco-Latin, Syriac, and Coptic."[16] This is not to deny the significant theology issues in play. It rather observes a necessary link between the theological and the cultural. Walls describes the sixth century as "a neglected Christian watershed—a great ecumenical failure," one in which the "division of the Church on cultural and linguistic lines . . . became routine, a

---

[15]Ibid., 23. This includes the critical rejection of the assumption that the "cultural encounter [in the Greco-Roman world] was the only possible encounter, and the pattern of synthesis was set once for all. Wherever the Christian message reached, it was under the garb of that set pattern" (25). Mundadan cites the observation from the Church History Association of India (CHAI) that the "history of Christianity in India has hitherto often been treated as an eastward extension of western ecclesiastical history." Church History Association of India (CHAI), "Scheme for a Comprehensive History of Christianity in India," *Indian Church History Review* 8, no. 2 (1974): 89.

[16]Andrew F. Walls, "World Christianity and the Early Church," in *A New Day: Essays on World Christianity in Honor of Lamin Sanneh*, ed. Akintunde E. Akinade (New York: Peter Lang, 2010), 25-26.

matter of convenience."[17] One part of this schism's enduring significance lies in establishing a pattern that later schisms (including that of the Reformation) followed and that during the colonial period became a type of modus operandi. The key ecumenical question today, by extension, concerns not the potential institutional unification of bodies developed, in the main, in the West, but how "African, Indian, Chinese, Korean, Hispanic, North American and East and West European expressions of Christian faith and life can live together and bring mutual enrichment and correction."[18] While this position lies distant from the established ecumenical method dealing with apostolicity, it is, in Walls's estimation, an immediate conclusion to be drawn from world Christianity and its intrusion on established territorial limits for Christian history and theology.

As to the identity of the "historical Christian faith," Walls observes the radical differences in form and theological concentration developed through the faith's historical course. Continuity lies not in place, language or institution. It is found in the centrality of the person of Jesus Christ, in a certain understanding of history, including the consciousness of belonging to a community connected across time and place, and in the use of Scripture, bread, wine and water.[19] A controlling point emerges at this point. Walls's interest as a church historian is not limited to the cultural; his concern is with "generational continuity."[20] The range of cultural particularities clothing these identifiable continuities should not be overlooked, because they too define the faith's historical progression, the "kinship of Christians across the generations."[21] They are part of the process of salvation because salvation includes the redemption of history. A definition of mission follows, one grounded (like Hoekendijk's) in history. Mission is no derivate of a territorial church—it is the nature of the church's historical continuity.

Bediako confirms the point. "If the world Christianity of our time discloses the logic of Christian history, it is the logic of Christian history as

---

[17]Ibid., 27.

[18]Ibid., 28.

[19]Andrew F. Walls, "The Gospel as Prisoner and Liberator of Culture," in *The Missionary Movement in Christian History: Studies in the Transmission of Faith* (Maryknoll, NY: Orbis Books, 1996), 6-7. For an in-depth examination of this position, see Andrew F. Walls, "Christianity," in *A New Handbook of Living Religions*, ed. John R. Hinnells (London: Penguin, 2003), 55-161.

[20]Walls, "Globalization," 72.

[21]Ibid.

mission."[22] Bediako does not mean by this that Christian history is a history of first encounter. It is missionary history because of the "symbiotic relationship between mission as 'cultural crossing' and theology as the process whereby the faith appropriated is lived, embodied and communicated."[23] Mission is first history because the process of cultural conversion is generational.[24] Christian expansion is generational, to continue with Sanneh, because it is not just a matter "of geographical range, but of cultural scope."[25] The identity of and maturity in the historical faith belongs to this definition of expansion.

Theorists of world Christianity are foremost historians. The importance of this point should not be lost. Their driving theological assumption, with Walls as a representative example, is that "in the Christian understanding of divine activity, salvation comes not only *in* history but *through* history; history is, as it were, the stuff, the material in which salvation takes place."[26] Focus falls on the continuity of divine action. "The redemptive purpose of God is cross-generational. It is not completed in one generation, only in the totality of the generations."[27] No single generation, be that the apostolic era, the period of the church councils or the Protestant Reformation, becomes definitive. Nor should the particular theological interests of a period come to determine the history as such. "Bad history," Walls avers, cannot be legitimized by the "plea that it is good theology."[28] In this respect, this consideration of history prefers the term "Christian" to that of "church" history. Approaching world Christianity through the lens of ecclesial institution (through the "church"), it is argued, includes a range of theological filters that direct attention away from the cross-cultural in that history.

---

[22]Kwame Bediako, "The Emergence of World Christianity and the Remaking of Theology," *Journal of African Christian Thought* 12, no. 2 (2009): 51.

[23]Ibid.

[24]Walls acknowledges the pioneering work of Charles Kraft in this regard. See, for example, Charles H. Kraft, "Christian Conversion or Cultural Conversion," *Practical Anthropology* 10, no. 4 (1963): 179-87.

[25]Lamin O. Sanneh, "Post-Western Wine, Post-Christian Wineskins? The Bible and the Third Wave Awakening," in Burrows, Gornik and McLean, *Understanding World Christianity*, 104.

[26]Walls, "Globalization," 70. See also Lamin O. Sanneh, *Disciples of All Nations: Pillars of World Christianity* (Oxford: Oxford University Press, 2007), 53.

[27]Walls, "Globalization," 71.

[28]Andrew F. Walls, "Eusebius Tries Again: The Task of Reconceiving and Re-visioning the Study of Christian History," in Shenk, *Enlarging the Story*, 18.

Such an approach, Sanneh argues, develops in service to "classical Christian thought" and inhibits investigation into "the tide of Christianity's global growth, expansion, and intercontinental connections."[29]

Apostolicity, as the historical continuity of the church, needs to be defined in terms of the church's actual historical course. From this perspective, Christian history has not been *progressive*, radiating out from a single heartland, a single geographical and cultural territory. The church has not been continuous as a visible cultural entity. It has been, Walls argues, *serial*.[30] Christian history is a story of the gospel crossing cultural boundaries. It is a history of both advance and recession. Where recession occurred, where Christianity became a minority or even died out in lands where it had been the majority faith, this "threatened eclipse of Christianity was averted by its cross-cultural diffusion. Crossing cultural boundaries has been the life-blood of historic Christianity."[31] While Christianity might diminish in one center, this does not indicate the demise of the faith. The barbarians, one might note with some irony, saved the faith. In this historical observation Walls finds a normative theological principle: "Christian faith must go on being translated, must continuously enter into vernacular culture and interact with it, or it withers and fades."[32] Though absent the formal terminology, Walls presents a theology of apostolicity. The church has been continuous in its historical course only because of its movement across cultural boundaries. Apostolicity is bound to the local appropriation of the gospel, and so its translation into local forms. The church apostolic is the church historically and so culturally pluriform.

---

[29]Sanneh, "World Christianity," 102-3. See also Lamin O. Sanneh, "Global Christianity and the Re-education of the West," *Christian Century* 112, no. 22 (1995): 715-18; Paul V. Kollman, "After Church History? Writing the History of Christianity from a Global Perspective," *Horizons* 31, no. 2 (2004): 336-37. This caution applies, on the one hand, to an understanding of the church's own cultural history. The operative image of the church that this history supports and promulgates, for Sanneh, is tied to the "Western territorial complex." Sanneh, "World Christianity," 103. On the other hand, as the subject of this history remains a Western body, so it grants no space for those in Africa or Asia to consider their own histories. Insofar as the "churches have been formed by someone else's history," Ross observes, so this history is "a foreign and alienating point of reference." Ross, "Doing Theology," 98.

[30]Walls, "Christianity in the Non-Western World," 30.

[31]Ibid., 32. This point, Walls notes, guided Kenneth Scott Latourette's work: Christian history is both recession and advance (30). Bediako makes the same point, observing that "both *accession* and *recession* belong within Christian religious history," meaning, by extension, that Christianity is without a "permanent centre." Bediako, "Emergence of World Christianity," 51.

[32]Walls, "Christianity in the Non-Western World," 29.

Excursus: The Moratorium on Missions

The call for a moratorium on missions provides an interesting example of the tendency to reduce the developments in world Christianity to a subset of "mission history" and without material significance for a wider theological discourse. In a famed 1971 speech delivered to the Mission Festival of the Reformed Church in America, John Gatu, then general secretary of the Presbyterian Church of East Africa, issued the call: "Missionary, Go Home." Gatu sought, for a period of not less than five years, the "withdrawal of foreign missionaries from many parts of the Third World."[33] Such withdrawal would serve a particular purpose: the churches from "the Third World must be allowed to find their own identity, and . . . the continuation of the present missionary movement is a hindrance to this selfhood of the church" (70). African Christian selfhood, something deemed necessary to the growth of the church, suffered because it evaluated the cultural and religious heritage of Africa according to an alien set of values. "Insofar as African religions are concerned, who is to decide that what my father or my grandfather believed was magic or superstition? Certainly not a missionary. He can only do so by applying Western values and degrees without the understanding of the social, cultural, and religious dynamics that led up to such practices" (71). Gatu's central point concerned not the activity of missions as such; "mission" constituted a form of Western ecclesiastical control. Gatu drew direct links between this devaluation of the African cultural milieu with the perceived need for ongoing missionary administration guided by Western standards of efficiency. Western funding sources maintained control, and the churches in Africa remained dependent. The moratorium sought space for the African church to develop its own ecclesiological forms, including the appropriation of its cultural heritage. Nor was this concern restricted to Africa. Gatu's call found immediate support from Latin American and Asian voices, notably Emérito P. Nacpil of the Philippines and José Míguez Bonino of Argentina.

Burgess Carr, general secretary of the All Africa Conference of Churches, furthered Gatu's position. God's mission is the "Holy Spirit communicating

---

[33]A gathered collection of the primary material is available in *In Search of Mission* (IDOC Documentation Participation Project, 1974), 49-86. The above Gatu quote appears on p. 70. Subsequent references are provided parenthetically within the text. For a summary of the moratorium debate, see Emele Mba Uka, *Missionaries Go Home? A Sociological Interpretation of an African Response to Christian Missions* (Berne: Peter Lang, 1989), 197-246.

through the Apostles the celebrated Magnalia Dei [the mighty acts of God] extending from Exodus to Resurrection. This message is communicated to each one in 'his [or her] own native language.' The Holy Spirit guarantees that. When God is the primary actor that is the way it is" (72). Carr continues that the Western church "distorted" mission by creating a category called "pagan" and used this as "the raw material used to attain [its own] salvation as well. Talk about theological heresy!" The growth of the Christian faith in Africa results not from the "work of 'missionaries' sent to rescue the perishing 'natives.'" It is rather "being done in Africa by the Africa Independent Churches who have placed evangelism at the very center of their life and not consigned it to peripheral structures staffed by 'experts' and financed by the local churches" (73). Turning to the thrust of the moratorium itself, Carr notes how it is "a debate about structures of exploitation, spiritual exploitation at that. Why should someone save his soul at the expense of emasculating my humanity? Why should I be portrayed as a perpetually helpless nobody, in order to re-enforce the racial and spiritual arrogance of people in Europe and North America?" (74). The objection is clear: culture belongs to the humanity of a person, and making the range of Western cultural forms necessary to the gospel succeeds only in disembodying the African Christian, in creating a superficial Christianity. Carr points to the primacy in African agency, meaning that the expansion of Christianity is not first a function of Western institutions but the translation of the gospel into "the center" of African life.

At the "Ecumenical Sharing of Personnel" WCC meeting held in Choully, July 1972, this desire for selfhood included a critical examination of received forms of the church. The moratorium, it argued, intended "to allow the receiving churches a time of critical questioning of the inherited structures and programs which may be cherished by some and yet are only relevant to a different age, and therefore remain a constant and unnecessary burden to the church" (44). What constituted the "inherited structures" under question the statement did not clarify. The goals of the moratorium were, however, forthrightly outlined:

1. To discover an authentic African form of Christianity which can in turn enrich all the Christian churches of the world;

2. To encourage African churches to leave the dependent attitudes many of us have adopted;

3. To help African churches to establish their own priorities in their work for Christ and to become fully missionary churches themselves;

4. To enable the traditionally missionary-sending churches in other lands to re-examine the nature of their mission and their future partnership with other churches. (44-45)

To give a concrete example of this vision, the document turns to the historical event of an "enforced 'moratorium,'" something later termed "orphaned missions," that is, the forced removal of Western leadership from the African churches during the two World Wars. When this occurred, "all of these African churches not only survived this enforced 'moratorium' but were strengthened by discovering their own self-reliance, setting their own priorities and learning their place in the universal Church" (45). The advent of local leadership promoted the expansion of the gospel. Though it might appear a rather startling plea today, it bears repeating that local leadership within the church remained a debated point even during the late 1970s.

In terms of its reception, this moratorium debate seems to have been interpreted as simply a "mission problem" and its discussion limited to mission circles. Western theorists focused on a perceived rejection of mission as such. Gerald Anderson framed the issue as one of "*integrity*—for both sides" (84). While the churches in the Third World struggle with questions of "authority and control as they seek to establish and express their own identity," the church in Europe and North America has to deal with the issue "of accountability and faithfulness to the mandate for world mission inherent in the gospel" (84). This twofold concern Anderson described as "the relation between selfhood and universality," the implication being that the African concern for selfhood should not be set in opposition to the universal intent embodied in the Western enterprise (84). A universal focus opened the local beyond itself. By contrast, a sweeping "moratorium would promote the domestication of the churches in their respective cultures. This in turn would promote the further encroachment on them of tribal religions" (85). The basis of this fear Anderson traces to a "cultural paganism [that] infests the churches in most areas of the world" and most particularly the churches in the North (85). This point he later repeats in defense of his position. Africa needs the "alien" missionary presence to offset this collapse into paganism, for it reminds the church of its dislocation. The point is not false, but it is an example of how a problem in the Northern church becomes projected onto the South, along with the assertion of mandatory controls before any comparative problem develops. At the same time the Northern church (even it acknowledges such a problem in theory) would reject any such controls if proposed by the South.

The responses to Anderson illustrate well how the moratorium debate focused on normative theological claims made by the Western church. Latin American theologian Ruben Lores countered in a rather aggressive tone: Anderson's supposed theological argument simply continued the imperialism the moratorium intended to depose. It claimed the "whole church" for the churches of Europe and North America and the "whole Gospel" for something that "amounts to the sectarian interpretation of the Gospel by each denomination" (55). The "universality of the Gospel and of the church," according to Lores, cannot be defined "by the presence of foreigners. We must not confuse foreigners with universality" (55). The Western church should encourage a "process of deforeignization . . . for the purpose of making the churches and the Gospel more meaningful in each culture" (56).

Musembe Kaisera also picked up the language of "cultural paganism" and summarized Anderson's message to non-Western churches thusly: "You people need us if you are going to keep from being overrun by paganism, and you need us to insure the integrity both of the Gospel and of the Church" (59). But for Kaisera this argument was a simple smokescreen. Anderson was "chafing a bit against the creative adaptability that is now taking place between Christianity and its cultural context in the Third world, a process that should have taken place when Christianity was first introduced" (59). One sees here, in other words, the continuing contest of Western theologians framing their positions in terms of an acultural, that is, universal, theological position, while non-Western theologians read this in terms of cultural imposition and control.

Though attention might be drawn to the heated language, many of the debate's substantial points share an evident similarity with the contemporary discussion of world Christianity: local appropriation is basic to maturity in the faith; external structures and the associated ecclesial controls amount to cultural controls; the contest is not between an established historic theology and local interests but between a particular cultural expression of the gospel that claims a normative status against the freedom of the gospel to be spoken in the local vernacular. For example, Paul Kalanda's interpretive essay on the moratium debate with the telling title "Consolidating Christianity in Africa" affirms that making Christianity meaningful for Africans must include "a systematic dialogue with the religious philosophy that lies behind the customs with which Christianity has to come to terms. Such dialogue is to be based not on the fact that there is full truth in its entirety in African traditional religion, but on an understanding of that truth as something towards which we are all growing."[34] This remains a central insight for the contemporary discussion.

As a final point, one should note the dating of the debate: 1971–1975. It occurred, in other words, coincidentally with the debates leading to the 1982 WCC statement *Baptism, Eucharist and Ministry*. Despite the attention given it at the 1972/3 CWME Bangkok conference, the moratorium debate, even while expressing concern over the cultural form of the prevailing ecclesiologies, failed to enter the conceptual horizon of the BEM "consensus" document. Yet the claimed advance of BEM includes the adoption of a methodology that relativizes any such cultural origins in favor of a transhistorical structure theologically named the people of God, a culture that includes structure and order but equally clothing, architecture and liturgical style. The contrast is indicative of the wider debate and the governing controls of apostolicity as conceived through the lens of schism.

6.3 Mirroring the New Testament Dynamic

Theorists of world Christianity draw direct parallels between what is occurring in Africa, Asia and Latin America today, what has occurred through the faith's historical course and the events recorded in the New Testament.[35] "World Christianity is not a development of the last century, it is the natural Christian condition. . . . Cultural diversity was built into the church within

---

[34]Paul Kalanda, "Consolidating Christianity in Africa," *Missiology* 4, no. 4 (1976): 402.

[35]Nor, it might be noted, is this observation of recent vintage. For Bediako, this parallel between the early church and contemporary processes in Africa was first indicated by Campbell N. Moody, *The Mind of the Early Converts* (London: Hodder & Stoughton, 1920), and later by John Foster, *Then and Now—The Historic Church and the Younger Churches* (London: SCM Press, 1942).

the New Testament period."[36] Walls argues not for a return to New Testament ecclesiology. Quite the opposite. The development of institution is not a false imposition on an early dynamic. Speaking the gospel through the conceptual landscape, in the idiom, and using the structures of Hellenistic culture is no distortion of the message. The conversion of culture and the accompanying enlargement of the tradition is basic to the gospel itself. It became acknowledged as such, Walls argues, with the formal decision not to require circumcision of Gentile believers at the Jerusalem Council in Acts 15.

The first church, both in practice and self-understanding, was Jewish. Peter interprets the events of Jesus Christ's life, death, resurrection and ascension as the fulfillment of the promises given to Israel (Acts 2:14-39). His audience, although composed of both local citizens and those visiting from afar, is Jewish, and the promised Messiah is his subject. As to the constitution and practices of this community, these maintained Jewish custom. This community gathered at the temple (Acts 2:46), maintained animal sacrifices and the purity laws (Acts 21:26), and devoted itself to "the prayers" (Acts 2:42), that is, "the temple liturgy," and this meant "congregating in a place where (beyond an outer court) none but Jews could go."[37] James, one of the first leaders, was known for his righteous commitment to the law. In all of this, Walls notes, the first church interpreted Jesus "from the perspective of Israel's history, hopes, and expectations." Such is evident in the inability to "conceive of Jesus' saving work without its political climax in the history of Israel because, in Jewish terms, salvation is unintelligible without the salvation of the nation."[38] Distinctive elements did differentiate this group from other observant Jews. The group held their property in common, shared meals together and sold possessions to distribute to those with need, especially widows and orphans (Acts 2:44-46; 4:32-35; 6:1-4). Distinct theological emphases appeared in the identification of Jesus Christ with "three key figures in the Scriptures of Israel—the Davidic Messiah who was the national savior, the Son of Man who would figure in the judgment of the world, and the Suffering Servant who sacrificed himself for his people."[39] Walls concludes that

---

[36]Walls, "World Christianity and the Early Church," 18.
[37]Walls, "Converts or Proselytes?," 2.
[38]Ibid.
[39]Ibid., 2-3.

the life of the first church "was 'Christian' because Jesus was at its center; yet it remained essentially and inalienably Jewish."[40] All of this indicates a discontinuity within continuity, including the call for Israel to "turn back" and be restored, to repent, be baptized in the name of Jesus Christ and receive the Holy Spirit.[41] To use Walls's language, this was "Jewish life and thought converted. It is life lived, and thinking done, in terms of the messianic age."[42] It was no new religion, nor did these Jewish believers need a "special name; they were Israel."[43] Nevertheless, Jesus Christ, as the fulfillment of the law, had given these believers a key for interpreting their religious, cultural and political heritage, one that set it in a new direction.

The type of internal crisis evident at the Jerusalem Council in Acts 15 belongs to this process of conversion. Pentecost, even with Peter's interpretive sermon focused on Israel, constituted the first step (Acts 2:1-13). According to Sanneh, this singular innovation "enabled the religion to adopt the multiplicity of geographical centers as legitimate destinations for the gospel."[44] Pentecost's full implications were not immediately clear, and one sees contests develop along cultural lines between "Hellenists" and "Hebrews" both within the Christian community (Acts 6:1) and without in the "synagogue of the Freedmen," composed of Cyrenians, Alexandrians and others from Cilicia and Asia. The scattering of the early church that followed in the wake of Stephen's stoning (Acts 6:8–8:3) stimulated a missionary expansion as these refugees moved into other language centers, including Samaria (Acts 8:4-25), Phoenicia, Cyprus and Antioch (Acts 11:19). But before developing the wider implications of this movement, Acts turns to the encounter between Peter and Cornelius (Acts 10:1-48). The Spirit falls even on Gentiles while coincidentally converting Peter's understanding of purity and the processes attendant to such. The resulting theological conclusion that

---

[40]Andrew F. Walls, "Old Athens and New Jerusalem: Some Signposts for Christian Scholarship in the Early History of Mission Studies," *International Bulletin of Missionary Research* 21, no. 4 (1997): 148.

[41]Walls, "Converts or Proselytes?," 3.

[42]Ibid., 4.

[43]Ibid., 3.

[44]Lamin O. Sanneh, "The Gospel, Language and Culture: The Theological Method in Cultural Analysis," *International Review of Mission* 84 (1995): 52. See also Lamin O. Sanneh, "Africa," in *Toward the Twenty-First Century in Christian Mission: Essays in Honor of Gerald H. Anderson*, ed. James M. Phillips and Robert T. Coote (Grand Rapids: Eerdmans, 1993), 92.

"God shows no partiality, but in every nation anyone who fears him and does what is right is acceptable to him" (Acts 10:34-35) becomes decisive for the Jerusalem Council. More than this, for Sanneh, it defines Christian history.[45]

The contention centered on the "conversion of the Gentiles" and the proposal that "unless you are circumcised according to the custom of Moses, you cannot be saved" prompted a gathering of the apostles and elders in Jerusalem. In contrast to positions that attribute the cultural openness of the fledgling Christian faith to a claimed universalism at the heart of Hellenistic culture, the resulting Apostolic Decree was no simple decision issued by the "Greek" Paul. Though the initiative came from Antioch (Acts 15:1-3), the proper location for the question was Jerusalem among the Jewish believers. Peter, as the one through whom God chose to speak the message to the Gentiles (Acts 15:7), gives the decisive testimony. And upon hearing of God's acting among the Gentiles, James delivers the final decision, observing God's creating a people from the Gentiles, and confirms this using the Hebrew Scriptures (Acts 15:13-21). One should not deny the facilitating historical factors for the spread of the gospel and the prompting of the question in its cross-cultural transmission and appropriation, but it is not a decision contingent on the "universalism" of Hellenistic culture. It is an act undertaken by Jewish actors and according to Jewish processes and standards.

The conversion of the Gentiles without the accompanying and scripturally mandated marks of the law, in the words of Sanneh, must have "struck the old-style Jewish believers as dangerous deviation from the established pillars of the received code" (an observation supported by Gal 2:11-14).[46] After all, there existed an established mode of Gentile conversion to the God of Abraham, Isaac and Jacob that circumvented this problem. To convert, Walls observes, meant incorporation into Israel: "incorporation was essential, since

---

[45]Sanneh, *Disciples of All Nations*, 3-5. Newbigin makes a similar point: "It is true that Cornelius was converted, but it is also true that 'Christianity' was changed. One decisive step was taken on the long road from the incarnation of the Word of God as a Jew of the first-century Palestine to summing up of *all things* in him." J. E. Lesslie Newbigin, *The Open Secret: An Introduction to the Theology of Mission* (Grand Rapids: Eerdmans, 1995), 182. It means that "the church cannot lay down in advance for such people what commitment will mean but must . . . learn from them new lessons about its own obedience. As a learning community that can only press forward from partial to fuller understanding of the Father's reign, the church will know that it cannot impose its own ethical insights at any one time and place upon those whom the Spirit calls into its company" (140).

[46]Sanneh, *Disciples of All Nations*, 10.

God's promises were to the nation."[47] A convert took on the marks of the covenant and undertook instruction in the law. A Gentile believer would undergo an extended process of proselytism. "Such a proposal would seem entirely natural to many in the Jerusalem community of believers in Jesus, and it is no surprise to find it was strongly urged."[48] If any culture might claim a special relationship to the divine Word and, by extension, make a legitimate case for cultural conformity, it is the one shaped by the Torah. And if the Jerusalem Council had decided for this set proselyte model, it "would have established fixed norms of Christian lifestyle, a common pattern of social custom to be practiced by all Christians, whatever their ethnic or cultural background. Its parameters would have been essentially Jewish."[49]

Becoming a proselyte means exchanging one set of beliefs and associated customs for those held by another people. "To become a proselyte involves the sacrifice of national and social affiliations. It involves a form of naturalization, incorporation into another milieu. But once the transition has been made, all the norms of conduct are set out; the way forward is safe. Precedent is built into the proselyte model; the proselyte inherits the accumulated experience of others."[50] It means following the established rules and living within the given structures.[51] From the perspective of the community that the proselyte joins, conversion centers on adopting what the community has previously received. In the case of a Gentile believer incorporated into Israel, continuity occurs not through ethnic or biological means but by way of teaching and ritual, by way of enculturation into a set cultural pattern. It circumscribes the

---

[47]Walls, "Old Athens and New Jerusalem," 147.

[48]Ibid.

[49]Ibid., 148.

[50]Ibid. Timothy Wiarda objects to approaches to Acts 15 that treat the law as "purely a cultural *product*," meaning, by extension, that "those who gathered at the Jerusalem Council had to wrestle with something other than simply the pressures of culture and ethnocentrism." Timothy Wiarda, "The Jerusalem Council and the Theological Task," *Journal of the Evangelical Theological Society* 46, no. 2 (2003): 235. The works he has in mind include David J. Hesselgrave and Edward Rommen, *Contextualization: Meanings, Methods, and Models* (Grand Rapids: Baker, 1989), 20-21; Charles H. Kraft, *Christianity in Culture: A Study in Dynamic Biblical Theologizing in Cross-Cultural Perspective* (Maryknoll, NY: Orbis Books, 1979), 340-41. Insofar as these authors depict the concern in flat cultural terms, the point is well made. But the position Wiarda opposes has greater complexity, especially as it finds contemporary correspondences. Walls is aware of the inseparability of the theological from the cultural form it assumes, both in terms of Jewish culture and in terms of the contemporary African experience.

[51]Walls, "Converts or Proselytes?," 6.

questions that might be asked. Should the proselyte model have been affirmed, Walls continues, "a good deal of what appears in the New Testament letters to early Christian communities would not have been needed."[52] There would have been no need to ask whether a Christian might eat meat that had been offered to idols because no proselyte would have eaten with a pagan neighbor.[53] There would have been no "circumcision school" and so no need to develop the range of contrasting theological positions such as justification by faith. One need only submit to the structures of the covenant. Nor, Walls argues, is this tendency limited to the New Testament: "the insistence on imposing our own religious culture, our own Torah and circumcision," is the church's oldest and most persistent heresy.[54] Despite the rejection of the proselyte model, it has remained a temptation through Christian history, becoming evident, by way of example, during the colonial period.

The Jerusalem Council forsook this established model. It agreed that God had purified the Gentiles by giving them the Holy Spirit, that God "made no distinction between them and us" (Acts 15:9), meaning that "followers of Jesus the Messiah, even if not ethnic Jews, had indeed entered Israel."[55] They did not require the marks of the law, did not need to be enculturated into Israel. Gentile believers were converts, and this, Walls argues, marked a "critical departure from Jewish tradition and experience." Guided by the desire to impose "no further burden" on Gentile believers (Acts 15:28), this decision "built cultural diversity into the church forever."[56] Sanneh agrees. With this decision, "territoriality ceased to be a requirement of faith."[57] Believers had no need to "serve a cultural apprenticeship," to "conform to one cultural ideal or standard to be saved."[58] Gentile believers were not to move from their particular cultural context into that of Judaism, nor were they to add something new to their old belief system.

---

[52]Walls, "Old Athens and New Jerusalem," 148.
[53]Ibid.
[54]Walls, "Converts or Proselytes?," 6. See also Hinne Wagenaar, "Stop Harassing the Gentiles: The Importance of Acts 15 for African Theology," *Journal for African Christian Thought* 6, no. 1 (2003): 44-54.
[55]Walls, "Converts or Proselytes?," 4. See also Walls, "Old Athens and New Jerusalem," 146-53.
[56]Walls, "Converts or Proselytes?," 5.
[57]Sanneh, *Disciples of All Nations*, 7.
[58]Ibid., 6, 7. See further Lamin O. Sanneh, "Should Christianity Be Missionary? An Appraisal and an Agenda," *Dialog* 40, no. 2 (2001): 87.

Conversion, Walls argues, "involves turning the whole personality with its social, cultural, and religious inheritance toward Christ, opening it up to him. It is about turning *what is already there*."[59] Conversion is the call to live within one's originating culture according to this new Christian identity, "disturbing, challenging, altering the conventions of that life, *but doing so from the inside*."[60] This introduced a measure of unpredictability into the Christian faith. Whereas the proselyte became enculturated into received patterns, for converts the "experience of old believers could be little help to them. . . . Such theological issues were beyond the experience and counsel of the oldest and the best and most experienced believers of a different cultural upbringing."[61] The answers present in the Jewish tradition could not simply transfer to the questions embodied in Hellenistic institutions and ways of life. Converts needed to turn their way of life toward Jesus. "They must think Christ into the patterns of thought they have inherited, into their networks of relationship and their processes for making decisions. And new issues, cultural or intellectual, where it is necessary to make a Christian choice, are arising all the time and with no exact parallels in the past."[62] The answers are not given in advance. By further implication, the vision of Christ developed by converts forms "among the elements of the preconversion life as he is received by faith there."[63] Conversion demands significant continuity with the local cultural heritage and leads to an expansion in the Christian tradition itself. To speak of Jesus Christ in another cultural milieu is to open that message to the range of questions, resources and idioms found in that culture, including those in the political and religious spheres.[64]

---

[59]Walls, "Converts or Proselytes?," 6.
[60]Walls, "Old Athens and New Jerusalem," 148.
[61]Walls, "Rise of Global Theologies," 24.
[62]Walls, "Converts or Proselytes?," 6.
[63]Ibid.
[64]For an early example of this process, Walls examines the terminological shift between *messiah* and *kyrios*. As Greek-language believers proclaimed Jesus in Antioch, the preferred Hebrew title of Messiah required translation into the local idiom. Though a literal translation might have sufficed, "Messiah" made sense in terms of Israel's history and religion but had no significance in a Hellenistic setting. These believers settled on the term *kyrios*, Walls argues, because it included a claim on the religious landscape and so "opened the way to a truly Hellenistic understanding of Jesus." Walls, "Old Athens and New Jerusalem," 146. Brian Stanley picks up Walls's argument, noting that "New Testament scholars now inform us that the term *kyrios* was well rooted in Palestinian Jewish culture, and that lordship had been ascribed to Jesus as early as the first Aramaic-speaking Jerusalem church." Brian Stanley, "Conversion to Christianity:

This proselyte/convert distinction, it might be further observed, indicates both a mission method and a way of religious existence. Mission develops, not destabilizes, the community, a point Walls illustrates by reference to Ephesians. While traditional exegetical treatments concentrate on the importance of the body and the cultural encounter of Jew and Gentile, such spatial aspects need to be supplemented with a historical frame. "The body functions in time as well as in space; time is also an element in which salvation is worked out: its various manifestations across time are necessary for its completion, for 'the completion of him who himself completes all things everywhere'" (Eph 1:19-23).[65] The point needs to be reiterated: the cultural element in conversion serves the historical continuity of the faith, or, the processes of cultural conversion themselves belong to Christian salvation.

> Christ takes flesh as he is received by faith in various segments of social reality at different periods, as well as in different places. And these different manifestations belong together; they are part of the same story. Salvation is complete when all the generations of God's people are gathered together, for only then is Christ's humanity complete. By the same token, the church has to be viewed across time. No one single segment of time encapsulates it; the segments belong together. The work of salvation is cross-generational.[66]

Such is the nature of the "body," and this temporal perspective means that the church includes a plurality of cultural forms. In Ephesus, two cultural communities belonged to the church, one Jewish and one Hellenistic. This is proper. As the coming together of diverse elements stimulates shared convictions about Jesus Christ, so each culture is to be converted to him. "The full stature of Christ is revealed only as a fresh cultural entity is incorporated into the church, which is his body."[67] This indicates the nature of the body's

---

The Colonization of the Mind?," *International Review of Mission* 92, no. 3 (2003): 323. He reasserts Walls's central contention, however, because whatever meaning *kyrios* might have had for Jewish believers, Gentile believers would have heard "a startling claim about the status of Jesus of Nazareth as one to whom could be applied, in a unique and exclusive sense, the term currently employed to refer to cult divinities, and, by extension through the imperial cult, to the Roman emperor" (323). The reception of this term within a Hellenistic milieu added a range of meanings not available to a Jewish audience and so expanded the understanding of who Jesus Christ was and is.

[65] Andrew F. Walls, "The Ephesian Moment: At a Crossroads in Christian History," in *Cross-Cultural Process in Christian History*, 74.

[66] Ibid.

[67] Walls, "Old Athens and New Jerusalem," 149.

own maturity. The "full stature of Christ" (Eph 4:13) occurs only in this cultural encounter and exchange. "Only 'together,' not on our own, can we reach his full stature."[68] Walls rejects the cultural relativism model where each expression is celebrated in isolation. "The Ephesian metaphors of the temple and of the body show each of the culture-specific segments as necessary to the body but as incomplete in itself."[69] Unity is central. This is to be one community (Eph 4:1-6), and table fellowship is the point at which this all comes together. This is the event representative of "diverse humanity redeemed by Christ and sharing in him."[70] Jewish law, however, prohibited eating with Gentiles, meaning that even while the Jews maintained their Jewish culture, it needed itself to be converted, turned to Christ. Maturity in the faith includes the retention of cultural particularities, for such growth in diversity is a necessary correlate of the obedient human response to the gospel. This one community in its cultural diversity is the power of the gospel, the destruction of the wall of partition and the creation of a holy temple (Eph 2:14-22). It is a community constituted in and shaped by love. Walls, in other words, sets the historical continuity, cross-cultural conversion, and body and its maturity in a necessary relationship and counts this as the nature and form of Christian unity.

6.4 Comprehending the Scope of Christian History

To recognize this New Testament dynamic is not to advocate a return to an idealized apostolic period. It establishes an early interpretive framework that finds confirmation through the same process occurring in Christian history and today in the ferment of world Christianity. One key difference is that while the early church focused on the relationship of two cultures, ongoing "Christian cross-cultural diffusion has brought many more into the church, and our own day has seen the greatest proliferation of all."[71] This only strengthens the point: what one sees in world Christianity is the very logic of Christian history.[72] This opens the scope of Christian history, first,

---

[68] Walls, "Ephesian Moment," 77.
[69] Ibid., 79.
[70] Ibid., 78.
[71] Walls, "Globalization," 72.
[72] Bediako, "Emergence of World Christianity," 51. Bediako illustrates this point through an extended parallel between what occurred within the patristic period and what is occurring now in

by finding that dynamic even in the perceived lineal course of the Western church, and second, through the detachment of Christian history from a singular passage coincidental with the European landmass by pointing to a wider range of historical continuities. The general hope, for Sanneh, is for a Christian history developed without a "preoccupation with the European heartland and its structures of power," and with a mind "to the frontier, scarce in institutional assets but with a teeming diversity that attests to the religion's genius for fostering a spirit of unity along with a variety of styles and idioms."[73] Whatever the critical element, it is in service to this positive vision of world Christianity.

The first stage in the argument challenges the dominant view of church history and its tracing a line from Jerusalem to the Mediterranean, to a consolidation in Rome, to the northern tribes, to western Europe, followed by the new colonies in America, and finally to Asia, Africa and Latin America. Included here is a normative evaluation of the Hellenization of the gospel: this initial episode of translation establishes a cultural form, and this form parallels the course of Western cultural history. It privileges these earlier cultural trajectories in relation to any later developments; that is, it is through this history that the Christian church is a visible continuous society.[74] The history serves a theology of apostolicity, which, in turn, renders the history itself unassailable. The problem, to cite Sanneh, is that "such a linear, Eurocentric understanding of Christianity happens to conflict with much of the available evidence."[75] Because of, it might be suggested,

---

the African context. Both periods highlight the central problem of the "Christian's response to the religious past as well as to the cultural tradition generally in which one stands, and the significance of that response for the development of theological answers to the culturally-rooted questions of the context." Kwame Bediako, *Theology and Identity: The Impact of Culture upon Christian Thought in the Second Century and in Modern Africa* (Oxford: Regnum Books, 1992), 7.

[73]Sanneh, *Disciples of All Nations*, 55.

[74]For Sanneh, two assumptions hamper a wider appreciation of world Christianity. First, "Christianity was already so firmly anchored in the Enlightenment milieu of its origins in the modern West that in whatever forms it emerged in the rest of the world it was bound to sow the seeds of its formative Western character. What is worldwide about Christianity is what the West did to the religion in the wake of the West's colonial expansion." The second assumption follows the first. Because world Christianity is itself the child of the West, "a reconstructed Christianity is little compatible with indigenous societies and cultures, and as such the concept of world Christianity is historically inaccurate. Christianity became a world religion only because Europe was a world power." Ibid., 217.

[75]Ibid., 54.

a theological definition of continuity, this history ignores the wider and long-standing geographical span of Christian faith. Walls notes the faith's expansion into India and Sri Lanka by the seventh century and how the "missionary whose Chinese name was A Lo Pen arrived in the capital of the T'ang Emperor in 635, much the same time as the faith was put before the king and council of Northumbria."[76] One might confirm the point by reference to the churches in Egypt, Syria, India, Ethiopia and Nubia, by way of slender example. The continuous history of the Christian faith includes this plurality of center.

To challenge the singularity of Western Christianity in relation to the faith's historical continuity is not to deny the importance of Western Christianity. It is to observe how a distorted image of Christian history supports limiting theological conclusions. This history becomes defined by the church's settled existence in a "Christian," that is, religiously homogeneous, culture and so assumes a parochial perspective with difference charted along institutional lines. This perspective, and the vision of continuity it underwrites, produces histories that underplay the diversities that belong to the continuity of this church. It promotes an understanding of schism that has little relevance beyond the competing bodies derived from European history. To quote Walls, the "assumption that Christianity exists in three more or less permanent modes: Roman Catholic, Protestant, and Orthodox . . . reflect events in Western history; they have in the West a significance that they cannot have in the non-Western world."[77] The assumed normative significance of this schism, however, illustrates how a singular church history claims "universal application."[78] Though it might, at the level of theological statement, cherish diversity of expression, the central subject remains a body conceived as the only child of the original encounter of Jew and Gentile and its institutional consolidation, beside which "anything else is an optional extra, determined by local needs."[79] History becomes stylized in support of a theological norm, and this in a way that submerges the processes of this history's own formation. For Sanneh, "Western Christianity is itself the upshot of a series of specific

---

[76]Walls, "Eusebius Tries Again," 10.
[77]Ibid., 13.
[78]Ibid., 14.
[79]Ibid.

vernacular adaptations and cultural adjustments no different in nature from the vernacular appropriation that was underway in non-Western societies."[80] What is happening in world Christianity is not alien to Western history.

In other words, one argument against this presumed lineal historical course demonstrates how that course is itself contingent on the processes of cross-cultural transmission and appropriation, how it is not continuous in the fashion of cultural continuity but embodies the dynamic evident in the New Testament. As a single example, Walls refers to the movement of the gospel from its Hellenistic-Roman setting into the northern tribes. The faith transformed from being "at home in the urban, literate, and technological culture of the Mediterranean basin to one that could take root among peasant herders and cultivators, military elites and semisettled raiders in western, northern, and eastern Europe." This process of thinking about Christ through the local languages, questions and structures paralleled what had occurred in the Hellenistic world. Evidence for this, Walls argues, is found in "the adoption of the faith into the frameworks of customary law of a multitude of peoples." Though his argument is light on detail, he illustrates the point, first, by reference to the theological development of the doctrine of the atonement. Anselm's position "makes sense in the categories of traditional Germanic law, with its principle of necessary compensation and its assumption of kinship solidarity."[81] The point, though simple, is theologically fundamental: thinking the gospel through the categories of the local culture is basic to its appropriation. Second, contemporary theological accounts of continuity themselves derive from this specific moment of the gospel's appropriation. Christendom refers not first to a political decision made by Constantine. Even in the primacy and legal protections this offered Christianity, cultural and religious pluralism was an irreducible characteristic

---

[80]Lamin O. Sanneh, *Summoned from the Margin: Homecoming of an African* (Grand Rapids: Eerdmans, 2012), 227. On the diversity present in Western Christianity, see Peter Brown, *The Rise of Western Christendom: Triumph and Diversity, A.D. 200–1000* (Malden, MA: Wiley-Blackwell, 2003). Walls argues, as an example of the point, that the Protestant need for a more direct link between Augustine and Luther tends to overlook the critical period of the conversion of the northern tribes. "So there is no study of the engagement between Christianity and the traditional religions of Europe, the very point where comparison of the experiences of African, Asian, and Western Christians can be most illuminating." Walls, "Globalization," 79.

[81]Walls, "Old Athens and New Jerusalem," 150. The singular source Walls refers to is James C. Russell, *The Germanization of Early Medieval Christianity: A Sociohistorical Approach to Religious Transformation* (New York: Oxford University Press, 1996).

of the Roman Empire.[82] The link forged between the Christian faith and a geographical territory, the assumption of a common cultural and religious identity, Walls argues, is related to the difficulties tribal peoples have in "dividing sacred and profane custom."[83] This helped secure a territorial Christianity. So assuming the identity of a people and their religion helped strengthen "the role of the Christian church in maintaining and transmitting, in residual form, the cultural legacy of Rome." Being Christian meant sharing "in a special history and literary tradition, as it were by adoption."[84] This complex cultural translation of the Christian heritage included a retroactive warrant for the culture of Rome and stimulated the perception that the Christian faith was coterminous with Europe. When Western Christendom moved beyond its own borders in the colonial period, this expectation of territorial Christianity marked its passage. As this history and language could be adopted, as there existed "a single inherited civilization," so this history was universal and capable of being adopted.[85] Walls's general point seems clear: the very theology of continuity that identifies church history with an institution in its Western course is itself a contingent development within a particular event of appropriation, the event of the barbarians becoming the people of God.

A second intrusion on this defining assumption of the church's Western historical course rests in the detailed histories of Christian bodies outside the West. It evaluates these other histories in their own terms and not at a relative distance to Western history or guided by the markers of institution and its complex of associated agendas.[86] Whatever early significance African Christianity might be granted in church history, contemporary African Christianity

---

[82]Walls, "Christianity in the Non-Western World," 35.

[83]Ibid.

[84]Ibid., 36.

[85]Ibid.

[86]For an attempt to present Christian history from this "world" perspective, see Dale T. Irvin and Scott W. Sunquist, *History of the World Christian Movement: Earliest Christianity to 1453* (Maryknoll, NY: Orbis Books, 2001); Dale T. Irvin and Scott W. Sunquist, *History of the World Christian Movement: Modern Christianity from 1454-1800* (Maryknoll, NY: Orbis Books, 2012). For a discussion focused more on the Latin American context, see Justo L. González, *The Changing Shape of Church History* (St. Louis, MO: Chalice Press, 2002), 2002. For one concerned with Asia, see Peter C. Phan, "A New Kind of Christianity, but What Kind?," *Mission Studies* 22, no. 1 (2005): 59-83; Phan, "Doing Theology in World Christianity: Different Resources and New Methods," *Journal of World Christianity* 1, no. 1 (2008): 27-53; Phan, "World Christianity: Its Implications for History, Religious Studies, and Theology," *Horizons* 39, no. 2 (2012): 171-88.

is often viewed as contingent on the gospel's presumed lineal passage from Rome to Europe to North America and then, by way of the Western mission enterprise, to Africa. By implication, this extended break between patristic Christianity and its contemporary revival becomes the dominant factor in African Christian history: Christianity's presence in Africa is as a Western import. Walls objects. On the one hand, Africa has never been without a Christian presence. "Africa has a continuous Christian history since sub-apostolic times, a history that antedates not only Western missions to Africa but the Islamic presence there."[87] Such is evident in the "unbroken historical continuity of the churches of Egypt and Ethiopia."[88] Nor is this limited to an imposed distinction between North Africa and the rest. Walls, drawing on recent archaeological evidence, notes a significant Christian presence in Nubia for close to a millennium. As to why this community needs to be "discovered," that is, why it was not preserved in the church's memory, perhaps indicates a wider complex of political and theological interests. It points, nevertheless, to a "degree of commonality between northern and sub-Saharan Africa" and the manner in which the "Christian faith linked people of northern Africa and mediterranean Africa before either Islam or the camel arrived there."[89] Whatever the contemporary nation-state divides, the Christianity of the North belongs to Africa as such.[90] Walls develops this conclusion on the basis of the wider significance of the name Ethiopia. "Ethiopian" in its present Christian usage means "Africa indigenously Christian, Africa *primordially* Christian: for a Christianity that has been continuously

---

[87]Walls, "Eusebius Tries Again," 11.

[88]Andrew F. Walls, "Africa in Christian History: Retrospect and Prospect," *Journal of African Christian Thought* 1, no. 1 (1998): 4.

[89]Ibid.

[90]It is worth citing Hegel's famous judgment that Africa is without history, interesting here because, as the early Christianity favored by the Western theological tradition focuses on northern Africa, Hegel states that "historical movements in [Africa]—that is in its northern part—belong to the Asiatic or European World. Carthage displayed there an important transitory phase of civilization; but, as a Phoenician colony, it belongs to Asia. Egypt will be considered in reference to the passage of the human mind from its Eastern to its Western phase, but it does not belong to the African Spirit. What we properly understand by Africa, is the Unhistorical, Undeveloped Spirit, still involved in the conditions of mere nature, and which had to be presented here only as on the threshold of the World's History." G. W. Friedrich Hegel, *The Philosophy of History,* trans. J. Sibree (Mineola, NY: Dover, 2004), 99. Whatever is deemed to be of value, in other words, is appropriated by and incorporated into Europe and its history while being denied to Africa. See also Babacar Camara, "The Falsity of Hegel's Theses on Africa," *Journal of Black Studies* 36, no. 1 (2005): 82-96.

in Africa for far longer than it has in Scotland, and infinitely longer than it has in the United States. African Christians today can assert their right to the *whole* history of Christianity in Africa, stretching back almost to the apostolic age."[91] Though presenting a different model of continuity, Christianity in Africa belongs to the history of the faith as such.

On the other hand, institutional interests create a unidirectional history. Though often overlooked when considered from the perspective of "sent" missionaries or church institutions, "Afro-America is part of the African history; it is an especially significant part of African Christian history."[92] By way of example, Walls refers to those eleven hundred people of African heritage who returned to Sierra Leone in 1792 after the American War of Independence, their establishment of a church and the subsequent conversion of slaves liberated from intercepted slave ships.[93] This story of migration and return is as much a part of African history as it is of Europe and America. The point is not benign. It includes a critical rejection of reading African Christianity through the lens of the institution, that is, through the history of another place, the significance of which is best illustrated by reference to "mission histories." As Paul Jenkins suggests, "An African church history that begins with missionary institutions—and especially one that begins with missionary initiatives—is almost bound to stress the foreign nature of the faith and its practices."[94] Such church history evaluates the relative success or failure of mission in terms of the establishment of the institution, its replication in a multitude of contexts and the numbers of converts and baptisms. Ogbu Kalu objects. Focusing on the parish while "ignoring the socio-political and economic structures of the cultural area" enshrines a range of ethnocentric assumptions. The starting point of an

---

[91] Walls, "Africa in Christian History," 4. See also Kwame Bediako, "Africa and Christian Identity: Recovering an Ancient Story," *Princeton Seminary Bulletin* 25, no. 2 (2004): 155.

[92] Walls, "Africa in Christian History," 5-6.

[93] Ibid., 6.

[94] Paul Jenkins, "The Roots of African Church History: Some Polemic Thoughts," *International Bulletin of Missionary Research* 10, no. 2 (1986): 68. Walls notes how attempts to make African church history "an appendage of a 'general' church history which is really a form of European clan history" succeeds only in distorting that history. Walls, "Eusebius Tries Again," 11. The same problem is evident in discussions of Christianity as a "universal religion," a point Sanneh illustrates by reference to the mission histories developed by Kenneth Scott Latourette and Stephen Neill. See Sanneh, "World Christianity," 95-100.

African church history "must be Africa itself and its complex cultures."[95] While the church's institutional structure is important, Christian history is more than the history of this structure. "It is the story," Kalu continues, "of the pilgrim people of God and their experiences of God's redeeming grace in the midst of their existence in various cultural and ecological milieux."[96]

One could populate this new historiography with more particular examples, but the central contention is clear. A plurality of histories and associated structural expressions is the direct result of apostolicity, that is, the nature of the faith's historical continuity. The basic metaphor of Christian history becomes, then, to cite Peter Phan, not a single "many-branched vertical tree, with the trunk representing the European *Corpus Christianum* of Christendom." It is one of "rhizomes, that is, plants with subterranean, horizontal root systems, growing below and above ground and moving crablike in all directions."[97] Christian history is not lineal and singular and reducible to the course of a simple institution. Christian history, following the path of conversion, is constituted by a series of cross-cultural encounters and the local appropriations of the gospel. It encompasses many histories, all of which contribute to the full stature of Christ.

6.5 APPROPRIATION AS TRANSLATION INTO VERNACULAR FORM

Though the parallels drawn between the appropriations of the gospel evident in world Christianity, the logic of Christian history and the basis of such in the New Testament are based in historical description, the linkage has prescriptive intent. It justifies the theological developments in Africa, Asia and Latin America and charts a future theological course. Sanneh formalizes this approach using the term "translation." Much rests on this point. Compared to Robert Jenson's avowed denial of translation because of its intrusion on

---

[95]Ogbu U. Kalu, "Doing Church History in Africa Today," in *Church History in an Ecumenical Perspective: Papers and Reports of an International Ecumenical Consultation Held in Basle October 12-17, 1981*, ed. Lukas Vischer (Bern: Evang. Arbeitsstelle Ökumene Schweiz, 1982), 79.

[96]Ogbu U. Kalu, "African Church Historiography: An Ecumenical Perspective," in *African Church Historiography: An Ecumenical Perspective; Papers Presented at a Workshop on African Church History, Held at Nairobi, August 3-8, 1986*, ed. Ogbu U. Kalu (Bern: Evang. Arbeitsstelle Ökumene Schweiz, 1988), 18.

[97]Peter C. Phan, "World Christianity and Christian Mission: Are They Compatible? Insights from the Asian Churches," *Asian Christian Review* 1, no. 1 (2007): 18. For an investigation into these "multiple trajectories" in Christian history, see Dale T. Irvin, *Christian Histories, Christian Traditioning: Rendering Accounts* (Maryknoll, NY: Orbis Books, 1998), 106-22.

the church's culture and so its apostolicity, Sanneh identifies translation with the gospel itself. "In contradiction to Christianity either as Scripture or as a dogmatic, creedal system," the faith is "a vernacular translation movement."[98] Note the terms of comparison: he sets translation in general contrast to the normative Protestant/Catholic binary. Clear implications for a theology of apostolicity follow. With translation, continuity rests in the local appropriation of the gospel, a point legitimated, it must be reiterated, by reference to the actual course of Christian history.

In almost identical fashion to Walls's proselyte/convert distinction, Sanneh draws a contrast between *diffusion* and *translation*.[99] With diffusion, "the 'missionary culture' is made the carrier and arbiter of the message. . . . By it religion expands by means of its founding cultural warrants and is implanted in other societies primarily as a matter of cultural adoption."[100] Though Sanneh defends the mission movement, he is forthright in acknowledging how diffusion shaped Western mission method. This perpetuated a model of "proselytization as cultural apprenticeship," producing a "fortress Christianity" that "wrenched" local believers from their contexts.[101] Further, "proselytization and colonization belonged together: a proselyte was a colonial subject, one who was politically required to submit."[102] Such a coordination should not come as

---

[98]Lamin O. Sanneh, *Translating the Message: The Missionary Impact on Culture* (Maryknoll, NY: Orbis Books, 2009), 7. As to his drawing a normative theological point from Christian history, the type of claims coming from observers of world Christianity have not often crossed the horizon of guild theologians. From a social science perspective, Marilyn Waldman objects to the methodological mixture because, for her, Sanneh the theologian overrules Sanneh the historian. Waldman's complaint focuses especially on Sanneh's treatment of Islam. Marilyn Robinson Waldman, "Translatability: A Discussion," *Journal of Religion in Africa* 22, no. 2 (1992): 159-64. Sanneh offers a stout defense; see Lamin O. Sanneh, "Translatability: A Discussion," *Journal of Religion in Africa* 22, no. 2 (1992): 168-72. For an argument similar to Waldman's from a more theological perspective, see Klaus Hock, "Translated Messages? The Construction of Religious Identities as Translatory Process," *Mission Studies* 23, no. 2 (2006): 261-76. For the purposes of this section, one need not draw any contrast with Islam to make the point: diffusion and translation correspond to two modes of Christian mission.

[99]Walls comments that "translation resembles conversion; indeed it is a working model of conversion, a turning of the processes of language (with the thought of which that language is the vehicle and the traditions of which it is the deposit) towards Christ." Andrew F. Walls, "The Translation Principle in Christian History," in *Missionary Movement in Christian History*, 29.

[100]Sanneh, *Translating the Message*, 33.

[101]Sanneh, "Should Christianity Be Missionary?," 88. Note how the language is identical to that used by Jenson. But, whereas for Jenson this justifies a process of enculturation, Sanneh rejects it as basic to proselytization and the improper imposition of a cultural Christianity.

[102]Ibid.

a surprise—it follows the ecclesiological assumptions of territorial Christendom and finds contemporary correspondence in the reified cultural expectations of ecumenical approaches to apostolicity. As this method advances a cultural form, so it establishes a range of conditions for the local context. Diffusion distrusts translation because, with "cultural apprenticeship as a Christian prerequisite," it involves "too radical a concession to indigenous values to be acceptable."[103] It permits a range of unexamined interpretive assumptions that define the faith and its authenticity.

To give but one example, Western missions operated with an unexamined distinction between the sacred and the profane. Though without basis in African cultures, this inserted a structural discontinuity between the gospel and the local context. It assumed, to cite Bediako, that "African culture—in terms of its religious, social and political values—constitutes a distinct entity, quite separate from the Good News about Jesus Christ."[104] Now with the "gospel" and "African culture" two self-contained systems, Edward Fasholé-Luke observes how conversion to Christianity demanded "a radical breaking away from the past, and being set in a new pattern of life; even if one still continues to live close to one's cultural and social situation."[105] In practical terms, the process of breaking away took form as the adoption of a Western way of life, stretching from surface elements like dress to deeper considerations like time, standards of efficiency and an economic understanding of

---

[103]Ibid. Sanneh considers this distrust of translation to be built into Western systems. "Standard theological models of Christianity have presented it as a closed circuit religion whose main pathways of communication and authority have been laid in the trusted channels of the Western canon. . . . In this view, translation spawns syncretism, sects, heresy, and apostasy, which are to religion what aberration, mutation, infection, and suicide are to an immutable organism." Sanneh, "Post-Western Wine, Post-Christian Wineskins?," 103.

[104]Kwame Bediako, "Facing the Challenge: Africa and World Christianity in the 21st Century—A Vision of the African Christian Future," *Journal of African Christian Thought* 1, no. 1 (1998): 56.

[105]Edward W. Fasholé-Luke, "The Quest for African Theologies," *Scottish Journal of Theology* 29 (1976): 160. Bediako, drawing on S. G. Williamson, notes that "the invitation to accept the Christian religion was also a call to participate in a western interpretation of reality. Thus converts were not merely required to abandon the worship of many gods for the worship of One God, but were taught to look upon traditional religion as the worship of nonentities. The missionary enterprise was seeking to implant its Christianity by the method of substituting for the Akan world-view, what was a European world-view." Kwame Bediako, *Christianity in Africa: The Renewal of a Non-Western Religion* (Maryknoll, NY: Orbis Books, 1995), 68-69, citing S. G. Williamson, *Akan Religion and the Christian Faith—A Comparative Study of the Impact of the Two Religions* (Accra: Ghana Universities Press, 1965), 170. Bediako continues that these planted Christian communities "have not really known how to relate to their traditional culture in terms other than those of denunciation or of separateness" (Bediako, *Christianity in Africa*, 69).

land. Especially where the message included the drive to civilize, the discontinuity supported a definition of "high culture" beside which African history and culture were dismissed as "primitive."[106] It equally dictated the forms of response. The imported structure was to be decorated with a façade of local color, meaning that an "authentic" African theology, to cite Bediako, would emerge as an "African equivalent of Western dogmatic formulations."[107] This itself presented a twofold challenge. On the one hand, because "Christian dogmatic formulations are the by-products of Christian self-definition," African theologians were unable to follow this course: the "self-definition" in question corresponded to a particular appropriation of the gospel within Western historical, political, economic, social and cultural narratives. Because African theology failed to follow this method, it reduced to a local variant beside a supposed universal theological tradition.[108] On the other hand, to oppose this assumption, to treat African culture and history as the "fundamental sub-stratum of [African] humanity and African identity," appeared to promote the "African cultural element" over the gospel, making it "prior and basic."[109] It was to place oneself outside the Christian community and its connections across time and space. The convert had to either stand within, as much as this was possible, the Western Christian tradition or be excluded from orthodox Christianity as such.

"Translation," in contrast to this model of diffusion, makes the "recipient culture . . . a valid and necessary locus of the proclamation, allowing the religion to arrive without the requirement of deference to the originating culture."[110] Or, the particular culture being addressed becomes the Christian center. The gospel "adopts each culture as its natural destination and a necessity of its life."[111] This challenges every instance of the gospel's cultural domestication because it is contrary to the message "to invoke cultural hegemony

---

[106]See, for example, Tite Tiénou, "The Invention of the 'Primitive' and Stereotypes in Mission," *Missiology* 19, no. 3 (1991): 295-303.

[107]Bediako, "Africa and Christain Identity," 159. Paul Jenkins too notes how "it is a somewhat arrogant—if unspoken—assumption in much writing about mission history that African people had to be taught how to phrase their questions and formulate their problems if they were to come to properly 'Christian' answers." Jenkins, "Roots of African Church History," 68.

[108]Bediako, "Africa and Christain Identity," 159.

[109]Bediako, "Facing the Challenge," 56.

[110]Sanneh, *Translating the Message*, 33.

[111]Ibid., 79.

as the prerequisite of conveying God's truth. Cultural hegemony violates the gospel by giving primacy to conveyance over the message."[112] As no singular culture mediates the gospel (including all the clerical, liturgical and structural sense the language of "mediate" implies), so agency shifts to local bodies. The emphasis typical of apostolicity inverts. "The act of historical transmission is really a secondary factor in the unveiling of the gospel, and the more critical stage is the vernacular embodiment of the message and the consequent 'feedback.'"[113] Historical transmission becomes real in its appropriation by an acting subject (community), its translation into vernacular forms.

Sanneh illustrates the process by reference to simple Bible translation. Because Christianity is without a sacred language, it can and must be spoken using local idiom. Significant consequences follow this simple observation. Culture is, at once, destigmatized and relativized: no culture is so crude as to lie beyond the gospel, and no culture is so refined as to have privileged access to God.[114] With this theological ratification, in using the local languages "Christianity invested in idioms and cultures that existed for purposes other than Christianity."[115] And because language, culture and religion are so intertwined, as Bediako suggests, "many Africans gained access to the original sources of Christian revelation mediated through African traditional religious terminology and ideas."[116] Jesus Christ is found in and expressed through the ideas and forms located in the local pre-Christian heritage.

Nothing illustrates this better, Sanneh argues, than the use of local names when speaking of the God of Abraham, Isaac and Jacob. "The name of God

---

[112]Ibid., 34.

[113]Lamin O. Sanneh, "Christian Mission in the Pluralist Milieu: The African Experience," *International Review of Mission* 74, no. 294 (1985): 203.

[114]Sanneh, "Gospel, Language and Culture," 53.

[115]Sanneh, *Disciples of All Nations*, 26.

[116]Kwame Bediako, "The Significance of Modern African Christianity—A Manifesto," *Studies in World Christianity* 1, no. 1 (1995): 54. Walls draws a direct parallel with Bede and the conversion of the kingdom of Northumbria. "The people of his own country initially responded to the proclamation of Christianity in terms of the expectations of their old religion and in terms of traditional goals. It could hardly be otherwise: it is hardly possible to take in a new idea except in terms of ideas we already have. . . . It was about essentially communal matters: ancestral custom, acceptable modes of life within the community, and the sanctions governing both." Walls, "Christianity in the Non-Western World," 35. All of this, for Burrows, illustrates the Latin axiom: "*Id quod recipitur secundum modum recipientis recipitur* ('Whatever is received is received according to the modality [mindset] of the receptor')." William R. Burrows, "Reconciling All in Christ: An Old New Paradigm for Mission," *Mission Studies* 15, no. 1 (1998): 86.

is basic to the structure of traditional societies. It forms and regulates agricultural rituals, territorial cults, agrarian festivals, the solar calendar, fertility ceremonies, mortuary observance, anniversary customs, units of generational measurement, naming rules, ethics, rank and status, gender relations, filial obligation, gift making, sacrificial offering, and so on."[117] To use these names in Bible translation is to embed the gospel in this pre-Christian religious system and its framing of the world. Translation resides not simply at a linguistic level. As it includes the fundamental thought constructs, structures of relationship and the means of their organization, so it finds expression at the structural and institutional level. It equally indicates the nature of theological development. Sanneh indicates how

> in particular cultural contexts and circumstances God has definite, particular qualities and attributes that do not belong to God in other contexts and circumstances. It is not that these qualities and attributes are incompatible with God generally defined, but that something more, in respect of the pool of qualities and attributes, is added by each particular context. Those qualities and attributes become the modes and individual ways in which God becomes real for particular people in particular situations and circumstances even though those situations and circumstances by their nature do not repeat themselves for everyone anywhere else or to the same degree.[118]

In the obedience of conversion, this message translates into new forms, assumes different accents, creates different moments and maintains continuity of meaning even in discontinuity of expression.

Translation does not confirm local culture in a static moment. As the gospel denies the divinization of any culture, so all cultures are open to change, to the processes of conversion. Nor does it stimulate an improper mixing of the gospel with local elements that require a later purification associated with a conception of Christian maturity at odds with translation.[119]

---

[117]Lamin O. Sanneh, *Whose Religion Is Christianity? The Gospel Beyond the West* (Grand Rapids: Eerdmans, 2003), 31.

[118]Sanneh, "Gospel, Language and Culture," 38-39.

[119]Apart from recognizing the negative polemic served by the charge, translation is distinguished from syncretism "by appealing to the process whereby the Christian message is appropriated into existing local frameworks but still remains recognizably Christian, much like what the Greeks in places like Alexandria, Antioch, Athens, and Ephesus did with the Jewish heritage of Jesus Christ. Syncretism represents the unresolved, unassimilated, and tension-filled mixing of Christian ideas with local custom and ritual, and that scarcely results in the kind of fulfilling

Translation is an ongoing process that is never final. Though each translation is itself incomplete, together their culmination and positive relationship reveals something of the fulness of Christ.[120] Nor does translation reduce to a kernel/husk model. Christianity exists in its being translated, in its being appropriated. It is not possible to disentangle Christianity from its cultural form, because it is not possible to have a language-less Christianity, a Christianity without a community. For Sanneh, "we cannot get at the gospel pure and simple. . . . The pure gospel, stripped of all cultural entanglements, would evaporate in a vague abstraction, although if the gospel were without its own intrinsic power it would be nothing more than cultural ideology."[121] To so affirm that the gospel does not exist without cultural form is not to reduce gospel to culture. The gospel is Jesus Christ and him crucified, the truth of which includes the human reconciled in this event, and so it is a community event and never apart from what belongs to human beings.

The gospel, because it can be expressed in every culture, relativizes all cultures. For Sanneh, the general position undoes any territorial approach. The coincidental destigmatization and relativization of culture promotes a cultural pluralism. With Pentecost the founding characteristic of the church in mission, Christianity relinquished "Jerusalem or any fixed universal centre,

---

change signaled by conversion and church membership." Sanneh, *Whose Religion Is Christianity?*, 44. This lays stress on the biblical text and on the ingrafting this entails into the history of Israel. For Walls, adoption into Israel ensures a form of critical historical dislocation. It "becomes a 'universalizing' factor, bringing Christians of all cultures and ages together through a common inheritance, lest any of us make the Christian faith such a place to feel at home that no one else can live there; and bringing into everyone's society some sort of outside reference." Walls, "Gospel as Prisoner and Liberator," 9. Walls even suggests that "the test between indigenization and syncretism is the capacity to incorporate the history of Israel and God's people and to treat it as one's own." Walls, "Africa and Christian Identity," 13.

[120]One should question, from this perspective, the language of *adiaphora* and the related presumed capacity to differentiate between the cultural and the non-cultural. The reactive tendency that charges that one must identify what particular practices or structures are "cultural" represents a wholesale failure to engage the issue. While such structures may be both historically and culturally located and thus subject to examination in terms of their "authenticity," designating them as *adiaphora* tends to present the issue in terms of a scale that slides from elements deemed necessary to the expression of the gospel to elements that might be disposed of without harm. No satisfactory criteria exist, however, for adjudicating between these points. Those things deemed necessary, such as baptism and the Lord's Supper, are always already clothed in cultural garb, and those more clearly identifiable cultural elements, such as the place of ancestors, are not so easily disregarded without weakening the witness of the local community, its capacity to answer the questions posed by its neighbors.

[121]Sanneh, "Gospel, Language and Culture," 47.

be it geographical, linguistic or cultural, and with the result of there being a proliferation of centres, languages and cultures within the church. Christian ecumenism is a pluralism of the periphery with only God at the centre."[122] The gospel neither exists as a culturally disembodied entity nor is it confined to a singular cultural form. "All cultural expressions remain at the periphery of truth, all equal in terms of access, but all equally inadequate in terms of what is ultimate and final."[123] No doubt certain communities have stressed their cultural heritage above that of the gospel, but recognizing the relative significance of culture militates against the slide into cultural captivity.[124] The appropriation of the gospel is meaningful in this acknowledgment of cultural relativity, in setting God at the center of creation and the unity of the nations gathered in worship around him. Nor is the church universal reduced to a multitude of independent histories. Each is a link in the historical continuity of the church. Plurality is basic to Christian maturity.

6.6 CONVERSION AND CONTINUITY WITH THE PRE-CHRISTIAN PAST

To this point, none of the binaries shaping the ecumenical discussion of apostolicity apply. Maturity is a function of pluralism, not the singularity of cultural expression. History, not territory, defines mission. Transmission is not guided by rules of exception but embodies the church's continuous historical course. Stability as cultural purification deteriorates into atrophy. Translation and so local appropriation constitute the body, not the replication of established structures. In short, "the church does not err in appropriating the requisite cultural materials to express the gospel. . . . The

---

[122]Ibid., 61.

[123]Ibid.

[124]Should such extremes occur, it is a position rightly criticized. Reflecting on Walls's two principles of "indigenization" and "pilgrim" (see Walls, "Gospel as Prisoner and Liberator," 9), Retief Müller points to two cautionary tales whereby the tendency to indigenization overwhelmed the pilgrim or, better, subsumed the pilgrim to serve the indigenizing narrative: the church in Nazi Germany and in apartheid South Africa. Retief Müller, "The 'Indigenizing' and 'Pilgrim' Principles of Andrew F. Walls Reassessed from a South African Perspective," *Theology Today* 70, no. 3 (2013): 311-22. To these two Protestant examples, one might add the relationship of the Roman Catholic Church to the Vichy Regime, or the colonialization of what is today "Latin" America. Note however that the caution, based on these examples, applies not first to developing but to "historic" ecclesiologies. Despite claims for some form of cultural transcendence, these have no inbuilt and automatic defense against this temptation and should not be seconded to promote ecclesiologies developed within a particular cultural milieu over those formed in other milieus.

error lies in making the religion exclusive to one cultural expression."[125] The difficulty with such a position lies in its critical intent. It is aimed against a form of the gospel experienced in Africa and Asia as Western in guise, one that makes claims for theological universality and so cultural neutrality, even while propounding a model of cultural replacement distancing local converts from their cultural heritage. No historic tradition understands itself in such parochial terms; none perceives its structures as promoting a particular cultural expression that establishes improper boundaries.

Here it should be observed that, along with historical continuity, maturity in the faith and spiritual growth constitute the main focus of the world Christianity debate. A central question, as posed by Walls, is whether "Africans become fully Christian only by embracing the mind-set of Western Christians and rejecting all the things that made them distinctively African."[126] As a general observation, the non-Western experience of Christianity, regardless of the tradition, has tended to include this element of cultural replacement. Each ecclesial body promoted a range of answers while overlooking the questions posed by the receiving culture. The imported theology did not address the world the African experienced, leaving broad stretches of life untouched and Africans with a bifurcated identity. However, to understand the church as located within a particular cultural expression, as is the charge laid against Western ecclesiologies, does not necessarily correspond to an improper cultural domestication of the gospel. It means that appropriation is basic to maturity in the faith. Even as he argues this point, Bediako remains adamant that "it is the gospel that is anterior or prior to culture and not our culture which is prior to the gospel. . . . It is the gospel, and not our culture, that defines us as human beings."[127] Christian identity develops in the community grounded in Jesus Christ and not in ethnic barriers. That the gospel remains the primary point of reference for the Christian community is not in question.

Memory and identity are basic to maturity in the faith. Affirmed from the perspective of conversion and the pre-Christian past, this means, to

---

[125]Sanneh, *Translating the Message*, 93.

[126]Andrew F. Walls, "Kwame Bediako and Christian Scholarship in Africa," *International Bulletin of Missionary Research* 32, no. 4 (2008): 189.

[127]Kwame Bediako, "Scripture as the Hermeneutic of Culture and Tradition," *Journal of African Christian Thought* 4, no. 1 (2001): 2.

continue with Bediako, that "theological consciousness presupposes religious tradition, and tradition requires memory, and memory is integral to identity: without memory we have no past, and if we have no past, we lose our identity."[128] If the entrance of Christianity included the importation of particular cultural expressions, that is, of theological forms developed in and addressed to another cultural milieu, and if this stimulated a false bifurcation between African and Christian identities, then the maturity of the African Christian rests in the reconciliation of this identity. It means the conversion of the pre-Christian past. To cite Walls, "the past cannot be suppressed, nor can it be left untouched by Christ. The past, with its identity-shaping cultural traditions, has to be converted, turned toward Christ."[129] Redemption includes this redemption of history. Sanneh can note how "the Scriptures . . . are preserved in a community of memory and observance." He affirms this, not because of some idea of continuity in tradition, but because of the processes of translation. In translated form "they continue to speak authoritatively to transmitter and recipient alike."[130] Even when

---

[128]Kwame Bediako, *Jesus in Africa: The Christian Gospel in African History and Experience* (Maryknoll, NY: Orbis Books, 2004), 51. See also Keith Ferdinando, "Christian Identity in the African Context: Reflections on Kwame Bediako's Theology and Identity," *Journal of the Evangelical Theological Society* 50, no. 1 (2007): 121-43.

[129]Walls, "Rise of Global Theologies," 26.

[130]Lamin O. Sanneh, *Encountering the West: Christianity and the Global Cultural Process; The African Dimension* (Maryknoll, NY: Orbis Books, 1993), 17. To further the point by way of contrast, it is more common to find this argument regarding memory developed in support of the church's apostolic tradition. An interesting example, precisely because he sets the issue in the context of the "global" church, can be found in Richard R. Gaillardetz, *Ecclesiology for a Global Church: A People Called and Sent* (Maryknoll, NY: Orbis Books, 2008). One characteristic of this church is its being "a people sustained by memory." This directs Gaillardetz to apostolicity. After surveying four early approaches, he decries how an ahistorical interpretation of the church's origins "saw office and doctrine as frozen in normative forms immune to historical change. . . . Apostolic office would over time become inculturated in the forms of empire, nobility, and monarchy, only to be set above the church as a transhistorical arbiter of belief and practice" (247). Gaillardetz does not examine the potential effects of this for world Christianity, confining the question to that of ecumenical unity; that is, the Protestant/Catholic schism retains priority. His positive suggestion begins with a definition of apostolicity as "communal identity . . . one in continuity with the faith of the apostles" (210, 211). This leads to an extended discussion of tradition, its development in post-Vatican II thinking and the similar lines of thought found in WCC statements. Apostolicity, by this definition, is not a static possession of the church but is rooted in the church's whole life as it seeks to be faithful to the gospel. As is now familiar, this shifts the focus to that which creates and sustains the community's culture. Apostolicity becomes a function of "communal memory," and identity is a function of "stories, symbols, and rituals that mediate our community's memory" (218). To lose this memory is to lose identity.

conceiving this community of memory in terms of the canon, it is not imported but stimulated by vernacular translation.

A clear location of continuity follows. For Fasholé-Luke, "conversion to Christianity must be coupled with cultural continuity. . . . If Christianity is to change its status from that of resident alien to that of citizen, then it must become incarnate in the life and thought of Africa and its theologies must bear the distinctive stamp of mature African thinking and reflection."[131] While conversion means cultural change (the conversion of culture), it does not mean the loss of cultural identity. Integrity and coherence become central terms. Following Kenneth Cragg's definition, the goal is "integrity in conversion, a unity of self in which one's past is genuinely integrated into present commitment."[132] The identity in question is a *Christian* identity, but

---

Arguing that memory is a biblical obligation rooted in the eucharist (Luke 22:19; 1 Cor 11:24), Gaillardetz observes how the church has preserved its memory through history: liturgy, canon, the testimony of communities and the "ministry of memory," that is, the apostolic office. Liturgy becomes basic to what follows, for ritual memory secures this "apostolicity of life" (222). Ritual imparts a "body knowledge" before any articulated belief, and "narrative accounts of the 'meaning' of a ritual must never be confused with the ritual itself and the knowledge or memory embedded within it" (222). Continuity is a function of ritual. "The vital liturgical life of the Christian church preserves a communal memory more powerful than any mere transmission of propositional beliefs. As the liturgy of the church is celebrated from generation to generation, the ritual knowledge gained by the corporate performance of the ritual funds the community's memory" (222). This sameness of ritual itself promotes Christian diversity, for the rituals, symbols and narratives basic to Christianity are "appropriated and passed on within distinct cultural matrices" (221-22). This, in Gaillardetz's estimation, safeguards the universal and historical structure of the Christian tradition while accounting for "the dynamic process of handing on and receiving the Christian faith in distinct sociocultural contexts" (221).

For our present discussion, Gaillardetz nowhere attends to local memory. His approach is unidirectional from a primal or culturally basic Christian memory to a second-order local appropriation. He nowhere investigates the origins of these ranging rituals and liturgies, remaining content to identity them with the early church and so without cultural or temporal texture. He grants the appropriation of ritual within distinct cultural contexts and the importance of diversity in the same liturgical practices. Yet the interpretation of these rituals, the local appropriation, contributes nothing to the pre-articulate memory contained in the ritual itself. They add color but not substance; "substantive apostolicity" is a function of the transmitted ritual. As the history and texture of the local cultural context lack any substantial relevance, Gaillardetz's program for a "global" church appears very much as the expansion of an established pattern that carries the substance of identity within it. Christian identity is a process of enculturation beside which local appropriation is non-determinative and secondary.

[131]Fasholé-Luke, "Quest for African Theologies," 172-73. Continuity, it must be noted, includes a local theological dialogue between those arguing for greater and lesser degrees of relationship to the religious past.

[132]Bediako, *Theology and Identity*, 4, citing Kenneth Cragg, "Conversion and Convertibility—with Special Reference to Muslims," in *Down to Earth: Studies in Christianity and Culture; The Papers of the Lausanne Consultation on Gospel and Culture*, ed. Robert T. Coote and John R. W. Stott

such identity requires interpreting the faith through traditional cultural categories. Such is possible because the religious past "is not so much a chronological past as an 'ontological' past, which, together with the profession of
the Christian faith, gives account of one and the same entity—namely, the
history of the religious consciousness of the African Christian."[133] This is no
rehash of the fulfillment theory because, as subordinate to the gospel, culture
holds no sacral power. Culture and the religious heritage become, in the
words of Sanneh, "our possession instead of our determiner."[134] The goal is
a mature Christianity, and such maturity includes the redemption of history,
the creation of an integral Christian identity.

In concrete terms, even if suitable answers may already exist in the
tradition, the processes of translation, appropriation and conversion
belong to generational continuity and need to be worked out in this historical frame. Bediako uses polygamy to illustrate what is at stake. The
Presbyterian Church of Ghana, with its received line of discipline outlined in its book of *Regulations, Practice and Procedure*, has proved
"unable to offer any substantial help to its members on the problem of
plural marriage simply because it has never adequately faced the problem
as an African church confronting an African problem."[135] Plural marriage
continues, with those who participate in it simply excluded from participation in the Lord's Supper. This approach he contrasts with churches like
the Musama Disco Christo Church, which prohibits polygamy on the
basis of a range of proof-texted biblical verses. Though lacking in theological sophistication and problematic in terms of method, the advance
lies in wrestling "with the problem of plural marriage as an African
problem" and in seeking a biblical position rather than trusting in an
imported system of regulations.[136] "In other words, being more alive to

---

(Grand Rapids: Eerdmans, 1980), 194. For Bediako, the attempt must be made to "achieve
integration between the African pre-Christian religious experience and African Christian commitment in ways that would ensure the integrity of African Christian identity and selfhood."
Bediako, *Jesus in Africa*, 49.

[133]Kwame Bediako, "The Roots of African Theology," *International Bulletin of Missionary Research*
13, no. 2 (1989): 59.

[134]Sanneh, "Gospel, Language and Culture," 54.

[135]Bediako, *Christianity in Africa*, 67.

[136]Ibid. See also C. M. Pauw's argument that African Independent Churches (AICs) should be interpreted not as a negative reaction but as a positive response to the Christian message within
the "total life context" of Africa. This includes the manner in which AICs work for "social and

the importance of these aspects of traditional culture, [the spiritual churches] apply their sense of Christian fellowship more radically to rec-reate the traditional African clan solidarity in Christian terms."[137] Insofar as plural marriage is grounded in clan solidarity, as an issue of conversion, the Musama Disco Christo Church is more likely to develop a position with which believers might identify. The "historical churches," by contrast, "because they present 'Christian' solutions which have not been thought through from the standpoint of the persisting traditional world-view of their members, prove in the end less helpful."[138] Bediako concludes that the charge of superficiality, of a dis-integrated Christianity, appears truer of those within the historic church structures.

The issue, as this example makes clear, is not simply one of doctrinal formulations—it is structural. Nor is the problem contingent on the impor-tation of structure as cultural artifact. It is the framing effect these struc-tures have on matters like time and space. Traditional African religious rituals and remedies addressed the range of concerns present within Af-rican life, notably its fragility. The well-known complaint regarding Chris-tianity's "foreignness," or, to cite Sanneh, the problem that converts may "be considered cultural orphans and traitors at the same time," perhaps gains greater theological traction when linked to the "superficiality" of the faith.[139] As the missionary faith ignored the traditional solutions, so it promoted a Christianity requiring supplement from traditional authorities.[140] An

---

cultural reintegration and renewal," assist members with "progress and development," emphasize "healing" and dealing with "powers and spiritual forces," and express a concern with "political response" and "missionary outreach." C. M. Pauw, "African Independent Churches as a 'People's Response' to the Christian Message," *Journal for the Study of Religion* 8, no. 1 (1995): 3-25.

[137]Bediako, *Christianity in Africa*, 67.

[138]Ibid., 68.

[139]Sanneh, *Encountering the West*, 16.

[140]For an illustration of this point from Asia, see Archie C. C. Lee, "Cross-textual Hermeneutics and Identity in Multi-scriptural Asia," in *Christian Theology in Asia*, ed. Sebastian C. H. Kim (Cambridge: Cambridge University Press, 2008), 198. In terms of Africa, Mercy Amba Oduyoye laments how "the missionaries told the Africans what they needed to be saved from, but when Africans needed power to deal with the spiritual realms that were real to them, the missionary was baffled. The ancestors were to be ignored; infant mortality and premature deaths were purely medical matters. Failure of rains and harvests were acts of God. Childlessness had nothing to do with witchcraft, nor was there any spiritual aspect to any other physical disorder or infirmity. The individual African in the process of being saved was told that witches do not exist, though the community continued to believe in the reality of evil that witchcraft represents. The mis-sionaries' superficial assessment of the indigenous culture and its hold on the people who belong

integrated Christian identity, by contrast, stimulates a range of alternate liturgies and practices that correspond to this range of questions and expectations. Tinyiko Maluleke, for example, argues that "the prefuneral-day night vigils, the foot-stamping, the repetitive choruses, the ceremonies of 'taking off the black mourning clothes,' the peculiarly African preaching style, the Manyano and the Amadodana traditions, the funeral 'celebration' etc.," must be "taken seriously as valid African appropriations of Christianity."[141] In the specific example of sickness and healing within the African church, and the relationship of such to the spiritual realm, this demands different forms of ministry. One example of this is the importance of the "prophet" in Christian leadership. Because developments in ecclesiology often match those of traditional clan structures, it has been possible to develop forms that, for Walls, are a "combination of the ritual and hierarchical with the charismatic and spontaneous. . . . Both features are part of African life. African life is ordered, has a sense of the appropriate time, place, and person; but it is also spontaneous, improvisatory, responsive."[142] African worship, in other words, is not beholden to the dichotomies that more generally shape Western Christianity. Though few studies reflect on the structures and ecclesiologies developing in Africa in relation to formal ecumenical considerations, it is clear that even "established" ecclesiologies have undergone development within the African context.[143] The point

---

to it led to the Africans' superficial acceptance of Christianity." Mercy Amba Oduyoye, *Hearing and Knowing: Theological Reflections on Christianity in Africa* (Maryknoll, NY: Orbis Books, 1986), 14. Because Christianity ignored these elements, believers had to go elsewhere.

[141] Tinyiko Sam Maluleke, "Christ in Africa: The Influence of Multi-Culturity on the Experience of Christ," *Journal of Black Theology in South Africa* 8, no. 1 (1994): 54.

[142] Andrew F. Walls, "The Challenge of the African Independent Churches: The Anabaptists of Africa?," in *Missionary Movement in Christian History*, 118. Elom Dovlo, summarizing Patrick Ryan, observes that although the Protestants were at the forefront of Bible translation, the "'literate orientation of word centred Protestant traditions which offer little in the way of sacramental concreteness to more symbolically oriented people . . .' is a major cause of the rise of spiritual churches. Clearly the access to the Bible empowered the leaders of the new churches to institute such sacramental concreteness and symbolical expressions that the Protestant missions lacked." Elom Dovlo, "African Culture and Emergent Church Forms in Ghana," *Exchange* 33, no. 1 (2004): 34-35, citing Patrick Ryan, "Is It Possible to Conduct a Unified History of Religions in West Africa?," *Universitas* 8 (1984): 107.

[143] Even with apparent instances of institutional continuity, one must acknowledge what Dovlo describes as the secret "retention of an African mindset" within mainline churches. Dovlo, "African Culture," 50. This reflects what Gerardus van der Leeuw has termed "transposition" or "the variation of the significance of any phenomenon, occurring in the dynamic of religion, while the form remains unchanged." Gerardus van der Leeuw, *Religion in Essence and*

might be simply stated: maturity in the Christian faith also necessitates structural change.

6.7 CULTURAL CHANGE, THE SUBSTANCE OF APOSTOLIC CONTINUITY

The merits of this world Christianity for a constructive definition of apostolicity lie in its basis in historical description. While key theoretical correspondences might be drawn between Hoekendijk and these advocates of world Christianity, the church of the latter is no abstraction. It is concrete and visible. Far from a novelty, a phenomenon of recent vintage, world Christianity embodies the logic of Christian history. Though it refuses set limits that read this history through the controlling assumptions of the Protestant/Catholic schism and its cartography of the ecclesial landscape, the emphasis throughout is the church as it exists. Christian history extends beyond the history of a particular institutional model. Reference to world Christianity assists the opening of Christian history so that it no longer serves a lineal cultural expression of the gospel but represents the pluriformity of the world church through its temporal course. This appreciation of history acknowledges that the churches outside Europe contribute something distinctive and original to the faith. To paraphrase Walls, translation enriches, not negates, the tradition.[144]

Despite the heavy theological investment, conceiving apostolicity as cultural continuity along a lineal historical course is untenable. Though the institution of the church claims a form of cultural transcendence derived from its historical passage, one might point to the very assumption that institution and order bear historical continuity as a theological instantiation of the Western cultural tradition. But this attempt to quantify what is or is not cultural leads to a pointless discussion typified often by a historic tradition rejecting the charges of cultural imposition while denigrating the

---

Manifestation: A Study in Phenomenology (New York: Harper & Row, 1963), 610-11. As an example of this process, see John Karanja, "The Role of Kikuyu Christians in Developing a Self-Consciously African Anglicanism," in *The Church Mission Society and World Christianity, 1799–1999*, ed. Kevin Ward and Brian Stanley (Grand Rapids: Eerdmans, 1999), 258-84; Kevin Ward, "African Identities in the Historic 'Mainline Churches': A Case Study of the Negotiation of Local and Global within African Anglicanism," in *African Identities and World Christianity in the Twentieth Century: Proceedings of the Third International Munich-Freising Conference on the History of Christianity in the Non-Western World (September 15-17, 2004)*, ed. Klaus Koschorke and Jens Holger Schjørring (Wiesbaden: Otto Harrassowitz Verlag, 2005), 49-62.

[144]Andrew F. Walls, "The Mission of the Church Today in the Light of Global History," *Word & World* 20, no. 1 (2000): 20.

initial complaint as an unwarranted intrusion occasioned by subjugating the gospel to culture. Such an approach, because the Western church remains the subject, misses the main point. No non-cultural gospel exists, and developing a cultural genealogy for every practice, liturgy or theological statement is an argument without end. The replication of this particular form in another cultural setting, and legitimating such a mission method through claims for historical continuity, can only produce a superficial and immature Christianity because it ensures cultural distance. The event of local appropriation, by contrast, works out the gospel in the language and structures through which it is received. "Safeguarding the deposit" refers not to the repetition of established forms but to their communication so that they are received by and shape the hearers. Nor do formal accounts of indigenization or contextualization go deep enough. These tend to assume the givenness of certain forms and their capacity to take on local clothing. Much of this continues the assumption of a lineal narrative confirmed by the many repetitions that contribute color but not substance. The claims associated with world Christianity are of a different order.

Recognizing this reshapes many theological predicates. The deterritorialization of the church, a singular positive consequence of the colonial era, does not lead to its disembodiment. The reactions to Hoekendijk revealed the deep-seated nature of the theological concern. World Christianity and its accompanying historiography demonstrate the fear of disembodiment to be a false necessity tied to the specific event of the faith's appropriation in northern Europe. No doubt the recognition of the non-territorial nature of the faith threatens a settled cultural arrangement and its accompanying theological ratification. But the vestigial polemic of the Protestant/Catholic schism does not apply. Quite the opposite. Theorists of world Christianity, because they refuse the operative binaries, affirm that God works in and through history and that the Holy Spirit structures the church. These theological axioms guided the decision of the Jerusalem Council and stimulated the non-territorial pluriformity and polycentricity basic to the Christian faith.

None of this undercuts the importance of institution. Local institutions must be redeemed as part of the conversion process, and without these no integral Christianity exists. The opposition of structural diversity to maturity in the faith is located within a proselyte model and needs to be rejected as such. Structures belong to the faith, and because historical continuity occurs in the faith's crossing of boundaries, so structures themselves are part of the conversion process. Definitions of "body" and "koinonia" detach from concepts of cultural purity and singularity because communion occurs within cultural pluriformity. Attaining the full stature of Christ is the unity of the church in its fullness of cultural expressions. Witness accompanies the process of conversion and is not a consequence of cultural purity.

The "continuity" determinative of the cultural approach to apostolicity is grounded in a historical fallacy, one linked to a perceived lineal Western course to the demerit of other histories. Moreover, definitions of unity, "legitimate" diversity and schism all correspond to this fallacy. Schism is defined as the opposite of apostolicity, the interruption of this institutional continuity. One might suggest that the very ecumenical framing of apostolicity, including its structural emphasis, is itself internal to the Western theological tradition and without traction among church bodies conceived as the offspring of schism—derivative at best and a physical manifestation of the church's sin at worst. Reference to world Christianity suggests an alternate definition. Schism is the petrification of the gospel, its consolidation into a religious culture focused on a range of considerations important in a set time and place, establishing an interpretive lens with which to judge all other positions. One might read the New Testament contest along these exact lines. Cultural diversity, without question, is a potential source of Christian division, but the contest apparent through the New Testament concerns the claimed necessity of an established cultural form and the manner of its enforcement. The problem lies not with cross-cultural difference but in the failure to acknowledge God's acting and the attempt to affirm established definitions of purity and the associated human controls.

To so redefine schism sets ecumenism within a larger frame. Unity refers to the whole Christian economy in its very pluriformity; that is, it is not limited to the narrow cultural and historical band inhabited by the institutional division of Protestant and Catholic.[145] Peter Phan, in a rather strong

---

[145]One of the key arguments for apostolicity as cultural continuity rests in the language of unity: cultural diversity threatens Christian unity and, as such, erodes Christian witness. Though the argument is common, one must question its actuality. This is not to deny the scandal of disunity. It is to suggest that the argument assumes a tacit but necessary connection between cultural sameness and structural unity. To quote Aylward Shorter, "The prospect of legitimising more

statement, notes how the application of this institutional history turned unity into a tool for the repression of cultural diversity. Appeals to unity masked "diversity and multiplicity in favor of an imagined and often enforced uniformity. There is not, nor has there ever been, one Christianity; rather there exist Christianities (in the plural), all over the world and all the time."[146] Exponents of world Christianity understand the unity of the faith as a function of its cultural range. For Sanneh, institutional Christianity's resistance to its proper pluralism constitutes a "rebellion of the branches against the tree."[147] He cautions against the two extremes of

> either lurching toward a single administrative instrument as an expression of unity or else succumbing to fragmentation as an answer to free choice. Neither is desirable. The unitary instrument is fraught with elements of compulsion and is deeply destructive of creativity, while fragmentation merely repeats the coercion of uniformity by making the fragments exclusive norms of the truth.[148]

An identical problem underlies both approaches. It is clear that the gospel affirms peoples in "their respective concrete identities."[149] That is, membership in the body of Christ does not produce "a composite montage of cultural differences" but brings such differences in "their teeming greatness into God's plan of salvation. As believers share in the divine fellowship they rise to the fullness of life whose source is God."[150] This is the nature of Christian maturity, of being part of the new creation in Jesus Christ. Unity is, as such, part of the conversion process, one that meant also the conversion of Peter in the encounter with Cornelius. While the early acceptance of the faith in a new cultural milieu might stimulate "the proliferation of

---

thorough-going cultural diversity in the church is, no doubt, daunting to leaders who accept the monocultural assumptions of the old mission paradigm. They fear that diversification will lead to disunity—even schism—yet the reverse is more likely. Schism is liable to occur whenever the Gospel is prevented from taking deep root in local churches, and even if it is avoided, there is a risk of internal heterodoxy under a veneer of monocultural uniformity." Aylward Shorter, "A Communion of Local Churches for the World," *South Pacific Journal of Mission Studies* 16 (1996): 10. Even more strongly from Dale Irvin, in terms of the ecumenical discussion, "cultural imperialism would seem to be inherent in the efforts to reconstruct the unity of the church on the basis of a common Tradition, or through convergence in ministry and sacraments." Irvin, *Christian Histories, Christian Traditioning*, 57.

[146]Phan, "World Christianity," 175.
[147]Sanneh, *Translating the Message*, 35.
[148]Sanneh, "Africa," 92.
[149]Sanneh, *Translating the Message*, 39.
[150]Ibid.

diversity in terms of national idioms, ethnic variety, worship styles, and aesthetic choices," and this might give "the appearance of disunity," it is the local growth in the faith that leads to unity.[151] Sanneh refers to a Filipino prayer that likens Christian unity to the life of a germinating grain: "Lord, make us realize that our Christianity is like a rice field, that when it is newly planted, the paddies are prominent; but as the plants take root and grow taller, these dividing paddies gradually vanish, and soon there appears only one vast continuous field."[152] Unity is grounded in Christian maturity and so in the processes of conversion and translation. To take unity seriously is to take Christian pluralism seriously.

All of this reconstitutes apostolicity. It is not the continuity of a cultural body in a lineal historical course. No such historical course exists. As the faith is non-territorial, so it is composed of redeemed histories. Nor is the church a singular cultural expression, the result of a singular cultural encounter between the Jewish and Hellenistic cultures. Apostolicity, the historical continuity of the church, rests in the event of cross-cultural encounter and the processes of conversion through the local appropriation of the gospel. This history is not the settled and measured development of a cultural entity but is marked by multiple instances of cross-cultural encounter and sometimes radical shifts in thinking. At base, world Christianity refuses the controlling duality of the cultivation of the faith over its proclamation. This liberates apostolicity to be construed in new ways.

---

[151]Sanneh, *Disciples of All Nations*, 168.
[152]Ibid., 168-69, citing *For All God's People: Ecumenical Prayer Cycle* (Geneva: World Council of Churches, 1978), 161.

7
. . . .

Jesus Christ, the One Ground of the Apostle

*Apostleship fundamentally points away from the self (from a
self-conscious preoccupation with the status of the apostolic agent) to
Christ as crucified and raised. The "grammar" of apostleship rests
upon the effectiveness and transparency of this witness.*

ANTHONY C. THISELTON[1]

7.1 BUILT ON THE FOUNDATION OF THE APOSTLES (AND PROPHETS)

Reference to world Christianity promotes a definition of apostolic continuity based in the gospel's movement across cultural boundaries, in its
transmission and local appropriation. A particular strength of this approach
lies in the commensurability of its method with the favored ecumenical
position—both rely on interpretation of history. Insofar as the history of
world Christianity reveals inadequacies with the narrative foundational to
the ecumenical position, it undercuts the theological edifice built on this
foundation. The deterritorialization of the church, its dislocation from a
lineal Western course, includes a multiplication of the histories constitutive
of the church's continuity. This method is not without its own shortcomings.
Focusing on the mechanics of history alone risks conflating the dynamic of
translation with simple sociological process. It can neglect the manner in
which, to cite John Webster, the "temporal economy, including the social
reality of the church in time, has its being not *in se* but by virtue of God who

---

[1]Anthony C. Thiselton, "Some Misleading Factors in the History of Interpretation of 'Apostle,'" in
The First Epistle to the Corinthians (Grand Rapids: Eerdmans, 2000), 673.

alone is *in se*."[2] The possibility of a community that is continuous in its movement across cultural boundaries, in other words, belongs not to the church itself. The identity of the church lies outside itself and in Jesus Christ and the power of the Spirit alone.

This chapter examines the theological possibility of the history described by world Christianity. It does this by considering the New Testament description of apostles and the apostolate. To some extent Hoekendijk foreshadows this constructive move. Much of his own positive account of the apostolate focuses on the appearance of the Messiah as the inauguration of the eschaton through the fulfillment of God's promises to Israel. The calling of the Gentiles is an immediate outworking of the in-breaking of the kingdom of God. Mission is defined in terms of history because it is and remains an act of God. The apostles are, by this definition, actors of the eschaton. This chapter picks up elements of this argument and especially, in conjunction with the findings of the previous chapter, the importance of history's redemption in the appropriation and translation of the gospel.

Defining the church's contemporary apostolicity by reference to the New Testament witness, it should be noted, constitutes no return to an imagined pristine primitive church before its institutional "perversion." Nor does it rehabilitate the charisma/institution opposition that shaped the discussion at the turn of the twentieth century. Such approaches, it is here argued, reflect the apologetic ends to which much of the New Testament scholarship on the "apostle" and the apostolic "office" is directed. Schism has had a distorting effect over this discussion, minimizing the complexity of the New Testament picture while overlooking its fundamental unity. Part of this distortion lies in the assumption of a sequential form of apostolic authority, one that is identified first with the person of the apostle and then transferred to the community grounded in that authority.

---

[2] John B. Webster, "'In the Society of God': Some Principles of Ecclesiology," in *Perspectives on Ecclesiology and Ethnography*, ed. Pete Ward (Grand Rapids: Eerdmans, 2012), 203. One might question Andrew Walls on this point. The importance he places on the incarnation as the "first divine act of translation into humanity" resides in its giving "rise to a constant succession of new translations." Andrew F. Walls, "The Translation Principle in Christian History," in *The Missionary Movement in Christian History: Studies in the Transmission of Faith* (Maryknoll, NY: Orbis Books, 1996), 27. Christology seemingly flattens to historical mechanics. God ceases to be the actor of God's own history.

Because this chapter references the available research, it shadows this line of argument. The basic contention, however, differs. Apostolic authority is corporate and centers on the processes of the gospel's appropriation, and while the apostle has a particular task, this both derives from and shares in the community's constitution—its being in Christ Jesus in the power of the Spirit. Apostolic authority resides in the conversion of this body to Jesus Christ, and basic to this is the conversion of prior histories, those of Jew and Gentile in this case, into his history.

When not read as a cypher for ecclesiastical politics, the New Testament witness presents a relatively clear picture of the apostle. An apostle is one whose ground and calling is Jesus Christ.[3] When aligned with this definition, the very complexity of the New Testament witness leads to a positive definition of mission, one that parallels the contours of "conversion" evident in world Christianity. Mission belongs to history's redemption, and just so is the movement across cultural boundaries. The identity of the Christian community exists not in itself but beyond it, in Jesus Christ. This apostolic movement to Christ is possible only in the power of the Spirit and his structuring of the body. With apostolicity being the church's participation in Jesus Christ's own history, its visibility is the visibility of the resurrection. This gives the church a freedom to follow the structure of the gospel, and so a freedom to follow the movement of the apostles in finding its identity in Jesus Christ as empowered by the Holy Spirit.

7.2 AN INTERPRETIVE HISTORY OF POLEMIC

It is generally observed that the New Testament presents no single cohesive picture of the nature and function of an apostle. To cite Rudolf Schnackenburg as a representative example, the biblical witness presents "a number of definitions which seem to stand in contradiction to one another. The clearest conceptions are to be found in Paul and Luke."[4] Leaving momentarily to one side the potential difference between Paul and Luke, Schnackenburg's

---

[3] I have elected to use the masculine pronoun in relation to the apostle because, while a case can be made for there being at least one female apostle (see Rom 16:7), the Twelve and Paul were males. It is, in this sense, a reflection of this very particular group and not a normative indication of present forms of ministry.

[4] Rudolf Schnackenburg, "Apostolicity: The Present Position of Studies," *One in Christ* 6, no. 3 (1970): 246.

strong language of "contradiction" indicates more the contemporary ecclesiastical concerns than the New Testament reality. As the Protestant/Catholic schism is read into the biblical variety, so the Bible's complexity functions as a Rorschach test confirming later doctrinal positions.[5] With this established and confirming picture in place, the New Testament witness hardens into an opposition of mutually exclusive positions, a contradiction.[6] The problem is known. Hans von Campenhausen, by way of example, chides both the Catholic and the Protestant traditions for presenting the "primitive community in terms of various mutually competitive tendencies in ecclesiastical politics."[7] Simply naming the problem, however, has failed to restrain its influence over the interpretive direction.

New Testament scholarship typically turns to J. B. Lightfoot's 1865 study as the first focused treatment on the Greek and Hebrew origins of ἀπόστολος (*apostolos*).[8] Given the great and persistent controversy surrounding apostolic succession, the lateness with which the question is addressed to the New Testament indicates the debate's primary location at the level of ecclesiastical politics. But to begin this investigation with Lightfoot is to posit the matter as first a problem of historical reconstruction, a problem resolved through an investigation into the social and

---

[5]On this point, see Hermann Vogelstein's characterization of the apostles as "an ecclesiastical central board of authorities," a managerial image much more reflective of his own *Sitz im Leben* than of the New Testament period. Hermann Vogelstein, "The Development of the Apostolate in Judaism and Its Transformation in Christianity," *Hebrew Union College Annual* 2 (1925): 115. Käsemann appears closer to the mark in observing that the New Testament witness "avoided the technical conception of office." Ernst Käsemann, "Ministry and Community in the New Testament," in *Essays on New Testament Themes* (London: SCM Press, 1964), 63.

[6]The gravity of the ecumenical concern tends to submerge the unities that might be found in the New Testament witness. For W. D. Davies, the New Testament does not "present us with a single fixed pattern of Church order which we are to regard as normative." W. D. Davies, *Christian Origins and Judaism* (London: Darton, Longman & Todd, 1962), 229. Though this seems self-evident, it fails to convince those who read New Testament ecclesiology as something *in nuce*, as something that develops (along with the canon) to its confirmation during the first ecumenical councils. Continuing with this line of logic, because Davies detaches the New Testament witness from the earliest interpretive tradition, his own observation might be interpreted as promoting an ecclesiastical agenda; that is, he represents a Protestant eschewal of tradition for an imagined return to a pristine New Testament image. Schism extends its shadow over the biblical text and its interpretation.

[7]Hans von Campenhausen, *Ecclesiastical Authority and Spiritual Power in the Church of the First Three Centuries* (London: Adam & Charles Black, 1969), 28.

[8]See J. B. Lightfoot, "The Name and Office of an Apostle," in *Saint Paul's Epistle to the Galatians* (London: Macmillan, 1914), 92-101.

theological origins of the term. This ignores the range of schismatic assumptions directing such reconstruction.

Anthony Thiselton differs from the majority by entering the discussion through the work of Ferdinand Christian Baur and the framework he developed in his 1845 *Paulus, der Apostel Jesu Christi*.[9] Baur's approach, informed by Hegel's method, posited an "early Catholicism" as the product of the conflict between Jewish and Gentile Christianities. Paul's claim to apostleship elevated Gentile Christians to a position of equality with Jewish believers, stimulating a dialectic between the "Pauline" and "Jerusalem" approaches and leading to a later synthesis of the two.

Though the generalizations basic to this position were challenged, Baur mapped the debate. First, while it may appear in modified form today, a contrast of Paul (missionary movement) against Luke (a settled college in Jerusalem) governs the discussion of the apostle and apostleship. Second, Baur treats the encounter between Jew and Gentile as singular and paradigmatic. The church is the synthesis obtained from the dialectic of "Christian universalism" and "Jewish particularism." Because the church emerges out of this encounter, no later cultural intercourse can have a similar foundational effect; the church is already the community of both Jew and Gentile, and this governs every later encounter with culture. Third, for Baur, "Christian universalism" constituted "the sole standard and rule of [Paul's] apostolic activity."[10] While this idea may appear benign, it attributes the church's universalism, that which made possible the mutual table fellowship of Jew and Greek, to a set cultural sphere: Hellenism. Paul's cross-cultural activity depends on these particular cultural roots. The very possibility of missionary movement lies in the Hellenization of the gospel.[11] Fourth, Baur applies the

---

[9]Thiselton, "Some Misleading Factors," 670. For an English translation of Baur's work, see Ferdinand Christian Baur, *Paul: The Apostle of Jesus Christ, His Life and Work, His Epistles and His Doctrine* (London: Williams and Norgate, 1878). For the essay that set the stage for this later work, see Ferdinand Christian Baur, "Die Christuspartei in der korinthischen Gemeinde, der Gegensatz des petrinischen und paulinischen Christentums in der ältesten Kirche, der Apostel Petrus in Rom," *Tübinger Zeitschrift für Theologie* 4 (1831): 61–206. For a discussion of patterns of universalism in Second Temple Judaism, see Terence L. Donaldson, *Judaism and the Gentiles: Jewish Patterns of Universalism (to 135 CE)* (Waco: Baylor University Press, 2007).

[10]Baur, *Paul*, 47.

[11]See as an example Wolfhart Pannenberg, "Notwendigkeit und Grenzen der Inkulturation des Evangeliums," in *Christentum in Lateinamerika: 500 Jahre seit der Entdeckung Amerikas*, ed. Geiko Müller-Fahrenholz (Regensburg: Verlag Friedrich Pustet, 1992), 148. One might note that while New

dialectic to the ecclesial politics of his time. For Wayne Meeks, the ingenuity of Baur's scheme lies in treating "Judaism" and "Hellenism" as "code words for complex sets of ideas masquerading as historical entities."[12] "Judaism" became a cypher for authoritarian Catholic structures and any other form of improper works-righteousness, while "Hellenism" found contemporary embodiment in the Lutheran Church. Though no longer appearing in such pronounced terms, this schismatic contest continues to inform the debate. All four of these framing assumptions are here contested.

To return to Bishop Lightfoot's contribution, at the time of his writing the election of Matthias to the Twelve was assumed to be an error by the early church, one undone by God's own action of calling Paul into the place vacated by Judas.[13] The Twelve remained, by this interpretation, a cohesive body. Lightfoot challenged this received approach by conceiving the "apostles" as a group wider than the Twelve, arguing that the "Twelve were primarily the Apostles of the Circumcision, the representatives of the twelve tribes. The extension of the Church to the Gentiles might be accompanied by an extension of the apostolate."[14] We will pursue this suggestion, albeit in modified form. As to Lightfoot's conclusion, the New Testament evidence does not limit "the Apostolate in the manner generally conceived."[15] Three points are key. First, Lightfoot demonstrated the role ecclesiastical politics played in the interpretation of the New Testament record. Second, Lightfoot's contribution lay in denying the assumed connection between the apostles and the episcopal office. Third, Lightfoot nonetheless set the significance of the New Testament discussion and its historical and linguistic reconstruction in terms of church order.[16]

Testament scholarship does not support Baur's treatment of Christian universalism, his treatment retains a certain dogmatic force when considering the contemporary nature of the church in relation to cultural diversity and the supposed normative nature of the first encounter between Greek and Jewish cultures. For a discussion of the New Testament's christological reworking of Jewish traditions of universalism, see Aaron Sherwood, *Paul and the Restoration of Humanity in Light of Ancient Jewish Traditions* (Leiden: Brill, 2013). My thanks to Sean Winter for the reference.

[12]Wayne A. Meeks, "Judaism, Hellenism, and the Birth of Christianity," in *Paul Beyond the Judaism/Hellenism Divide*, ed. Troels Engberg-Pedersen (Louisville, KY: Westminster John Knox, 2001), 19.

[13]For comment on this approach, see Holger Mosbech, "Apostolos in the New Testament," *Studia Theologica* 2, no. 2 (1948): 177.

[14]Lightfoot, "Name and Office of an Apostle," 95.

[15]Ibid., 99. This latitude Lightfoot finds also in the early church fathers (99-101).

[16]For a summary of the discussion that occupied especially German scholarship during the last part of the nineteenth and first part of the twentieth centuries, see James Tunstead Burtchaell,

Edwin Hatch, recognizing the direct challenge Lightfoot posed to a sac-
erdotal interpretation of episcopal succession, issued a response in his 1881
text *The Organization of the Early Christian Churches*. This acknowledged
one line of critique: polity in the New Testament maintained a "fluid state";
it had not yet "congealed into a fixed form."[17] Hatch even grants that the
whole of the church's organization derived from the secular political orders
of the period. This constituted no problem. Hatch affirmed historical development as itself the "mode" of divine operation, with the "divine order" of
the church determined "not by exegesis, but by history."[18] Hatch shifted the
focus from the open and various orders apparent within the New Testament
to the development of order in history. The importance of the biblical
witness rested not in its fluid variety but in containing the seeds of a later
catholic order. The argument is, of course, familiar today.

Adolf von Harnack translated Hatch's text into German and developed an
alternate interpretation. With assistance of the then newly discovered *Didache*,
Harnack saw the apostles, prophets and teachers as charismatic enthusiasts—
they did not hold particular offices.[19] However, while Harnack differed on the
issue of formal office, he retained Hatch's historical framework: this early charismatic order became institutionalized through its temporal course and did
so in service to the church's mission.[20] Rudolph Sohm engaged the debate by
concentrating on "charisma."[21] He too accepted a normative historical shift but

---

From Synagogue to Church: Public Services and Offices in the Earliest Christian Communities (Cambridge: Cambridge University Press, 1992). While his final position seeks to justify the structures
of the Roman Catholic Church, Burtchaell nonetheless acknowledges the problems with traditional justifications. This leads him to conclude that "polity itself is not all that determinative in
the church" (353), while he retains the importance of "institution" as necessary to both the
church's continuity and unity.

[17]Edwin B. Hatch, *The Organization of the Early Christian Churches* (London: Rivingtons, 1881),
20-21.

[18]Hatch, *The Organization of the Early Christian Churches*, 209, 21.

[19]Adolf von Harnack, *Lehre der Zwölf Apostel nebst Untersuchungen zur ältesten Geschichte der
Kirchenverfassung und des Kirchenrechts* (Leipzig: J.C. Hinrichsäsche Buchhandlung, 1884).

[20]See Adolf von Harnack, *The Mission and Expansion of Christianity in the First Three Centuries*
(Gloucester, MA: Peter Smith, 1972), 431-44.

[21]See Rudolph Sohm, *Kirchenrecht I: Die Geschichtlichen Grundlagen* (Leipzig: Duncker & Humblot,
1892), 19-23. For Harnack's response, see Adolf von Harnack, "Kirchliche Verfassung und
kirchliches Recht im 1. und 2. Jahrhundert," *Protestantische Realenzyklopädie für Theologie und
Kirche* 20 (1908): 508-46. For a summary of the Harneck/Sohm debate, see Wilhelm Maurer, "Die
Auseinandersetzung zwischen Harnack und Sohm und die Begründung eines evangelischen
Kirchenrechtes," *Kerygma und Dogma* 6, no. 3 (1960): 194-213. On Sohm's definition of "charisma," see Peter Haley, "Rudolph Sohm on Charisma," *Journal of Religion* 60, no. 2 (1980): 185-97;

judged the latter in negative terms, rejecting the idea of legal regulation as necessary to the church. The assumption of historical development remained intact but bequeathed a binary opposition of institution versus charisma. This approach would find its polar opposite in the work of Karl Holl, who overcame the charismatic reading by enforcing a sharp distinction between Paul and Jerusalem. Whatever Paul's more christological and missionary development, the church in Jerusalem remained authoritative and enjoyed a juridical status.[22] The assumption of a historical development and its inclination toward a set institutional form now had its roots in, and so was continuous with, the New Testament. Though tracing an extensive discussion, this brief note highlights the thematic directions: Paul is to be contrasted with Jerusalem; charisma (mission) is properly opposed to institution; the historical development of office in the early church becomes interpretive of the New Testament. These assumptions continue to frame the contemporary reflection on the New Testament's picture of the apostle, apostolic authority and the church's apostolicity.

One finds this interpretive pattern in treatments of the Hebrew term *shaliach* as informing the New Testament development of *apostolos*. Though Lightfoot pioneered the connection, it emerged as key in a 1933 article by Karl Rengstorf.[23] *Shaliach* was a Jewish legal institution whereby a person received a commission to carry the authority of another; that is, the person was a plenipotentiary. The apostle assumed this same responsibility in relation to Jesus Christ. Though Rengstorf himself balanced the concept by advancing the "missionary element" in the New Testament as "radically" distinguishing the apostle from the Jewish *shaliach* institution, some found

Enrique Nardoni, "Charism in the Early Church Since Rudolph Sohm: An Ecumenical Challenge," *Theological Studies* 53, no. 4 (1992): 646-62. For an interesting discussion on the relationship between Sohm and Max Weber, see David N. Smith, "Faith, Reason, and Charisma: Rudolf Sohm, Max Weber, and the Theology of Grace," *Sociological Inquiry* 68, no. 1 (1998): 32-60.

[22]Karl Holl, "Der Kirchenbegriff des Paulus in seinem Verhältnis zu dem der Urgemeinde," in *Gesammelte Aufsätze zur Kirchengeschichte II* (Tübingen: J.C.B. Mohr, 1928), 62-63.

[23]See Karl Heinrich Rengstorf, "ἀποστέλλω, ἀπόστολος," in *Theologisches Wörterbuch zum Neuen Testament I*, ed. Gerhard Kittel (Stuttgart: W. Kohlhammer, 1933), 397-448. For the English translation, see Karl Heinrich Rengstorf, "ἀποστέλλω, ἀπόστολος," in *Theological Dictionary of the New Testament*, ed. Gerhard Kittel and Gerhard Friedrich (Grand Rapids: Eerdmans, 1964), 389-447. For Lightfoot's contribution, see Lightfoot, "Name and Office of an Apostle," 93. After Lightfoot, significant developments appeared in Hermann Vogelstein, "Die Entstehung und Entwicklung des Apostolats im Judentum," *Monatsschrift für die Geschichte und Wissenschaft des Judentums* 49, no. 7/8 (1905): 427-49; Samuel Krauß, "Die jüdischen Apostel," *Jewish Quarterly Review* 17, no. 2 (1905): 370-83.

in this connection an immediate warrant for apostolic succession.[24] In the hands of Dom Gregory Dix, as one notable example,

> the shaliach's action irrevocably commits even his divine principal; for God has conditioned Himself by His own word of promise. The evangelical view of the apostles and the meaning of their office is quite clear. They are not officers of the Christian society but the envoys of God. As Jesus "the Apostle and High-priest of our confession," is the shaliach or plenipotentiary of God so after His ascension the Twelve are His plenipotentiaries, empowered like Him by the Messianic Spirit to fulfil and continue His own Messianic mission.[25]

As to the final interpretive significance of *shaliach* for the New Testament apostle, a later negative reaction has given way to a more complex picture where the *shaliach* is one contributing element within a novel development.[26] But the overall point being made here is simple. As Ernest Best observes, "Those who see its origin in the Jewish term *shaliach* favour Jerusalem. Those who reject this origin probably favour Antioch."[27] The main interpretive categories are determined by and serve a historical debate concerning ecclesiastical order and suppose elements such as a necessary consolidation of order and a binary opposition of Paul against Luke.

---

[24]Rengstorf, "ἀποστέλλω, ἀπόστολος," 432 (Eerdmans translation).

[25]Gregory Dix, "The Ministry in the Early Church," in *The Apostolic Ministry: Essays on the History and the Doctrine of Episcopacy*, ed. Kenneth E. Kirk and Cecilia M. Ady (London: Hodder & Stoughton, 1946), 230. For further along these lines, see A. G. Herbert's argument that interprets Jesus' being sent by God in terms of *shaliach* and finds in this "the essential idea of the Nicene formula." A. G. Herbert, "Ministerial Episcopacy," in Kirk and Ady, *Apostolic Ministry*, 500. Herbert thereby linked episcopal order to the orthodox Christian faith: to deny that order means to deny Nicaea. For a reaction to Dix from an evangelical direction, see Leon Morris, *Ministers of God* (London: Inter-Varsity Fellowship, 1964).

[26]For a survey of the subsequent debate, see Francis H. Agnew, "The Origin of the NT Apostle-Concept: A Review of Research," *Journal of Biblical Literature* 105, no. 1 (1986): 75-96. For critical treatments of *shaliach*, see Günter Klein, *Die zwölf Apostel: Ursprung und Gehalt einer Idee* (Göttingen: Vandenhoeck & Ruprecht, 1961); Walter Schmithals, *Das kirchliche Apostelamt: Eine historische Untersuchung* (Göttingen: Vandenhoeck & Ruprecht, 1961). For an appraisal of Klein and Schmithals, see Birger Gerhardsson, *Die Boten Gottes und die Apostel Christi* (Lund: Gleerup, 1962). It may be, of course, that the New Testament trades on different senses of the term depending on the meaning being conveyed. For example, Thomas Wieser applies the *shaliach* tradition to Paul's conversion. "According to Acts 9:2 Paul leaves Jerusalem for Damascus as a *Shaliach* in the Jewish tradition, vested with full powers of the High Priest. This authority is challenged by the authority of the risen Lord. What happened on the road to Damascus was a power struggle." We see here "the victory of the power of Christ over the authority of the High Priest." Thomas Wieser, "Notes on the Meaning of the Apostolate," *International Review of Mission* 64 (1975): 130.

[27]Ernest Best, "Paul's Apostolic Authority?," *Journal for the Study of the New Testament* 27 (1986): 5.

The New Testament witness does not address the anachronistic concerns of the Protestant/Catholic schism. Much of the discussion is apologetic in nature; that is, justifying arguments are imposed on the New Testament with subsequent interpretive lines drawn. A categorical division appears between Jerusalem and Paul with developments read through this filter, and this contest submerges potential lines of unity.[28] To the extent that world Christianity relocates the discussion of apostolicity, detaching it from the hermeneutical limits of schism, the following argument agrees with J. Andrew Kirk: the "development from a functional to a theological stage, or vice versa, does not exist at all; individual 'theologies of apostleship' within the New Testament ought to be considered the twentieth-century anachronism they undoubtedly are."[29] Instead, Kirk argues, the New Testament views on apostolicity "represent a diversity in unity which points to a view of apostleship of the early church which, when taken together, is much more flexible than we often allow."[30] While the New Testament definition of apostle lacks clarity when investigated from the perspective of order, it is clear regarding the christological ground of the apostolate and its determining significance for the Christian communities grounded in the witness of the apostles. This mission stimulates the diversity of both a more located and a more mobile apostolate.

EXCURSUS: JOHN D. ZIZIOULAS ON THE TWO FORMS OF APOSTOLICITY

To give one example of this apologetic approach to apostolicity, John Zizioulas identifies two main trajectories within the New Testament's "complex" picture of the apostle: one historical and one eschatological.[31]

First, the historical trajectory depicts the apostles as sent individuals, entrusted with a mission and dispersed into the world.[32] This includes a

---

[28]For Rudolf Schnackenburg, by way of example, insofar as "Paul did not know of a uniform concept of apostleship which had clear-cut criteria," it "makes no sense to play the 'charismatic' and 'institutional' concepts of an apostle one against the other." Rudolf Schnackenburg, "Apostles Before and During Paul's Time," in *Apostolic History and the Gospel: Essays Presented to F. F. Bruce*, ed. W. Ward Gasque and Ralph P. Martin (Exeter, UK: Paternoster, 1970), 301, 302.

[29]J. Andrew Kirk, "Apostleship Since Rengstorf: Towards a Synthesis," *New Testament Studies* 21, no. 2 (1975): 262.

[30]Ibid., 254.

[31]For a similar line of critique, see Irvin, "Ecumenical Dislodgings," 192-93.

[32]John D. Zizioulas, *Being as Communion: Studies in Personhood and the Church* (Crestwood, NY: St. Vladimir's Seminary Press, 1985), 172. Subsequent references are provided parenthetically within the text.

widening of the apostle concept so that it moves beyond the Twelve and the extraordinary witnesses, such as Paul, to include a wider group of missionaries endowed with the charisma to proclaim the gospel. Their missionary significance lies in the link forged between Jesus Christ and the formation of the church. "Thus the idea of mission and that of historical process go together in the New Testament and lead to a scheme of continuity in a linear movement: God sends Christ—Christ sends the apostles—the apostles transmit the message of Christ by establishing Churches and ministers" (173). Zizioulas's first "historical" approach develops a model of continuity that is "retrospective," a "consciousness of continuity with the past," an observation that holds whether one understands this as occurring "through various media or by way of copying as faithfully as possible this normative period" (178). A rather precise definition of mission follows. It is an action limited to the current historical period and consists of a lineal handing on of what has been received.

In the second trajectory, the apostles have an "eschatological function." The apostles are not sent individuals but constitute a "college." As a college, the apostles are the "*foundations* of the church in a presence of the Kingdom of God here and now" (175). Zizioulas acknowledges that mission, especially as it appears within the Pauline corpus, possesses an eschatological character, but this eschatology of orientation (mission) differs from eschatology as a "state of existence which reveals itself here and now. As orientation, eschatology appears to be the *result of historical process* as the climax of mission . . . whereas as state of existence it confronts history already now with *a presence from beyond history*" (174n11). As the eschatological function implies the presence of the kingdom here and now, so it implies "the *convocation* of the dispersed people of God from the ends of the earth to one place" (174). This, of necessity, "*presupposes the end of mission*," meaning simply that the church's sending through history comes to an end (174n11). Thus Zizioulas subjects the two New Testament trajectories to a clear ordering, with the first "historical" (provisional) and the second "eschatological" (final and pristine).

Zizioulas's generous definition of who the apostles were comes to the fore at this point. His identification of James as an apostle (a move supported by Hippolytus of Rome but resisted within Catholicism with its focus on Peter as the first pope), while perhaps validated by his historical trajectory, actually serves Zizioulas's eschatological approach and its relation to "permanent" church structures.

> With the disappearance of the Twelve from the Jerusalem Church (dispersion
> for mission?) the scheme "Apostles and presbyters" is replaced with that of
> "James and the presbyters" (Acts 21:18). The significance of this scheme lies in the
> eschatological nature of the Jerusalem Church as the center of the earth, where
> all mission converges in its final consummation (Romans 15:19). Paul must be
> reconciled with "James and the presbyters" precisely because the latter represent
> the eschatological court of the Church. Thus we have from the beginning a
> structure emerging from the eschatological state of the Church's convocation. It
> is more than significant to notice how this model is transferred to the Eucharist
> and through that to the Episcopacy after the fall of Jerusalem. (175n16)[33]

This apostolic prioritization of James is basic to the distinction Zizioulas draws and informs his entire ecclesiology. His argument for a structure of convocation, a shifting of this structure into the eucharist, and through the eucharist to episcopal order, prioritizes the apostolicity of church structures above, and establishes its control over, the missionary apostolate. This latter observation is pertinent given how discussion of church structure finds it necessary to set such structures over against the cross-cultural dynamism evident through the New Testament—the eschatological and permanent over the temporal and provisional.

The very eschatological permanence of the church means that its reality must be understood in terms of "continuity" and of "transmission or normativity" (178). The chuch's structures result from the Spirit drawing the *eschata* into history. In so acting, the Spirit "changes linear history into a *presence*" (180). This presence, because it is the presence of the kingdom, has the structure of communion. Specifically, in the eucharist the church celebrates the structure of the kingdom. From this flows the whole shape of the church's life and ministry. Zizioulas seeks thus not to resolve the tension of the historical and the eschatological, but understands the eucharist as accomplishing a synthesis of the two, the "*only reality in the Church which is at once an institution and an event*" (205). The eucharist is the privileged moment in which the "Kingdom comes epicletically, i.e., *without emerging as an expression of*

---

[33]See also 195n87, where he gives a formulaic outline of the logic.

the historical process, although it is manifested through historical forms" (207). Zizioulas coincidentally affirms the "eschatological" nature of fundamental church structures while providing latitude for historical particularities.

Mission, given its own historical limits and this acting of the Spirit, does not of itself inform such things as the fundamental communion structure of the church. Any external movement, while it may be deemed necessary as a way of connecting the church to the world, remains external to the church. Instead, "structure" determines mission because, for Zizioulas, structure refers not to institution but to the form in which the community relates to God and to the world. "This is due to the fact that Church structure and ministry are not simply matters of convenient and efficient arrangements, but 'modes of being,' ways of relating between God, the Church and the world" (244). So long as they do not introduce a "fundamentally different way of the Church's relating herself to God and the world," a range of ministerial forms can develop in relation to a particular time and place. A simple difference in form does not, of itself, determine whether a church may or may not be recognized as a church. Yet, insofar as these structures must express the right relationship of God to the world, it is not the case that the "existential and eschatological conditioning of past structures" permits a simple plurality of ministerial forms (244). As "the baptismal structure of this community is not basically changed by this conditioning," so "the eucharistic structure must be understood as implying something permanent, its permanence being dictated by its existential and eschatological nature" (245). In this way, Zizioulas satisfies the Orthodox interest in autochthonous expressions within the framework of established hierarchy and structure.

Understanding the church in terms of an eschatological apostolicity establishes clear limits on the form of mission. First and foremost, the church does not relate to the world by way of a dichotomy. Mission does not consist of the church "*addressing* the world" but "in being *com-passion* with it." The church's eucharistic nature "assumes" the world and refers it back to the creator. As its ministry is relational, so "the only acceptable method of mission for the church is the *incarnational* one" (244). Mission *ad extra* occurs in organic relation to the actual local eucharistic community. With mission as the historical expression of eucharistic ontology, it permits a variety corresponding to the particular needs of a time and place but is governed by the fundamental distinction between "mobile" and "permanent" ministries, with "mission," of course, the "mobile" (225n43). Mobile ministries ensure that the church does not

> become unrelated to the world, but they cannot acquire permanent forms, being always dependent upon the needs of the particular place and time in which the Church finds herself. From this point of view the ministries *ad extra* differ from those *ad intra*, in that the latter are essentially permanent, dictated by the Church's eucharistic structure as the community gathers together in its baptismal distinctiveness from the world. (225)

As an existential expression of an eschatological ontology, mission is cordoned off from the church and its structures as historical accident.

At this point, the limitations imposed on a missionary apostolicity become evident. The key pattern is one of permanent church structures and of a necesary relationship between the eucharist, the community and episcopal order. The church does not exist outside this set order because it fails to mediate between God and the world. Any externality, any missionary sending of the church beyond itself, is secondary and derivative because it is limited to history and transient—not part of the church's permanent character, not belonging to the kingdom of God. This dictates Zizioulas's interpretation of the apostle and apostleship within the New Testament.

7.3 THE UNITY OF THE APOSTLES: WITNESSES TO JESUS CHRIST

For all the differences within New Testament scholarship, one might indicate a loose consensus concerning the shape of an apostle. First, an apostle is an eyewitness to Jesus Christ, his life and ministry and especially his resurrection (Acts 1:21-26; 1 Cor 9:1-2; 15:7-8; Gal 1:12). Second, an apostle is one who has received a commission from Jesus Christ according to the will of God (Acts 1:24; Rom 1:1; 1 Cor 1:1; 2 Cor 1:1; Gal 1:1, 15-16; Eph 1:1; Col 1:1; 1 Tim 1:1; 2:7; 2 Tim 1:1, 11). Third, an apostle is commissioned to proclaim the gospel of Jesus Christ, the coming kingdom of God and the resurrection of the dead (Acts 4:33; Eph 3:2-7; 2 Tim 1:10-11). Fourth, this witness is confirmed in power, for it is accompanied by the Spirit (Acts 2:43-44; Rom

15:18-19; 2 Cor 4:10; 12:1-12; Gal 6:17).[34] Before turning to each point in turn, the single constituting element is clear: Jesus Christ himself. The nature and function of an apostle and of apostolic authority is wholly contingent on this ground. Whatever ecclesiological ramifications might be drawn, they derive from and are defined in the closest relation to Jesus Christ.[35]

As an eyewitness to Jesus Christ's life, death and resurrection from the dead, the apostle, as Rengstorf suggests, witnesses "to historical facts rather than to myths, and consciously and necessarily so in view of the fact that what he proclaims contradicts all human experience."[36] The historical facts contradict history itself (i.e., death is not the end), meaning that the apostle's whole message lies in what occurred. Apostleship thus points away from the apostle as an agent and to Jesus Christ, the whole of the gospel. For this reason von Campenhausen enters his examination of the apostle through Jesus' own authority during his earthly ministry. Foremost here is the identity of the gospel with Jesus Christ's own person: "the divine action that he proclaims possesses a 'humanness' which is precisely the thing that offends and enrages the most pious of his compatriots."[37] It is this humanness that directs his whole ministry; that is, his authority is not external to but lies in his mission. "He is at the same time the one who is sent and the one who from the start and in his inmost self matches the demands of that mission. . . . He stands completely on God's side. Nor is he the holder of any office in the customary sense, he appeals

---

[34]Ferdinand Hahn gives a nice example of the logic using the clauses of 2 Cor 5:20. Ferdinand Hahn, "Der Apostolat im Urchristentum," *Kerygma und Dogma* 20 (1974): 64-65. For other similar models, see C. K. Barrett, *The Signs of an Apostle: The Cato Lecture 1969* (Cumbria, UK: Paternoster, 1996), 67; Robert D. Culver, "Apostles and the Apostolate in the New Testament," *Bibliotheca Sacra* 134, no. 534 (1977): 136; Mosbech, "Apostolos in the New Testament," 170.

[35]One might raise a slight criticism against the otherwise good comment by Jürgen Roloff on this point. For him, Paul regards this *"christological grounding* [of the apostolate] through the commission of the risen One [as] only one component to which in addition are joined the *subordination to the gospel* and the *orientation toward the church.* The apostolate is, for Paul, an authorized service in the name and commission of Christ, the *origin* of which lies in an historical and unique act of sending by the risen One, the *content* of which is the gospel, itself grounded in the resurrection of Christ, pointing back to the word and way of the incarnated One, and proclaimed in the doctrine and life of the apostles, the *goal* of which is the building of the church as the eschatological people of God founded in this unique historical witness." Jürgen Roloff, "Apostel/Apostolat/Apostolizität: I. Neues Testament," in *Theologische Realenzyklopädie,* ed. Gerhard Krause and Gerhard Müller (Berlin: Walter de Gruyter, 1978), 437. In response, it would be better to understand the subordination to the gospel and the orientation toward the church and all that follows in terms of, and not "in addition to," the christological grounding of the apostolate.

[36]Rengstorf, "ἀποστέλλω, ἀπόστολος," 436.

[37]Campenhausen, *Ecclesiastical Authority,* 8.

to no official commissioning; for commission and office are combined in his person."[38] Jesus' message is not secondary to him. In him is the power and the glory of the kingdom of God. With his death and resurrection, with this event of history's contravention, the "name" of Jesus Christ as the Lord of all heaven and earth is revealed. In this name, the authority of Jesus Christ, this coincidence of his message and his person, is present.

The apostles act in power because they act in the name of Jesus Christ (Acts 4:7-10). As "only Jesus had this authority 'in himself,'" so "the disciples receive it 'in his Name,' and only in his Name and in the power of the Spirit given by him can they remain what they have become; or, to put it another way, it is Jesus himself who takes them into his service, works in them, abides with them, and employs them in his cause."[39] The disciples' authority lies not in their own "power or piety" (Acts 3:12) but in the proclamation of the gospel. As eyewitnesses, the history of Jesus Christ, his suffering under Pontius Pilate, his being raised from the dead and the present power of his name is the whole of their testimony (Acts 3:12-16). This gospel, because it is Jesus Christ himself, is not words alone. To witness in the name of Jesus Christ is to witness likewise in the coincidence of "claim and person," meaning that the apostle becomes participant in his history.[40] C. K. Barrett reinforces the point: the apostle as eyewitness is "drawn into the eschatological events of the crucifixion and resurrection of Jesus . . . into this historical manifestation of the non-historical, of the power and majesty of God."[41] The authority of the apostle lies in becoming part of Jesus Christ's history, and so under his coincidence of person and message. This is possible because the apostle has received a commission from God, a commission marked by power.

To receive a commission to proclaim the gospel is to remain dependent on God's initiative and so to act in correspondence with Jesus Christ himself.[42] Grace is the ground of the apostolic calling (Rom 1:5; 1 Cor 3:10;

---

[38]Ibid., 10.

[39]Ibid., 25.

[40]Ibid.

[41]Barrett, *Signs of an Apostle*, 43. See also Rengstorf, "ἀποστέλλω, ἀπόστολος," 437. Anton Fridrichsen's major contribution to the debate lies in locating apostleship within the eschatological framework of New Testament theology. See Anton Fridrichsen, *The Apostle and His Message* (Uppsala: Lundequistaka, 1947), 3.

[42]Kirk, "Apostleship Since Rengstorf," 255-56. Not all witnesses to earthly ministry, such as the five hundred mentioned in 1 Cor 15:6, become, by virtue of this, apostles.

15:10).[43] God is sovereign, and through God's act of grace, the apostle, to cite John Howard Schütz, is "the instrument of God's acting, just as Christ was" (2 Cor 5:18-20). Here the apostle remains a mediate instrument, "the relationship of the apostle to God is *through* Christ."[44] Because of this mediating action of Christ, the apostle is not simply identifiable with an itinerant missionary.[45] The apostle is one called by Christ and set apart for the gospel. Insofar as this is true, the apostle corresponds to Jesus Christ's own earthly ministry and the missionary form of its authority, in his proclamation of the kingdom of God. In such correspondence to Christ, every apostle is sent; every apostle is a missionary. Thus von Campenhausen: "In every case the apostles are missionaries, and to that extent the popular conception of the apostolate and of 'apostolic ministry' is entirely correct. . . . But the modern concept of a missionary is not wide enough to characterise fully the status and weight of apostolic authority."[46] The point is key, for it indicates the inconsistency accompanying an anachronistic assumption concerning the nature of mission. To suggest that the ἀπόστολος is properly differentiated from the ἐπίσκοπος by virtue of its missionary sensibility is not to presume a territorial distinction, one determined by a contrast between geographical movement and residential location.[47] This latter distinction is an assumption through which the text is read, not a definition of the apostolate to which the New Testament witnesses. It does not hold for the description of the apostle because, as Hahn observes, the commission to preach the gospel does not include any distinction between a mission internal to the community and one external to the community.[48] The commission of Jesus Christ is to proclaim the eschatological message of the kingdom of God in

---

[43]See the links drawn between grace, apostleship and mission in A. Satake, "Apostolat und Gnade bei Paulus," *New Testament Studies* 15, no. 1 (1968): 96-107.

[44]John Howard Schütz, *Paul and the Anatomy of Apostolic Authority* (Cambridge: Cambridge University Press, 1975), 205.

[45]The point needs to be made because, first, not all such missionaries receive the title apostle. (Not all those who accompany Paul are called apostle. Notable here is the distinction between Paul and Timothy in 2 Cor 1:1 and Col 1:1 and the wider witnessing group mentioned in Phil 1:14-18.) Second, Eph 4:11 draws a distinction between apostle and evangelist, which suggests that the apostolic charism was of wider significance than evangelistic proclamation alone.

[46]Campenhausen, *Ecclesiastical Authority*, 22.

[47]C. K. Barrett, "*Shaliah* and Apostle," in *Donum Gentilicium: New Testament Studies in Honor of David Daube*, ed. Ernst Bammel, C. K. Barrett and W. D. Davies (Oxford: Oxford University Press, 1978), 99.

[48]Hahn, "Der Apostolat im Urchristentum," 70.

claim and person. It is this relationship between sending and proclamation that underlies the development of the novel term "apostle." Apostles are servants of the gospel, preaching the present Messiah and the already broken-out eschatological salvation.[49] The unity of the apostles rests in the unity of their commission and witness, the unity of the apostolic mission.[50]

The content of this commission is to make the gospel known. The apostle, Thiselton argues, in that he points away from himself to Christ and is himself a *"sign' of living out* the dying-and-being-raised of Christ," is a "public, visible *witness*."[51] Such visibility is an event in history, but its nature corresponds to the event to which it witnesses; it shares in the visibility of the resurrection. As Barrett observes, whereas the cross was reportable, the resurrection was known only to a few. What is generally visible in the apostolic witness is "the sign of the Cross."[52] Such visibility reduces the apostle to a fool (1 Cor 4:10) as he preaches a message that is foolishness compared to the standards of wisdom (Rom 1:14). What is seen is the dependence of the apostle on the one who sent him. Mission defines visibility. To see the resurrection, by contrast, is wholly contingent on God revealing Godself. As a direct consequence, first, the gospel is properly distinguished from the community and its own historical visibility, for it remains God's own act. The gospel is beyond the community even as it is the community's sole ground. For this reason Peter Stuhlmacher, in remarkable similarity to Hoekendijk, develops a schema of "gospel—apostolate—community."[53] This should not be understood as a historical sequence. It refers to the gospel as the single authority because in the gospel Christ is himself present. The apostolate is the movement of community toward the ground in which it exists. Second, the apostle communicates this authority, the authority of the gospel, to the church, meaning that the visibility of the community is the sign of the cross. In being a public, visible witness, the church participates in the mission and authority of the apostles, in the authority that belongs to it with its foundation. This mission

---

[49]The necessary link between apostolate and gospel Hahn finds grounded in the Old Testament (Is 61:1) and its significance in the New Testament (Lk 1:19). Hahn, "Der Apostolat im Urchristentum," 70-73.

[50]Kirk, "Apostleship Since Rengstorf," 262. See also Campenhausen, *Ecclesiastical Authority*, 29.

[51]Thiselton, "Some Misleading Factors," 669.

[52]Barrett, *Signs of an Apostle*, 44.

[53]Peter Stuhlmacher, "Evangelium—Apostolat—Gemeinde," *Kerygma und Dogma* 17 (1971): 35.

is identified with the corporate nature of the resurrection and just so the essential sending of the whole community.[54] The shift from the apostle to apostolicity lies in this continuity of mission. Significant here is the contribution of the Fourth Gospel. While it nowhere employs the term ἀπόστολος, its focus falls on Jesus Christ himself being sent (Jn 3:17, 34; 5:36-38; 6:29, 57; 10:36; 17:3, 8, 18, 21, 23; 20:21; cf. Heb 3:1), his sending the disciples (Jn 4:38; 17:18; 20:21) and, by implication, the church's own basis in this christological ground (1 Jn 4:14). That is, the noun ἀπόστολος gives way for the verb ἀποστέλλω.[55] The public nature of this witness is missionary; it is the cruciform movement of the church in the authority given to it in its constitution and corresponding to the apostles called by Christ.

For their ministry the apostles receive power sufficient to their witness. Evident here is the performance of miracles, including healing and exorcism, and the struggle against the "principalities and powers" in confirmation of the gospel. The power in question enables the apostle to live a cruciform life, a life that is itself an "explication of the gospel," making imperative the support of a local community.[56] It is the power to identify with the broken and crucified Christ. For this reason Ernest Best isolates apostleship from (ecclesial) authority. The apostle is a function, not a position (1 Cor 12:27); the power of an apostle lies not in an office.[57] Paul does not identify his authority with a type of religio-cultural expertise associated with the method of proselytization.[58]

---

[54]Hahn, "Der Apostolat im Urchristentum," 69. See also H. P. Owen, "Resurrection and Apostolate in St. Paul," *Expository Times* 65, no. 11 (1954): 324-28.

[55]See Rengstorf, "ἀποστέλλω, ἀπόστολος," 423-24, 443-44; Barrett, *Signs of an Apostle*, 62-68; Calvin Mercer, "Jesus the Apostle: 'Sending' and the Theology of John," *Journal of the Evangelical Theological Society* 35, no. 4 (1992): 457-62.

[56]Roloff, "Apostel/Apostolat/Apostolizität," 439.

[57]Best, "Paul's Apostolic Authority?," 10. Best continues that "we are much happier dealing with 'offices' than with 'functions.' If 'apostle' was originally descriptive of a function it was natural as time went by that it should be transformed into an office. Officials always exercise authority. So we connect authority with the apostolic office and then with those who exercise the function" (21). Best even questions the notion of a foundational position reserved for the apostles alone, for when the apostles are described as the foundation of the church, the prophets are treated as an equal authority, "and these are prophets of the New Testament and not of the Old" (19).

[58]Though his conclusion presents as a cypher for ecclesiastical politics, Käsemann's discussion of the legitimacy of an apostle follows Best's contention. Käsemann suggests that those questioning Paul's apostolic credentials in 2 Cor 10–13 expected a type of formal and juridical authority from the original community and, by this measure, a clear connection to the historical Jesus. Paul needed to demonstrate his "subordination to Jerusalem." Ernst Käsemann, *Die Legitimität des Apostels: Eine Untersuchung zu 2 Korinther 10-13* (Darmstadt: Wissenschaftliche Buchgesellschaft, 1956), 34. The legitimacy of the apostle, according to these opponents, follows a "principle

He followed the singular authority of the gospel, leading to the calling of a people who were previously no people. By extension, his authority lies where the gospel is embodied, the communities where he was the "founding father" (cf. 2 Pet 3:2).[59] A similar concern prompts Thomas Wieser to frame apostolic power in terms of the identity question. "The substantive issue over which the Early Church struggled was the question: 'Can a Gentile become a Christian without first becoming a Jew?'"[60] Apostolic power lay in this turning of a people to Jesus Christ and so in the redemption of history. This challenged the lines of power (religious, economic and political) in both Jewish and Hellenistic culture, as evidenced by Paul's conflict with both Gentile and Jewish authorities.[61] For Wieser,

> the power of the Apostolate resides in the power of the risen Lord and in the Spirit. Peter's first sermon in Jerusalem culminates in the affirmation that "God has made this Jesus . . . both Lord and Messiah" ([Acts] 2:36). This is power-language, and it is also employed by Paul before Agrippa when he declares that the purpose of his mission is "to open their (the Gentiles') eyes and to turn them from darkness to light, from the dominion of Satan to God" ([Acts] 26:18). He thereby gives notice to the (puppet) king of the change of power which has taken place. In other words, Paul takes the case far beyond the charges which the Jews have brought against him. The real merits of the case have now been spelled out and they challenge the king and the Roman governor to step down from the judgement seat and to become party to the case.[62]

---

of tradition" and was properly interpreted and controlled in juridical terms. Apostolic responsibility lay in observation and control in relation to theological/cultural developments (37n114). While this picture of Paul's opposers is perhaps more caricature than commentary, Käsemann's contribution lies in his positive contrast. Paul's counterargument grounds the authority of the apostle in his weakness (see 38-43) and so in his dependence on God and the power of the Spirit. The Lord is the only authority in the apostolate, and his authority the only available measure and control for the apostles (49).

[59] Best, "Paul's Apostolic Authority?," 17.

[60] Wieser, "Notes on the Meaning of the Apostolate," 132. Wieser, writing in 1975, draws similar conclusions to those of the "translation" school today. "The decision by the Early Church to 'lay no further burden' upon the Gentiles (Acts 15:28) has implications for the role of the Jewish tradition in relation to Christianity. It is one, but no longer the only, valid option of cultural identity in relation to Christian identity" (132). One might point to Peter's encounter with Cornelius, but it is also illustrated by the collection for Jerusalem (1 Cor 16:1-4; 2 Cor 8:1-9:15; Rom 15:14-32).

[61] Ibid., 135.

[62] Ibid. Wieser refers this authority to the experience of Christians in a minority context, and so without recourse to any institutional authority; only in this setting "can the claim, the proclamation, of the Lordship of Jesus Christ as a power in this world be appreciated as the act of faith which it is, and not as an exercise in triumphalism" (136).

The christological ground constituting the function and authority of the apostle (directly related to which are both the wonders of the Spirit and Paul's own sharing in Christ's suffering) directs the apostle to the processes of conversion, to the ground and growth of communities with no other foundation (cultural, political, social, economic or gendered [Col 3:1-11]) than that of Jesus Christ himself.

7.4 The Twelve and the Redemption of History

Grounding the apostolic commission in Jesus Christ himself and his ongoing mission relativizes the focus on formal ecclesial authority structures. This permits a rereading of the contest between Paul and Luke that informs so much of the discussion.[63] One could, following the dominant account, loosely characterize these differences in terms of a charismatic and missionary apostolate associated with Paul against Luke's depiction of the apostles as a residential college located in Jerusalem and concerned with matters of theological and structural oversight.[64] An assumed ordering accompanies and explains this difference. Paul represents an earlier and fluid concept of the apostle beside a later consolidation by Luke. Luke indicates, so it is argued, settled institutions of the type perhaps already evident in the Pastoral Epistles and that find confirmation in the structures deemed to be widespread if not normative in the sub-apostolic period. An early eschatological mission, one not itself capable of historical continuity, develops into an institution that embodies the mission and enables its survival. So goes the logic.

Such an account, however, Kirk regards as "based on a set of unproved assumptions about the beginning of new movements and the development and evolution of structures rather than on a sound approach to the exegesis of the

---

[63]For a good summary of the divergence and convergence of the two, and especially the fundamental christological agreement, see Jörg Frey, "Apostelbegriff, Apostelamt und Apostolizität: Neutestamentliche Perspektiven zur Frage nach der 'Apostolizität' der Kirche," in *Kirchliche Amt in apostolischer Nachfolge I, Grundlagen und Grundfragen* (Göttingen: Vandenhoeck & Ruprecht, 2004), 126-38.

[64]For Schuyler Brown, as but one example, Acts "itself reveals a spontaneity in early missionary activity which is in tension with the role assigned to the twelve as missionary supervisors. The mission to Samaria is carried out by the Hellenists, who were persecuted in Jerusalem after Stephen's martyrdom (Acts 8. 1). Significantly, this group of missionaries, led by Philip, is distinguished from 'the apostles,' who remained undisturbed in the holy city." Schuyler Brown, "Apostleship in the New Testament as an Historical and Theological Problem," *New Testament Studies* 30, no. 3 (1984): 477.

relevant passages."[65] Much truth lies in Kirk's observation, especially as the controlling assumptions reflect the apologetic trajectories of schism. One might suggest, given the general agreement this evolutionary reading finds across the Protestant/Catholic divide (albeit often interpreted in oppositional terms), that the highlighted differences in Paul and Luke reflect the duality of apostolicity, the primacy of the cultivation of the faith with its settled location over a derivative and territorially conceived mission. Tying the apostolate to Christology and so pneumatology suggests an alternate approach. The mission of the apostles, in proclaiming the gospel that is Jesus Christ in claim and action and with power, concentrated on the local appropriation of the gospel, the integration of Jewish and Gentile histories into the history of Jesus Christ. Their commission and the identity of their authority lay in forming the eschatological people of God, a people grounded in the resurrection of the dead and so the new creation. The residential mission of the Twelve and the transient mission of Paul are, from this perspective, identical.

Lightfoot's contribution lay in disrupting the identification between the "apostles" and the "Twelve," in questioning this latter group's singular and coherent presence as a ruling "college."[66] It remains the case, however, that Luke attributes a significance to the apostles not found in any other Gospel (Lk 6:13; 9:10; 17:5; 22:14; 24:10; cf. Mt 10:2; Mk 6:30) and apart from one occasion (Acts 14:4, 14; cf. Lk 11:49) maintains an identity between the apostles, in the plural, and the Twelve (Acts 1:2, 25, 26; 2:14, 37; 6:2, 6; cf. 2:14, 37, where Peter is differentiated from the Eleven or the apostles). A valid question develops as to the significance of this body. Andrew Clark gives a fourfold answer. The apostles are, first, the "nucleus of a restored Israel," which includes a necessary relationship to Jerusalem (Acts 3:12, 25-26; 4:2, 8, 10; 5:12-16, 20, 25; 10:42; 13:31); second, witnesses to the resurrection; third, authoritative teachers; fourth,

---

[65]Kirk, "Apostleship Since Rengstorf," 258.

[66]Potential examples of this wider definition of apostle include 1 Cor 9:5; 15:5-10 (where Paul draws a distinction between Cephas and "the twelve" and between James and "the apostles"); Gal 1:19 (James, Jesus' brother, is called an apostle); Rom 16:7 (Andronicus and Junia are described as "prominent among the apostles," meaning either that they were known by the apostles or that they were well known as apostles; note, however, that if they are to be considered apostles, Junia is a female name; see Eldon Jay Epp, *Junia: The First Woman Apostle* [Minneapolis: Fortress, 2005]); 1 Thess 2:7 (Paul speaks of himself and colleagues as apostles of Christ); Acts 14:4, 14; 1 Cor 9:5-6 (the apostleship of Barnabas); 2 Cor 11:13; Rev 2:2 (false apostles). See further Andrew C. Clark, "Apostleship: Evidence from the New Testament and Early Christian Literature," *Vox Evangelica* 19 (1989): 56-64.

missionaries to Israel.[67] Important is both this variety in description and the underlying unity. The apostles are "transitional" precisely in the continuity they embody between accompanying Jesus from his early ministry to becoming authoritative witnesses to his life, death and resurrection.[68] All of this confirms the above christological ground of the apostolic ministry.

The Twelve are identified with the history of Jesus Christ, becoming themselves "eschatological regents."[69] Any importance that might accrue to them rests not in their own persons but in this continuity in discontinuity (including the defection of Judas and betrayal of Peter [Lk 22:54-62]) between Jesus Christ and the eschatological mission to the Gentiles.[70] This is evident, first, in the election of Matthias to fill the position vacated by Judas and his necessary qualification as one who had accompanied the Eleven from the time of Jesus' baptism to his ascension (Acts 1:21-22). Matthias's importance lies in this continuity with the pre-Easter history of Jesus Christ and, as a direct consequence, with his being a witness to the resurrection.[71] The coordinated observation turns to the martyrdom of James the brother of John by Herod (Acts 12:2). Unlike Judas, who is removed from the Twelve by virtue of his betrayal, James's death does not impact his membership in the group; he is not replaced. For von Campenhausen, "this can only mean that the real and imperishable significance of the Twelve was not connected with the contemporary life of the community at all."[72] Their role, for Luke, lies in the continuity of Jesus Christ's own history, not in their being an ongoing institution.

Second, the continuity function is evident in the authority Luke attributes to the Twelve. Mission becomes significant at this point. As Barrett suggests,

---

[67]See Andrew C. Clark, "The Role of the Apostles," in *Witness to the Gospel: The Theology of Acts*, ed. I. H. Marshall and D. Peterson (Grand Rapids: Eerdmans, 1998), 73-81.

[68]Ibid., 90.

[69]Jacob Jervell, "The Twelve on Israel's Thrones: Luke's Understanding of the Apostolate," in *Luke and the People of God: A New Look at Luke–Acts* (Minneapolis: Augsburg, 1972), 95.

[70]Nor is the precise constitution of the Twelve clear (compare Mt 10:2-4; Mk 3:16-19; Lk 6:14-16; Acts 1:13, 26). See Dietrich-Alex Koch, "The Origin, Function and Disappearance of the 'Twelve,'" in *Hellenistisches Christentum: Schriftverständnis—Ekklesiologie—Geschichte*, ed. Friedrich Wilhelm Horn (Göttingen: Vandenhoeck & Ruprecht, 2008), 141-42; John P. Meier, "The Circle of the Twelve: Did It Exist During Jesus' Public Ministry?," *Journal of Biblical Literature*, no. 116 (1997): 646. Von Campenhausen also notes how the lists lack "all personal or biographical detail." Campenhausen, *Ecclesiastical Authority*, 15.

[71]See Frey, "Apostelbegriff, Apostelamt und Apostolizität," 134.

[72]Campenhausen, *Ecclesiastical Authority*, 16.

Luke's anxiety to represent the church in its mission to the world as the outcome of, and as continuous with, Jesus and his mission to Israel, leads him to tie down the notion of apostleship to the group of twelve whom he could describe as having been close disciples and companions of Jesus during his ministry, and to represent these twelve as responsible through Peter, for initiating the Gentile mission (Acts 10:1-48), and collectively sanctioning and controlling it (8:14-17; 11:1-18, 22; 15:22-29).[73]

From this perspective, Luke's harmonization of the primitive church's history and his restriction of Paul's apostleship serve to connect the history of Jesus Christ to the conversion of the Gentiles. Paul is no renegade. His subordination to the Twelve includes the evident parallel between his mission to the Gentiles and the mission of the Twelve to Israel (seen in Peter's mission to Cornelius [Acts 10], the concern expressed in Jerusalem and the ensuing debate [Acts 11:1-18] and, in the last mention of Peter in Acts, Peter's own testimony that God chose him to bear the gospel to the Gentiles [Acts 15:7-11]).[74] Paul and the wider conversion of the Gentiles, in other words, belongs to the same history (1 Cor 15:3-8). This explains the diminishing authority of the Twelve through Acts. Often observed is the disappearance of the Twelve after the Jerusalem Council (Acts 16:4). Less noted is the shift in role already evident in Stephen's sermon (Acts 7). In this moment the message expanded to the Gentiles, but it is equally the moment when the mission to the Jews changed.[75] This coincides with a developing parallel between Peter and Paul and the elevation of James and the "elders" in the processes of decision making (Acts 15:2, 4, 6, 22, 23; 16:4), culminating in Paul's final visit to Jerusalem, where he meets with James, a non-apostle by Luke's account, and the elders alone (Acts 21:17-26).[76] The authority of the Twelve lies in the historical continuity it ensures and so in its mission to the Jews and the coordinated mission to the Gentiles. To cite Wieser on this point, "the fact that the Twelve were followed by other Apostles, principally

---

[73]Barrett, *Signs of an Apostle*, 52-53.
[74]See the informative discussion in Clark, "Role of the Apostles," 85-89.
[75]See Jervell, "The Twelve on Israel's Thrones," 77. Kirk regards it as "extremely significant that the twelve apostles fade from the picture once the Gentile mission is under way. Thus the *church* in Jerusalem sends *Barnabas* to Antioch (xi. 22), whereas, before, the *apostles* sent *Peter* and *John* to Samaria (viii. 14)." Kirk, "Apostleship Since Rengstorf," 263.
[76]See Best, "Paul's Apostolic Authority?," 19.

Paul, is for Luke evidence of the continuance of God's history of salvation."[77] Within this continuity, the continuity of Jesus Christ's own history, Luke attributes only secondary importance to issues of organization because, as Rengstorf suggests, "through the Holy Spirit the risen Lord himself leads and governs his church."[78] Apart from grounding it in the history of Jesus Christ, which includes the type of discussion found at the Jerusalem Council, the Twelve have no further governing role in the mission to the Gentiles.

One final point concerns the "mission" of the Twelve. If, as Wieser maintains, the power of the apostolate lies in the identity question, in faithfulness to the risen Jesus Christ through the local appropriation of the gospel, then it is necessary to question the governing distinction between the settled Twelve in Jerusalem and the itinerant Paul, a supposed residential ministry to be distinguished from an external mission.[79] The assumption is one of discontinuity, often read backwards from an early missionary ferment to a settled pastoral ministry.[80] This needs to be questioned

---

[77]Wieser, "Notes on the Meaning of the Apostolate," 131.

[78]Karl Heinrich Rengstorf, "Faith and Order in the New Testament," in *Current Issues in New Testament Interpretation: Essays in Honor of Otto A. Piper*, ed. William Klassen and Graydon F. Snyder (London: SCM Press, 1962), 49. As to the ecclesiological question, it does not seem possible to draw direct connections between Luke and church structures. Jervell rejects any notion that "the Twelve institute the offices, transfer authority and install office-holders." Jervell, "The Twelve on Israel's Thrones," 95. He also questions whether Luke is at all concerned with the church as an institution given that the "technical ecclesiological terms common at the time Luke wrote are lacking in Acts" (111n78). To further the point with Joseph Fitzmeyer, if Luke is interested in the "organized Christian community or structured church, he does not conceal its changeable and ephemeral character." Joseph A. Fitzmeyer, *The Gospel According to Luke I-IX: Introduction, Translation, and Notes* (New York: Doubleday, 1982), 255. Luke is more concerned with "the growth of the church in various parts of the eastern Mediterranean world and with the speaking of the Word of God through it to the 'end of the earth' (Acts 1:8) than in the details of church-structure" (256).

[79]See, for example, Clark's definition of witness in relation to Peter and the notion that "the apostles are closely associated with a stationary role in Jerusalem rather than a missionary one." Clark, "Role of the Apostles," 180.

[80]On this point, especially when connections are drawn between the Twelve and a later church order, Kirk notes the contrast of a functional against an eschatological view. The Twelve as an order represented a process of consolidation after an early eschatological ferment. In opposition, Kirk asks, "If it is true, as the majority of writers seem to think, that the functional is the most primitive form of the apostolic ministry[,] how can it also be maintained that the church's earliest period was dominated by a severe eschatological crisis which would consistently have undermined the functional task of the apostles?" Kirk, "Apostleship Since Rengstorf," 255. Apart from the ecclesiastical interests such a division supports, it appears contrary to the logic of the text. Luke places the importance of the Twelve precisely in this eschatological setting, with its significance diminishing as the history of the church progresses. For Holmberg, it is the Gentile mission (i.e., the eschatological mission) that caused this shift in focus from the Twelve (i.e., as

because it imposes a certain understanding of mission: mission is properly external and defined in terms of geographical movement. A confused logic follows whereby the proper missionary context of the apostolic vocation, which in the case of the Twelve is identified as a mission to the Jews, becomes immediately qualified by the observation, to quote Jervell, that "the term 'missionary' is not sufficient and may obscure their role."[81] In response, Luke's concern for continuity is christological, identified with the calling of Jesus Christ and confirmed by the power of the Spirit. The mission of the Twelve, especially insofar as they constitute an eschatological symbol of the renewed Israel, consists of calling Israel to repentance, turning the people of God to their Messiah (see the issue of authority in relation to the Jewish council: Acts 8:1, 14, 18; 9:27; 11:1; 15:2, 4, 6, 22, 23; 16:4). Jerusalem is central as the place where God would be made manifest and as the place from which God's word would go out. The Twelve's "mission to the Jews" demanded this residential location because it is basic to the Jewish religious heritage and to God's promises made to Israel (a point illustrated by the mission of Peter and John to Samaria in Acts 8:14-17). Mission is the conversion of the history of Israel, its conversion to the history of its Messiah. The mission identified with Israel expands to include the Gentiles, but the form does not change. It remains christologically determined—the Gentiles are to turn to Christ, which means a turning of their own religious and historical heritage, which, by extension, takes a different shape. The presence or absence of geographical movement does not determine mission as a descriptor of the apostolic ministry.

---

supposed settled ministry). "The original idea about what God's 'messianic' mission among the Jews would look like had to be expanded, almost exploded, by the fact forced upon the Jewish-Christian church that the Gentiles belonged in the church as well. Thus, God's Spirit showed the church unmistakably that God is able to bypass his earlier institutions and innovate." Bengt Holmberg, "Jewish *Versus* Christian Identity in the Early Church?," *Revue Biblique* 105, no. 3 (1998): 421.

[81] Jervell, "The Twelve on Israel's Thrones," 93. For Jervell, because the Twelve called Israel to repentance, they had a "prophetic role." The assumption is clear: mission is a geographical and cross-cultural movement. When this is not present, it is not mission. However, even at a flat sociological level, Gerd Theissen is able to differentiate between two types of missionaries: "itinerant charismatics" and "community organizers." Gerd Theissen, "Legitimation and Subsistence: An Essay on the Sociology of Early Christian Missionaries," in *The Social Setting of Pauline Christianity: Essays on Corinth* (Philadelphia: Fortress, 1982), 27-68. That is, the restrictions on mission as a theological concept appear much more a form of ecclesiological projection than related to the variety of definition evident in the biblical text.

7.5 NEGOTIATING CONVERSION AS THE NATURE OF THE APOSTOLIC MINISTRY

Shifting this discussion of the apostle to apostolicity, to this authority's corporate form, we immediately note the lack of New Testament scholarship examining apostleship in relation to the communities rooted in this mission. On this point, the polemic framing the debate exerts its greatest force. When the community becomes the focus, apostleship narrows to structure and the formal demarcation of authority. Even while the event of translating the gospel across cultural borders belongs to the nature of apostolicity as a direct consequence of its christological ground, this does not appear within the literature as a positive and continuing theological factor. The controlling assumption remains that of an early missionary and eschatological spirit that consolidates into a particular institutional expression.

The church apostolic as the product of these mechanics, so it would seem, represents a later and settled trajectory, one deemed determinative for church history as such. A twofold consequence follows. First, apostolicity reduces to a flat contest of either structure's given nature or its freedom to change. For Barrett, as representative of one side of the debate, the "nature of the [apostolic] task will vary from age to age and from place to place, and the church's organization, structure, and method must change to meet changing circumstances; indeed, changing, adaptable structures might be said to be a better mark of apostolicity than an order received from remote ages and carefully preserved."[82] While reference to world Christianity and so to pluriform Christian histories confirms structural variety as belonging to apostolic continuity, the weakness in Barrett's position lies in reducing structures to the circumstantial. The importance of structural expression in world Christianity lies in the processes of the gospel's appropriation and so translation, and against the method of assuming a form of Christian expression organized elsewhere. Maturation in the faith resides in this redemption of history and the turning of this cultural identity to Christ, not in the assumption of answers and their structural expression to questions posed in other times and places. Structure, by extension, while governed by Christian witness and not reducible to a single form, is not a façade

---

[82]Barrett, *Signs of an Apostle*, 91.

changeable without consequence for the underlying framework. Structure belongs itself to the content of the message, the embodiment of Jesus Christ in the language and history of a people gathered by the power of the Spirit. Placing the freedom of structural change in the circumstantial fails to grasp the importance of institution at this level of appropriation and its centrality for the processes of conversion and maturation in the faith.

Second, with the structural issue detached from the processes of conversion, the apostle and apostolic authority appear detached from the gospel's appropriation. As one consequence, John Barclay observes how "interpreting Paul as a cultural critic and exploring his vision of community in which there is 'neither Jew nor Gentile' is an agenda still largely unaddressed by Pauline scholars."[83] Though noted of Paul, the concern can be more generally applied to the question of apostleship through the New Testament. The direct correlation between the ground of apostleship in Christ and the apostle being a "cultural critic," with all that this means for "table fellowship," is not, so it would seem, a defining characteristic of the apostolic ministry.[84] Alternately stated, should one reject the range of assumptions that restrict the apostolic ministry to the limits afforded by schism, it seems clear that the christological ground of the apostolate itself impels the processes of cross-cultural transmission and the question of a common life. The apostle directs the apostolic community beyond itself to its ground in Christ. The question of "structure" corresponds to this issue of identity and community in Christ, to the common table in the encounter between local appropriations of the gospel without the reduction to a third, mediating culture.

If Barclay's observation holds and New Testament scholarship has neglected the issue of intercultural encounter and order and, by extension, failed to investigate apostleship from the perspective of conversion, his constructive position advances the discussion. He establishes the problem of this community as "neither Jew nor Gentile" through Daniel Boyarin's

---

[83]John M. G. Barclay, "'Neither Jew nor Greek': Multiculturalism and the New Perspective on Paul," in *Ethnicity and the Bible*, ed. Mark G. Brett (Leiden: Brill, 1996), 206.

[84]On this question, attention has focused much more at the social science level and the description of group dynamics and boundary markers. For an interesting discussion of Jew/Gentile dynamic within a "Christian" community from a social science perspective, see Philip F. Esler, "Group Boundaries and Intergroup Conflict in Galatians: A New Reading of Galatians 5:13–6:10," in Brett, *Ethnicity and the Bible*, 215-40.

A Radical Jew: Paul and the Politics of Identity.[85] Boyarin's argument attributes Paul's universalism to "a Hellenistic desire for the One, which among other things produced an ideal of a universal human essence, beyond difference and hierarchy." Boyarin judges this relationship in negative terms. Paul "required that all human cultural specificities . . . be eradicated."[86] Equality becomes equated with sameness, resulting not in a "cultural uniformity" (a diversity of language and dress remains) but in treating matters of religious and cultural heritage (including the law) as "adiaphora, matters of indifference," when set in relation to Christ.[87] Boyarin's objection recognizes in this "tolerance" of cultural identity markers of an undoing of cultural difference, a reduction of difference to a matter of taste and so a denigration of those who find their identity in these differences.[88] The problem, at base, is one of cultural absorption. Since "there is no such thing as cultural unspecificity, merging of all people into one common culture means ultimately (as it has meant in the history of European cultural imperialism) merging all people into the dominant culture."[89] Though one should not pretend an immediate connection, neither should one leave unobserved the similar contours evident in contemporary ecumenical statements concerning apostolicity, especially in the claim for a transcendent (by virtue of its passage through time and space) culture that integrates historical and cultural contingencies as confirmation of its very universalism. Nor should one overlook the similar account of diversity, one that does not expect uniformity in expression but subsumes difference to established order.

Barclay's counter to Boyarin begins with the social context of Judaism in Paul's time and with a distinction between "'acculturation' (the adoption of Hellenistic speech, literary forms, values and philosophies) and 'assimilation' (social integration into Hellenistic society)."[90] Though acculturated, diasporic

---

[85]Daniel Boyarin, *A Radical Jew: Paul and the Politics of Identity* (Berkeley: University of California Press, 1994). Barclay's treatment occurs in Barclay, "'Neither Jew nor Greek,'" 206-9.

[86]Ibid., 8.

[87]Ibid., 9.

[88]Boyarin supports James Dunn's interpretation of the "works of the law" as boundary markers; see ibid., 53. For an example of Dunn's contribution, see James D. G. Dunn, "Works of the Law and the Curse of the Law (Galatians 3.10-14)," *New Testament Studies* 31, no. 4 (1985): 523-42.

[89]Boyarin, *Radical Jew*, 8. Boyarin makes the same point vis-à-vis gender: "The erasure of gender seems always to have ended up positing maleness as the norm to which women can 'aspire'" (8).

[90]Barclay, "'Neither Jew nor Greek,'" 209.

Jews resisted assimilation through a common life shaped by ancestral customs, including monotheism (prohibiting participation in non-Jewish religion), circumcision (limiting marriage possibilities), dietary laws (limiting social interaction) and Sabbath observance (limiting employment relations).[91] Such customs demarcated the borders between Jewish and Greek cultures. With his conviction that the Gentiles were also heirs of the promise, Paul sought "an alternative form of community which could bridge ethnic and cultural divisions by creating new patterns of common life."[92] Paul attempted this not through a spiritualization of social customs, for he sought a community "embodied in social reality."[93] Instead, he *relativized* cultural specificities. Paul, Barclay argues, maintained his respect for circumcision (Rom 3:1-2) and insisted on the priority of the Jews in the promises of God (Rom 9:4-5). Christ, however, is Lord of all who acknowledge him as such "whatever their cultural identity. Thus Jews and Gentiles are simultaneously *affirmed* as Jews and Gentiles and *humbled* in their cultural pretensions. . . . No one culture is despised or demonized, but by the same token none is absolutized or allowed to gain hegemony."[94] Nor did Paul promote the gospel as creating a "third race," a blending of Jewish and Greek cultures through which emerged a composite "universal" culture. Christ is not installed as "the founder of a new culture."[95] Rather, "commitment to Christ can simultaneously

---

[91]Ibid.

[92]Ibid., 210.

[93]Ibid.

[94]Ibid., 211. As a further example, for John Riches, Paul rejects not cultural "particularity, not diversity *as such*, but cultural exclusivism, the absolutizing of cultural boundaries. The new creation is forged in an encounter with the stranger in which the old distinctions are subverted and new forms of life permitted to emerge." John K. Riches, "'Neither Jew nor Greek': The Challenge of Building One Multicultural Religious Community," *Concilium*, no. 1 (1995): 41-42.

[95]Barclay, "'Neither Jew nor Greek,'" 211. For William Campbell too, "Paul did *not* hold that Christians should lose their cultural identity as Jew or Gentile and become one new humanity which is neither." William S. Campbell, *Paul's Gospel in an Intercultural Context: Jew and Gentile in the Letter to the Romans* (Frankfurt am Main: Peter Lang, 1992), 9. As an opposing example, Holmberg asserts that "the fundamental identity, common to Jews and Gentiles in the church, is neither Jewish nor Gentile, but simply *Christian*." Holmberg, "Jewish *Versus* Christian Identity," 415. The "common, fundamental Easter experience [of Jew and Gentile believers], which is at the same time their conversion and salvation experience" (418), led them to slide "out of their earlier identities" and become "something no one had ever been before. This *reciprocal identity displacement*, which is at the same time a *unification process*, started early in the history of the church" (422). Holmberg might, from this perspective, be criticized for conceiving the common table fellowship in terms of a loss in Jewish identity (410-11), implying that the early Christians would both question and leave their Jewishness behind in service to the "common, fundamental

encompass various cultural particularities."[96] Unity should not be confused with cultural homogeneity, nor oversight with structural controls.

The similarity between Barclay's position and that advanced by students of world Christianity should be clear. Against Boyarin's characterization of a universal "Christian" culture cherishing diversity while eliminating difference, cultural identity is affirmed in Jesus Christ while coincidentally subjugated to him. Such an agreement is important in this context because it draws the notion of apostolicity as the translation and appropriation of the gospel into Paul's own apostolic ministry. Paul's apostolate expresses his "corporate christology," and the cultural relationship that follows is the church apostolic.[97] The confirmation of cultural identity in Christ Jesus means turning that identity to him. The Spirit leads this community beyond itself, and in this cultural encounter the lines of identity become evident. This process is never internal to the church alone but is, by virtue of its replacement of and so challenge to cultural authorities, part of the wider political context.[98]

7.6 A Body Whose Identity Lies in Jesus Christ and So Beyond Itself

It seems reasonable to argue that the framework of schism has created this lacuna within New Testament studies. The examination of apostolicity is directed to a certain end. So to draw this New Testament discussion together in more systematic terms, apostolicity should not be confused with the transfer of an original and individual grounding authority to a community. The authority of the apostle is the authority that already constitutes the church as a creature of the gospel. The key point is christological. Whatever

---

Christian identity of the church [that] is more important than inherited ethno-religious self-definitions" (425). One might counter Holmberg by observing that the ground of unity lies in the mutual conversion to Christ, which means the turning of ethno-religious self-definitions to him, and not in their abandonment. "Christian" identity is only ever an embodied identity.

[96]Barclay, "'Neither Jew nor Greek,'" 211. For John Riches, Paul is "not *building* a multicultural community at all. He is announcing the advent of a new community in Christ and issuing a call to people to enter it and to be reconciled." Riches, "'Neither Jew nor Greek,'" 41.

[97]For a discussion of this, see the helpful David G. Horrell, "'No Longer Jew or Greek': Paul's Corporate Christology and the Construction of Christian Community," in *Christology, Controversy, and Community: New Testament Essays in Honour of David R. Catchpole*, ed. David G. Horrell and Christopher M. Tuckett (Leiden: Brill, 2000), 321-44.

[98]The type of translation process, its link with mission and the church being the "body" of Christ, is well illustrated by reference to Eduard Schweizer's discussion of Col 1:15-20 in Eduard Schweizer, "The Church as the Missionary Body of Christ," *New Testament Studies* 8, no. 1 (1961): 1-11.

might be said of the church (its witness, structure and historical continuity) follows from its ground in Christ Jesus and the "foundation of the apostles"— and the prophets (Eph 2:20). With this ground, the identity of the community lies beyond itself. It lies in Jesus Christ.[99] In other words, apostolicity is the movement of the community beyond itself, the movement of the body toward its head. The community finds its identity in this movement.[100] This lays great stress on the power of the Spirit, who constitutes the community in its being directed beyond itself.

One potential misinterpretation when framing apostolicity in relation to world Christianity lies in reducing it to a natural process of identity formation, to the mechanics of history and culture detached from any discussion of God's own acting. As this type of "historical project," to cite John Webster, the church is "more than a rather indeterminate set of cultural negotiations in which [it] figures out some kind of identity for itself. The church is not finished; it learns itself over time; it does not possess itself wholly, because its source of life is the infinity of God."[101] While Webster's own argument does not concern apostolicity, the central contention lies close to the argument developed in relation to world Christianity and its parallel in the New Testament church. Christian identity is not secured within the borders of a single historical narrative that follows the contours of a supposed center of Christian power and the controls of form and interpretation managed by such. The church finds its identity beyond itself, in the history of Jesus Christ. In this resides the possibility of conversion, the possibility of multiple Christian histories. The church's proper externality is that of Jesus Christ himself, meaning that the crossing of cultural boundaries is an immediate consequence of the identity of the church in this ground.

---

[99]Hans-Peter Großhans locates this "beyondness" in the truth of the gospel and so treats apostolicity as the basic mark of the church; see Hans-Peter Großhans, *Die Kirche—irdischer Raum der Wahrheit des Evangeliums* (Leipzig: Evangelische Verlagsanstalt, 2003), 294-99. For further on the centrality of the gospel as a power that communicates itself, see Peter T. O'Brien, *Gospel and Mission in the Writings of Paul: An Exegetical and Theological Analysis* (Grand Rapids: Baker, 1995), 53-81.

[100]James Hawkey makes a similar point in the context of the contemporary ecumenical discussion. As the early church participated in the sending of the Spirit into "human temporality," so it "discovered itself not to be just a community of disciples, but rather of *apostles.*" By implication, "the dynamic of apostolicity is about a kind of unrestricted sending of the community beyond itself, which in turn reveals something essential about that community's identity." James Hawkey, "Excavating Apostolicity: Christian Communities and Secular Cultures," *Ecumenical Review* 62, no. 3 (2010): 272.

[101]Webster, "'In the Society of God,'" 217.

The continuity basic to apostolicity is the continuity of Jesus Christ's own history. This is not reducible to a single form. To follow Karl Barth, Jesus Christ's life is a "*self-multiplying* history," evoking "its own reflection in the world."[102] This history Barth conceives as the living history of the objective acting of God to reconcile the world to himself and the subjective response of the human. This is true first of Jesus Christ, and as such it is true of other human beings called by him. It is on this basis that Barth identifies the being of the community as "a predicate" of Jesus Christ's own being, a being "taken up and hidden in His, and absolutely determined and governed by it."[103] The advantage of this position lies in undoing any false identification of the church with Jesus Christ, while maintaining a "*real identity*" between the two as a gift of God and in the power of the Spirit.[104] It lies, in other words, in dislocating the body from any singular historical and cultural form and placing the possibility and form of conversion in the integration of human histories into Jesus Christ's own history, the living intercourse between the act of God reconciling the world to himself and the human act of response. The christological ground of apostolicity means this opening of closed histories, their turning to and so redemption in Christ. The human histories gathered into the history of Jesus Christ remain, in Barth's estimation, an "after-history" (*Nachgeschichte*), meaning that they remain contingent on the completion of reconciliation in Jesus Christ. But, precisely as participant in his history, they exist within a "surplus space," the surplus of God's own radiant and declarative being, and by this become and are real histories.[105] For apostolicity, the multiple histories of world Christianity find their possibility in the one history of Jesus Christ, for in this history they are redeemed. It is in the integration of particular histories in the one living history of Jesus Christ that the community provisionally represents the alteration of the world that has taken place in him. The relativization and affirmation of culture identified by Sanneh in the process of translation is a consequence of the church's participation in the history of Jesus Christ, the church's having its identity beyond itself.

---

[102]CD IV/3.2, 212; KD IV/3.2, 242.

[103]CD IV/2, 655; KD IV/2, 741. For a development of this point in both christological and pneumatological terms, see CD IV/3.2, 752-62; KD IV/3.2, 861-72.

[104]CD IV/2, 655; KD IV/2, 743.

[105]CD IV/1, 736-37; KD IV/1, 823.

This beyondness of the community, its being in Jesus Christ, is the ground of the church's structuring. For Catholic theologian Jürgen Werbick, it makes possible a clear identification of the church's apostolic structure—which is given with the call to follow Christ. It means "participation, in power, in the sending of Jesus Christ *and* participation, in powerlessness, in his witness to the kingdom of God, meaning thus a *visible* witness to the promise as to the challenge of God's coming lordship for humanity; it means taking and bearing the 'passion' of God in this world, his passion for this world."[106] Apostolicity determines, in Werbick's estimation, the "hermeneutic of discipleship," the processes of conversion.[107] Or, the beyondness of the church is its being sent, its apostolicity. Only those who are sent participate in Jesus Christ's own sending, and his own self-identification with those who are sent takes the form of his presence among them. This presence is the "solidarity of the One sent (and his Father) with those being sent."[108] The church receives its structure as the whole apostolic community follows Jesus Christ's own way through time. Because of this ground, visibility is a necessary element of apostolicity, but, equally in this ground, visibility is defined in relation to apostolicity as this eschatological missionary sending, the being of the church in Jesus Christ and so beyond itself.

Such visibility directly corresponds to the content of the apostolic message. It is the visibility of Jesus Christ's own history, that is, the visibility of his resurrection from the dead. The truth of the church as Christ's body is, to cite Barth, "not a matter of a general but a very special visibility."[109] The church is not accidentally but essentially visible; the elements basic to its historical existence are not matters indifferent to its life. The church is as it takes place, meaning that it is a matter of historical human actions, including ecclesial order, institution, cultus, teaching, theology and hospitality. As this human fellowship, it is visible to all.[110] Nor is it possible to look through this form to find a real

---

[106]Jürgen Werbick, *Kirche: Ein ekklesiologischer Entwurf für Studium und Praxis* (Freiburg: Herder, 1994), 86.

[107]Werbick, *Kirche*, 91.

[108]Werbick, *Kirche*, 88. Based on this Werbick argues that structural continuity cannot guarantee apostolicity. He opposes treating apostolicity as a "formula of legitimation," its reduction to an ideology (90-91).

[109]CD IV/1, 658; KD IV/1, 731.

[110]CD IV/1, 653; KD IV/1, 728.

church behind it.[111] However, the visibility of the church cannot be other than that which is true now of Jesus Christ himself. The truth of its visibility, what it actually is as the people of the new creation, is not generally visible to all but corresponds to the manner in which "the glory of the humanity justified in Him is *concealed*."[112] As with the ministry of the apostles, what can generally be seen is the cross, and the church can so bear the marks of messianic passion because it lives in the power of the resurrection. Only with Jesus Christ's return will the Christian community be seen as it, in truth, is.

In relation to this visibility, apostolicity, Barth argues, gives the church its "concrete criterion, the one and only *nota ecclesiae*, not in competition with the decisive determination of the church by the existence and work of its living Lord, but as the true and authentic interpretation of this basic determination."[113] Apostolicity refers the church to its ground in Jesus Christ. This concrete criterion is a spiritual criterion, for only by the power of the Spirit does the church become visible as the body it is. Apostolicity is the history of Jesus Christ taking place.[114] Thus, in a programmatic statement, as the apostleship of the apostles consisted of pointing beyond themselves, witnessing in the power of the Spirit to Jesus Christ as the light of the world, so the church apostolic "can never in any respect be an end in itself. . . . As Christ's community it points beyond itself."[115] Two consequences follow.

First, form does not itself bear visibility, because no form can make visible the truth of the community. The visibility of the church's identity in the gospel is the visibility of the resurrection; it remains an act of God's own self-revelation. No sacred sociological form exists, and the church is free to structure itself according to its witness. Yet this simple confirmation of freedom does not exhaust the point. The gospel has, to use Webster's phrase, a "self-organizing power."[116]

---

[111]CD IV/1, 653-54; KD IV/1, 730.

[112]CD IV/1, 656; KD IV/1, 733.

[113]CD IV/1, 714; KD IV/1, 797-98.

[114]CD IV/1, 721; KD IV/1, 805.

[115]CD IV/1, 724; KD IV/1, 809.

[116]John Webster warns that "apostolicity has less to do with transmission and more to do with identity or authenticity, with the 'Christianness' of the church's teaching and mission." John B. Webster, "The Self-Organizing Power of the Gospel of Christ: Episcopacy and Community Formation," in *Word and Church: Essays in Christian Dogmatics* (Edinburgh: T&T Clark, 2001), 208. Transmission, in this context, refers to the simple replication of structures. "Authenticity," Webster maintains, "cannot by its very nature be 'transmitted,' because it is not capable of being embodied without reside in ordered forms. Forms cannot guarantee authenticity, simply because

The freedom the church has in creating forms in service to its mission does not render these structures accidental. The gospel creates communities. World Christianity illustrates the coincidence and importance of both these aspects. It is a positive statement of God's own superfluity, and only reading the issue through the lens of schism makes it appear a negative point.

This church's freedom, second, is directed. The center of the church is in Jesus Christ's own history. This is no abstraction. As Jesus Christ is the one sent by the Father for the world (Jn 3:16), so the church exists for the world as Jesus Christ did and does. The apostolate means sharing in Jesus Christ's own mission. The church's commission to be light in the world, to continue with Barth, is not "only an immediate or more distant deduction from the gift of its being and existence."[117] This commission is not "additional" to an otherwise defined being of the church. Difficulty arises with this position when the so-called time of mission is restricted to the period between Jesus Christ's ascension and his return in glory. A determining assumption follows: as this mission does not belong to the eschaton, so it is of merely relative significance for the church here and now. Jürgen Moltmann, by way of example, develops apostolicity in simple missionary terms. "It is only in fulfilling the mission itself that the church can be called apostolic."[118] Such mission indicates the hermeneutical nature of the church's movement through history. "The biblical witness is witness to a historic forward-moving mission in the past, and hence in the light of the present mission it can be understood for what it really is."[119] But so defining apostolicity comes at a price. As "the church's special historical designation," apostolicity is limited to history. Whereas the three marks of one, holy and catholic will "continue in eternity, and are also the characteristics of the church when it is glorified in the kingdom, the apostolic mission will come to an end when it is fulfilled."[120] This position detaches the church's apostolicity from the history of Jesus Christ and so from the eschatological identity of the church. By way

---

forms are themselves not immune to the critical question of their own authenticity" (208).

[117]CD IV/3.2, 787; KD IV/3.2, 900.

[118]Jürgen Moltmann, *The Church in the Power of the Spirit: A Contribution to Messianic Ecclesiology,* trans. Margaret Kohl (Minneapolis: Fortress, 1993), 312.

[119]Ibid., 283. For further on Moltmann's understanding of the relationship between hermeneutics and mission, see 272-303.

[120]Ibid., 357.

of counter, apostolicity is the ground of the church in this living history, and it will not be otherwise in the kingdom of God. As Barth maintains, the community will not be divested of this "very being *ad extra*" with the return of Jesus Christ. Instead, this being "will be manifested in its visibility and worldliness at the fulfillment of His return."[121] This being *ad extra* is only true in Christ by the power of the Spirit. It will not be removed, but be seen as it is, in the final revelation of Jesus Christ as the Lord of all creation.

7.7 THE ONE JESUS CHRIST AND THE PLURALITY OF APOSTOLICITY

The New Testament presents a complex picture of the apostle. Important differences exist between the Pauline and Lukan accounts, but their interpretation needs to be detached from the schismatic end to which it is often directed. No New Testament ground advances or supports such interpretive assumptions. The permanent importance of Judaism for the Christian faith notwithstanding, there is no basis to treat "Jew" and "Gentile" as the two prototypical cultural entities exhaustive for the limits of the gospel's cross-cultural transmission. Nor does the New Testament regard the early church as a stage of temporary ferment awaiting stabilization into a singular church order and history. Nor does the gospel's capacity to move across cultural boundaries reside outside of it and in Hellenistic culture. Nor does the New Testament regard the appropriation of the gospel in different cultural settings as an impediment to maturity in the faith. Nor, as is central to Luke's argument, does the movement from Jesus Christ's earthly ministry through the Twelve to the Gentile mission in any way interrupt the historical continuity of the gospel. The opposite is clearly the case. All these assumptions reflect more the concerns of apologetic ecclesiastical politics than attending to the available New Testament evidence.

Detached from the interpretive mechanics of schism, the New Testament picture becomes clearer and, in outline, finds general support. Paul and Luke both ground the nature and work of an apostle in Jesus Christ. The apostles are eyewitnesses to his life, death and resurrection, are called by Jesus Christ according to God's will, are commissioned to proclaim the gospel of Jesus Christ and receive the power of the Holy

---

[121]CD IV/3.2, 724; KD IV/3.2, 829.

Spirit as testimony to the truth of their witness. Anything that might be said about church structures derives from this same ground, and it is evident from the New Testament witness that cultural and so structural diversity belongs to the communities grounded in the apostolate. One might extend the point: such diversity is a direct correlate of the apostolate's christological ground and calling—not secondary or accidental, but part of the full stature of Jesus Christ's body. Such is possible only in the power of the Spirit. The importance of table fellowship should not go unnoticed here. The New Testament identifies the problem as theologically basic and, as such, basic to the processes of cultural engagement. Nor does the proposed solution within the New Testament lie in a shared visible ministry. Paul does not himself locate the problem and its solution in office and recognized particular authorities. The solution lies in the return to the christological ground of the community, to the significance of each history in Christ and so to the relativization of each culture, on the one hand, and their destigmatization, on the other: even Gentiles receive the Spirit; God shows no partiality.

Though a further area of agreement lies in the missionary shape of the apostolate, commentators often express some uncertainty regarding this point due to the "located ministry" of the Twelve in Jerusalem. A tension results whereby mission characterizes the apostolic ministry while coincidentally appearing somehow unnecessary. The effect is evident in how discussions addressing the missionary intent of the apostle in the New Testament fail to draw this into the contemporary ecclesiological discussion.[122]

---

[122]Wolfgang Beinert, for example, argues that the New Testament defines apostolicity in five main ways: it is, first, a christological concept; second, a missionary concept; third, a personal concept, meaning that it indicates the dynamic of discipleship and one's belonging to Christ; fourth, it is related to God's own self-revelation because it is determined by the resurrection and ascension of Jesus of Nazareth; fifth, it is an eschatological category and so indicates the universal sending of the church into the world. Wolfgang Beinert, "Apostolisch: Anatomie eines Begriffs," in *Kirchliche Amt in apostolischer Nachfolge II, Ursprünge und Wandlungen* (Göttingen: Vandenhoeck & Ruprecht, 2006), 279-80. After noting the general interpretive patterns of apostolicity articulated in the traditions, and the danger of apostolicity reducing to an ideology, Beinert identifies it with the work of the Spirit. Apart from the Spirit, apostolicity understood as the canon or as office has no meaning. As first pneumatological, apostolicity is an "eschatological gift" given by God to the church (284). As a sign of the eschaton, apostolicity is a hermeneutical process, the movement of the church to the world "in the care of the burning fire of the Holy Spirit" (284). Beinert's treatment throughout speaks to the missionary intent of the apostle. Yet, as his argument progresses, this initial position gives way to established lines of

The acknowledged essential missionary character of the apostle gives way to the familiar binary of established structures necessary to the cultivation of the faith against a structural freedom for the purposes of missionary proclamation. Such an approach, however, presumes a link between mission and territory—the missionary act takes place in geographical movement. While this assumption derives from and reinforces established ecclesiological models and associated patterns of mission, it does not derive from the New Testament witness. In the New Testament, the nature of mission is defined by the christological ground of the apostle, the missionary calling to point beyond the self and to Christ, the subjection of this ministry to God's own self-revelation in the power of the Spirit and the eschatological pentecost by which Jesus Christ's own mission extends to the whole world. These elements hold true for both Paul and Luke. The difference between them, in other words, concerns not the definition of mission. This difference gives mission its positive shape. Mission turns the history and culture of a people to Jesus Christ and only so in the power of the Spirit.

It was necessary to the mission of the Twelve to remain in Jerusalem because the conversion of the Jewish people meant a fulfillment of God's promises. Such fulfillment leads not to a destruction of that people, their religious heritage and cultural identity. It means a redemption also of that history through its turning to the Messiah, a setting of that culture on its ground in Christ. Exactly the same is true of Paul's ministry. Gentiles do not need to become Jews. Gentiles remain Gentiles and are valued as such in Christ, meaning that they are to turn their own way of life to him. Nor does Paul postulate a third culture as a harmonization of the Jew and Gentile encounter, one that undoes the particularities of especially the Jewish people. Mission is this redemption of history and, as such, the movement of the gospel across cultural boundaries. It means that the missionary act takes a community form conditioned by all those elements necessary to human societies. Precisely in proclaiming the gospel as "good news," mission assumes different forms in different historical and cultural settings. Wolfgang Beinert can thus conclude, "Faithfulness to the kerygma leads to the plurality of

---

concern. While Beinert's conclusion expresses an openness of the problem of apostolic succession, it is not at all clear how his earlier argument drawn from his own understanding of the biblical material informs his later argument shaped as it is by the Protestant/Catholic schism.

theologies, ways of life, churchly constitutional models, all of which already confronts us in the time of the New Testament."[123] This "one mission of Christ divides itself into many missions: apostolicity is realized in plurality."[124] Beinert's conclusion, of course, confirms the fundamental notion that it is the power of the Spirit that structures and sustains the church.

This mission, while mandating historical and cultural diversity, does not oppose (to use Webster's words) the "self-organizing power of the gospel." It exists subject to this power; the gospel must find structural expression in the body. This view of mission equally cautions against depicting church structures in simple functionalist terms. The very importance of inculturation lies in the gravity of structures for the local community and the necessity of these structures for Christian witness. One can, from this perspective, agree with those who conceive church structures in terms of historical development, for these are a part of the history and processes of conversion. But it is equally to deny the normativity of a singular history. Development can occur because no culture is the divine culture; all can be turned to Christ. This is the central New Testament lesson.

The ministry of the apostle lies in the ministry of the risen Lord Jesus Christ. Likewise, the apostolicity of the church lies in the livingness of the living Lord Jesus Christ. Apostolicity means that the church does not possess its own identity. The church finds this identity in the history of Jesus Christ. This is the possibility of historical continuity, for it is the continuity of the resurrected Jesus Christ and his abundance through which every history is redeemed. Because it is the history of Jesus Christ, it takes the form of participation in his being sent to and for the world and thus the integration of multiple histories into his and only so by the testimony of the Spirit.

---

[123]Wolfgang Beinert, "Die Apostolizität der Kirche als Kategorie der Theologie," *Theologie und Philosophie* 52 (1977): 175. Nor does structure guarantee faithfulness in doctrine. As Beinert observes, "the major heretics of the early church were almost all bishops whose succession was above suspicion, e.g., Nestorius, Apollinaris, Eutyches, etc." Beinert, "Apostolisch: Anatomie eines Begriffs," 292.

[124]Beinert, "Die Apostolizität der Kirche als Kategorie der Theologie," 178.

Apostolicity

The Livingness of the Living Word

For all its importance in the cause of Christian unity, the treatments of apostolicity within ecumenical discourse appear ill equipped to deal with the polycentrism and pluriformity of world Christianity. In this context, the global expansion of the gospel seems somehow in the wrong, an outworking of the Protestant/Catholic schism and a dilution of Christian identity. None of this is to deny the challenge of unity and its fundamental role in witness. Unity speaks to the power of God in bringing together groups otherwise divided along blood, economic, cultural, linguistic, social, political and gender lines; unity lies in the redemption of history definitive of mission. Ecumenical treatments fall down, not because of structural diversity, but because of a shared opposition and related ordering: the cultivation of the faith is defined apart from, and gains a determinative priority over, the communication of the faith. Historical continuity is conceived in these terms, privileging a single historical and cultural course and promoting institution as the determining factor. Defining cultivation at some distance from communication frames continuity in terms of the geographically located and residential. This shapes the theological evaluation of continuity, stability, order and maturity in the faith, and so directs Christian witness. At issue is not the church's being a body, a community of the new creation. The gospel of reconciliation is to be proclaimed by a reconciled and reconciling people. The issue concerns the constriction of this body, its reduction to a single history and so culture, which denies the power of Christian unity.

Nor does this asymmetrical ordering of cultivation and communication correspond to the dividing lines demarcing episcopal order. It frames the whole debate, the agreed on point underlying the Protestant/Catholic schism and on which current proposals trade. Instead of beginning with the issue of episcopal order, ecumenical documentation approaches apostolicity through the missionary ground of church. Apostolicity now refers to the whole life of the community, and the "apostolic tradition" to the range of practices and institutions that build up this community in its appropriate *habitus*. This broadening of apostolicity focuses on the community's life while affirming the key theological link between institution, cultivation and continuity at the heart of the debate. Or, the naming of the "apostolic tradition" corresponds to the priority of cultivation as apostolicity's necessary end, and this includes the selective non-inclusion of certain practices and structures (the avoidance of the structures mentioned in Eph 3:11, as one example). Without reference to anything beyond the community when conceiving the nature of its witness, all interest lies in the complex of liaisons constitutive of community and its identity. As a culture, the church apostolic remains continuous even as it changes with each generation and encounters other cultural bodies. Culture bears and expresses the body's missionary witness, and it confirms the processes of cultivation as basic. The question of office remerges at this point, secondary and in service to this people, but as a necessary extension of this particular culture. Diversity becomes a diversity of gift, confirming that its order grows out of, maintains and directs this culture, that certain people are called to shepherd the community in its gospel identity. As an identifiable culture, the historical and cultural origins of institutional forms become relativized, even while they establish the governing controls for difference in relation to the community.

One should not deny the power of the cultural position. Apostolicity as cultural continuity gives clear direction concerning the nature of Christian growth while allowing for historical change. One clear limitation, however, lies in the mission method it promotes. In simple terms, the orthodox and normative theology of apostolicity enlists a mission method of cultural replication. Accepting this as a problem is, of course, a major component of the challenge. Much of the theological work done in the postcolonial period consigns such method to renegade and independent missions, isolating the sending ecclesiologies from any responsibility for what occurred in proclaiming the gospel, baptizing in the name of the Father, Son and Spirit, making disciples and building the body. The judgment is a nonsense, a powerful one, but a nonsense nonetheless.

This judgment exists because of a peculiar variance in the definition of mission. As a summary concept for the nature of the community, the ground in which the community is cultivated and the end to which it is directed, mission retains the highest priority. It becomes the communication of "identity" as borne by the "communion" basic to Christian existence and so by its structures. With Christian witness identified in terms of the growth and maturation of the faith, and in terms of the gifts, practices and artifacts basic to this growth, mission then becomes the activity of replicating the structures basic to this witness. Discipleship into a Christian identity becomes the process of enculturation, of learning the language, the patterns, the interpretive measures, the questions and answers of this culture. Mission develops as a contest with other cultural forms in different geographical locations. Though the possibility exists for cultural forms to give shape to the wider tradition, such remains possible only under the governing structures by which historical continuity is maintained.

While this witness serves the world, while it presumes some external effect, its mechanics are internal and associated with a certain approach to purity, stability and maturity. This internality establishes the parameters and method for the church's movement beyond itself. Such a mission becomes secondary and derivative, motivated by some external accident and taking shape according to that circumstance. But while the institutional manner of delivery may vary, the content remains consistent: this secondary mission replicates the structures basic to the building up of the primary mission. If the true witness to the gospel results from a Christian *habitus*, then it results from the structures and practices necessary to its cultivation. A fundamental contest develops when growth is conceived as contingent on a particular cultural form and so opposed to the disruption occasioned by cross-cultural encounter. The aggrandizing of the internal mission and the coordinated elimination of an external mission in the postcolonial period succeeds only in reifying the problem. The more a community focuses on its internals, the more its external movement consists of transmitting its culture and the practices, interpretive means, histories, authorities and myths integral to such.

This colonialist charge applies irrespective of the presence or absence of episcopal order. Historically, it made no difference whether a church body promoted an established order or granted the freedom to shape order. Both approaches mandated a form of Christian expression experienced locally as a foreign import. Maturity in the faith emerges as the key point. An immature faith develops when faith remains external to the context, and this foreignness occurs with the failure to convert the local heritage and associated structures.

Here the problem of schism has enduring significance. In recognizing a particular body as apostolic, the church validates a lived expression of the gospel. This body represents a faithful interpretation of its ground and apostolic calling in Jesus Christ. Herein lies the ecumenical challenge. Schism as apostolicity's opposite is the petrification of the gospel. It is the consolidation of a particular historical expression of the living Word into a normative religious culture and the promotion of its interpretative artifacts as themselves necessary to the gospel. Schism results in the competition of now set cultural narratives, with the associated forms of cultivation, promoted as the best expression of, and so witness to, the gospel. As the contest of lived interpretations of the gospel, schism becomes the contest of one tailored history against another. Recognition becomes a tool of power and ideology.

Schism lays improper conditions for the church's apostolicity, and when one refuses its framing premises, other theological resources come to the fore, notably the reality of world Christianity with its pluriformity and polycentrism. A solution to the ecumenical problem requires a better parsing and incorporation of the lived cultural appropriations of the gospel. Whatever ecclesiastical power remains within Europe and North America, the Christian population centers reside now in Latin America, Africa and Asia. This is the church visible and concrete. And while world Christianity might appear a novel development contingent on Western missionary expansion, it is this expectation of a singular institutional history that world Christianity disproves. The faith's geographical expansion revealed the very cultural location of Western Christianity, and this necessitates the gospel's deterritorialization. To reiterate: the point of agreement is maturity in the faith and the necessary role of community and institutions. The difficulty emerges with an approach to cultivation for which cross-cultural missionary transmission is not simply absence but negatively judged—it intrudes on the processes and structures necessary to cultivation. This mission disrupts a presumed identity of embodiment and territory. Insofar as this identity is treated as basic, to promote mission is to "disembody" the church and replace it with a "dynamic." So goes the logic, and it is unsustainable in the perspective of world Christianity. Negatively stated, the problem of colonization reveals territorial definitions of the church to be false. Positively stated, maturity in the faith rests on the gospel's local appropriation, on the conversion of local structures and histories into the history of Jesus Christ. Conversion is a process both non-territorial and embodied. Though the ecclesiological ramifications of the position remain unattended at an ecumenical level, no single cultural form is the normative expression of the gospel. It follows as an immediate correlate that the gospel is not bound to a single history. The territorial diversity cannot be limited to cultural diversity alone but speaks also to a diversity of histories.

Nor is this conclusion to be drawn from world Christianity alone. The strength of the discussion lies in the evident parallels between the history of world Christianity and the formation of believing communities in the New Testament. Before developing this point, it is necessary to create space for the comparison: schism turns the New Testament discussion to its own ends. In depicting the first church as driven by an eschatological hope and without concern for its own continuity, the faith's embodiment appears dependent on the processes of historical development and on the particularity of the resulting structure. But there is no basis to assume that mission, specifically the mission of the apostles, is without means for historical continuity; there is no basis to assume that this mission failed to ground believing communities concerned with growth in the faith. Such a position reflects much more a distorted definition of mission, one derived from a territorial definition of the church, than one derived from the New Testament witness. Instead of finding the singularity of Christian history in the (eschatological) history of Jesus Christ and in the conversion of multiple histories into his, Jesus Christ's history is reduced to a single cultural form. One might suggest that to conceive the church as an "eschatological *detour*," to use Jenson's language (STII, 171), is to conceive the church apart from its apostolic ground.

Likewise, the body of scholarship investigating apostleship within the New Testament addresses the material to the existing Catholic/Protestant schism. Questions of personal authority, office and formal structure trump investigation into the apostolic grounding of communities and the corporate nature of apostolic authority. Investigation along this latter line bears constructive fruit. The apostolate lies in the conversion of the Jewish and Gentile histories into Jesus Christ's own, and so in the creation of the one people of God within the particularity of both. The importance of the apostles lies in their relation to this living Word: their continuity with Jesus Christ's earthly ministry and their service to his prophetic ministry. For this service they received the power of the Spirit. Their authority lies not in themselves but in their being instruments of the risen Lord, in their pointing beyond themselves to the reconciliation of the world accomplished in him. The apostle is one sent in the calling of Jesus Christ and in the power of the Spirit. To heed the authority of the apostles is to engage in this same movement. This authority the church receives with its grounding. Standing under the Word, the church hears the call to follow Jesus Christ in his own apostolic mission in, to and for the world and receives the gifts of the Spirit for this witness. The church apostolic follows the apostles in no other way than in pointing beyond itself. Apostolic authority lies in turning peoples and histories to Christ; it lies in the communities as themselves witnesses to the kingdom of God.

The church's apostolicity, its continuity through history, has occurred only as the gospel has moved across cultural boundaries and been appropriated in the language, thought forms and structures of this other history. These histories do not remain as they are in this encounter. On the contrary, it is through the process of conversion, of turning all things to Jesus Christ, that these histories are redeemed and the expression of the gospel through local structures is both possible and necessary. This mission reveals the operative binaries of the Protestant/Catholic schism to be false. Missionary translation affirms the centrality of structure in the appropriation of the gospel. It results not in a groundless dynamic without the means for historical continuity, for, precisely in the processes of translation, the gospel structures a community. With this the case, no structure can be a priori affirmed because no structure is without an accompanying range of interpretive means that are themselves developed responses to complex questions. Christian maturity is based in this translation. Maturity is not the result of being enculturated into questions asked in other places but results from being reconciled to God and so developing answers to local questions, from the integration of this local history into that of Jesus Christ's own. The developments in world Christianity can be seen as new because they draw redeemed histories into the one body of Christ. They are basic to the church attaining the full stature of Christ. But, equally, this does not suggest a new form of continuity different from the faith's actual historical course.

In this process of conversion, the church structures itself according to a cultural heritage. Claiming the lordship of Jesus Christ will challenge local religious and political authorities, meaning that the church engages in a wider cultural dialogue. None of this prioritizes a particular cultural form, even one with an extended temporal lineage, in relation to other forms. It is because no culture can be sacralized that each culture can be converted, that every history can be redeemed. As Sanneh suggests, "Christianity is embroiled in this profound tension, confidently affirming God in the channels of cultural particularity and just as confidently rejecting any one expression as definitive of the truth."[1] Mission, by extension, is not a derivative and replicative action of a territorial body. It is the movement of this eschatological living Word, the integration of every history into the history of the resurrection. Precisely as such, mission is the movement of the gospel across cultural boundaries, recognizing this movement as necessary to maturity in the gospel at a local level and in terms of the fullness of Christ. Because the identity of the church is beyond it and in Jesus Christ, the church cannot remain content in its own parochial setting. In other words, the very possibility of conversion includes this movement of being sent and the proclamation of the living Word beyond these borders. Maturation in the faith necessitates this movement of reconciliation with difference, a movement that does not deny that difference but affirms it as also part of the body. This is the possibility and tension of apostolicity.

Apostolicity is the community's participation in Jesus Christ's own history, the history of the resurrection of the dead. This history is concrete and visible—it takes place. It is a matter of communities and of what properly belongs to such, including structures, institutions and order. But it is equally the history and visibility of the eschaton, not given to sight apart from God's own revelation of the kingdom. Apostolicity remains a spiritual criterion. It is not destined to pass away with the visible appearance of the kingdom but awaits the earthly revelation of Jesus Christ as the Lord of history. Apostolicity as the

---

[1]Lamin O. Sanneh, *Translating the Message: The Missionary Impact on Culture* (Maryknoll, NY: Orbis Books, 2009), 81.

visibility of the resurrection is an eschatological promise. It will be fulfilled in the eschaton, meaning that it will be then and there perfected in what it here and now is. As the history of the resurrection of the dead, this history follows no singular course, for it is the redemption of history itself, including the disruption of death. Jesus Christ's history is self-multiplying. His own apostolic movement into and for the world means the integration of multiple histories into his. The church finds its identity, not in itself and the gifts given to it, but beyond itself in the history of Jesus Christ. The church apostolic is the church determined by its living Lord and his mission. Apostolicity is the concrete interpretation of this christological determination. Apostolicity is the church following the living Word, its being sent into and for the world. The church's form, in other words, is given with the call to follow Jesus Christ and in the power of the Spirit as it witnesses to the truth of the gospel. Faithfulness to its apostolic foundations means that the church must move beyond the borders of its own particular history to proclaim the gospel of history's redemption. Nor is unity institutionally secured. Unity is a living event in which the one body seeks the full stature of Christ. It is a matter of maturity in Christ and so of humbling every cultural pretension to the law of love. Apostolicity, as this participation in the sending of Jesus Christ in the power of the Spirit, and so in the sending of the apostles, is the hermeneutic of discipleship. Apostolicity is true in this plurality. Recognizing this directs us again to the richness of the gospel, for only the Lamb that was slain is able to set the voices of every tongue, nation and tribe in their proper harmony.

Bibliography

Adjei, Ako. "Imperialism and Spiritual Freedom: An African View." *American Journal of Sociology* 50, no. 3 (1944): 189-98.

Agnew, Francis H. "The Origin of the NT Apostle-Concept: A Review of Research." *Journal of Biblical Literature* 105, no. 1 (1986): 75-96.

Albrecht, Gloria H. *The Character of Our Communities: Toward an Ethic of Liberation for the Church.* Nashville: Abingdon, 1995.

Allen, Roland. *Missionary Methods: St. Paul's or Ours?* London: Robert Scott, 1912.

Alternative Globalization Addressing Peoples and Earth (AGAPE): A Background Document. Geneva: World Council of Churches, 2005.

Althaus-Reid, Marcella. "'A Saint and a Church for Twenty Dollars': Sending Radical Orthodoxy to Ayacucho." In *Interpreting the Postmodern: Responses to Radical Orthodoxy*, edited by Rosemary Radford Ruether and Marion Grau, 107-18. London: T&T Clark, 2006.

Amin, Samir. *Eurocentrism.* New York: Monthly Review Press, 1989.

Andersen, Wilhelm. *Towards a Theology of Mission: A Study of the Encounter Between the Missionary Enterprise and the Church and Its Theology.* London: SCM Press, 1955.

Apostolicity and Succession: House of Bishops Occasional Paper. London: Church House Publishing, 1994.

Avis, Paul D. L. *A Ministry Shaped by Mission.* London: T&T Clark, 2005.

———. *Reshaping Ecumenical Theology: The Church Made Whole?* London: T&T Clark, 2010.

———. "Rethinking Ecumenical Theology." In *Paths to Unity: Explorations in Ecumenical Method*, edited by Paul D. L. Avis, 91-106. London: Church House Publishing, 2004.

Baago, Kaj. "Post-colonial Crisis of Missions." *International Review of Mission* 55 (1966): 322-32.

Balz, Heinrich. *Der Anfang des Glaubens: Theologie der Mission und der jungen Kirchen*. Neuendettelsau: Erlanger Verlag für Mission und Ökumene, 2010.

Baptism, Eucharist and Ministry. Geneva: World Council of Churches, 1982.

Barclay, John M. G. "'Neither Jew nor Greek': Multiculturalism and the New Perspective on Paul." In *Ethnicity and the Bible*, edited by Mark G. Brett, 197-214. Leiden: Brill, 1996.

Barrett, C. K. "*Shaliah* and Apostle." In *Donum Gentilicium: New Testament Studies in Honor of David Daube*, edited by Ernst Bammel, C. K. Barrett and W. D. Davies, 88-102. Oxford: Oxford University Press, 1978.

———. *The Signs of an Apostle: The Cato Lecture 1969*. Cumbria, UK: Paternoster, 1996.

Barry, F. R. *The Relevance of the Church*. New York: Charles Scribner's Sons, 1936.

Barth, Karl. *Church Dogmatics*. Edited by G. W. Bromiley and T. F. Torrance. 4 vols. In 12 parts. Edinburgh: T&T Clark, 1957.

Baum, Gregory. "Two Question Marks: Inculturation and Multiculturalism." In *Christianity and Cultures: A Mutual Enrichment*, 101-6. Maryknoll, NY: Orbis Books, 1994.

Baur, Ferdinand Christian. "Die Christuspartei in der korinthischen Gemeinde, der Gegensatz des petrinischen und paulinischen Christentums in der ältesten Kirche, der Apostel Petrus in Rom." *Tübinger Zeitschrift für Theologie* 4 (1831): 61-206.

———. *Paul: The Apostle of Jesus Christ, His Life and Work, His Epistles and His Doctrine*. London: Williams and Norgate, 1878.

Becker, Karl. "The Church and Vatican II's *Subsistit* Terminology." *Origins* 35 (2006): 514-22.

Bediako, Kwame. "Africa and Christian Identity: Recovering an Ancient Story." *Princeton Seminary Bulletin* 25, no. 2 (2004): 153-61.

———. "Africa and Christianity on the Threshold of the Third Millennium: The Religious Dimension." *African Affairs* 99 (2000): 303-23.

———. *Christianity in Africa: The Renewal of a Non-Western Religion*. Maryknoll, NY: Orbis Books, 1995.

———. "The Emergence of World Christianity and the Remaking of Theology." *Journal of African Christian Thought* 12, no. 2 (2009): 50-55.

———. "Facing the Challenge: Africa and World Christianity in the 21st Century—A Vision of the African Christian Future." *Journal of African Christian Thought* 1, no. 1 (1998): 52-57.

———. *Jesus and the Gospel in Africa: History and Experience*. Maryknoll, NY: Orbis Books, 2004.

———. *Jesus in Africa: The Christian Gospel in African History and Experience.* Maryknoll, NY: Orbis Books, 2004.

———. "The Roots of African Theology." *International Bulletin of Missionary Research* 13, no. 2 (1989): 58-62.

———. "Scripture as the Hermeneutic of Culture and Tradition." *Journal of African Christian Thought* 4, no. 1 (2001): 2-11.

———. "The Significance of Modern African Christianity—A Manifesto." *Studies in World Christianity* 1, no. 1 (1995): 51-67.

———. *Theology and Identity: The Impact of Culture upon Christian Thought in the Second Century and in Modern Africa.* Oxford: Regnum Books, 1992.

Beidelman, T. O. "Contradictions Between the Sacred and the Secular Life: The Church Missionary Society in Ukaguru, Tanzania, East Africa, 1876–1914." *Comparative Studies in Society and History* 23, no. 1 (1981): 73-95.

Beinert, Wolfgang. "Apostolisch: Anatomie eines Begriffs." In *Kirchliche Amt in apostolischer Nachfolge II, Ursprünge und Wandlungen*, 274-303. Göttingen: Vandenhoeck & Ruprecht, 2006.

———. "Die Apostolizität der Kirche als Kategorie der Theologie." *Theologie und Philosophie* 52 (1977): 161-81.

Beintker, Michael. "The Study 'The Church of Jesus Christ' from the Protestant Point of View." In *Consultation Between the Conference of European Churches (CEC) and the Leuenberg Church Fellowship (LCF) on Ecclesiology: Report on the Consultation Papers and Final Communiqué*, edited by Wilhelm Hüffmeier and Viorel Ionita, 73-88. Frankfurt am Main: Verlag Otto Lembeck, 2003.

Békés, Gellert. "The Growing Awareness of the Una Sancta: Convergencies in Ecumenical Ecclesiology." *Journal of Ecumenical Studies* 16, no. 4 (1979): 691-704.

Bell, Daniel. *The Cultural Contradictions of Capitalism.* New York: Basic Books, 1976.

Bellagamba, Anthony. *Mission and Ministry in the Global Church.* Maryknoll, NY: Orbis Books, 1992.

Bellah, Robert N., Steven M. Tipton, William M. Sullivan, Richard Madsen and Ann Swidler. *Habits of the Heart: Individualism and Commitment in American Life.* Berkeley: University of California Press, 1985.

Benedict XVI. "Faith, Reason and the University: Memories and Reflections." *Islamic Studies* 45, no. 4 (2006): 595-604.

Benn, Christoph. "The Theology of Mission and the Integration of the International Missionary Council and the World Council of Churches." *International Review of Mission* 76, no. 3 (1987): 380-402.

Berger, Peter L. "A Market Model for the Analysis of Ecumenicity." *Social Research* 30, no. 1 (1963): 77-93.

Berger, Teresa. "A Note on Notions of Catholicity in Ecumenical Reflection." *Studia Liturgica* 26 (1996): 315-22.

Berkhof, Hendrikus. *Christian Faith: An Introduction to the Study of the Faith.* Grand Rapids: Eerdmans, 1986.

———. "De Apostoliciteit der Kerk." *Nederlandse Theologisch Tijdschrift* 2 (1947): 146-60, 193.

———. "Kerk en Zending." *In de Waagschaal* 6 (1951): 260, 264.

Berkouwer, G. C. *Studies in Dogmatics: The Church.* Translated by James E. Davison. Grand Rapids: Eerdmans, 1976.

Bernstein, Richard J. "The Hermeneutics of Cross-Cultural Understanding." In *Cross-Cultural Conversation: Initiation*, edited by Anindita N. Balslev, 29-42. Atlanta: Scholars Press, 1996.

Best, Ernest. "Paul's Apostolic Authority?" *Journal for the Study of the New Testament* 27 (1986): 3-25.

Best, Thomas F., and Martin Robra. *Ecclesiology and Ethics: Ecumenical Ethical Engagement, Moral Formation and the Nature of the Church.* Geneva: World Council of Churches, 1997.

Beusekom, J. H. van. *Het experiment der gemeenschap: Een onderzoek naar plaats en functie van de 'orde' in de reformatorische kerken.* The Hague: Voorhoeve, 1958.

Bevans, Stephen B. "Ecclesiology Since Vatican II: From a Church with a Mission to a Missionary Church." *Verbum SVD* 46, no. 1 (2005): 27-56.

Beyerhaus, Peter. "Mission und Einheit: Die theologische Entscheidung für die Integration von Weltmission und Ökumene." In *Ökumenische Erneuerung in der Mission*, edited by Heinrich Stirnimann, 9-24. Freiburg: Paulus Verlag, 1970.

Bimwenyi, K. Oscar. "Inculturation en Afrique et Attitude des de l' Evangelisation." *Bulletin of African Theology* 5 (1981): 5-17.

Blanco, Pablo. "The Theology of Joseph Ratzinger: Nuclear Ideas." *Theology Today* 68, no. 2 (2011): 153-73.

Blasi, Anthony J. "A Market Theory of Religion." *Social Compass* 56, no. 2 (2009): 263-72.

Blaut, James M. *The Colonizer's Model of the World: Geographical Diffusionism and Eurocentric History.* New York: Guilford Press, 1993.

Blauw, Johannes. "Das Missionsdenken in den Niederlanden 1945–1955." *Evangelisches Mission-Magazin* 106 (1956): 116-26.

Bosch, David J. "Systematic Theology and Mission: The Voice of an Early Pioneer." *Theologia Evangelica* 5, no. 3 (1972): 165-89.

———. "Theological Education in Missionary Perspective." *Missiology* 10, no. 1 (1982): 13-34.

———. *Transforming Mission: Paradigm Shifts in Theology of Mission*. Maryknoll, NY: Orbis Books, 1991.

Bourdieu, Pierre. *Outline of a Theory of Practice*. Cambridge: Cambridge University Press, 1977.

Bouteneff, Peter, and Alan D. Falconer. *Episkopé and Episcopacy and the Quest for Visible Unity: Two Consultations*. Geneva: World Council of Churches, 1999.

Boyarin, Daniel. *A Radical Jew: Paul and the Politics of Identity*. Berkeley: University of California Press, 1994.

Boyd, Robin H. S. *India and the Latin Captivity of the Church: The Cultural Context of the Gospel*. Cambridge: Cambridge University Press, 1974.

Brechter, Suso. "Decree on the Church's Missionary Activity." In *Commentary on the Documents of Vatican II*, edited by Herbert Vorgrimler, 87-181. New York: Herder & Herder, 1967.

Brown, G. Gordon. "Missions and Cultural Diffusion." *American Journal of Sociology* 50, no. 3 (1944): 214-19.

Brown, Peter. *The Rise of Western Christendom: Triumph and Diversity, A.D. 200–1000*. Malden, MA: Wiley-Blackwell, 2003.

———. *Through the Eye of a Needle: Wealth, the Fall of Rome, and the Making of Christianity in the West, 350–550 AD*. Princeton, NJ: Princeton University Press, 2012.

Brown, Raymond E. "The Unity and Diversity in New Testament Ecclesiology." *Novum Testamentum* 6, no. 4 (1963): 298-308.

Brown, Schuyler. "Apostleship in the New Testament as an Historical and Theological Problem." *New Testament Studies* 30, no. 3 (1984): 474-80.

Brunner, Emil. "One Holy Catholic Church." *Theology Today* 4, no. 3 (1947): 318-31.

Bühlmann, Walbert. *The Coming of the Third Church: An Analysis of the Present and Future of the Church*. Maryknoll, NY: Orbis Books, 1977.

Burleigh, J. H. S., T. F. Torrance and F. W. Camfield. "Concerning the Ministry." *Scottish Journal of Theology* 1, no. 2 (1948): 184-206.

Burrows, Mark S. "Globalization, Pluralism, and Ecumenics: The Old Question of Catholicity in a New Cultural Horizon." *Journal of Ecumenical Studies* 29, no. 3/4 (1992): 346-67.

Burrows, William R. "Conversion: Individual and Cultural." In *Understanding World Christianity: The Vision and Work of Andrew F. Walls*, edited by

William R. Burrows, Mark R. Gornik and Janice A. McLean, 109-26. Maryknoll, NY: Orbis Books, 2011.

———. "Mission and Missiology in the Pontificate of John Paul II." *International Bulletin of Missionary Research* 30, no. 1 (2006): 3-8.

———. *New Ministries: The Global Context.* Maryknoll, NY: Orbis Books, 1980.

———. "Reconciling All in Christ: An Old New Paradigm for Mission." *Mission Studies* 15, no. 1 (1998): 79-98.

Burtchaell, James Tunstead. *From Synagogue to Church: Public Services and Offices in the Earliest Christian Communities.* Cambridge: Cambridge University Press, 1992.

Cabral, Amilcar. *Return to the Source: Selected Speeches.* New York: Monthly Review Press, 1974.

"The Calling of the Church to Mission and Unity." *Ecumenical Review* 4, no. 1 (1951): 66-71.

Camara, Babacar. "The Falsity of Hegel's Theses on Africa." *Journal of Black Studies* 36, no. 1 (2005): 82-96.

Camp, Bruce K. "A Theological Examination of the Two-Structure Theory." *Missiology* 23, no. 2 (1995): 197-209.

Campbell, William S. *Paul's Gospel in an Intercultural Context: Jew and Gentile in the Letter to the Romans.* Frankfurt am Main: Peter Lang, 1992.

Campenhausen, Hans von. *Ecclesiastical Authority and Spiritual Power in the Church of the First Three Centuries.* London: Adam & Charles Black, 1969.

Carter, David. "Legitimacy of Development Within the Apostolic Tradition." *One in Christ* 29, no. 3 (1993): 226-34.

———. "Some Reflections on Apostolicity." *One in Christ* 31, no. 3 (1995): 237-50.

Carvalhaes, Claudio. "Communitas: Liturgy and Identity." *International Review of Mission* 100, no. 1 (2011): 37-47.

"Catholicity and Apostolicity." In *Faith and Order, Louvain 1971: Study Reports and Documents,* 133-68. Geneva: World Council of Churches, 1971.

Cavanaugh, William T. "The Empire of the Empty Shrine: American Imperialism and the Church." *Cultural Encounters* 2, no. 2 (2006): 7-29.

———. *Theopolitical Imagination: Discovering the Liturgy as a Political Act in an Age of Global Consumerism.* London: T&T Clark, 2002.

———. "The World in a Wafer: A Geography of the Eucharist as Resistance to Globalization." *Modern Theology* 15, no. 2 (1999): 181-96.

Chantraine, Georges. "The Missionary Tasks Received from Vatican II." *Communio* 12 (1985): 312-18.

Chapman, Mark D. "The Politics of Episcopacy." *Anglican and Episcopal History* 69, no. 4 (2000): 474-503.

Charles, Pierre. *Dossiers de l'action missionnaire*. Louvain-Bruxelles: Editions de L'Aucam, 1938.

———. *Études missiologiques*. Bruges: Desclee de Brouwer, 1956.

"Church as Communion." In *Growth in Agreement II: Reports and Agreed Statements of Ecumenical Conversations on a World Level, 1982–1998*, edited by Jeffrey Gros, Harding Meyer and William G. Rusch, 328-43. Geneva: World Council of Churches, 2000.

"The Church as Mission in Its Very Life." *International Review of Mission* 101, no. 1 (2012): 105-31.

The Church for Others, and the Church for the World: A Quest for Structures for Missionary Congregations. Geneva: World Council of Churches, 1967.

Church History Association of India (CHAI). "Scheme for a Comprehensive History of Christianity in India." *Indian Church History Review* 8, no. 2 (1974): 89-90.

"The Church: Local and Universal." In *Growth in Agreement II: Reports and Agreed Statements of Ecumenical Conversations on a World Level, 1982–1998*, edited by Jeffrey Gros, Harding Meyer and William G. Rusch, 862-75. Geneva: World Council of Churches, 2000.

The Church: Towards a Common Vision. Geneva: World Council of Churches, 2013.

Clark, Andrew C. "Apostleship: Evidence from the New Testament and Early Christian Literature." *Vox Evangelica* 19 (1989): 49-82.

———. "The Role of the Apostles." In *Witness to the Gospel: The Theology of Acts*, edited by I. H. Marshall and D. Peterson, 169-90. Grand Rapids: Eerdmans, 1998.

Coffele, Gianfranco. *Johannes Christiaan Hoekendijk: Da una teologia della missione ad una teologia missionaria*. Rome: Universita Gregoriana, 1976.

Collet, Giancarlo. *Das Missionsverständnis der Kirche in der gegenwärtigen Diskussion*. Mainz: Matthias-Grünewald-Verlag, 1984.

Collins, Paul M. "Communion: God, Creation and Church." In *Receiving "The Nature and Mission of the Church": Ecclesial Reality and Ecumenical Horizons for the Twenty-First Century*, edited by Paul M. Collins and Michael A. Fahey, 21-41. London: Continuum, 2008.

Comaroff, Jean, and John L. Comaroff. "Christianity and Colonialism in South Africa." *American Ethnologist* 13, no. 1 (1986): 1-22.

———. *Of Revelation and Revolution*. Vol. 1, *Christianity, Colonialism, and Consciousness in South Africa*. Chicago: University of Chicago Press, 1991.

Comblin, José. *Called for Freedom: The Changing Context of Liberation Theology.* Maryknoll, NY: Orbis Books, 1998.

"Communal, Collegial, Personal: Report of Group I." In *Episkopé and Episcopacy and the Quest for Visible Unity: Two Consultations,* edited by Peter Bouteneff and Alan D. Falconer, 48-56. Geneva: World Council of Churches, 1999.

Congar, Yves M. J. "The Necessity of the Mission 'Ad Gentes.'" *Studia Missionalia* 51 (2002): 157-65.

———. "Theologische Grundlegung (Nr. 2-9)." In *Mission nach dem Konzil,* edited by Johannes Schütte, 134-72. Mainz: Matthias-Grünewald-Verlag, 1967.

Congdon, David W. *The Mission of Demythologizing: Rudolf Bultmann's Dialectical Theology.* Minneapolis: Fortress, 2015.

Connor, Timothy G. *The Kenotic Trajectory of the Church in Donald MacKinnon's Theology: From Galilee to Jerusalem to Galilee.* London: T&T Clark, 2011.

Costas, Orlando E. *Christ Outside the Gate: Mission Beyond Christendom.* Maryknoll, NY: Orbis Books, 1982.

———. *The Church and Its Mission: A Shattering Critique from the Third World.* Wheaton, IL: Tyndale House, 1974.

———. "Contextualization and Incarnation." *Journal of Theology for Southern Africa* 29 (1979): 23-30.

Countryman, L. William. *The Language of Ordination: Ministry in an Ecumenical Context.* Philadelphia: Trinity Press International, 1992.

Cragg, Kenneth. "Conversion and Convertibility—with Special Reference to Muslims." In *Down to Earth: Studies in Christianity and Culture; The Papers of the Lausanne Consultation on Gospel and Culture,* edited by Robert T. Coote and John R. W. Stott, 193-208. Grand Rapids: Eerdmans, 1980.

Cressey, Martin H. "Three Games in a Long Ecumenical Set: Leuenberg, Meissen and Porvoo on Ministry and Episkopé." In *Episkopé and Episcopacy and the Quest for Visible Unity: Two Consultations,* edited by Peter Bouteneff and Alan D. Falconer, 122-26. Geneva: World Council of Churches, 1999.

Culver, Robert D. "Apostles and the Apostolate in the New Testament." *Bibliotheca Sacra* 134, no. 534 (1977): 131-43.

Dahl, Nils A. "The Doctrine of Justification: Its Social Function and Implications." In *Studies in Paul: Theology for the Early Christian Mission,* 95-120. Minneapolis: Augsburg, 1977.

Dalferth, Ingolf U. "Ministry and the Office of Bishop According to Meissen and Porvoo." In *Visible Unity and the Ministry of Oversight: The Second Theological Conference Held Under the Meissen Agreement Between the Church of England*

and the Evangelical Church in Germany, edited by Ingolf Dalferth and Rupert Hoare, 9-48. London: Church House Publishing, 1997.

———. "Visible Unity and Episcopal Office." In *Einheit bezeugen: Zehn Jahre nach der Meissener Erklärung: Beiträge zu den theologischen Konferenzen von Springe und Cheltenham zwischen der EKD und der Kirche von England*, edited by Ingolf Dalferth and Paul Oppenheim, 207-15. Frankfurt am Main: Verlag Otto Lembeck, 2003.

Danaher, William J. "Catholicity and Globalization in the Anglican Tradition." *Internationale Kirchliche Zeitschrift* 100 (2010): 147-61.

Daniélou, Jean. *The Lord of History: Reflections on the Inner Meaning of History*. London: Longmans, 1958.

Davidson, Allan K. "Culture and Ecclesiology: The Church Missionary Society and New Zealand." In *The Church Mission Society and World Christianity, 1799–1999*, edited by Kevin Ward and Brian Stanley, 198-227. Grand Rapids: Eerdmans, 1999.

Davies, W. D. *Christian Origins and Judaism*. London: Darton, Longman & Todd, 1962.

Davison, Andrew, and Alison Milbank. *For the Parish: A Critique of Fresh Expressions*. London: SCM Press, 2010.

Dedji, Valentin. "Between Christ and Caesar: The Politics of Mission and Ecumenism Encountering African Myths and Realities." In *The Unity We Have and the Unity We Seek: Ecumenical Prospects for the Third Millennium*, edited by Jeremy Morris and Nicholas Sagovsky, 135-64. London: T&T Clark, 2003.

De Mey, Peter. "Is the Connection of 'Catholicity' and 'Globalization' Fruitful? An Assessment of Recent Reflections on the Notion of Catholicity." *Bulletin ET* 13 (2002): 169-81.

d'Espine, Henri. "The Apostolic Succession as an Ecumenical Issue (a Protestant View)." *Ecumenical Review* 4, no. 2 (1952): 151-60.

Devanandan, Paul D. "Called to Witness." *Ecumenical Review* 14, no. 2 (1962): 154-63.

De Witte, Pieter. "'The Apostolicity of the Church' in Light of the Lutheran-Roman Catholic Consensus on Justification." *Ecclesiology* 7, no. 3 (2011): 317-35.

Dibeela, Moiseraele Prince. "Conversion, Evangelism and Market." *International Review of Mission* 97, no. 386/387 (2008): 187-97.

Dix, Gregory. "The Ministry in the Early Church." In *The Apostolic Ministry: Essays on the History and the Doctrine of Episcopacy*, edited by Kenneth E. Kirk and Cecilia M. Ady, 183-304. London: Hodder & Stoughton, 1946.

Dodson, Patrick L., Jacinta K. Elston and Brian F. McCoy. "Leaving Culture at the Door: Aboriginal Perspectives on Christian Belief and Practice." *Pacifica* 19, no. 3 (2006): 249-62.

Donaldson, Terence L. *Judaism and the Gentiles: Jewish Patterns of Universalism (to 135 CE)*. Waco: Baylor University Press, 2007.

Douglas, Ian T. "The Clash of Global Christianity: A Review of 'The Next Christendom: The Coming of Global Christianity' by Philip Jenkins." *World & I* 18, no. 2 (2003): 222.

Dovlo, Elom. "African Culture and Emergent Church Forms in Ghana." *Exchange* 33, no. 1 (2004): 28-53.

Dulles, Avery R. *The Catholicity of the Church*. Oxford: Clarendon, 1985.

———. "The Catholicity of the Church and Globalization." *Seminarium* 40 (2000): 259-68.

———. "The Emerging World Church: A Theological Reflection." *Proceedings of the Catholic Theological Society of America* 39 (1984): 1-12.

———. "True and False Reform." *First Things*, no. 135 (2003): 14-19.

Dunch, Ryan. "Beyond Cultural Imperialism: Cultural Theory, Christian Missions, and Global Modernity." *History and Theory* 41, no. 3 (2002): 301-25.

Dunn, James D. G. "Was Judaism Particularist or Universalist?" In *Judaism in Late Antiquity*. Part 3, vol. 2, *Where We Stand: Issues and Debates in Ancient Judaism*, edited by Jacob Neusner and Alan J. Avery-Peck, 57-73. Leiden: Brill, 1999.

———. "Works of the Law and the Curse of the Law (Galatians 3.10-14)." *New Testament Studies* 31, no. 4 (1985): 523-42.

Dürr, Johannes. *Sendende und werdende Kirche in der Missionstheologie Gustav Warneck's*. Basel: Basler Missionsbuchhandlung, 1947.

Dussel, Enrique. "Beyond Eurocentrism: The World-System and the Limits of Modernity." In *The Cultures of Globalization*, edited by Fredric Jameson and Masao Miyoshi, 3-31. Durham, NC: Duke University Press, 1998.

Ebeling, Gerhard. "Das hermeneutische Ort der Gotteslehre bei Petrus Lombardus und Thomas von Aquin." *Zeitschrift für Theologie und Kirche* 61 (1964): 281-326.

Elbourne, Elizabeth. "Word Made Flesh: Christianity, Modernity, and the Cultural Colonialism in the Work of Jean and John Comaroff." *American Historical Review* 108, no. 2 (2003): 435-59.

"Episcope, Niagara Falls, September 1987." In *Growth in Agreement II: Reports and Agreed Statements of Ecumenical Conversations on a World Level, 1982–1998*, edited by Jeffrey Gros, Harding Meyer and William G. Rusch, 11-37. Geneva: World Council of Churches, 2000.

Epp, Eldon Jay. *Junia: The First Woman Apostle*. Minneapolis: Fortress, 2005.

Esler, Philip F. "Group Boundaries and Intergroup Conflict in Galatians: A New Reading of Galatians 5:13–6:10." In *Ethnicity and the Bible*, edited by Mark G. Brett, 215-40. Leiden: Brill, 1996.

Evans, Gillian R. *The Church and the Churches: Toward an Ecumenical Ecclesiology*. Cambridge: Cambridge University Press, 2002.

"Facing Unity, Rome, Italy, 3 March 1984." In *Growth in Agreement II: Reports and Agreed Statements of Ecumenical Conversations on a World Level, 1982–1998*, edited by Jeffrey Gros, Harding Meyer and William G. Rusch, 443-84. Geneva: World Council of Churches, 2000.

Fahey, Michael A. "Continuity in the Church Amid Structural Changes." *Theological Studies* 35, no. 3 (1974): 415-40.

"Faith and Order By-Laws, 3.1." In *Faith and Order at the Crossroads: Kuala Lumpur 2004; The Plenary Commission Meeting*, edited by Thomas F. Best, 450. Geneva: World Council of Churches, 2005.

Falconer, Alan D. "The Church: God's Gift to the World—On the Nature and Purpose of the Church." *International Review of Mission* 90, no. 359 (2001): 389-400.

———. "En Route to Santiago: The Work of the Faith and Order Commission from Montreal 1963 to Santiago de Compostela 1993." *Ecumenical Review* 45, no. 1 (1993): 44-54.

Fasholé-Luke, Edward W. "The Quest for African Theologies." *Scottish Journal of Theology* 29 (1976): 159-75.

Ferdinando, Keith. "Christian Identity in the African Context: Reflections on Kwame Bediako's Theology and Identity." *Journal of the Evangelical Theological Society* 50, no. 1 (2007): 121-43.

Fitzmeyer, Joseph A. *The Gospel According to Luke I–IX: Introduction, Translation, and Notes*. New York: Doubleday, 1982.

Flannery, Austin, ed. *Vatican Council II: The Conciliar and Post Conciliar Documents*. Northport, NY: Costello, 1996.

Flett, John G. "What Does It Mean for a Congregation to Be a Hermeneutic?" In *The Gospel and Pluralism Today: Reassessing Lesslie Newbigin in the 21st Century*, edited by Scott W. Sunquist and Amos Yong, 195-213. Downers Grove, IL: IVP Academic, 2015.

———. *The Witness of God: The Trinity, Missio Dei, Karl Barth and the Nature of Christian Community*. Grand Rapids: Eerdmans, 2010.

For All God's People: Ecumenical Prayer Cycle. Geneva: World Council of Churches, 1978.

Foster, John. *Then and Now—The Historic Church and the Younger Churches.* London: SCM Press, 1942.

Fowl, Stephen E. "Learning to Be a Gentile: Christ's Transformation and Redemption of Our Past." In *Christology and Scripture,* 22-40. London: T&T Clark, 2007.

Frazier, William. "A Monumental Breakthrough in the Missiology of Vatican II and Its Reception by Ongoing Leadership in the Church." *International Bulletin of Missionary Research* 34, no. 3 (2010): 139-44.

Frey, Jörg. "Apostelbegriff, Apostelamt und Apostolizität: Neutestamentliche Perspektiven zur Frage nach der 'Apostolizität' der Kirche." In *Kirchliche Amt in apostolischer Nachfolge I, Grundlagen und Grundfragen,* 91-188. Göttingen: Vandenhoeck & Ruprecht, 2004.

Freytag, Walter. "Mission im Blick aufs Ende." *Evangelische Missions Zeitschrift* 3 (1942): 321-33.

Fridrichsen, Anton. *The Apostle and His Message.* Uppsala: Lundequistaka, 1947.

Fuchs, Lorelei F. *Koinonia and the Quest for an Ecumenical Ecclesiology: From Foundations Through Dialogue to Symbolic Competence for Communionality.* Grand Rapids: Eerdmans, 2008.

Furberg, Tore. "The Sending and Mission of the Church in the Porvoo Common Statement." In *Apostolicity and Unity,* 201-15. Grand Rapids: Eerdmans, 2002.

Gaillardetz, Richard R. *Ecclesiology for a Global Church: A People Called and Sent.* Maryknoll, NY: Orbis Books, 2008.

Gairdner, W. H. T. *Echoes from Edinburgh, 1910: An Account and Interpretation of the World Missionary Conference.* New York: Fleming H. Revell, 1910.

Gallaher, Brandon. "'Waiting for the Barbarians': Identity and Polemicism in the Neo-Patristic Synthesis of Georges Florovsky." *Modern Theology* 27, no. 4 (2011): 659-91.

Geertz, Clifford. "Common Sense as a Cultural System." *Antioch Review* 33, no. 1 (1975): 5-26.

Gehlin, Sara. "Quest for Unity, Quest for Diversity: Ecumenical Challenges in a Time of Globalization." *Ecumenical Review* 62, no. 3 (2010): 308-16.

Gensichen, Hans-Werner. "Grundfragen der Kirchwerdung in der Mission: Zur Gespräch mit J. C. Hoekendijk." *Evangelische Missions Zeitschrift* 8 (1951): 33-46.

———. "New Delhi and the World Mission of the Church." *Lutheran World* 9, no. 2 (1962): 133-43.

George, Kondothra M. "Cross-Cultural Interpretation: Some Paradigms from the Early Church." *International Review of Mission* 85 (1996): 217-26.

Gerhardsson, Birger. *Die Boten Gottes und die Apostel Christi*. Lund: Gleerup, 1962.

Gibaut, John St-Helier. "Catholicity, Faith and Order, and the Unity of the Church." *Ecumenical Review* 63, no. 2 (2011): 177-85.

Gifford, Paul. *African Christianity: Its Public Role*. London: C. Hurst, 1998.

The Gift of Authority: Authority in the Church III. Toronto: Anglican Book Centre, 1999.

Gilhuis, J. C. "Ecclesiocentrische aspecten van het zendingswerk met name bij de ontwikkeling daarvan in Indonesië, bijzonder op Midden-Java." Diss., Vrije Universiteit, 1955.

Gittins, Anthony J. "The Universal in the Local: Power, Piety, and Paradox in the Formation of Missionary Community." In *Mission and Culture: The Louis J. Luzbetak Lectures, 2000–2010*, edited by Stephen B. Bevans, 133-87. Maryknoll, NY: Orbis Books, 2012.

Goldstone, Brian, and Stanley Hauerwas. "Disciplined Seeing: Forms of Christianity and Forms of Life." *South Atlantic Quarterly* 109, no. 4 (2010): 765-90.

González, Justo L. *The Changing Shape of Church History*. St. Louis, MO: Chalice Press, 2002.

Goodall, Norman, ed. *The Uppsala Report 1968: Official Report of the Fourth Assembly of the World Council of Churches Uppsala July 4–20, 1968*. Geneva: World Council of Churches, 1968.

Gorringe, Timothy J. *Furthering Humanity: A Theology of Culture*. Surrey, UK: Ashgate, 2004.

Gray, Francis. "The Apostolic Succession as an Ecumenical Issue (an Anglican View)." *Ecumenical Review* 4, no. 2 (1952): 139-50.

Großhans, Hans-Peter. *Die Kirche—irdischer Raum der Wahrheit des Evangeliums*. Leipzig: Evangelische Verlagsanstalt, 2003.

Gründer, Horst. "Christian Mission and Colonial Expansion: Historical and Structural Connections." *Mission Studies* 12, no. 1 (1995): 18-29.

Gurney, T. A. "Modern Imperialism and Mission." *Church Missionary Intelligencer* 27 (1902): 481-89.

Gustafson, James. "The Voluntary Church: A Moral Appraisal." In *Voluntary Associations: A Study of Groups in Free Societies*, edited by D. B. Robertson, 299-322. Richmond, VA: John Knox Press, 1966.

Gutiérrez, Gustavo. *A Theology of Liberation: History, Politics, and Salvation*. Translated by Caridad Inda and John Eagleson. Maryknoll, NY: Orbis Books, 1988.

Hahn, Ferdinand. "Der Apostolat im Urchristentum." *Kerygma und Dogma* 20 (1974): 54-77.

Haight, Roger D. "Comments on Robert T. Sear's Article." *Theological Studies* 37, no. 4 (1976): 680-82.

———. "Mission: The Symbol for Understanding the Church Today." *Theological Studies* 37, no. 4 (1976): 620-51.

Haley, Peter. "Rudolph Sohm on Charisma." *Journal of Religion* 60, no. 2 (1980): 185-97.

Hallencreutz, Carl F. *Kraemer Towards Tambaram: A Study in Hendrik Kraemer's Missionary Approach.* Uppsala: Gleerup, 1966.

Halliburton, John. "Bishops Together in Mission and Ministry: The Understanding of Episcopacy in the Porvoo Common Statement." *Theology* 101 (1998): 253-62.

Hardt, Michael, and Antonio Negri. *Empire.* Translated by Michael Hardt. Cambridge, MA: Harvard University Press, 2000.

Harnack, Adolf von. "Kirchliche Verfassung und kirchliches Recht im 1. und 2. Jahrhundert." *Protestantische Realenzyklopädie für Theologie und Kirche* 20 (1908): 508-46.

———. *Lehre der Zwölf Apostel nebst Untersuchungen zur ältesten Geschichte der Kirchenverfassung und des Kirchenrechts.* Leipzig: J.C. Hinrichsäsche Buchhandlung, 1884.

———. *The Mission and Expansion of Christianity in the First Three Centuries.* Gloucester, MA: Peter Smith, 1972.

Hartenstein, Karl. "Was haben wir von Tambaram zu lernen?" In *Das Wunder der Kirche unter den Völkern der Erde: Bericht über Weltmissions-Konferenz in Tambaram*, edited by Martin Schlunk, 193-203. Stuttgart: Evangelischer Missionsverlag, 1939.

Hatch, Edwin B. *The Organization of the Early Christian Churches.* London: Rivingtons, 1881.

Hauerwas, Stanley. "Discipleship as a Craft, Church as a Disciplined Community." *Christian Century* 108, no. 27 (1991): 881-84.

———. "The Importance of Being Catholic: Unsolicited Advice from a Protestant Bystander." In *In Good Company.* Notre Dame, IN: University of Notre Dame Press, 1995.

———. "In Defense of Cultural Christianity." In *Sanctify Them in the Truth: Holiness Exemplified*, 157-73. Edinburgh: T&T Clark, 1998.

Hawkey, James. "Excavating Apostolicity: Christian Communities and Secular Cultures." *Ecumenical Review* 62, no. 3 (2010): 270-81.

Healy, Nicholas M. *Church, World and the Christian Life: Practical-Prophetic Ecclesiology.* Cambridge: Cambridge University Press, 2000.

Hegel, G. W. Friedrich. *The Philosophy of History.* Translated by J. Sibree. Mineola, NY: Dover, 2004.

Herbert, A. G. "Ministerial Episcopacy." In *The Apostolic Ministry: Essays on the History and the Doctrine of Episcopacy,* edited by Kenneth E. Kirk and Cecilia M. Ady, 439-534. London: Hodder & Stoughton, 1946.

Herms, Eilert. "Unity, Witness, Mission: A Hypothetical Statement on Each of the Terms in the Title and Some Remarks on Further Possible Developments in the Meissen Process." In *Einheit bezeugen: Zehn Jahre nach der Meissener Erklärung; Beiträge zu den theologischen Konferenzen von Springe und Cheltenham zwischen der EKD und der Kirche von England,* edited by Ingolf Dalferth and Paul Oppenheim, 471-85. Frankfurt am Main: Verlag Otto Lembeck, 2003.

Hesselgrave, David J., and Edward Rommen. *Contextualization: Meanings, Methods, and Models.* Grand Rapids: Baker, 1989.

Hexham, Irving. "Violating Missionary Culture: The Tyranny of Theology and the Ethics of Historical Research." In *Mission und Gewalt,* edited by Ulrich van der Heyden, Jürgen Becher and Holger Stoecker, 193-206. Stuttgart: Franz Steiner Verlag, 2000.

Hillman, Eugene. "Ministry: Missionary and/or Pastoral." *New Theology Review* 14, no. 2 (2001): 76-79.

Hobhouse, Walter. *The Church and the World in Idea and in History.* London: Macmillan, 1910.

Hock, Klaus. "Translated Messages? The Construction of Religious Identities as Translatory Process." *Mission Studies* 23, no. 2 (2006): 261-76.

Hoedemaker, L. A. "Die Welt als theologisches Problem: Kritischer Rückblick auf die niederländische Theologie des Apostolates." *Zeitschrift für dialektische Theologie* 2, no. 1 (2004): 9-20.

———. "Hoekendijk's American Years." *Occasional Bulletin of Missionary Research* 1, no. 2 (1977): 7-10.

———. "The Legacy of J. C. Hoekendijk." *International Bulletin of Missionary Research* 19, no. 4 (1995): 166-70.

———. "Mission and Unity: The Relevance of Hoekendijk's Vision." In *Changing Partnership of Missionary and Ecumenical Movements: Essays in Honour of Marc Spindler,* edited by Leny Lagerwerf, Karel Steenbrink and F. J. Verstraelen, 26-35. Leiden-Utrecht: Interuniversity Institute for Missiological and Ecumenical Research, 1995.

Hoekendijk, J. C. "The Call to Evangelism." *International Review of Missions* 39 (1950): 162-75.

———. "Christ and the World in the Modern Age." *Student World* 54, nos. 1-2 (1961): 75-82.

———. "The Church in Missionary Thinking." *International Review of Missions* 41 (1952): 324-36.

———. *The Church Inside Out*. Philadelphia: Westminster, 1966.

———. "Die Welt als Horizont." *Evangelische Theologie* 25 (1965): 467-84.

———. "Ende und Anfang der Verkündigung." *Quatember* 17, no. 2 (1953): 70-76.

———. "Evangelism—The 'Raison d'être' of the Church." *Ecumenical Review* 4, no. 4 (1952): 431-34.

———. "The Evangelization of Man in Modern Mass Society." *Ecumenical Review* 2 (1949): 206-8.

———. "Evangelization of the World in this Generation." *International Review of Mission* 59 (1970): 23-31.

———. "Gesprek onder-weg." *In de Waagschaal* 6 (1951): 348-50.

———. "Kirche." In *Theologie für Nichttheologen II*, edited by Hans Jürgen Schultz, 100-105. Berlin: Kreuz-Verlag, 1964.

———. *Kirche und Volk in der deutschen Missionswissenschaft*. Munich: Chr. Kaiser Verlag, 1967.

———. "Mission—a Celebration of Freedom." *Union Seminary Quarterly* 21, no. 2 (1966): 135-44.

———. "Mission—Heute!" In *Mission—Heute! Zeugnisse holländischen Missionsdenkens: Vorgetragen auf einer Tagung des Bruderringes evangelischer Missionsseminare und des Studentenbundes für Mission in Oegstgeest bei Leiden, 23.–28. Mai 1953*, 5-12. Bethel: Studentenbund für Mission, 1954.

———. "Mission in der Krise." *Evangelische Missions Zeitschrift* 6, no. 3 (1949): 1-7.

———. "Mission und Oekumene." *Evangelisches Mission-magazin* 95 (1951): 145-56.

———. "'Morphological Fundamentalism.'" In *Planning for Mission: Working Papers on the New Quest for Missionary Communities*, edited by Thomas Wieser, 134. New York: U.S. Conference for the World Council of Churches, 1966.

———. "Notes on the Meaning of Mission(-ary)." In *Planning for Mission: Working Papers on the New Quest for Missionary Communities*, edited by Thomas Wieser, 37-48. New York: U.S. Conference for the World Council of Churches, 1966.

Hoffman, Ronan. "The Development of Mission Theology in the Twentieth Century." *Theological Studies* 23, no. 3 (1962): 419-41.

Hofmeyr, Isabel. "Studying Missionaries in a Post-National World." *African Studies* 63, no. 1 (2004): 119-29.

Hogg, William Richey. "Vatican II's Ad Gentes: A Twenty-Year Retrospective." *International Bulletin of Missionary Research* 9, no. 4 (1985): 146-54.

Holl, Karl. "Der Kirchenbegriff des Paulus in seinem Verhältnis zu dem der Urgemeinde." In *Gesammelte Aufsätze zur Kirchengeschichte II*, 44-67. Tübingen: J.C.B. Mohr, 1928.

Hollenweger, Walter J. "Die Kirche für andere—ein Mythos." *Evangelische Theologie* 37, no. 5 (1977): 425-43.

———. "Johannes Christian Hoekendijk: Pluriformität der Kirche." *Reformatio* 16, no. 10 (1967): 663-77.

Holmberg, Bengt. "Jewish *Versus* Christian Identity in the Early Church?" *Revue Biblique* 105, no. 3 (1998): 397-425.

Hopewell, James F. *Congregation: Stories and Structures*. Philadelphia: Fortress, 1987.

Horrell, David G. "'No Longer Jew or Greek': Paul's Corporate Christology and the Construction of Christian Community." In *Christology, Controversy, and Community: New Testament Essays in Honour of David R. Catchpole*, edited by David G. Horrell and Christopher M. Tuckett, 321-44. Leiden: Brill, 2000.

Huber, Wolfgang. "Die wirkliche Kirche: Das Verhältnis von Botschaft und Ordnung als Grundproblem evangelischen Kirchenverständnisses im Anschluß an die 3. Barmer These." In *Folgen christlicher Freiheit: Ethik und Theorie der Kirche im Horizont der Barmer Theologischen Erklärung*, 147-68. Neukirchen-Vluyn: Neukirchener Verlag, 1983.

Hüffmeier, Wilhelm, ed. *The Church of Jesus Christ: The Contribution of the Reformation Towards Ecumenical Dialogue on Church Unity*. Frankfurt am Main: Verlag Otto Lembeck, 1995.

Hütter, Reinhard. "The Church as 'Public': Dogma, Practices and the Holy Spirit." *Pro Ecclesia* 3, no. 3 (1994): 334-61.

———. *Suffering Divine Things: Theology as Church Practice*. Translated by D. Scott. Grand Rapids: Eerdmans, 2000.

Ibuka, K. "The Problem of Co-Operation Between Foreign and Native Workers." In *World Missionary Conference, 1910: The History and Records of the Conference Together with Addresses Delivered at the Evening Meetings*, 294-305. Edinburgh: Oliphant, Anderson & Ferrier, 1910.

Idowu, E. Bolaji. "The Predicament of the Church in Africa." In *Christianity in Tropical Africa: Studies Presented and Discussed at the Seventh International African Seminar, University of Ghana, April 1965*, edited by Christian G. Baëta, 417-37. Oxford: Oxford University Press, 1968.

————. *Towards an Indigenous Church*. London: Oxford University Press, 1965.

In Search of Mission. IDOC Documentation Participation Project, 1974.

Irvin, Dale T. *Christian Histories, Christian Traditioning: Rendering Accounts*. Maryknoll, NY: Orbis Books, 1998.

————. "Ecumenical Dislodgings." *Mission Studies* 22, no. 2 (2005): 187-205.

————. "From One Story to Many: An Ecumenical Reappraisal of Church History." *Journal of Ecumenical Studies* 28, no. 4 (1991): 537-54.

————. *Hearing Many Voices: Dialogue and Diversity in the Ecumenical Movement*. Lanham, MD: University Press of America, 1994.

————. "Towards a Hermeneutics of Difference at the Crossroads of Ecumenics." *Ecumenical Review* 47, no. 4 (1995): 490-502.

Irvin, Dale T., and Scott W. Sunquist. *History of the World Christian Movement: Earliest Christianity to 1453*. Maryknoll, NY: Orbis Books, 2001.

————. *History of the World Christian Movement: Modern Christianity from 1454–1800*. Maryknoll, NY: Orbis Books, 2012.

Jansen-Schoonhoven, Evert. "Der Artikel 'Vom Apostolat der Kirche' in der Kirchenordnung der niederländischen reformierten Kirche." In *Basileia: Walter Freytag zum 60. Geburtstag*, edited by Jan Hermelink and Hans Jochen Margull, 278-84. Stuttgart: Verlag der rheinischen Missionsgesellschaft Wuppertal-Barmen, 1959.

————. *Variaties op het thema 'zending'*. Kampen: J. H. Kok, 1974.

————. "Wort und Tat im Zeugendienst: 'Comprehensive Approach' als Missionmethode." In *Mission—Heute! Zeugnisse holländischen Missionsdenkens: Vorgetragen auf einer Tagung des Bruderringes evangelischer Missionsseminare und des Studentenbundes für Mission in Oegstgeest bei Leiden, 23.–28. Mai 1953*, 43-51. Bethel: Studentenbund für Mission, 1954.

Janssen, Allan J. *Kingdom, Office, and Church: A Study of A. A. van Ruler's Doctrine of Ecclesiastical Office*. Grand Rapids: Eerdmans, 2006.

Jenkins, Daniel T. "The Apostolic Ministry Today." *Theology Today* 4, no. 4 (1948): 474-84.

Jenkins, Paul. "The Roots of African Church History: Some Polemic Thoughts." *International Bulletin of Missionary Research* 10, no. 2 (1986): 67-71.

Jenkins, Philip. *The Next Christendom: The Coming of Global Christianity*. New York: Oxford University Press, 2002.

————. "The Next Christianity." *The Atlantic* 290, no. 3 (2002): 53-68.

Jenson, Robert W. "Catechesis for Our Time." In *Marks of the Body of Christ*, edited by Carl E. Braaten and Robert W. Jenson, 137-49. Grand Rapids: Eerdmans, 1999.

———. "Christ as Culture 1: Christ as Polity." *International Journal of Systematic Theology* 5, no. 3 (2003): 323-29.

———. "Christ as Culture 3: Christ as Drama." *International Journal of Systematic Theology* 6, no. 2 (2004): 194-201.

———. "Christian Civilization." In *God, Truth, and Witness: Engaging Stanley Hauerwas*, edited by L. Gregory Jones, Reinhard Hütter and C. Rosalee Velloso da Silva, 153-63. Grand Rapids: Brazos, 2005.

———. "The Church as Communio." In *The Catholicity of the Reformation*, edited by Carl E. Braaten, 1-12. Grand Rapids: Eerdmans, 1996.

———. "The Church's Responsibility for the World." In *The Two Cities of God: The Church's Responsibility for the Earthly City*, edited by Carl E. Braaten and Robert W. Jenson, 1-10. Grand Rapids: Eerdmans, 1997.

———. "Creator and Creature." *International Journal of Systematic Theology* 4, no. 2 (2002): 216-21.

———. "Election and Culture: From Babylon to Jerusalem." In *Public Theology in Cultural Engagement*, edited by Stephen R. Holmes, 48-61. Milton Keynes, UK: Paternoster, 2008.

———. "God's Time, Our Time: An Interview with Robert W. Jenson." *Christian Century* 123, no. 9 (2007): 31-35.

———. *Systematic Theology I: The Triune God*. New York: Oxford University Press, 1997.

———. *Systematic Theology II: The Works of God*. New York: Oxford University Press, 1999.

———. *Unbaptized God: The Basic Flaw in Ecumenical Theology*. Minneapolis: Fortress, 1992.

———. "You Wonder Where the Spirit Went." *Pro Ecclesia* 2, no. 3 (1993): 296-304.

Jervell, Jacob. "The Twelve on Israel's Thrones: Luke's Understanding of the Apostolate." In *Luke and the People of God: A New Look at Luke–Acts*, 75-112. Minneapolis: Augsburg, 1972.

John Paul II. "Address of John Paul II to the Aborigines and Torres Strait Islanders in 'Blatherskite Park,' Alice Springs, General Audience 27 September 1989." *Insegnamenti di Giovanni Paolo II* 12, no. 2 (1989): 679.

———. "Address to Aborigines and Torres Strait Islanders of Australia (29 November 1986)." *Origins* 16, no. 26 (1986): 473-77.

———. *Redemptoris Missio: On the Permanent Validity of the Church's Missionary Mandate*. Washington, DC: United States Catholic Conference, 1990.

———. *Ut unum sint: On Commitment to Ecumenism*. Boston, MA: Pauline Books and Media, 1995.

Jones, Gareth. "Visibility as Ecclesiological Criterion." In *Einheit bezeugen: Zehn Jahre nach der Meissener Erklärung; Beiträge zu den theologischen Konferenzen von Springe und Cheltenham zwischen der EKD und der Kirche von England*, edited by Ingolf Dalferth and Paul Oppenheim, 343-56. Frankfurt am Main: Verlag Otto Lembeck, 2003.

Jongeneel, Jan A. B. "The Missiology of Gisbertus Voetius: The First Comprehensive Protestant Theology of Missions." *Calvin Theological Journal* 16 (1991): 47-79.

Jüngel, Eberhard. *Justification: The Heart of the Christian Faith*. Edinburgh: T&T Clark, 2001.

Kähler, Martin. *Schriften zu Christologie und Mission: Gesamtausgabe der Schriften zur Mission*. Munich: Chr. Kaiser Verlag, 1971.

Kalanda, Paul. "Consolidating Christianity in Africa." *Missiology* 4, no. 4 (1976): 395-404.

Kalu, Ogbu U. "African Church Historiography: An Ecumenical Perspective." In *African Church Historiography: An Ecumenical Perspective; Papers Presented at a Workshop on African Church History, Held at Nairobi, August 3–8, 1986*, edited by Ogbu U. Kalu, 9-27. Bern: Evang. Arbeitsstelle Ökumene Schweiz, 1988.

———. "Doing Church History in Africa Today." In *Church History in an Ecumenical Perspective: Papers and Reports of an International Ecumenical Consultation Held in Basle October 12–17, 1981*, edited by Lukas Vischer, 77-91. Bern: Evang. Arbeitsstelle Ökumene Schweiz, 1982.

———. "Unconquered Spiritual Gates: Inculturation Theology in Africa Revisited." *Journal of Inculturation Theology* 1, no. 1 (1994): 25-37.

Kandler, Karl Hermann. "Kirche als Exodusgemeinde: Bemerkungen zur Theologie J. C. Hoekendijks." *Kerygma und Dogma* 17, no. 4 (1971): 244-57.

Kang, Namsoon. "Whose/Which World in World Christianity? Toward World Christianity as Christianity of Worldly-Responsibility." In *A New Day: Essays on World Christianity in Honor of Lamin Sanneh*, edited by Akintunde E. Akinade, 31-48. New York: Peter Lang, 2010.

Karanja, John. "The Role of Kikuyu Christians in Developing a Self-Consciously African Anglicanism." In *The Church Mission Society and World Christianity, 1799–1999*, edited by Kevin Ward and Brian Stanley, 254-84. Grand Rapids: Eerdmans, 1999.

Karrer, O. "Apostolische Nachfolge und Primat." In *Fragen der Theologie heute*, edited by Johannes Feiner, 175-206. Zürich: Benziger, 1957.

Käsemann, Ernst. *Die Legitimität des Apostels: Eine Untersuchung zu 2 Korinther 10–13*. Darmstadt: Wissenschaftliche Buchgesellschaft, 1956.

————. "Ministry and Community in the New Testament." In *Essays on New Testament Themes*, 63-94. London: SCM Press, 1964.

————. "Paul and Early Catholicism." In *New Testament Questions of Today*, 236-51. London: SCM Press, 1969.

Kasper, Walter. "Die apostolische Sukzession als ökumenisches Problem." In *Lehrverurteilungen—kirchentrennend?*, edited by Karl Lehmann and Wolfhart Pannenberg, 329-49. Göttingen: Vandenhoeck & Ruprecht, 1986.

Keane, Webb. *Christian Moderns: Freedom and Fetish in the Mission Encounter*. Berkeley: University of California Press, 2007.

Keysser, Christian. *A People Reborn*. Pasadena, CA: William Carey Library, 1980.

Khodr, Georges Metr. "Church and Mission." *St. Vladimir's Seminary Quarterly* 6, no. 1 (1962): 16-25.

King, Richard. "Cartographies of the Imagination, Legacies of Colonialism: The Discourse of Religion and the Mapping of Indic Tradition." *Evam* 3, nos. 1-2 (2004): 245-62.

Kinney, John W. "The Theology of John Mbiti: His Sources, Norms and Method." *Occasional Bulletin of Missionary Research* 3, no. 2 (1979): 65-68.

Kirk, J. Andrew. "Apostleship Since Rengstorf: Towards a Synthesis." *New Testament Studies* 21, no. 2 (1975): 249-64.

Kirk, Kenneth E., and Cecilia M. Ady, eds. *The Apostolic Ministry: Essays on the History and the Doctrine of Episcopacy*. London: Hodder & Stoughton, 1946.

Klein, Günter. *Die zwölf Apostel: Ursprung und Gehalt einer Idee*. Göttingen: Vandenhoeck & Ruprecht, 1961.

Koch, Dietrich-Alex. "The Origin, Function and Disappearance of the 'Twelve.'" In *Hellenistisches Christentum: Schriftverständnis—Ekklesiologie—Geschichte*, edited by Friedrich Wilhelm Horn, 126-44. Göttingen: Vandenhoeck & Ruprecht, 2008.

Kollman, Paul V. "After Church History? Writing the History of Christianity from a Global Perspective." *Horizons* 31, no. 2 (2004): 322-42.

Komonchak, Joseph A. "Modernity and the Construction of Roman Catholicism." *Cristianesimo nella Storia* 18 (1997): 353-85.

Koyama, Kosuke. "New World—New Creation: Mission in Power and Faith." *Mission Studies* 10, nos. 1-2 (1993): 59-77.

Kraemer, Hendrik. *The Christian Message in a Non-Christian World*. London: Harper and Brothers, 1938.

————. *The Communication of the Christian Faith*. Philadelphia: Westminster, 1956.

————. *Religion and the Christian Faith*. Philadelphia: Westminster, 1956.

Kraft, Charles H. "Christian Conversion or Cultural Conversion." *Practical Anthropology* 10, no. 4 (1963): 179-87.

———. *Christianity in Culture: A Study in Dynamic Biblical Theologizing in Cross-Cultural Perspective*. Maryknoll, NY: Orbis Books, 1979.

Krauß, Samuel. "Die jüdischen Apostel." *Jewish Quarterly Review* 17, no. 2 (1905): 370-83.

Küng, Hans. *The Church*. New York: Sheed & Ward, 1967.

Laing, Mark T. B. "The International Impact of the Formation of the Church of South India: Bishop Newbigin Versus the Anglican Fathers." *International Bulletin of Missionary Research* 33, no. 1 (2009): 18-24.

Landau, Paul S. "Hegemony and History in Jean and John L. Comaroff's *Of Revelation and Revolution*." *Africa* 70, no. 3 (2000): 501-19.

Latourette, Kenneth Scott. "The Study of the History of Missions." *International Review of Mission* 14, no. 1 (1925): 108-15.

Lee, Archie C. C. "Cross-textual Hermeneutics and Identity in Multi-scriptural Asia." In *Christian Theology in Asia*, edited by Sebastian C. H. Kim, 179-204. Cambridge: Cambridge University Press, 2008.

Le Guillou, Marie-Joseph. "Mission as an Ecclesiological Theme." In *Re-thinking the Church's Mission*, edited by Karl Rahner, 81-130. New York: Paulist Press, 1966.

Lenka Bula, Puleng, ed. *Choose Life, Act in Hope: African Churches Living Out the Accra Confession; A Study Resource on the Accra Confession: Covenanting for Justice in the Economy and Earth*. Geneva: World Alliance of Reformed Churches, 2009.

Lightfoot, J. B. "The Name and Office of an Apostle." In *Saint Paul's Epistle to the Galatians*, 92-101. London: Macmillan, 1914.

Lindbeck, George A. "The Church." In *Keeping the Faith: Essays to Mark the Centenary of Lux Mundi*, edited by G. Wainwright, 178-208. Philadelphia: Fortress, 1988.

Link, Hans-Georg. *Apostolic Faith Today: A Handbook for Study*. Geneva: World Council of Churches, 1985.

"The Local and the Universal Dimensions of the Church Reformation-Catholic Dialogue Commission: A Report Offered to the Leadership of the Uniting Protestant Churches in the Netherlands, the Old Catholic Church, and the Roman Catholic Church in the Netherlands." *Exchange* 37, no. 4 (2008): 396-443.

Loffeld, E. "Convergences actuelles en Theologie missionnaire." *Eglise Vivante* 15 (1963): 49.

Löffler, Paul. "The BEM Document from a CWME Perspective." *Ecumenical Review* 39, no. 3 (1987): 327-31.

Loughlin, Gerard. "Christianity at the End of the Story or the Return of the Master-Narrative." *Modern Theology* 8, no. 4 (1992): 365-84.

Lubac, Henri de. *The Motherhood of the Church: Followed by Particular Churches in the Universal Church.* San Francisco: Ignatius, 1982.

Lüpke, Johannes von. "Was macht die Kirche zur Kirche? Grundlagen evange-lischen Kirchenverständnisses." In *Kirche—dem Evangelium Strukturen geben,* edited by Hellmut Zschoch, 28-44. Neukirchener-Vluyn: Neukirchener, 2009.

Lutheran World Federation. "Episcopal Ministry Within the Apostolicity of the Church: The Lund Statement by the Lutheran World Federation—a Com-munion of Churches, Lund, Sweden, 26 March 2007." *Ecumenical Review* 59, nos. 2-3 (2007): 389-408.

MacIntyre, Alasdair. *After Virtue.* Notre Dame, IN: University of Notre Dame Press, 2007.

Mackay, John A. "With Christ to the Frontier." In *Renewal and Advance: Christian Witness in a Revolutionary World,* edited by Charles W. Ranson, 198-205. London: Edinburgh House Press, 1948.

MacKinnon, Donald M. "Kenosis and Establishment." In *The Stripping of the Altars,* 13-40. London: Collins, 1969.

Majeke, Nosipho. *The Role of the Missionaries in Conquest.* Johannesburg: So-ciety of Young Africa, 1953.

Mallampalli, Chandra. "World Christianity and 'Protestant America': Historical Narratives and the Limits of Christian Pluralism." *International Bulletin of Missionary Research* 30, no. 1 (2006): 8-13.

Mallon, Colleen Mary. *Traditioning Disciples: The Contributions of Cultural An-thropology to Ecclesial Identity.* Eugene, OR: Pickwick, 2011.

Maluleke, Tinyiko Sam. "Christ in Africa: The Influence of Multi-Culturity on the Experience of Christ." *Journal of Black Theology in South Africa* 8, no. 1 (1994): 49-64.

Manecke, Dieter. *Mission als Zeugendienst: Karl Barths theologische Begründung der Mission im Gegenüber zu den Entwürfen von Walter Holsten, Walter Freytag und Joh. Christiaan Hoekendijk.* Wuppertal: Rolf Brockhaus Verlag, 1972.

Manson, Thomas W. *The Church's Ministry.* London: Hodder & Stoughton, 1948.

Margull, Hans J. *Hope in Action: The Church's Task in the World.* Translated by Eugene Peters. Philadelphia: Muhlenberg Press, 1962.

———. "Structures for Missionary Congregations." *International Review of Mission* 52, no. 4 (1963): 433-46.

———. "Strukturfragen werden wichtig: Anmerkung zur 'Laien'—Arbeit und zur missionarischen Verkündigung." *Ökumenische Rundschau* 11 (1962): 17-23.

———. "We Stand in Our Own Way." *Ecumenical Review* 17, no. 4 (1965): 321-31.

———. *Zeugnis und Dialog: Ausgewählte Schriften*. Ammersbek bei Hamburg: Verlag an der Lottbek, 1992.

Marzheuser, Richard. "Globalization and Catholicity: Two Expressions of One Ecclesiology?" *Journal of Ecumenical Studies* 32, no. 2 (1995): 179-93.

Matthey, Jacques. "Melbourne: Mission in the Eighties." In *Your Kingdom Come: Mission Perspectives; Report on the World Conference on Mission and Evangelism, Melbourne, Australia 12–25 May, 1980*, edited by Jacques Matthey, xi-xviii. Geneva: World Council of Churches, 1980.

———, ed. *"You are the Light of the World": Statements on Mission by the World Council of Churches, 1980–2005*. Geneva: World Council of Churches, 2005.

Maurer, Wilhelm. "Die Auseinandersetzung zwischen Harnack und Sohm und die Begründung eines evangelischen Kirchenrechtes." *Kerygma und Dogma* 6, no. 3 (1960): 194-213.

Mbiti, John S. "Theological Impotence and the Universality of the Church." In *Mission Trends No. 3: Third World Theologies*, edited by Gerald H. Anderson and Thomas F. Stransky, 6-18. Grand Rapids: Eerdmans, 1976.

———. "The Ways and Means of Communicating the Gospel." In *Christianity in Tropical Africa: Studies Presented and Discussed at the Seventh International African Seminar, University of Ghana, April 1965*, edited by Christian G. Baëta, 329-47. Oxford: Oxford University Press, 1968.

McDonnell, Kilian. "The Ratzinger/Kasper Debate: The Universal Church and Local Churches." *Theological Studies* 63, no. 2 (2002): 227-50.

McGavran, Donald A. "Essential Evangelism: An Open Letter to Dr. Hoekendijk." In *The Conciliar-Evangelical Debate: The Crucial Documents, 1964–1976*, edited by Donald A. McGavran, 56-66. South Pasadena, CA: William Carey Library, 1977.

McGuckian, Michael C. "The Apostolic Succession: A Reply to Francis A. Sullivan." *New Blackfriars* 86 (2005): 76-93.

McMahon, Christopher. "Theology and the Redemptive Mission of the Church: A Catholic Response to Milbank's Challenge." *Heythrop Journal* 51, no. 5 (2010): 781-94.

Meeks, M. Douglas. "The Future of Theology in a Commodity Society." In *The Future of Theology: Essays in Honor of Jürgen Moltmann*, edited by Miroslav Volf, 253-66. Grand Rapids: Eerdmans, 1996.

Meeks, Wayne A. "Judaism, Hellenism, and the Birth of Christianity." In *Paul Beyond the Judaism/Hellenism Divide*, edited by Troels Engberg-Pedersen, 17-27. Louisville, KY: Westminster John Knox, 2001.

Meier, John P. "The Circle of the Twelve: Did It Exist During Jesus' Public Ministry?" *Journal of Biblical Literature*, no. 116 (1997): 635-72.

Mercer, Calvin. "Jesus the Apostle: 'Sending' and the Theology of John." *Journal of the Evangelical Theological Society* 35, no. 4 (1992): 457-62.

Meyendorff, John. "The Orthodox Church and Mission: Past and Present Perspectives." *St. Vladimir's Theological Quarterly* 16, no. 2 (1972): 59-71.

Meyer, Harding. "Differentiated Participation: The Possibility of Protestant Sharing in the Historic Office of Bishop." *Ecumenical Trends* 34, no. 9 (2005): 9-15.

Míguez Bonino, José. "Comments on 'Unity of the Church, Unity of Mankind.'" *Ecumenical Review* 24, no. 1 (1972): 47-50.

———. "Historical Praxis and Christian Identity." In *Frontiers of Theology in Latin America*, edited by Rosino Gibellini, 260-83. Maryknoll, NY: Orbis Books, 1979.

———. "A 'Third World' Perspective on the Ecumenical Movement." *Ecumenical Review* 34, no. 2 (1982): 115-24.

Milbank, John. *Theology and Social Theory: Beyond Secular Reason*. Oxford: Basil Blackwell, 2006.

Miller, Vincent J. "Where Is the Church? Globalization and Catholicity." *Theological Studies* 69, no. 2 (2008): 412-32.

"The Ministry in the Church, 1981." In *Growth in Agreement I: Reports and Agreed Statements of Ecumenical Conversations on a World Level, 1972–1982*, edited by Harding Meyer and Lukas Vischer, 248-75. Geneva: World Council of Churches, 1984.

"Mission in the Context of Empire." *International Review of Mission* 101, no. 1 (2012): 195-211.

"Mission in the Context of Empire: CWM Theology Statement 2010." *International Review of Mission* 100, no. 1 (2011): 108-25.

Moltmann, Jürgen. *The Church in the Power of the Spirit: A Contribution to Messianic Ecclesiology*. Translated by Margaret Kohl. Minneapolis: Fortress, 1993.

Moody, Campbell N. *The Mind of the Early Converts*. London: Hodder & Stoughton, 1920.

Moody, Christopher. "Apostolicity and the Call of the Kingdom." *Theology* 94 (1991): 86-91.

Morris, Leon. *Ministers of God*. London: Inter-Varsity Fellowship, 1964.

Mosbech, Holger. "Apostolos in the New Testament." *Studia Theologica* 2, no. 2 (1948): 166-200.

Müller, Retief. "Christianity and Globalisation: An Alternative Ethical Response." *HTS Teologiese Studies / Theological Studies* 67, no. 3 (2011): 1-7.

———. "The 'Indigenizing' and 'Pilgrim' Principles of Andrew F. Walls Reassessed from a South African Perspective." *Theology Today* 70, no. 3 (2013): 311-22.

Mundadan, A. Mathias. "The Changing Task of Christian History: A View at the Onset of the Third Millennium." In *Enlarging the Story: Perspectives on Writing World Christian History*, edited by Wilbert R. Shenk, 22-53. Maryknoll, NY: Orbis Books, 2002.

Murphy, Francesca Aran. *God Is Not a Story: Realism Revisited*. Oxford: Oxford University Press, 2007.

Nardoni, Enrique. "Charism in the Early Church Since Rudolph Sohm: An Ecumenical Challenge." *Theological Studies* 53, no. 4 (1992): 646-62.

The Nature and Mission of the Church: A Stage on the Way to a Common Statement. Geneva: World Council of Churches, 2005.

The Nature and Purpose of the Church: A Stage on the Way to a Common Statement. Geneva: World Council of Churches, 1998.

Neill, Stephen. *Creative Tension*. London: Edinburgh House Press, 1959.

———. *The Ministry of the Church: A Review by Various Authors of a Book Entitled "The Apostolic Ministry."* London: Canterbury Press, 1947.

———. *The Unfinished Task*. London: Edinburgh House Press, 1957.

Neve, Herbert T. "The Diversity of Unity." *International Review of Mission* 60 (1971): 339-55.

Newbigin, J. E. Lesslie. "Common Witness and Unity." *International Review of Mission* 69 (1980): 158-60.

———. "Context and Conversion." *International Review of Mission* 68, no. 3 (1979): 301-12.

———. *The Gospel in a Pluralist Society*. Geneva: World Council of Churches, 1989.

———. *Honest Religion for Secular Man*. London: SCM Press, 1967.

———. *The Household of God: Lectures on the Nature of the Church*. London: SCM Press, 1953.

———. "Integration—Some Personal Reflections 1981." *International Review of Mission* 70, no. 4 (1981): 247-55.

———. "Mission to Six Continents." In *The Ecumenical Advance: A History of the Ecumenical Movement, 1948–1968*, edited by Harold E. Fey, 171-97. London: SPCK, 1970.

———. *One Body, One Gospel, One World: The Christian Mission Today*. London: International Missionary Council, 1958.

———. *The Open Secret: An Introduction to the Theology of Mission*. Grand Rapids: Eerdmans, 1995.

———. "Reply to Konrad Raiser." *International Bulletin of Missionary Research* 18, no. 2 (1994): 51-52.

———. *The Reunion of the Church: A Defence of the South India Scheme*. London: SCM Press, 1960.

———. *A South India Diary*. London: SCM Press, 1960.

———. "Which Way for 'Faith and Order'?" In *What Unity Implies: Six Essays After Uppsala*, edited by Reinhard Groscurth, 115-32. Geneva: World Council of Churches, 1969.

———. *A Word in Season: Perspectives on Christian World Missions*. Grand Rapids: Eerdmans, 1994.

Nielsen, Erik W. "The Role of the I.M.C.: Some Reflections on the Nature and Task of the I.M.C. in the Present Situation." In *The Ghana Assembly of the International Missionary Council, 28th December, 1957 to 8th January, 1958*, edited by Ronald Kenneth Orchard, 185-240. London: Edinburgh House Press, 1958.

Nissiotis, Nikos A. *Die Theologie der Ostkirche im ökumenischen Dialog*. Stuttgart: Evangelisches Verlagswerk, 1968.

Noort, Gerrit. "Emerging Migrant Churches in the Netherlands: Missiological Challenges and Mission Frontiers." *International Review of Mission* 100, no. 1 (2011): 4-16.

Nwatu, Felix. "'Colonial' Christianity in Post-Colonial Africa?" *Ecumenical Review* 46, no. 3 (1994): 352-60.

O'Brien, Peter T. *Gospel and Mission in the Writings of Paul: An Exegetical and Theological Analysis*. Grand Rapids: Baker, 1995.

O'Collins, Gerald. "Origins of Apostolic Continuity in the New Testament." In *Ecclesia tertii millennii advenientis: Omaggio al P. Angel Anton Professore de ecclesiologia alla Pontificia Universita Gregoriana nel suo 70. compleanno*, edited by Fernando Chica, Sandro Panizzolo and Harald Wagner, 830-41. Monferrato: Piemme, 1997.

O'Donovan, Oliver. "What Kind of Community Is the Church? The Richard Hooker Lectures 2005." *Ecclesiology* 3, no. 2 (2007): 171-93.

Oduyoye, Mercy Amba. *Hearing and Knowing: Theological Reflections on Christianity in Africa*. Maryknoll, NY: Orbis Books, 1986.

O'Gara, Margaret. "Apostolicity in Ecumenical Dialogue." *Mid-Stream* 37, no. 2 (1998): 175-212.

Okure, Teresa. "The Church in the World: A Dialogue on Ecclesiology." In *Theology and Conversation: Towards a Relational Theology*, edited by Jacques Haers and P. De Mey, 393-438. Leuven: Peeters, 2003.

364

"On Intercultural Hermeneutics: Report of a WCC Consultation, Jerusalem, December 1995." *International Review of Mission* 85, no. 337 (1996): 241-52.

"The Ordained Ministry." In *Faith and Order, Louvain 1971: Study Reports and Document*, 78-101. Geneva: World Council of Churches, 1971.

Owen, H. P. "Resurrection and Apostolate in St. Paul." *Expository Times* 65, no. 11 (1954): 324-28.

Pannenberg, Wolfhart. "Notwendigkeit und Grenzen der Inkulturation des Evangeliums." In *Christentum in Lateinamerika: 500 Jahre seit der Entdeckung Amerikas*, edited by Geiko Müller-Fahrenholz, 140-54. Regensburg: Verlag Freidrich Pustet, 1992.

———. "The Significance of Eschatology for Understanding the Apostolicity and Catholicity of the Church." In *The Church*, 44-68. Philadelphia: Westminster, 1970.

———. *Systematic Theology*. Grand Rapids: Eerdmans, 1998.

Paulson, Graham. "Towards an Aboriginal Theology." *Pacifica* 19, no. 3 (2006): 310-20.

Pauw, C. M. "African Independent Churches as a 'People's Response' to the Christian Message." *Journal for the Study of Religion* 8, no. 1 (1995): 3-25.

Pekridou, Aikaterini. "The Plenary Discussion on the Ecclesiology Study of Faith and Order, The Nature and Mission of the Church: The Meeting and Its Process." *Ecumenical Review* 62, no. 3 (2010): 254-69.

Pew Forum on Religion & Public Life. *Global Christianity: A Report on the Size and Distribution of the World's Christian Population*. Washington, DC: Pew Research Center's Forum on Religion & Public Life, 2011.

Phan, Peter C. "Doing Theology in World Christianity: Different Resources and New Methods." *Journal of World Christianity* 1, no. 1 (2008): 27-53.

———. "A New Kind of Christianity, but What Kind?" *Mission Studies* 22, no. 1 (2005): 59-83.

———. "World Christianity and Christian Mission: Are They Compatible? Insights from the Asian Churches." *Asian Christian Review* 1, no. 1 (2007): 14-31.

———. "World Christianity: Its Implications for History, Religious Studies, and Theology." *Horizons* 39, no. 2 (2012): 171-88.

Pierard, Richard V. "Völkisch Thought and Christian Missions in Early Twentieth Century Germany." In *Essays in Religious Studies for Andrew Walls*, edited by James Thrower, 138-49. Aberdeen: Department of Religious Studies, University of Aberdeen, 1986.

Pieris, Aloysius. "The Non-semitic Religions of Asia." In *Mission in Dialogue:*

The SEDOS Research Seminar on the Future of Mission, edited by Mary Motte and Joseph R. Lang, 426-41. Maryknoll, NY: Orbis Books, 1982.

Porter, Andrew N. "'Cultural Imperialism' and Protestant Missionary Enterprise, 1780–1914." *Journal of Imperial and Commonwealth History* 25, no. 3 (1997): 367-91.

Price, Frank Wilson. "Missions and Imperialism." *Occasional Bulletin* 10, no. 7 (1959): 1-6.

Puglisi, James F. "Catholic Learning Concerning Apostolicity and Ecclesiality." In *Receptive Ecumenism and the Call to Catholic Learning: Exploring a Way for Contemporary Ecumenism*, edited by Paul D. Murray, 181-96. Oxford: Oxford University Press, 2008.

Quick, Oliver Chase. "The Jerusalem Meeting and the Christian Message." *International Review of Mission* 17, no. 4 (1928): 445-54.

Radcliffe, Timothy. *I Call You Friends*. London: Continuum, 2001.

Rahner, Karl. "Towards a Fundamental Theological Interpretation of Vatican II." *Theological Studies* 40, no. 4 (1979): 716-27.

Raiser, Konrad. "Festes Fundament? Die Apostolizität der Kirche im ökumenischen Gespräch." *Ökumenische Rundschau* 60, no. 1 (2011): 80-94.

———. "Mission oder Bestandssicherung?" In *Jahrbuch Mission 1987*, edited by Joachim Wietzke, 8-19. Hamburg: Missionshilfe Verlag, 1987.

———. "'... That the World May Believe': The Missionary Vocation as the Necessary Horizon for Ecumenism." *International Review of Mission* 88 (1999): 187-96.

Ramsey, A. Michael. *The Gospel and the Catholic Church*. London: Longmans, Green, 1956.

Ramsey, Paul. "Liturgy and Ethics." *Journal of Religious Ethics* 7, no. 2 (1979): 139-71.

Ranger, Terence O. "Christianity, Capitalism and Empire: The State of the Debate." *Transformation* 23, no. 2 (2006): 67-70.

———. "Religious Movements and Politics in Sub-Saharan Africa." *African Studies Review* 29, no. 2 (1986): 1-69.

Ratzinger, Joseph. "Culture, Identity and Church Unity." *Ecumenical Review* 57, no. 3 (2005): 358-60.

———. "In the Encounter of Christianity and Religions, Syncretism Is Not the Goal." *L'Osservatore Romano (weekly edition)*, April 26, 1995, 5-8.

———. "Nicht nur eine Frage der Kompetenzverteilung: Das Verhältnis von Universalkirche und Ortskirche aus der Sicht des Zweiten Vatikanischen Konzils." *Frankfurther Allgemeine Zeitung*, December 12, 2000, 46.

Rausch, Thomas P. "Unity and Diversity in New Testament Ecclesiology: Twenty-Five Years After Käsemann and Brown." *Irish Theological Quarterly* 54, no. 2 (1988): 131-39.

Rayan, Samuel. "The Lima Text and Mission." *International Review of Mission* 72 (1983): 199-206.

———. "Mission After Vatican II: Problems and Positions." *International Review of Mission* 59 (1970): 414-26.

"Renewal in Mission: The Report as Adopted by the Assembly." *International Review of Mission* 58 (1969): 354-60.

Rengstorf, Karl Heinrich. "ἀποστέλλω, ἀπόστολος." In *Theological Dictionary of the New Testament*, edited by Gerhard Kittel and Gerhard Friedrich, 389-447. Grand Rapids: Eerdmans, 1964.

———. "ἀποστέλλω, ἀπόστολος." In *Theologisches Wörterbuch zum Neuen Testament I*, edited by Gerhard Kittel, 397-448. Stuttgart: W. Kohlhammer, 1933.

———. "Faith and Order in the New Testament." In *Current Issues in New Testament Interpretation: Essays in Honor of Otto A. Piper*, edited by William Klassen and Graydon F. Snyder, 166-92. London: SCM Press, 1962.

"Report of the Joint Lutheran-Roman Catholic Study Commission on the 'Gospel and the Church,' 1972 ('Malta Report')." In *Growth in Agreement I: Reports and Agreed Statements of Ecumenical Conversations on a World Level, 1972–1982*, edited by Harding Meyer and Lukas Vischer, 168-89. Geneva: World Council of Churches, 1984.

Richard, Lucien. "Vatican II and the Mission of the Church: A Contemporary Agenda." In *Vatican II: The Unfinished Agenda—A Look to the Future*, edited by Lucien Richard, Daniel J. Harrington and John W. O'Malley, 57-70. New York: Paulist Press, 1987.

Riches, John K. "'Neither Jew nor Greek': The Challenge of Building One Multicultural Religious Community." *Concilium*, no. 1 (1995): 36-44.

Robbins, Joel. "Continuity Thinking and the Problem of Christian Culture: Belief, Time, and the Anthropology of Christianity." *Current Anthropology* 48, no. 1 (2007): 5-38.

Roberts, Nathaniel. "Is Conversion a 'Colonization of Consciousness'?" *Anthropological Theory* 12, no. 3 (2012): 271-94.

Roelvink, Henrik. "The Apostolic Succession in the Porvoo Statement." *One in Christ* 30 (1994): 344-54.

Roloff, Jürgen. "Apostel/Apostolat/Apostolizität: I. Neues Testament." In *Theologische Realenzyklopädie*, edited by Gerhard Krause and Gerhard Müller, 430-45. Berlin: Walter de Gruyter, 1978.

Ross, Kenneth R. "Doing Theology with a New Historiography." *Journal of Theology for Southern Africa*, no. 99 (1997): 94-98.

Rusch, William G. "Introduction." In *Episkopé and Episcopacy and the Quest for Visible Unity: Two Consultations*, edited by Peter Bouteneff and Alan D. Falconer, 1-11. Geneva: World Council of Churches, 1999.

———. "Structures of Unity: The Next Ecumenical Challenge—A Possible Way Forward." *Ecclesiology* 2, no. 1 (2005): 107-22.

Russell, James C. *The Germanization of Early Medieval Christianity: A Sociohistorical Approach to Religious Transformation*. New York: Oxford University Press, 1996.

Rütti, Ludwig. *Zur Theologie der Mission: Kritische Analysen und neue Orientierungen*. Munich: Chr. Kaiser Verlag, 1972.

Ryan, Patrick. "Is It Possible to Conduct a Unified History of Religions in West Africa?" *Universitas* 8 (1984): 98-112.

Ryan, Seamus. "Vatican II: The Rediscovery of the Episcopate." *Irish Theological Quarterly* 33, no. 3 (1966): 208-41.

Rynne, Xavier. *The Third Session: The Debates and Decrees of Vatican Council II, September 14 to November 21, 1964*. New York: Farrar, 1965.

Sachs, William L. *The Transformation of Anglicanism: From State Church to Global Communion*. Cambridge: Cambridge University Press, 1993.

Samson, Jane. "The Problem of Colonialism in the Western Historiography of Christian Missions." *Religious Studies and Theology* 23, no. 2 (2004): 3-25.

Sanneh, Lamin O. "Africa." In *Toward the Twenty-First Century in Christian Mission: Essays in Honor of Gerald H. Anderson*, edited by James M. Phillips and Robert T. Coote, 84-97. Grand Rapids: Eerdmans, 1993.

———. "Christian Mission in the Pluralist Milieu: The African Experience." *International Review of Mission* 74, no. 294 (1985): 199-211.

———. *Disciples of All Nations: Pillars of World Christianity*. Oxford: Oxford University Press, 2007.

———. *Encountering the West: Christianity and the Global Cultural Process; The African Dimension*. Maryknoll, NY: Orbis Books, 1993.

———. "Global Christianity and the Re-education of the West." *Christian Century* 112, no. 22 (1995): 715-18.

———. "The Gospel, Language and Culture: The Theological Method in Cultural Analysis." *International Review of Mission* 84 (1995): 47-64.

———. "The Horizontal and the Vertical in Mission: An African Perspective." *International Bulletin of Missionary Research* 7, no. 4 (1983): 165-71.

———. "Post-Western Wine, Post-Christian Wineskins? The Bible and the Third Wave Awakening." In *Understanding World Christianity: The Vision and Work of Andrew F. Walls*, edited by William R. Burrows, Mark R. Gornik and Janice A. McLean, 91-107. Maryknoll, NY: Orbis Books, 2011.

———. "Should Christianity Be Missionary? An Appraisal and an Agenda." *Dialog* 40, no. 2 (2001): 86-98.

———. *Summoned from the Margin: Homecoming of an African.* Grand Rapids: Eerdmans, 2012.

———. "'They Stooped to Conquer': Vernacular Translation and the Socio-Cultural Factor." *Research in African Literatures* 23, no. 1 (1992): 95-106.

———. "Translatability: A Discussion." *Journal of Religion in Africa* 22, no. 2 (1992): 168-72.

———. *Translating the Message: The Missionary Impact on Culture.* Maryknoll, NY: Orbis Books, 2009.

———. *West African Christianity: The Religious Impact.* Maryknoll, NY: Orbis Books, 1983.

———. *Whose Religion Is Christianity? The Gospel Beyond the West.* Grand Rapids: Eerdmans, 2003.

———. "World Christianity and the New Historiography: Historical and Global Interconnections." In *Enlarging the Story: Perspectives on Writing World Christian History*, edited by Wilbert R. Shenk, 94-114. Maryknoll, NY: Orbis Books, 2002.

Satake, A. "Apostolat und Gnade bei Paulus." *New Testament Studies* 15, no. 1 (1968): 96-107.

Schillebeeckx, Edward. *The Church with a Human Face: A New and Expanded Theology of Ministry.* New York: Crossroad, 1987.

Schlabach, Gerald. *Unlearning Protestantism: Sustaining Christian Community in an Unstable Age.* Grand Rapids: Brazos, 2010.

Schlindler, David L. "Catholicity and the State of Contemporary Theology: The Need for an Onto-Logic of Holiness." *Communio* 14 (1987): 426-50.

Schmemann, Alexander. *Church, World, Mission: Reflections on Orthodoxy in the West.* Crestwood, NY: St. Vladimir's Seminary Press, 1979.

———. "The Missionary Imperative in the Orthodox Tradition." In *The Theology of the Christian Mission*, edited by Gerald H. Anderson, 250-57. New York: McGraw-Hill, 1961.

Schmithals, Walter. *Das kirchliche Apostelamt: Eine historische Untersuchung.* Göttingen: Vandenhoeck & Ruprecht, 1961.

Schnackenburg, Rudolf. "Apostles Before and During Paul's Time." In *Apostolic History and the Gospel: Essays Presented to F. F. Bruce*, edited by W. Ward Gasque and Ralph P. Martin, 287-303. Exeter, UK: Paternoster, 1970.

———. "Apostolicity: The Present Position of Studies." *One in Christ* 6, no. 3 (1970): 243-69.

Schreiter, Robert J. "Globalization, Postmodernity and the New Catholicity." In *For All People: Global Theologies in Contexts*, 13-31. Grand Rapids: Eerdmans, 2002.

———. *The New Catholicity: Theology Between the Global and the Local*. Maryknoll, NY: Orbis Books, 1997.

Schulz, Klaus Detlev. "The Lutheran Debate over a Missionary Office." *Lutheran Quarterly* 19, no. 3 (2005): 276-301.

Schütz, John Howard. *Paul and the Anatomy of Apostolic Authority*. Cambridge: Cambridge University Press, 1975.

Schuurman, Barend Martinus. "Discipelschap en Apostolaat." *Eltheto* (1919): 45-57.

Schweizer, Eduard. "The Church as the Missionary Body of Christ." *New Testament Studies* 8, no. 1 (1961): 1-11.

Schwöbel, Christoph. "'The Church of Jesus Christ': The Leuenberg Study on the Church and Its Significance for the Ways Forward from Meissen." In *Einheit bezeugen: Zehn Jahre nach der Meissener Erklärung; Beiträge zu den theologischen Konferenzen von Springe und Cheltenham zwischen der EKD und der Kirche von England*, edited by Ingolf Dalferth and Paul Oppenheim, 436-51. Frankfurt am Main: Verlag Otto Lembeck, 2003.

———. "God as Conversation: Reflections on a Theological Ontology of Communicative Relations." In *Theology and Conversation: Towards a Relational Theology*, edited by Jacques Haers and P. De Mey, 43-67. Leuven: Peeters, 2003.

Scott, Benjamin G. McNair. *Apostles Today: Making Sense of Contemporary Charismatic Apostolates; A Historical and Theological Appraisal*. Eugene, OR: Pickwick, 2014.

Sears, Robert T. "Comments on Rodger D. Haight's Article." *Theological Studies* 37, no. 4 (1976): 649-51.

———. "Trinitarian Love as Ground of the Church." *Theological Studies* 37, no. 4 (1976): 652-82.

Seumois, Andreas. *Auf dem Wege zu einer Definition der Missionstätigkeit*. Möchengladbach: Kühlen, 1948.

Shaw, Mark. "Robert Wuthnow and World Christianity: A Response to Boundless Faith." *International Bulletin of Missionary Research* 36, no. 4 (2012): 170-84.

Shenk, Wilbert R. "Challenging the Academy, Breaking Barriers." In *Understanding World Christianity: The Vision and Work of Andrew F. Walls*, edited by William R. Burrows, Mark R. Gornik and Janice A. McLean, 35-50. Maryknoll, NY: Orbis Books, 2011.

———. "Toward a Global Church History." *International Bulletin of Missionary Research* 20, no. 2 (1996): 50-57.

Sherwood, Aaron. "Faith, Culture and the Global Village." *South Pacific Journal of Mission Studies* 16 (1996): 31-38.

———. *Paul and the Restoration of Humanity in Light of Ancient Jewish Traditions.* Leiden: Brill, 2013.

Shorter, Aylward. "A Communion of Local Churches for the World." *South Pacific Journal of Mission Studies* 16 (1996): 6-14.

Skreslet, Stanley H. "Thinking Missiologically About the History of Mission." *International Bulletin of Missionary Research* 31, no. 2 (2007): 59-65.

Smith, David N. "Faith, Reason, and Charisma: Rudolf Sohm, Max Weber, and the Theology of Grace." *Sociological Inquiry* 68, no. 1 (1998): 32-60.

Smith, James K. A. *Desiring the Kingdom: Worship, Worldview, and Cultural Formation.* Grand Rapids: Baker Academic, 2009.

Sohm, Rudolph. *Kirchenrecht I: Die Geschichtlichen Grundlagen.* Leipzig: Duncker & Humblot, 1892.

"Some Aspects of the Church Understood as Communion." *Origins* 22 (1992): 108-12.

Speelman, Gé. "Continuity and Discontinuity in Conversion Stories." *Exchange* 35, no. 3 (2006): 304-35.

Stanley, Brian. "Afterword: The CMS and the Separation of Anglicanism from 'Englishness.'" In *The Church Mission Society and World Christianity, 1799–1999*, edited by Kevin Ward and Brian Stanley, 344-52. Grand Rapids: Eerdmans, 1999.

———. *The Bible and the Flag: Protestant Missions and British Imperialism in the Nineteenth and Twentieth Centuries.* Leicester, UK: Apollos, 1990.

———. "Conversion to Christianity: The Colonization of the Mind?" *International Review of Mission* 92, no. 3 (2003): 315-31.

———. "Where Have Our Mission Structures Come From?" *Transformation* 20, no. 1 (2003): 39-46.

Staples, Peter. "Apostolicity." In *Dictionary of the Ecumenical Movement*, edited by Nicolas Lossky, José Míguez Bonino, John Pobee, Thomas F. Stransky, Geoffrey Wainwright and Pauline Webb, 44-48. Geneva: World Council of Churches; Grand Rapids: Eerdmans, 1991.

Stockwell, Eugene L. *Claimed by God for Mission: The Congregation Seeks New Forms*. New York: World Outlook Press, 1965.

Stone, Bryan P. "The Ecclesiality of Mission in the Context of Empire." In *Walk Humbly with the Lord: Church and Mission Engaging Plurality*, edited by Viggo Mortensen and Andreas Østerlund Nielsen, 105-12. Grand Rapids: Eerdmans, 2011.

Stout, Jeffrey. *Democracy and Tradition*. Princeton, NJ: Princeton University Press, 2004.

Stransky, Thomas F. "From Vatican II to Redemptoris Missio: A Development in the Theology of Mission." In *Good News of the Kingdom*, 137-47. Maryknoll, NY: Orbis Books, 1993.

———. "The Mission of the Church: Post-Vatican II Developments in 'Official' Roman Catholic Theology." *One in Christ* 35, no. 1 (1999): 51-68.

Stuhlmacher, Peter. "Evangelium—Apostolat—Gemeinde." *Kerygma und Dogma* 17 (1971): 28-45.

Suess, Paulo. "A Confused Mission Scenario: A Critical Analysis of Recent Church Documents and Tendencies." In *Christianity and Cultures: A Mutual Enrichment*, 107-19. Maryknoll, NY: Orbis Books, 1994.

Sullivan, Francis A. *From Apostles to Bishops: The Development of the Episcopacy in the Early Church*. Mahwah, NJ: Paulist Press, 2001.

———. "Response to Karl Brecker, S.J., on the Meaning of Subsistit In." *Theological Studies* 67 (2006): 395-409.

Sundermeier, Theo. "Konvivenz als Grundstruktur ökumenischer Existenz heute." In *Ökumenische Existenz heute*, edited by W. Huber, D. Ritschl and Theo Sundermeier, 49-100. Munich: Chr. Kaiser Verlag, 1986.

———. "Missio Dei Today: On the Identity of Christian Mission." *International Review of Mission* 92, no. 4 (2003): 579-87.

Sundermeier, Theo, and Volker Küster. *Die Bilder und das Wort: Zum Verstehen christlicher Kunst in Afrika und Asien*. Göttingen: Vandenhoeck & Ruprecht, 1999.

Tamez, Elsa. *The Amnesty of Grace: Justification by Faith from a Latin American Perspective*. Translated by Sharon H. Ringe. Eugene, OR: Wipf & Stock, 2002.

Tanner, Kathryn. *Theories of Culture: A New Agenda for Theology*. Minneapolis: Fortress, 1997.

ter Haar, Gerrie. "Strangers in the Promised Land: African Christians in Europe." *Exchange* 24, no. 1 (1995): 1-33.

Theissen, Gerd. "Legitimation and Subsistence: An Essay on the Sociology of

Early Christian Missionaries." In *The Social Setting of Pauline Christianity: Essays on Corinth*, 27-68. Philadelphia: Fortress, 1982.

A Theological Reflection on the Work of Evangelism. Geneva: World Council of Churches, 1963.

Thiselton, Anthony C. "Some Misleading Factors in the History of Interpretation of 'Apostle.'" In *The First Epistle to the Corinthians*, 669-73. The New International Greek Testament Commentary. Grand Rapids: Eerdmans, 2000.

Thurian, Max. *Churches Respond to BEM: Official Responses to the "Baptism, Eucharist and Ministry" Text*. Geneva: World Council of Churches, 1987.

Tiénou, Tite. "The Invention of the 'Primitive' and Stereotypes in Mission." *Missiology* 19, no. 3 (1991): 295-303.

Tillard, J. M. R. "Episcopacy: A Gift of the Spirit." In *Episkopé and Episcopacy and the Quest for Visible Unity: Two Consultations*, edited by Peter Bouteneff and Alan D. Falconer, 65-79. Geneva: World Council of Churches, 1999.

Together in Mission and Ministry: The Porvoo Common Statement with Essays on Church and Ministry in Northern Europe; Conversations Between the British and Irish Anglican Churches and the Nordic and Baltic Lutheran Churches. London: Church House Publishing, 1993.

Tomkins, Oliver S., ed. *The Third World Conference on Faith and Order, Lund 1952*. London: SCM Press, 1953.

Toolan, David. "The Catholic Taboo Against Schism: Strained but Holding." *Religion and Intellectual Life* 7, no. 1 (1989): 36-50.

"Towards a Common Understanding." In *Growth in Agreement II: Reports and Agreed Statements of Ecumenical Conversations on a World Level, 1982–1998*, edited by Jeffrey Gros, Harding Meyer and William G. Rusch. Geneva: World Council of Churches, 2000.

Toy, John. "Is Porvoo Working?" *Theology* 104 (2001): 3-14.

A Treasure in Earthen Vessels: An Instrument for an Ecumenical Reflection on Hermeneutics. Geneva: World Council of Churches, 1998.

Tumsa, Gudina, and Paul E. Hoffman. "The Moratorium Debate and the ECMY." In *Witness and Discipleship: Leadership of the Church in Multi-Ethnic Ethopia in a Time of Revolution; The Essential Writings of Gudina Tumsa, General Secretary of the Ethiopian Evangelical Church Mekane Yesus (1929–1979)*, 45-54. Addis Ababa: Gudina Tumsa Foundation, 2003.

Tutu, Desmond. "Whither African Theology." In *Christianity in Independent Africa*, edited by Edward W. Fasholé-Luke, Richard Gray, Adrian Hastings and Godwin Tasie, 364-69. London: Rex Collings, 1978.

Uka, Emele Mba. *Missionaries Go Home? A Sociological Interpretation of an African Response to Christian Missions.* Berne: Peter Lang, 1989.

Ukwuegbu, Bernard. "'Neither Jew nor Greek': The Church in Africa and the Quest for Self-Understanding in the Light of the Pauline Vision and Today's Context of Cultural Pluralism." *International Journal for the Study of the Christian Church* 8, no. 4 (2008): 305-18.

Van der Borght, Eduardus A. J. G. "No Longer Strangers or Pilgrims in the Church? Socio-cultural Identities in the Faith and Order Document: Nature and Mission of the Church." In *Strangers and Pilgrims on Earth: Essays in Honour of Abraham van de Beek,* edited by Eduardus A. J. G. Van der Borght and P. van Geest, 431-44. Leiden: Brill, 2011.

van der Leeuw, Gerardus. *Religion in Essence and Manifestation: A Study in Phenomenology.* New York: Harper & Row, 1963.

Vandervelde, George. "Costly Communion: Mission Between Ecclesiology and Ethics." *Ecumenical Review* 49, no. 1 (1997): 46-60.

———. "The Meaning of 'Apostolic Faith' in World Council of Churches' Documents." In *Apostolic Faith in America,* edited by Thaddeus Daniel Horgan, 20-25. Grand Rapids: Eerdmans, 1988.

van Kooten, Reinier. *Hoe apostolaire bewogenheid een onbeweegbare kerk in beweging brengt.* Apeldoorn: Labarum Academic, 2013.

van Ruler, A. A. "De kerk is ook doel in zichzelf." In *Verwachtingen Voltooiing: Een bundel theologische opstellen en voordrachten,* 53-66. Nijkerk: Callenbach, 1978.

———. "De Kolonie." In *Visie en Vaart.* Amsterdam: Nijkerk, 1947.

———. *De vervulling van de wet: Een dogmatische studie over de verhouding van openbaring en existentie.* Nijkerk: G. F. Callenbach, 1947.

———. *Gestaltwerdung Christi in der Welt: Über das Verhältnis von Kirche und Kultur.* Neukrichen Kr. Moers: Verlag der Buchhandlung des Erziehungsvereins, 1956.

———. "A Theology of Mission." In *Calvinist Trinitarianism and Theocentric Politics: Essays Toward a Public Theology,* trans. John Bolt, 199-226. Lewiston, NY: Edwin Mellen, 1989.

Vicedom, Georg F. *The Mission of God: An Introduction to a Theology of Mission.* Translated by Gilbert A. Thiele and Dennis Hilgendorf. St. Louis, MO: Concordia, 1965.

Visser 't Hooft, W. A., ed. *The First Assembly of the World Council of Churches, Held at Amsterdam, August 22nd to September 4th, 1948.* London: SCM Press, 1949.

———, ed. *The New Delhi Report: Third Assembly of the World Council of Churches.* London: SCM Press, 1962.

———. "The Threefold Christian Calling." *Student World* 54, nos. 1-2 (1961): 26-39.

Vogelstein, Hermann. "The Development of the Apostolate in Judaism and Its Transformation in Christianity." *Hebrew Union College Annual* 2 (1925): 99-123.

———. "Die Entstehung und Entwicklung des Apostolats im Judentum." *Monatsschrift für die Geschichte und Wissenschaft des Judentums* 49, no. 7/8 (1905): 427-49.

Volf, Miroslav. "Soft Difference: Theological Reflections on the Relation Between Church and Culture in 1 Peter." *Ex Auditu* 10 (1994): 15-30.

Volpe, Medi Ann. *Rethinking Christian Identity: Doctrine and Discipleship.* Malden, MA: Wiley-Blackwell, 2012.

Vondey, Wolfgang. "Pentecostal Perspectives on The Nature and Mission of the Church: Challenges and Opportunities for Ecumenical Transformation." In *Receiving "The Nature and Mission of the Church": Ecclesial Reality and Ecumenical Horizons for the Twenty-First Century*, edited by Paul M. Collins and Michael A. Fahey, 55-68. London: Continuum, 2008.

Wagenaar, Hinne. "Stop Harassing the Gentiles: The Importance of Acts 15 for African Theology." *Journal for African Christian Thought* 6, no. 1 (2003): 44-54.

Wagner, C. Peter. *Church Growth and the Whole Gospel: A Biblical Mandate.* San Francisco: Harper & Row, 1981.

Wainwright, Geoffrey. "Is Episcopal Succession a Matter of Dogma for Anglicans? The Evidence of Some Recent Dialogues." In *Community, Unity, Communion*, 164-79. London: Church House Publishing, 1998.

Waldman, Marilyn Robinson. "Translatability: A Discussion." *Journal of Religion in Africa* 22, no. 2 (1992): 159-64.

Walls, Andrew F. "Africa and Christian Identity." *Mission Focus* 6 (1978): 11-13.

———. "Africa in Christian History: Retrospect and Prospect." *Journal of African Christian Thought* 1, no. 1 (1998): 2-15.

———. "The Challenge of the African Independent Churches: The Anabaptists of Africa?" In *The Missionary Movement in Christian History: Studies in the Transmission of Faith*, 111-18. Maryknoll, NY: Orbis Books, 1996.

———. "Christianity." In *A New Handbook of Living Religions*, edited by John R. Hinnells, 55-161. London: Penguin, 2003.

———. "Christianity in the Non-Western World: A Study in the Serial Nature of Christian Expansion." In *The Cross-Cultural Process in Christian History: Studies in the Transmission and Appropriation of Faith*, 27-48. Maryknoll, NY: Orbis Books, 2002.

———. "Converts or Proselytes? The Crisis over Conversion in the Early Church." *International Bulletin of Missionary Research* 28, no. 1 (2004): 2-6.

———. "Culture and Coherence in Christian History." In *The Missionary Movement in Christian History: Studies in the Transmission of Faith*, 16-25. Maryknoll, NY: Orbis Books, 1996.

———. "The Ephesian Moment: At a Crossroads in Christian History." In *The Cross-Cultural Process in Christian History: Studies in the Transmission and Appropriation of Faith*, 72-81. Maryknoll, NY: Orbis Books, 2002.

———. "Eusebius Tries Again: The Task of Reconceiving and Re-visioning the Study of Christian History." In *Enlarging the Story: Perspectives on Writing World Christian History*, edited by Wilbert R. Shenk, 22-53. Maryknoll, NY: Orbis Books, 2002.

———. "Globalization and the Study of Christian History." In *Globalizing Theology: Belief and Practice in an Era of World Christianity*, edited by Craig Ott and Harold A. Netland, 70-82. Grand Rapids: Baker Academic, 2006.

———. "The Gospel as Prisoner and Liberator of Culture." In *The Missionary Movement in Christian History: Studies in the Transmission of Faith*, 3-15. Maryknoll, NY: Orbis Books, 1996.

———. "A History of the Expansion of Christianity *Reconsidered*: Assessing Christian Progress and Decline." In *The Cross-Cultural Process in Christian History: Studies in the Transmission and Appropriation of Faith*, 3-26. Maryknoll, NY: Orbis Books, 2002.

———. "Kwame Bediako and Christian Scholarship in Africa." *International Bulletin of Missionary Research* 32, no. 4 (2008): 188-93.

———. "The Mission of the Church Today in the Light of Global History." *Word & World* 20, no. 1 (2000): 17-21.

———. "Missionary Societies and the Fortunate Subversion of the Church." In *The Missionary Movement in Christian History: Studies in the Transmission of Faith*, 241-54. Maryknoll, NY: Orbis Books, 1996.

———. "Of Ivory Towers and Ashrams: Some Reflections on Theological Scholarship in Africa." *Journal of African Christian Thought* 3, no. 1 (2000): 1-5.

———. "Old Athens and New Jerusalem: Some Signposts for Christian Scholarship in the Early History of Mission Studies." *International Bulletin of Missionary Research* 21, no. 4 (1997): 146-53.

———. "The Rise of Global Theologies." In *Global Theology in Evangelical Perspective: Exploring the Contextual Nature of Theology and Mission*, edited by Jeffrey P. Greenman and Gene L. Green, 19-34. Downers Grove, IL: IVP Academic, 2012.

———. "'Such Boastings as the Gentiles Use . . .': Some Thoughts on Imperialist Religion." In *An African Miscellany for John Hargreaves*, edited by Roy Bridges, 109-16. Aberdeen: Aberdeen University Africa Studies Group, 1983.

———. "Towards Understanding Africa's Place in Christian History." In *Religion in a Pluralistic Society: Essays Presented to Professor C. G. Baëta*, edited by J. S. Pobee, 180-89. Leiden: Brill, 1976.

———. "The Translation Principle in Christian History." In *The Missionary Movement in Christian History: Studies in the Transmission of Faith*, 26-42. Maryknoll, NY: Orbis Books, 1996.

———. "World Christianity and the Early Church." In *A New Day: Essays on World Christianity in Honor of Lamin Sanneh*, edited by Akintunde E. Akinade, 17-30. New York: Peter Lang, 2010.

Ward, Kevin. "African Identities in the Historic 'Mainline Churches': A Case Study of the Negotiation of Local and Global Within African Anglicanism." In *African Identities and World Christianity in the Twentieth Century: Proceedings of the Third International Munich-Freising Conference on the History of Christianity in the Non-Western World (September 15–17, 2004)*, edited by Klaus Koschorke and Jens Holger Schjørring, 49-62. Wiesbaden: Otto Harrassowitz Verlag, 2005.

Warneck, Gustav. *Evangelische Missionslehre: Ein missionstheoretischer Versuch.* Gotha: Friedrich Andreas Perthes, 1903.

Warren, Max A. *Caesar, the Beloved Enemy: Three Studies in the Relation of Church and State.* London: SCM Press, 1955.

———. "Why Missionary Societies and Not Missionary Churches?" *Student World* 53, no. 1-2 (1960): 149-56.

Weber, Hans R. "The Laity in the Apostolic Church." *Ecumenical Review* 10, no. 3 (1958): 286-93.

Weber, Otto. "Die Kirchenordnung der Niederländischen Reformierten Kirche von 1950." *Zeitschrift für evangelisches Kirchenrecht* 2 (1953): 225-69.

Webster, John B. *Confessing God: Essays in Christian Dogmatics II.* London: T&T Clark, 2005.

———. "The Goals of Ecumenism." In *Paths to Unity: Explorations in Ecumenical Method*, edited by Paul D. L. Avis, 1-12. London: Church House Publishing, 2004.

———. "'In the Society of God': Some Principles of Ecclesiology." In *Perspectives on Ecclesiology and Ethnography*, edited by Pete Ward, 200-222. Grand Rapids: Eerdmans, 2012.

———. "Locality and Catholicity: Reflections on Theology and the Church." *Scottish Journal of Theology* 45 (1992): 1-17.

———. "On Evangelical Ecclesiology." In *Confessing God: Essays in Christian Dogmatics II*, 153-93. London: T&T Clark, 2005.

———. "The Self-Organizing Power of the Gospel of Christ: Episcopacy and Community Formation." In *Word and Church: Essays in Christian Dogmatics*, 191-210. Edinburgh: T&T Clark, 2001.

Webster, John C. B. *Historiography of Christianity in India*. New Delhi: Oxford University Press, 2012.

———. "Writing a Social History of Christianity in India." *International Bulletin of Missionary Research* 32, no. 1 (2008): 10-12.

Werbick, Jürgen. *Kirche: Ein ekklesiologischer Entwurf für Studium und Praxis*. Freiburg: Herder, 1994.

Werner, Dietrich. *Wiederentdeckung einer missionarischen Kirche: Breklumer Beiträge zur ökumenischen Erneuerung*. Hamburg: EB-Verlag, 2005.

West, Charles C. "Ecumenics, Church and Society: The Tradition of Life and Work." *Ecumenical Review* 39, no. 4 (1987): 462-69.

Western European Working Group. "Zonal Structures for the Church." In *Planning for Mission: Working Papers on the New Quest for Missionary Communities*, edited by Thomas Wieser, 208-14. New York: U.S. Conference for the World Council of Churches, 1966.

Westhelle, Vitor. "The Church's Crucible: Koinonia and Cultural Transcendence." *Currents in Theology and Mission* 31, no. 3 (2004): 211-18.

Wiarda, Timothy. "The Jerusalem Council and the Theological Task." *Journal of the Evangelical Theological Society* 46, no. 2 (2003): 233-48.

Wieser, Thomas, ed. "Notes on the Meaning of the Apostolate." *International Review of Mission* 64 (1975): 129-36.

———. *Planning for Mission: Working Papers on the New Quest for Missionary Communities*. New York: U.S. Conference for the World Council of Churches, 1966.

Wilken, Robert L. "The Church as Culture." *First Things*, no. 142 (2004): 31-36.

———. "The Church's Way of Speaking." *First Things*, no. 155 (2005): 27-31.

Willebrands, John. "The Future of Ecumenism." *One in Christ* 11 (1975): 310-23.

Williams, C. Peter. "The Church Missionary Society and the Indigenous Church in the Second Half of the Nineteenth Century: The Defense and Destruction of the Venn Ideals." In *Converting Colonialism: Vision and Realities in Mission History, 1706–1914*, edited by Dana L. Robert, 86-111. Grand Rapids: Eerdmans, 2007.

Williams, Colin W. *Where in the World? Changing Forms of the Church's Witness.* New York: National Council of the Churches of Christ in the U.S.A., 1963.

Williams, Peter. "'Not Transplanting': Henry Venn's Strategic Vision." In *The Church Mission Society and World Christianity, 1799–1999*, edited by Kevin Ward and Brian Stanley, 147-72. Grand Rapids: Eerdmans, 1999.

Williams, Rowan. "Doing the Works of God." In *A Ray of Darkness: Sermons and Reflections*, 221-32. Cambridge, MA: Cowley, 1995.

———. "Incarnation and the Renewal of Community." In *On Christian Theology*, 225-38. Oxford: Blackwell, 2000.

———. "The Judgment of the World." In *On Christian Theology*, 29-43. Oxford: Blackwell, 2000.

———. *Mission and Christology.* Brynmawr: Welsh Members Council, Church Mission Society, 1994.

———. "Ways Forward from Meissen: What Kind of Unity in Witness and Mission?" In *Einheit bezeugen: Zehn Jahre nach der Meissener Erklärung; Beiträge zu den theologischen Konferenzen von Springe und Cheltenham zwischen der EKD und der Kirche von England*, edited by Ingolf Dalferth and Paul Oppenheim, 486-93. Frankfurt am Main: Verlag Otto Lembeck, 2003.

Williamson, S. G. *Akan Religion and the Christian Faith—A Comparative Study of the Impact of the Two Religions.* Accra: Ghana Universities Press, 1965.

Winter, Michael M. *Mission or Maintenance: A Study in New Pastoral Structures.* London: Darton, Longman & Todd, 1973.

Winter, Ralph D. "Churches Need Missions Because Modalities Need Sodalities." *Evangelical Missions Quarterly* 7, no. 4 (1971): 193-200.

———. "Two Structures of God's Redemptive Mission." *Missiology* 2, no. 1 (1974): 121-39.

———. "The Warp and the Woof of the Christian Movement." In *The Warp and the Woof: Organizing for Mission*, edited by Ralph D. Winter and R. Pierce Beaver, 52-62. South Pasadena, CA: William Carey Library, 1970.

Wong, Kam Ming. "Catholicity and Globality." *Theology Today* 66, no. 4 (2010): 459-75.

Wright, John R. "Catholicity and Globalization: A Perspective from the Episcopal Church." *Internationale Kirchliche Zeitschrift* 100 (2010): 75-89.

Wuthnow, Robert. *Boundless Faith: The Global Outreach of American Churches.* Berkeley: University of California Press, 2009.

———. "Church Realities and Christian Identity in the 21st Century." *Christian Century* 110, no. 16 (1993): 520-23.

Yeago, David S. "The Church as Polity? The Lutheran Context of Robert W. Jenson's Ecclesiology." In *Trinity, Time, and Church: A Response to the Theology of Robert W. Jenson*, edited by Colin E. Gunton, 201-37. Grand Rapids: Eerdmans, 2000.

Yoder, John Howard. *Ecumenical Movement and the Faithful Church*. Scottdale, PA: Mennonite Publishing House, 1985.

Zizioulas, John D. "Apostolic Continuity and Orthodox Theology: Towards a Synthesis of Two Perspectives." *St. Vladimir's Theological Quarterly* 19, no. 2 (1975): 75-108.

———. *Being as Communion: Studies in Personhood and the Church*. Crestwood, NY: St. Vladimir's Seminary Press, 1985.

Author Index

Subject Index

Scripture Index

MISSIOLOGICAL
ENGAGEMENTS

Series Editors: Scott W. Sunquist,
Amos Yong and John R. Franke

Missiological Engagements: Church, Theology and Culture in Global Contexts charts interdisciplinary and innovative trajectories in the history, theology and practice of Christian mission at the beginning of the third millennium.

Among its guiding questions are the following: What are the major opportunities and challenges for Christian mission in the twenty-first century? How does the missionary impulse of the gospel reframe theology and hermeneutics within a global and intercultural context? What kind of missiological thinking ought to be retrieved and reappropriated for a dynamic global Christianity? What innovations in the theology and practice of mission are needed for a renewed and revitalized Christian witness in a postmodern, postcolonial, postsecular and post-Christian world?

Books in the series, both monographs and edited collections, will feature contributions by leading thinkers representing evangelical, Protestant, Roman Catholic and Orthodox traditions, who work within or across the range of biblical, historical, theological and social scientific disciplines. Authors and editors will include the full spectrum from younger and emerging researchers to established and renowned scholars, from the Euro-American West and the majority world, whose missiological scholarship will bridge church, academy and society.

Missiological Engagements reflects cutting-edge trends, research and innovations in the field that will be of relevance to theorists and practitioners in churches, academic domains, mission organizations and NGOs, among other arenas.

Finding the Textbook You Need

The IVP Academic Textbook Selector
is an online tool for instantly finding the IVP books
suitable for over 250 courses across 24 disciplines.

ivpacademic.com